Helen Paynter is a seasoned biblical scholar who has devoted herself to the study of violence and scripture. *Blessed Are the Peacemakers* is a superb distillation of her careful engagement of this topic over the years. Whether one is a Christian just-war proponent (as I am) or a pacifist, every reader will not only find much rich, biblically rooted material to ponder, but each one will likewise be challenged to look afresh at what it means to be a peacemaker for Christ in this world.

> PAUL COPAN, Pledger Family Chair of Philosophy and Ethics,
> Palm Beach Atlantic University, and author of *Is God a Moral Monster?*
> and *Is God a Vindictive Bully?*

One way to read Paynter's work is as the story of Peace, from its creation at the beginning of the world to its consummation in the age to come. The book takes the reader across the biblical canon, stopping at insightfully chosen, familiar texts, to surprise us with sightings of Peace. At every point, the "then" of the biblical text is made immediate and urgent with the everyday realities of "now." It calls both scholar and common reader, the global south as much as the north, to attend to Peace, and delight in the prosperity of its paths.

> HAVILAH DHARAMRAJ, academic dean and head of the department of
> Old Testament, South Asia Institute of Advanced Christian Studies,
> Bangalore, India

In the news, on our streets, and in our own hearts and actions, violence rears its ugly and dangerous head. Why is violence so pervasive, and is there any hope? In *Blessed Are the Peacemakers*, Helen Paynter addresses these and other issues (war, capital punishment, gun control, structural racism) with deep biblical insight and cultural awareness. I highly recommend this profound study for all who desire to understand and implement a hopeful and redemptive Christian response to the violence of our world.

> TREMPER LONGMAN III, distinguished scholar and professor emeritus
> of biblical studies, Westmont College

Paynter's *Blessed Are the Peacemakers* is truly an impressive volume! Her wise and thoughtful guidance through the dense foliage of Scripture's troubling texts renders the biblical panoramas of peace and peacemaking even more breathtaking. This book is theoretically informed, exegetically rich, and eminently pastoral and practical. From dealing with challenging violent texts to boots-on-the-ground issues like gun control, capital punishment, racism, and migration, this volume provides insightful and realistic guidance for Christians who want to respond well to the problems of violence in Scripture and in the world today.

> MATTHEW LYNCH, associate professor of Old Testament, Regent College

Boldly facing the pervasiveness of human violence and the charges of Christianity's complicity in it, Paynter employs rigorous research to delineate various theories, supplemented by stories and discussion questions, so that readers can begin to arrive at their own decisions on timely and timeless issues. *Blessed Are the Peacemakers* can serve as a resource for consultation on almost any issue dealing with violence, an exegetical guide to key biblical texts, and a practical instruction for faithful living. This will become an indispensable book to support individuals and churches who desire to live justly and peaceably amid a violent world, aiding their desire to live out the hope of God's kingdom now.

> AMY PEELER, Kenneth T. Wessner Chair of Biblical Studies, Wheaton College

In *Blessed Are the Peacemakers*, Rev. Dr. Helen Paynter offers a broad and sweeping treatment of human violence in the Bible with an eye toward how it might inform contemporary ethics. Writing accessibly with erudition and grace, Paynter explores a wide range of Christian views, providing suggestions for how to navigate some of the most pressing issues of our time. While not everyone will agree with all her conclusions—I myself differ at points—all should celebrate her commitment to read Scripture in ways that promote peace. *Blessed Are the Peacemakers* is a substantial contribution to the conversation that Christians need to have about what it means to be faithful to God in a violent world.

ERIC A. SEIBERT, professor of Old Testament, Messiah University,
and author of *Disarming the Church: Why Christians Must Forsake Violence to Follow Jesus and Change the World*

A deeply thoughtful, compassionate, and challenging examination of human violence—in Scripture, in history, and in our chaotic and terrifying modern age. Drawing from a vast array of sources, Paynter offers a wealth of insights and applications. I benefited greatly from her hard work—and from her tender heart for a broken world. I'm sure you will too.

JOSEPH W. SMITH III, author of *Sex and Violence in the Bible* and *Transparency: A Cure for Hypocrisy in the Modern Church*

In *Blessed Are the Peacemakers*, Helen Paynter offers a scholar's seasoned reflection on the biblical text and human violence. Attuned to many forms of violence, Paynter selects key texts and demonstrates an approach that is hermeneutically honest and theologically adept. Her work exhibits an astonishing range of thinking across the biblical corpus and the scholarly literature, and the volume's pages are filled with wise insight, compassion, and always hope. Of value to scholars and a gift to the church, it is a work I will return to again as a resource for my own teaching, writing, and thinking.

LISSA M. WRAY BEAL, professor of Old Testament, Wycliffe College,
Toronto, Canada

Prompted by questions from contemporary society and informed by the best of biblical scholarship and Christian theology, Helen Paynter has written an immensely insightful book that addresses the problem of human violence and what the Bible says about it. *Blessed Are the Peacemakers* should be required reading for all who want to understand how Scripture speaks about and to violence in our world. Paynter makes a clear and convincing case that the Bible calls us to live without violence as we submit ourselves to the sovereignty of God.

JEROME F. D. CREACH, Robert C. Holland Professor of Old Testament,
Pittsburgh Theological Seminary

textbook*plus⁺*

Equipping Instructors and Students with
FREE RESOURCES for Core Zondervan Textbooks

Available Resources for Blessed Are the Peacemakers

Teaching Resources

- Instructor's manual
- Presentation slides
- Chapter quizzes
- Midterm and final exams
- Sample syllabus

Study Resources

- Flashcards
- Exam study guides

*How To Access Resources

- Go to www.ZondervanAcademic.com
- Click "Sign Up" button and complete registration process
- Find books using search field or browse using discipline categories
- Click "Teaching Resources" or "Study Resources" tab once you get to book page to access resources

www.ZondervanAcademic.com

BIBLICAL THEOLOGY FOR LIFE

BLESSED ARE THE PEACEMAKERS

A Biblical Theology of
Human Violence

HELEN PAYNTER

general editor JONATHAN LUNDE

ZONDERVAN
ACADEMIC

ZONDERVAN ACADEMIC

Blessed Are the Peacemakers
Copyright © 2023 by Helen Paynter

Requests for information should be addressed to:
Zondervan, *3900 Sparks Dr. SE, Grand Rapids, Michigan 49546*

Zondervan titles may be purchased in bulk for educational, business, fundraising, or sales promotional use. For information, please email SpecialMarkets@Zondervan.com.

ISBN 978-0-310-16037-3 (audio)

Library of Congress Cataloging-in-Publication Data

Names: Paynter, Helen, author. | Lunde, Jonathan, 1960- editor.
Title: Blessed are the peacemakers : a biblical theology of human violence / Helen Paynter, Jonathan Lunde, general editor.
Other titles: Biblical theology for life
Description: Grand Rapids : Zondervan, 2023. | Series: Biblical theology for life | Includes index.
Identifiers: LCCN 2023016743 (print) | LCCN 2023016744 (ebook) | ISBN 9780310125549 (paperback) | ISBN 9780310125556 (ebook)
Subjects: LCSH: Violence--Religious aspects--Christianity. | Violence--Biblical teaching. | BISAC: RELIGION / Biblical Studies / General | SOCIAL SCIENCE / Violence in Society
Classification: LCC BT736.15 .P393 2023 (print) | LCC BT736.15 (ebook) | DDC 241/.697--dc23/eng/20230622
LC record available at https://lccn.loc.gov/2023016743
LC ebook record available at https://lccn.loc.gov/2023016744

Cover design: Ron Huizinga
Cover image: © Gremlin / GettyImages
Interior image (ch. 12): Romanova Ekaterina/Shutterstock
Interior design: Kait Lamphere

Printed in the United States of America

23 24 25 26 27 28 29 30 31 32 33 34 35 36 37 /TRM/ 20 19 18 17 16 15 14 13 12 11 10 9 8 7 6 5 4 3 2 1

CONTENTS

QUEUING THE QUESTIONS

ARRIVING AT ANSWERS

REFLECTING ON RELEVANCE

DETAILED TABLE OF CONTENTS

QUEUING THE QUESTIONS

ARRIVING AT ANSWERS

REFLECTING ON RELEVANCE

ACKNOWLEDGMENTS

All speech is answering speech. This is true in the family. As we begin to lisp our first words, we echo and then learn to reply to the words that we have heard since the cradle. It is true in our faith. Our first prayer is a response to the words God has spoken over us: words of creation, words of blessing, words of invitation, words of command. And it is true in every scholarly endeavor. Every time we pick up a pen (well, switch on the computer) to write, we are—consciously or unconsciously—replying to the words of others.

So it is fitting that here I attempt to acknowledge some of the voices whose words I am echoing and to which I am attempting to respond. I cannot express my debt to those who taught me to love Scripture—my parents Bruce and Eleanor Batchelor, my early Sunday school teachers (I think particularly of John Waldron and Nick Perry), and my husband Stephen. I must also acknowledge my gratitude to those who introduced me to the wonders of biblical theology. I think of a former minister, Mike Pears, whose preaching first attuned me to the deep themes of Scripture; of the work of Desmond Alexander and Stephen Dempster, which blew my mind when I first encountered it; of Ernest Lucas and John Nolland, who formally taught me the subject; and of my good friend Trevor Laurence who constantly astonishes me with his fresh insights.

I must also here record my gratitude to those who have read and commented on drafts of this work. Thank you to Mark Welch, Peter King, Trevor Laurence, and Marc Wilson. Many thanks to my commissioning editor, Jon Lunde, who managed to combine great encouragement with an appropriately critical eye. And always, my greatest debt is to my husband Stephen, who is my first, my most thorough, and my most loving critic. Of course, any errors that remain are my own responsibility.

But the "speech" that I am answering is not only represented in those who have taught me or whose written work I have appreciated. It is also represented in a thousand conversations, sermons, and visits with those who are practicing peacemaking on the ground, and who are seeking to discover and inhabit the ways of Jesus more fully. I have lost count of the number of interactions that have inspired, challenged, and provoked me. I think of my dear colleagues—past and present—at the Bristol Baptist College, with whom I have chewed over many tough issues. (And I am grateful, too, that the College granted me sabbatical time that enabled me to complete this project.) I am grateful to my students in the various institutions where I have taught or supervised, who have so often taught me in return. In terms of peacemaking, I think of Werner Mischke and Kristin Caynor of the Ephesians 2 Gospel Project; of Bekah Legg and the amazing domestic abuse charity Restored;

of those who gave the Lent lectures for the Centre for the Study of Bible and Violence in 2022; of my friends in the Anabaptist network here in the UK; of the 2017 Middle East consultation held at the Arab Baptist Theological Seminary, Beirut; of the gracious and faithful Palestinian theologians of the Bethlehem Bible College and its conference titled Christ at the Checkpoint. I think of the many churches who have asked me to speak to them about biblical violence and whose congregations have so often stirred and provoked me with their questions. I think of the Ukrainian Christians from the Eastern European Institute of Theology whom I met on Zoom in December 2022, speaking to them about violence while missiles were falling on their cities. And I think of my colleagues and dear friends at the Centre for the Study of Bible and Violence. I am privileged to lead this group of people whose diversity of theological perspective and denominational adherence does not diminish but rather enriches our mutual respect, dialogue, and love.

Ultimately, this book is my stuttering but devoted answering speech to the triune God: the Father who spoke the first word, the Son who is the Word made flesh, and the Spirit who inspired the word of God we call Scripture and continues to bring light and truth forth from it. Everlasting Father, Prince of Peace, may this bring you glory.

This book is dedicated to all who work for the cause of peace in the name of Christ. May it enrich and resource you.

ABBREVIATIONS

ABRL	Anchor Bible Reference Library
BibInt	*Biblical Interpretation*
DDD	*Dictionary of Deities and Demons in the Bible.* Edited by Karel van der Toorn, Bob Becking, and Pieter W. van der Horst. Leiden: Brill, 1995. 2nd rev. ed. Grand Rapids: Eerdmans, 1999
ESV	English Standard Version
CBQ	*Catholic Biblical Quarterly*
JBL	*Journal of Biblical Literature*
JEH	*Journal of Ecclesiastical History*
JETS	*Journal of the Evangelical Theological Society*
JSOT	*Journal for the Study of the Old Testament*
JSOTSup	Journal for the Study of the Old Testament Supplement Series
KJV	King James Version
MT	Masoretic Text
NICNT	New International Commentary on the New Testament
NICOT	New International Commentary on the Old Testament
NIGTC	New International Greek Testament Commentary
NIVAC	NIV Application Commentary
NovT	*Novum Testamentum*
NSBT	New Studies in Biblical Theology
NTT	New Testament Theology
SGBC	Story of God Bible Commentary
WBC	Word Biblical Commentary

SERIES PREFACE

The question "What does the Bible have to say about that?" is, in essence, what the Biblical Theology for Life series is all about. Not unlike other biblical explorations of various topics, the volumes in this series articulate various themes in biblical theology, but they always do so with the "So what?" question rumbling about and demanding to be answered. Too often, books on biblical theology have focused mainly on *description*—simply discerning the teachings of the biblical literature on a particular topic. But contributors to this series seek to straddle both the world of the text and the world in which we live.

This means that their descriptions of biblical theology will always be understood as the important *first* step in their task, which will not be completed until they draw out that theology's practical implications for the contemporary context. Contributors therefore engage both in the *description* of biblical theology and in its contemporary *contextualization*, accosting the reader's perspective and fostering application, transformation, and growth. It is our hope that these informed insights of evangelical biblical scholarship will increasingly become enfleshed in the sermons and discussions that transpire each week in places of worship, in living rooms where Bible studies gather, and in classrooms around the world. We hope that this series will lead to personal transformation and practical application in real life.

Every volume in this series has the same basic structure. In the first section, entitled "Queuing the Questions," authors introduce the main questions they seek to address in their books. Raising these questions enables you to see clearly from the outset what each book will be pursuing, inviting you to participate in the process of discovery along the way. In the second section, "Arriving at Answers," authors develop the biblical theology of the topic they address, focusing their attention on specific biblical texts and constructing answers to the questions introduced in section one. In the concluding "Reflecting on Relevance" section, authors contextualize their biblical-theological insights, discussing specific ways in which the theology presented in their books addresses contemporary situations and issues, giving you opportunities to consider how you might live out that theology in the world today.

Long before you make it to the "Reflecting on Relevance" section, however, we encourage you to wrestle with the implications of the biblical theology being described by considering the "Relevant Questions" that conclude each chapter. Frequent sidebars spice up your experience, supplementing the main discussion with significant quotations, illustrative historical or contemporary data, and fuller explanations of the content.

In sum, the goal of the Biblical Theology for Life series is communicated by its title. On the one hand, its books mine the Bible for theology that addresses a wide range of topics so you may know "the only true God, and Jesus Christ, whom [he] . . . sent" (John 17:3). On the other hand, contributing authors contextualize this theology in ways that allow the *life*-giving Word (John 1:4; 20:31) to speak into and transform contemporary *life*.

Series Editor
Jonathan Lunde

PART 1

QUEUING THE QUESTIONS

CHAPTER 1

THE HUMAN PROBLEM OF VIOLENCE

Blessed are those who find wisdom,
those who gain understanding . . .
Her ways are pleasant ways,
and all her paths are peace.
Proverbs 3:13, 17

What drives human violence? The cause of violence is one of the great questions that people of every age have asked. It has been explored in sacred texts, classical myths, philosophy, and fiction. It is one of the great questions that we will bring to our study of Scripture.

The atheist writer Steven Pinker believes that violence is declining in our day.[1]

[The decades since World War II have been] decades of progress for racial minorities, women, children, gay people, and animals. . . . In every case, quantifiable measures of violence—hate crimes and rape, wife-beating and child abuse . . . all point downward.[2]

Others are less sure. David Bentley Hart, for example, considers that Pinker is far too optimistic, demonstrating "the ecstatic innocence of a faith unsullied by prudent doubt."[3]

But even Pinker is surprised by his own conclusions. After all, he argues, the biological urge is against us. Trends of violence reduction have to contend with powerful forces that oppose them. These include:

The dehumanization and demonization of outgroups; men's sexual rapacity and their proprietary sentiments toward women; manifestations of parent-offspring conflict such as infanticide and corporal punishment; the moralization of sexual disgust in homophobia; and our meat hunger, thrill of the hunt, and boundaries of empathy based on kinship, reciprocity, and charisma.[4]

---

1. Whether any trend toward improvement proves to be sustainable will, of course, be left to future historians to decide.

2. Steven Pinker, *The Better Angels of Our Nature: The Decline of Violence in History and Its Causes* (London: Penguin, 2011), 572.

3. David Bentley Hart, "The Precious Steven Pinker," *First Things*, January 2012, www.firstthings.com/article/2012/01/the-precious-steven-pinker.

4. Pinker, *Better Angels of our Nature*, 572.

In other words, as Pinker sees it, the problem comes down to human biology. Patterns that lead to violence are hardwired within us.

Is this an interpretation that Scripture would agree with? If so, does it mean that violence is inherent and intractable? Is there any hope for a world at peace? Can human nature be overcome, as Pinker claims is happening, by a growth in empathy and with the benefits of a global perspective? Or are we doomed to squabble violently until the end of time?

In Pinker's view, there is another barrier to violence reduction, and this one we will find very close to home.

> As if biology didn't make things bad enough, the Abrahamic religions ratified some of our worst instincts with laws and beliefs that have encouraged violence for millennia: the demonization of infidels, the ownership of women, the sinfulness of children, the abomination of homosexuality, the dominion over animals and denial to them of souls.[5]

Pinker accuses the Abrahamic religions of making things worse, serving as reactionary influences that oppose human progress toward peace. As a Christian writer, I cannot answer for the Jewish and Muslim faiths, of course. But this challenge is hard to ignore because there are elements of our Scripture that would seem to support his claim. And there are certainly periods in the history of the church that would provide evidence for a claim that the Christian faith has a violent tendency.

So this brings us to another great question; one that we must squarely face.

Is the Bible part of the problem?

Or, to put it another way:

Is the Christian faith inherently violent?

If it seems odd to begin our study of the Bible's teaching about human violence by listening to the voice of an atheist scholar, it should not. Pinker presents questions we should face honestly. Our answers will be of little value if we have not taken into account the most robust challenges that can be offered.

It is the task of this book to consider questions such as these by hosting a conversation between Scripture and (contemporary and historical) thinkers on the subject of violence, all with attention to violence's (contemporary and historical) victims. And by so doing, perhaps we can discern, and learn to walk in, wisdom's paths of peace.

---

5. Pinker, *Better Angels of our Nature*, 572.

DEFINITIONS AND PRELIMINARY QUESTIONS

We should begin with a definition. Many definitions of violence have been offered, but I propose a simple one, which will underlie all that follows:

Violence is the use of force or coercion in a way that causes harm to another.

While this is a reasonable working definition of violence, we will put some boundaries around it to limit the scope of our inquiry.

- "The use of"—by humans. The question of divine violence will arise but will not form the main focus of our study.
- "The use of"—by systems as well as by individuals. This means our definition encompasses various forms of group violence, including that conducted by the nation state.
- "Force or coercion"—while violence is often physical in nature, this is not the only form it takes, and our inquiry will also at times encompass verbal, emotional, and structural violence.
- "Causes harm"—which may be visible or invisible and includes severe emotional harm such as post-traumatic stress disorder.
- "To another"—we will principally be considering violence that causes harm to another human being. This does not deny the reality of violence against animals and against the planet, which may enter our discussion from time to time. While acknowledging the gravity of self-harm, this is not within the scope of our inquiry here.

Because violence is so prevalent and has such enormous impact on people's lives, it has been the subject of a great deal of research and investigation. Sociologists, political scientists, historians, physicians, and anthropologists—to name but a few—have all attempted to explain it. Their contributions are often highly insightful and provocative, and they can help us to shape the questions that we bring to Scripture.

Here, then, we will briefly consider some of the most significant contributions to the field. They vary in the type of violence they are examining and in the approach they take. Some take a "neutral," observational approach, which tends to result in pragmatic solutions—this is what will work. Others take an "ideological" approach that makes no pretense to neutrality but seeks to make the world a better place. This observational/ideological distinction is, of course, too simple a dichotomy. Many people with deep convictions and high principles work hard to generate solutions that will make a difference in the real world. But it highlights the tension that exists between the *ideal* and the *possible*; a tension to which we will return in the final section of the book.

> The prison system is an example of the interplay between ideology and pragmatism in public policy. Why do we lock criminals up? Some people will give pragmatic reasons: to keep violent people off the streets, to deter others from offending, to rehabilitate offenders. Others offer the ideological perspective that crime demands retribution. When a notorious criminal is convicted, especially if their offence has been against children, the public mood is highly retributive. *Lock him up and throw away the key! I hope he rots in prison!*
>
> In cases of less serious crime, the pragmatic-ideological tension is even more obvious. Many have argued that incarceration for minor offenses has little value in reducing the likelihood of repeat offending.[6] But the use of incarceration continues to be pushed strongly, especially by parties on the right of the political divide.[7] In the UK, the rhetoric of being "tough on crime" noticeably ramps up around election time when Conservative Party candidates are seeking election. In the US, support for the "three strikes and you are out"[8] policy tends to split along party lines, with Republicans positioning themselves as being the party that takes crime seriously.[9]

Each of the theorists we will consider here will raise for us some important questions, which we will carry forward to our study of Scripture.

1. How does the model align with the testimony of Scripture? For example, what view of humanity (anthropology) is proposed or presupposed? Does it consider humans to be inherently good or evil? Are we parasites upon the planet or rulers of it?
2. How does the model compare with a Christian theological understanding of the world? For example, is it a "closed system," with no room for divine activity? Or, as another example, is the model ultimately hopeful or pessimistic? If hopeful, what is that hope based upon, and how well does that align with what the Bible teaches and promises?
3. Once we have considered how well the model aligns with Scripture, we can reverse the perspective and ask to what extent it might offer a lens for reading Scripture. Does it aid our interpretation of difficult texts? Does it offer a model that is expressed in different terms than the biblical account, but has

---

6. See, e.g., the meta-analysis in Patrice Villettaz, Gladys Gillieron, and Martin Killias, "The Effects on Re-offending of Custodial vs. Noncustodial Sanctions: An Updated Systematic Review of the State of Knowledge," *Campbell Systematic Reviews* 11.1 (2015): 1–92.

7. Travis C. Pratt, *Addicted to Incarceration: Corrections Policy and the Politics of Misinformation in the United States* (Los Angeles: Sage, 2019).

8. This refers to the policy that a person with two previous con-victions who is convicted of a third offense must serve a mandatory life sentence in prison.

9. The ideology is not all one-way, of course. The liberal anti-incarceration push is also driven by conviction as much as pragmatism. See the discussion in the introduction of John Paul Wright and Matt DeLisi, *Conservative Criminology: A Call to Restore Balance to the Social Sciences* (New York: Routledge, 2016), 1–13.

sufficient points of contact to provide a helpful perspective? Or is it seeking
to answer a completely different set of questions?

4. Finally, if the theory attempts to offer solutions to the problem of violence,
we need to critically examine their usefulness. Our approach to this question
will be strongly linked to the conclusions we have drawn from the preceding
questions.

With these preliminary comments in mind, we now turn to consider some of
the big ideas about violence currently in circulation.

VIOLENCE AND THE ORDINARY PERSON

Zygmunt Bauman was born in 1925 into a Jewish-Polish family. At the outbreak
of hostilities in 1939, they fled east to the USSR, and he served in the First Polish
Army during the second half of World War II. He then became a sociologist and
ultimately one of the leading writers on the Holocaust.[10]

One of Bauman's great contributions was to argue that the Holocaust was *not an
anomaly*. It would be comforting, he suggests, to view it as an aberration committed
by evil and psychotic miscreants and sadists. Then we could view it as unrepeatable,
or at least rare and perhaps preventable. But the SS officers who perpetrated the worst
atrocities were not mad. Rather, they had responded to three factors that enable
normal people to commit the sorts of atrocities that were seen in those dark days.
These are: authorization, routinization, and dehumanization.[11]

Authorization[12]

In the hierarchical setting of an army at war, an individual soldier's normal moral
code is replaced by the duty to obey the orders of a superior, resulting in a lack of a
sense of personal responsibility for the actions taken. This provides a psychological
route for the avoidance of a sense of guilt.

Routinization[13]

Reducing a large mission into a series of small, routine, and mechanical steps, which
may be divided between a number of individuals, reduces the number of morally
charged decisions that need to be made by any one person. In other words, it reduces
the number of times that the individual is faced with the moral choice of whether
to commit the atrocity or not.

This is related to the argument made by Hannah Arendt in her reflection upon

---

10. Zygmunt Bauman, *Modernity and the Holocaust* (Ithaca: Cornell University Press, 2000).

11. Here Bauman is drawing upon Herbert Kelman's work on "sanctioned massacres." See Herbert C. Kelman, "Violence without

Moral Restraint: Reflections on the Dehumanization of Victims and Victimizers," *Journal of Social Issues* 249.4 (1973): 25–61.

12. Kelman, "Violence without Moral Restraint," 38–46.

13. Kelman, "Violence without Moral Restraint," 46–48.

the trial of Adolf Eichmann in Jerusalem in 1961. Perhaps surprisingly, Eichmann showed little evidence of hatred for Jewish people. Rather, he was an accomplished administrator, someone who took delight in making certain processes integral to the genocide (such as the Auschwitz train timetables) ran smoothly. This led Arendt to coin the controversial phrase "banality of evil." It was not a phrase intended to exonerate Eichmann but to point toward the very mundane face that evil can wear.[14]

Dehumanization[15]

The final step is to render the intended victims inhuman by stripping them of identity and community. As examples, Bauman offers the technological capacity for killing at arm's length, particularly the gas chambers, where the murderers were "optically separated" from their victims.[16] This removes the last moral constraint that might otherwise prevent the soldier from committing the murder. Ironically, however, this process serves to dehumanize the victimizer too.

Consequently, Bauman argues that the Holocaust was not committed by psychopaths but by individuals whose moral restraint was eroded by dint of these three stages of moral stripping. But he takes the argument beyond the individual, to ask how a society could come to tolerate such mass killing. What was revealed at the Holocaust was not some warped perversion of civilized society but the other face that civilization has worn all along. Every element that combined to permit it was "normal."[17]

These chilling conclusions are borne out by the work of the historian Christopher Browning, who looked at involvement that was even more direct than Eichmann's.[18] On July 13, 1942, five hundred men of the German Reserve Police Battalion 101 entered the Polish village of Józefów and began an action that only ended after thirty-eight thousand civilian Jews had been shot at close range, and a further forty-five thousand deported to the extermination camp Treblinka.[19] What is unusual about this massacre is that it was conducted not by the SS or their like, but by a rearguard unit of nonprofessional soldiers—*ordinary men*. They were dockworkers, shop owners, teachers, and so on.[20] But at least 80 percent of them participated in the close-range shooting of men, women, and children.[21]

They were not obliged to. Wilhelm Trapp, their commander, understood that they were being asked to do a terrible thing.

14. Hannah Arendt, *Eichmann in Jerusalem: A Report on the Banality of Evil* (London: Penguin Classics, 2006). Amos Elon's introductory essay in this edition (vii–xiii) helpfully evaluates Arendt's argument and the public response to it.

15. Kelman, "Violence without Moral Restraint," 48–52.

16. Bauman, *Modernity and the Holocaust*, 26.

17. Bauman, *Modernity and the Holocaust*, 8.

18. Christopher R. Browning, *Ordinary Men: Reserve Police Battalion 101 and the Final Solution in Poland* (London: Penguin, 1992).

19. Browning, *Ordinary Men*, 142.

20. Browning, *Ordinary Men*, 46–48.

21. Browning, *Ordinary Men*, 159.

Pale and nervous, with choking voice and tears in his eyes, Trapp visibly fought to control himself as he spoke. The battalion, he said plaintively, had to perform a frightfully unpleasant task. This assignment was not to his liking, indeed it was highly regrettable, but the orders came from the highest authorities. . . . If any of the older men among them did not feel up to the task that lay before him, he could step out.[22]

Those who availed themselves of this option, or who later were unable to stomach the actual process of close-range shooting, were deployed to less direct roles such as cordon duty.

Twenty years later, the state prosecutor began an investigation into this action. Two hundred and ten men from the unit were still alive, and they were brought in for questioning and trial. Christopher Browning later analyzed the transcripts of their trials and interviews, and of covertly recorded conversations with cellmates. The question he was seeking to answer was: What could bring these ordinary men to commit the atrocities that they did? Using the findings of Stanley Milgram's now famous electric-shock experiment to help him, he tested some theories.[23]

They were not specially selected for the task. In fact, Browning suggests that, as those passed over for full military service, they had experienced a sort of negative selection.[24] As we have seen, they were not under duress, though careerism seems to have played a part for some.[25] Ideological indoctrination did not prove to be particularly significant. These men had not, by and large, been members of the Nazi Party until after 1933. They experienced the general propaganda aimed at soldiers, but nothing that was designed to condition men to direct action such as this.[26] The most important factors, Browning concludes, were the sense of peer pressure, along with a desire not to seem weak,[27] and the process of gradual brutalization.[28]

In 1971, Philip Zimbardo and colleagues ran the now infamous Stanford Prison experiment.[29] From a group of healthy, young, male student volunteers, carefully screened for their stability, maturity, and lack of evidenced antisocial behavior, twenty-four were selected and randomly assigned to be a "prisoner" or a "guard" in a simulated prison. They were to be paid $15 per day if they completed the two-week assignment. The guards were told that the experiment was designed to test

22. Browning, *Ordinary Men*, 2.

23. In the early 1970s, Stanley Milgram conducted a series of experiments where test subjects were induced to give (unknown to them, fake) electric shocks to actors, in order to test their willingness to inflict pain in response to instructions. They were told that the experiment was to test the use of pain to aid learning. Two thirds of participants administered what they believed to be the maximum dose of 450 volts, labeled in their sight, "danger—severe shock" (Stanley Milgram, *Obedience to Authority: An Experimental View* [New York: HarperCollins, 2009]).

24. Browning, *Ordinary Men*, 164.

25. Browning, *Ordinary Men*, 169–71.

26. Browning, *Ordinary Men*, 176–84.

27. Browning, *Ordinary Men*, 185–86.

28. Browning, *Ordinary Men*, 160–63.

29. Craig Haney, Curtis Banks, and Philip Zimbardo, "A Study of Prisoners and Guards," *Naval Research Reviews* 26 (1973): 1–17.

the responses of the prisoners (which was true) but not that it was also testing their behavior. Certain prohibitions were placed upon the guards (no physical brutality), but within those limits they were free to run the prison as they saw fit.

Very quickly some of the guards began to overstep their agreed protocols. Over the course of a few days, the compulsory ten-minute roll call was taking several hours. Some guards chose to stay beyond their shift for voluntary, unpaid overtime. In lieu of physical violence, there was a good deal of verbal abuse and aggression. This increased daily even though prisoner resistance had ceased. Some guards attempted to deprive inmates of sleep. When the experiment was terminated early, despite the promise of no financial loss, some guards complained bitterly.

Not all the guards behaved similarly, however. Of the twelve, two or three resisted this trend, treated prisoners kindly, and did small favors for them. Around half could be categorized as "tough but fair"; they were not excessively brutal but nor did they show any leniency. And a third of the group seemed to take a sadistic delight in their role.

> Being a guard carried with it . . . the freedom of exercising an unprecedented degree of control over the lives of other human beings. This control was invariably expressed in terms of sanctions, punishment, demands, and with the threat of manifest physical power. There was no need for the guards to rationally justify a request as they did their ordinary life, and merely to make a demand was sufficient to have it carried out. Many of the guards showed in their behaviour and revealed in post experimental statements that this sense of power was exhilarating. The use of power was self-aggrandizing and self-perpetuating. . . . The most hostile guards on each shift moved spontaneously into the leadership roles of giving orders. . . . Not to be tough and arrogant was to be seen as a sign of weakness by the guards, and even those "good" guards who did not get as drawn into the power syndrome as the others respected the implicit norm of *never* contradicting or even interfering with the action of a more hostile guard on their shift.[30]

Remember, these young men had all been screened as stable, mature, and not antisocial just a few days previously.

Zimbardo's experimental findings were echoed in Browning's real-life study. Just as the pseudo prison guards fell into three broad categories in their response to the power they were given, so did Wilhelm Trapp's men. A few members of the battalion were completely unable to stomach the shootings and recused themselves immediately. The majority got on with the job, although some with weaker stomachs

---

30. Haney, Banks, and Zimbardo, "Study of Prisoners and Guards," 14.

needed to be excused before the massacre was completed. And there were some—a minority, but a sizable one—who enthusiastically volunteered for the opportunity.[31] Browning closes his book with these chilling words:

> Everywhere society conditions people to respect and defer to authority, and indeed could scarcely function otherwise. Everywhere people seek career advancement. In every modern society, the complexity of life and the resulting bureaucratization and specialization attenuate the sense of personal responsibility of those implementing official policy. Within virtually every social collective, the peer group exerts tremendous pressures on behaviour and sets moral norms. *If the men of Reserve Police Battalion 101 could become killers under such circumstances, what group of men cannot?*[32]

Bauman, Kelman, Milgram, Zimbardo, and Browning do not all agree on the process by which it happens, but they are united on one thing: apparently normal people—and societies—are capable of great evil. None of these theorists is a theologian, and so none is asking ultimate questions about the human soul. But their work certainly raises these issues. Is human violence an aberration, or is it something that we are all capable of, given the right set of circumstances? This is a troubling possibility, but it is one that we will need to take seriously as we move forward in our study.

The second, and related, insight that these theorists offer is the influence that dehumanizing of the enemy has upon the human capacity for violence. It is much easier to kill when we do not see the personhood of the human whose life we are ending. This might be because we have been taught to view them that way, or because we have technologies that facilitate killing at a distance. As we shall see, the Bible has much to say about human personhood, and we need to bring this to bear upon the issue of lethal technology.

The third theme that has emerged from this study is the idea that brutalization reduces the threshold for committing subsequent violent actions. It is empirically demonstrable that many combatants become desensitized over time to the killing of others. We will consider the idea of moral injury in chapter 14, but this discussion brings us to the role of shame in the perpetration of violence.

THE ROLE OF SHAME IN INTERPERSONAL VIOLENCE

James Gilligan is a psychiatrist, the former medical director of the Bridgewater State Hospital for the criminally insane, and director of mental health for the Massachusetts

---

31. Browning, *Ordinary Men*, 168.   32. Browning, *Ordinary Men*, 189 (italics added).

prison system. In these roles he has gained extensive experience with (mostly) men who have committed criminally violent acts. In his seminal book *Violence: Reflections on a National Epidemic*,[33] he sets out the conclusions that he has drawn and makes a compelling case for the reform of both our conceptualization of, and our response to, individual violence. Note his use of the medical term "epidemic." Again and again, Gilligan returns to such language, not as a metaphor, nor to consign the criminally violent to the morally neutral category of "sick," but because he views the problem of violence in the USA as a public-health issue:

> The only way to explain the causes of violence, so that we can learn how to prevent it, is to approach violence as a problem in public health and preventive medicine, and to think of violence as a symptom of life threatening (and often lethal) pathology, which, like all forms of illness, has an etiology or cause, a pathogen.[34]

In saying this, Gilligan is thereby bypassing the question of morality, considering it a category error. He does not seek to invalidate such questions but rather to exclude them from his inquiry. Moral (and legal) evaluations of conduct are just that—*evaluations*; Gilligan is seeking to discover *causes*.[35]

Gilligan's studies identified that the explanation for most criminal violence lies in the near ubiquity of deep *shame* among violent criminals. He defines shame as "the absence or deficiency of self-love."[36] Violent crime is irrational, self-destructive, and linked to self-loathing. Such shame frequently has its roots in an abusive upbringing or severe trauma.

> I have yet to see a serious act of violence that was not provoked by the experience of feeling shamed and humiliated, disrespected and ridiculed, and that did not represent the attempt to prevent or undo this "loss of face."[37]

This extreme sense of shame results in what Gilligan terms "living death." Prison inmates describe themselves as robots, zombies, vampires, or believe that they are already decomposing.

> To speak of these men as "the living dead" is not a metaphor I have invented, but rather the most direct and literal, least distorted way to summarize what these men have told me when describing their subjective experience of themselves. . . . When they say they feel dead they mean they cannot feel anything—neither emotions nor even physical sensations. I have seen many who admit to killing others without so much as a flicker of remorse or any other emotion.[38]

---

33. James Gilligan, *Violence: Reflections on a National Epidemic* (New York: Random House, 1996).

34. Gilligan, *Violence*, 92.

35. Gilligan, *Violence*, 92.

36. Gilligan, *Violence*, 47.

37. Gilligan, *Violence*, 110.

38. Gilligan, *Violence*, 33.

This helps to explain the enormously high levels of self-harm in prison and also serves as a caution against believing that capital punishment acts as a deterrent: "The men I know are so spiritually dead that they long for physical death as well."[39]

Gilligan is not seeking to exonerate or excuse violence by this explanation. He considers the sense of shame to be a necessary but not sufficient cause for violent actions. But by viewing it as a public-health issue, he points toward the sickness in society that provides the soil in which such pathologies grow.

Gilligan's work is undertaken in male US penitentiaries, and we cannot immediately assume that it translates equally to any other setting. It has, however, been found applicable in other contexts,[40] and as such deserves serious consideration even if it has not yet been acclaimed as universally explicative. However, its applicability to women offenders remains moot. Gilligan himself links the phenomenon he has identified to male perpetration of violence and women's experience of violence.

> The horror of dependency is what causes violence. The emotion that causes the horror of dependency is shame. Men, much more than women, are taught that to want love or care from others is to be passive, dependant, unaggressive and unambitious or, in short, unmanly; and that they will be subjected to shaming, ridicule, and disrespect if they appear unmanly in the eyes of others. Women, by contrast, have traditionally been taught that they will be honoured if, and only if, they accept a role that restricts them to the relatively passive aim of arranging to be loved by men and to depend on men for their social and economic status. . . . This set of injunctions decreases women's vulnerability to behaving violently, but it also inhibits women from participating actively or directly in the building of civilisation in part by reducing them to the role of men's sex objects.[41]

Gilligan moves beyond diagnosis to offer some suggestions for a way forward. As we might imagine, his targets are those structures and institutions that ritually and systematically humiliate people, particularly young men, with special reference to the penal system. He concludes his book with these words: "Perhaps reforming the social, economic, and legal institutions that systematically humiliate people can do more to prevent violence than all the preaching and punishing in the world."[42]

These words signify a slight theological turn that Gilligan makes toward the end of his argument. Having seen the raw underbelly of the American penal system, he is clearly disillusioned with it, considering it a self-defeating policy that actually increases violence in society.[43] After comparing prisons to hell because of the

---

39. Gilligan, *Violence*, 42.
40. See, for example, Danny Hoffman, *The War Machines: Young Men and Violence in Sierra Leone and Liberia* (Durham: Duke University Press, 2011), 105.
41. Gilligan, *Violence*, 237.
42. Gilligan, *Violence*, 239.
43. Gilligan, *Violence*, 185.

conditions and the "living death" which we noted above, he then makes the deeper point that they are symbolically connected in the public imagination.

> Throughout history . . . the societies that construct prisons have specifically wanted to make the prisons resemble hell, as much as possible, from their architecture to the relationships between the various groups of people involved in them.[44]

In this way, medieval images of hell portrayed demons inflicting upon the damned the same tortures experienced by real people in the criminal systems of the day: criminal trials were often fashioned like the last judgment, judges were parallel to God himself, and prison officers became modeled on hell's demons, which in medieval theology tortured the damned.[45] Gilligan's point is that this ancient symbolism has an ongoing effect in the popular imagination; prison is the place for just punishment, and hellish conditions are therefore acceptable.

Gilligan's work raises significant questions for us as we move into our reading of Scripture. Do we agree that the themes of self-love and shame find resonance there? Does Scripture endorse Gilligan's perspective? Does it offer a way forward that addresses his concerns?

His theological turn then becomes more explicit as he considers the human need for forgiveness.

> The death of God is such a tragedy not because we no longer have anyone to uphold the moral law, but because we have no one who is capable of forgiving us.

Gilligan is using the term "death of God" in the way that Enlightenment philosophers used it—to refer to the functional irrelevance of God in society and the widespread lack of belief in him. His words may be written with a sense of pessimism, but we who know of a God who forgives may find here the grounds for hope. If so, this poses a strong challenge to the church, and we will carry this question forward into the later parts of this book.

We will now consider a different understanding of violence, particularly with regard to its more organized forms. This will contrast with Gilligan's strong assertion that violence is irrational and argues that it can be explained on the basis of economic analysis.

RELIGIOUS VIOLENCE?

Religion causes violence—this is a dogma that almost every reader of this book will have encountered as a truism at some time. Indeed, the claims of a relationship

---

44. Gilligan, *Violence*, 157.   45. Gilligan, *Violence*, 157–61.

between religion and violence are so manifold that Matthew Rowley has constructed a taxonomy of three hundred such claims in the academic literature.[46] For example, some claim that religion is inherently violent, while others suggest that the problem lies with the instrumentalization of religion. Some center their criticism on over-dogmatic leadership, and others focus on the role of emotion in religion's violent turn.

On first inspection, this weight of criticism looks damning for religious adher-ents. And the rhetoric around such claims is often inflammatory. The sociologist Mark Jurgensmeyer has described a "dark alliance between religion and violence."[47] Redoubtable atheist Christopher Hitchens wrote,

> Violent, irrational, intolerant, allied to racism and tribalism and bigotry, invested in ignorance and hostile to free inquiry, contemptuous of women and coercive toward children: organized religion ought to have a great deal on its conscience.[48]

But, as Rowley goes on to argue, many of the examples he identifies in his taxonomy, and the sheer scope of the claims made, should give pause for thought. Some of the claims seem to be mutually contradictory—religion's dogmatism and religion's ambiguity, perhaps. Others are very complex, such as the Jonestown mass suicide,[49] whose leader, Jim Jones, was an ordained minister but also a professing atheist.[50] Reductive claims of a simple correlation between religion and violence fail to take account of the fact that not everyone responds to violent texts (for example) in the same way. Correlation does not necessarily indicate causation.

The dogma that religion causes violence has also been robustly disputed by theologian William T. Cavanaugh. Cavanaugh shows that many definitions of religion introduce a false dichotomy between religious and secular belief systems. Not only is this anachronistic for the majority of times in history, but it also reflects an Enlightenment attitude that characterizes religious belief as irrational and backward and the secular world, by contrast, as enlightened and progressive.

> I have no doubt that ideologies and practices of all kinds . . . can and do promote violence under certain conditions. What I challenge as incoherent is that there is something called religion . . . which is necessarily more inclined toward violence than are ideologies and institutions that are identified as secular.[51]

46. Matthew Rowley, "What Causes Religious Violence? Three Hundred Claimed Contributing Causes," *Journal of Religion and Violence* 2.3 (2014): 361–402.

47. Mark Jurgensmeyer, *Terror in the Mind of God: The Global Rise of Religious Violence*, 4th ed. (Berkeley: University of California Press, 2017), xiv.

48. Christopher Hitchens, *God Is Not Great: How Religion Poisons Everything* (Toronto: McClelland & Stewart, 2008), 56.

49. Over nine hundred members of the California based Peoples Temple cult committed suicide at Jonestown, on November 18, 1978 (see www.britannica.com/event/Jonestown).

50. Rowley, "What Causes Religious Violence?," 361–400.

51. William T. Cavanaugh, *The Myth of Religious Violence: Secular Ideology and the Roots of Modern Conflict* (Oxford: Oxford University Press, 2009), 5.

Considering one influential book making this type of claim, Charles Kimball's *When Religion Turns Evil*,[52] Cavanaugh examines five signs claimed to be evidence of a religion becoming toxic. These are: absolute truth claims, blind obedience, establishment of the "ideal time" for action, assertion that the end justifies the means, and a declaration of holy war. But none of these, as Cavanaugh shows, is limited to religious ideology. With particular attention to the "secular" ideology of nationalism, he gives examples from recent US history to show how this frequently operates just like a religion. Indeed, if one defines "absolutism" (Kimball's first sign) as a willingness to kill, Cavanaugh points out that far more Americans—even those who consider themselves Christian—are willing to kill (or countenance killing) for their nation than for God.[53]

The uncritical assertion of religion's link with violence provides "a stock character, the religious fanatic, to serve as enemy," and thereby serves to justify "secular" violence in the public discourse.[54] Because of *their* (irrational, religious, illegitimate) violence, *we* have to make recourse to (rational, secular, legitimate) violence: "We find ourselves obliged to bomb them into liberal democracy."[55] The final two sentences of a paper he wrote in 2004 are still challenging today:

> The beliefs of the Jim Joneses and Osama bin Ladens of the world are a significant part of the problem of violence in the 21st century. At least equally significant is the evangelical zeal with which "free trade," liberal democracy, and American hegemony are offered to—or forced upon—a hungry world.[56]

What can we learn from these theorists in view of our questions outlined earlier? The claims of religion's inextricable complicity with violence often have strong ideological motivations. None of the theorists we have been considering would deny that violence and religion may and do coexist, but rather they caution against simplistic correlations or false dichotomies.

A case in point is the mistaken assumption that someone who speaks in religious terms is necessarily motivated by their religion. We all function within a certain worldview, which provides us with an operative set of metaphors. When we want to provide explanation or make an argument, we tend to make our case using these ideas. Adherents to a particular religion, operating among other believers, will tend to frame their argument and motivations in religious terms, which may not reflect the primary motivation for their violence.[57] As Matthew Rowley puts it, "Because humans are meaning makers and meaning seekers, because religion and sacred

---

52. Charles Kimball, *When Religion Becomes Evil: Five Warning Signs* (New York: HarperCollins, 2008).

53. William T. Cavanaugh, "Sins of Omission: What 'Religion and Violence' Arguments Ignore," *The Hedgehog Review* 6.1 (2004): 34–50.

54. Cavanaugh, *Myth of Religious Violence*, 5.

55. Cavanaugh, *Myth of Religious Violence*, 4.

56. Cavanaugh, "Sins of Omission," 50.

57. J. D. Wright, and Y. Khoo, "Empirical Perspectives on Religion and Violence," *Contemporary Voices: St Andrews Journal of International Relations* 1.3 (2019): 75–100.

texts help interpret events, and because killing compels interpretation, justifying or describing conflict through one's religious worldview is normative."[58]

Nonetheless, there are certain features of religions that do lend themselves to violent instrumentalization. Confining ourselves to comments on Christianity, these include: monotheism; biblical texts that appear to promote violence, including the characterization that God is a warrior; and eschatology.

Monotheism

Regina Schwartz has argued that monotheistic religions tend toward violence because of their emphasis on exclusivism and therefore the "scarcity" of divine blessing.

> When everything is in short supply, it must all be competed for—land, prosperity, power, favor, even identity itself. In many biblical narratives, the one God is not imagined as infinitely giving, but as strangely withholding. Everyone does not receive divine blessings. Some are cursed—with dearth and with death—as though there were a cosmic shortage of prosperity. . . . While I was heartened to discover that the Bible does offer glimpses of a monotheistic plenitude instead of scarcity—the heavens rain enough bread to feed everyone—those moments have not held the same command in our politics, in our culture, and in our imaginations that the biblical myth of scarcity has.[59]

This argument deserves careful consideration. Note that it does not wholly rest upon what Scripture *says* but also upon how it has been *used*. And while Schwartz's thesis has been critiqued, not least because of her underestimate of polytheistic violence, it should not be summarily dismissed. Even a cursory reading of history will identify just such narratives on display to justify violence—against the Jews in Europe in the Middle Ages, for instance.

Biblical Violence

Biblical texts that appear to promote violence can be a contributing factor to violent action, sometimes being used to justify (i.e., to seek to provide a justification for) or engender submission to violence. Examples abound, but here are three.

- The annihilation of the Amalekites (e.g., Deut 25:17–19) has been used to justify the crusades, religious persecution of the Catholics, and the extermination of the native Americans.[60] More recently, the texts commanding the annihilation of the Amalekites were used to promote the ideology of degeneracy: that some peoples are too hereditarily corrupt to be permitted

58. Matthew Rowley, *God, Religious Extremism and Violence* (Cambridge: Cambridge University Press, forthcoming).

59. Regina M. Schwartz, *The Curse of Cain: The Violent Legacy of Monotheism* (Chicago: University of Chicago Press, 1997), xi.

60. Helen Paynter, *Dead and Buried: Attending to the Voice of the Victim in the Old Testament and Today: Toward an Ethical Reading of the Old Testament Texts of Violence* (Oxford: Centre for Baptist History and Heritage, 2018).

to procreate. (Degeneracy ideology evolved into the eugenics movement.[61]) These words were written by Massachusetts clergyman John Hayley in 1876:

> Had the women and children been spared, there would soon have been a fresh crop of adult Amalekites, precisely like their predecessors. Or suppose merely the children had been saved . . . they might, from their hereditary disposition and proclivities to evil have proved a most undesirable and pernicious element in the nation. It was, doubtless, on the whole, the best thing for the world that the Amalekite race should be exterminated.[62]

- Kerry Noble was the leader of the cult Christian Identity and founder of the paramilitary group Covenant, Sword, and Arm of the Lord. Noble wrote a pamphlet titled "The Lord God is a Man of War." In 1984, Noble was arrested while carrying a bomb into a gay-affirming church.[63]
- The Bible is not infrequently used by domestic abusers in Christian homes to manipulate their wives into compliance with the abuse. In my own research, I have heard testimony from women who were told—by their abusers—that the Bible tells them to obey their husbands *in all things*; that God hates and utterly prohibits divorce; and that Sarah and Esther were good examples of how a wife should submit to her husband.[64]

Eschatology

There are many varieties of Christian eschatological belief, which can be broadly categorized into premillennial, postmillennial, and amillennial types. What we believe about the end times undoubtedly shapes the way that we behave in the present. By what means the end will come, and whether humans have a role to play in the final battle, may work itself out in ways that lead to violence. Further, one's eschatology has a strong effect on one's attitude toward Jews and Palestinians.

Premillennial dispensationalists tend to be philo-Semitic and often have strong ideological commitments toward the state of Israel. This may work itself out in a prejudice against Palestinians and, indeed, in destabilizing interventions in the Middle East. Palestinian theologian Munther Isaac has written,

---

61. Trent Goodbaudy, *The Rebirth of Mankind: Homo Evolutis* (Portland: PDXdzyn, 2012), 25–27.

62. Quoted in Philip Jenkins, *Laying Down the Sword: Why We Can't Ignore the Bible's Violent Verses* (New York: HarperOne, 2011), 114.

63. Jurgensmeyer, *Terror in the Mind of God*, 149.

64. Clearly there is significant diversity on the proper interpretation of biblical commands to wives to submit. This remark is not intended to engage with that debate but rather to indicate the range of ways that abusive husbands sometimes exceed what even the most conservative of interpreters would permit. I explore this much more fully in Helen Paynter, *The Bible Doesn't Tell Me So: Why You Don't Have to Submit to Domestic Abuse and Coercive Control* (Abingdon: Bible Reading Fellowship, 2020).

In [a Zionist] ideology, the Palestinians have become the unchosen "other." As with the Canaanites before them, the interest of the "people of God" trumps their own value and worth. A theology that privileges a people group produces prejudice, and even bigotry. For Christian Zionists, Palestinians are often an irrelevant afterthought. They are secondary to the interests of Israel.[65]

A very different example can be found in the aforementioned racist and anti-Semitic group Christian Identity, which came into being in the mid-twentieth century. Its adherents believe that the lost tribes of Israel migrated to the British Isles (Isaac's sons = Saxons), an ideology that supported imperial expansion; and that racial separation is part of God's design for the world.[66] This is so-called "two-seed" theology, where the primal sin was Eve's copulation with Satan, which is the origin of the Jews. This combines with a millennial eschatology to terrifying effect:

> Two-seed theory leads to an apocalyptic conclusion, for the seed lines are said to have been continually at war. . . . Eventually, in Identity's millennial vision the war between Jews and their nonwhite allies on one side and whites on the other will reach a final stage, in a climactic battle—Armageddon as race war. . . . The pull of the end time led some to try to become instruments of eschatological acceleration.[67]

It cannot be denied that religions often exercise enormous influence over their adherents. In particular, the power of a religious text, with the authority it exercises over many believers, can be a great force for good or ill. As I have written elsewhere:

> Most Christians do not read Greek or Hebrew. Most are not biblical specialists or theologians. And while many Christians believe in the perspicuity of scripture to every believer, there is still a gap between the ancient text and the modern reader that someone is filling. Someone is translating the scripture for them. Someone is probably interpreting it to them. If scripture carries authority in the mind of the believer because they consider it to be the word of God, then the person who translates it for them, and the person who interprets it to them bear some of that authority, and functionally exercises authority in their lives.[68]

Those of us who are church leaders should take this as a warning about the power we wield when we stand up in the pulpit.

---

65. Munther Isaac, *The Other Side of the Wall: A Palestinian Christian Narrative of Lament and Hope* (Bethlehem: Bethlehem Bible College, 2022), 56.

66. Michael Barkun, "Millennialism on the Radical Right in America," in *The Oxford Handbook of Millennialism*, ed. Catherine Wessinger (Oxford: Oxford University Press, 2011), 650–52.

67. Barkun, "Millennialism on the Radical Right," 653–54.

68. Helen Paynter, "I Believe in the Afterlife (of the Word)," in *Global Perspectives on Bible and Violence*, ed. H. Paynter and M. Spalione (Sheffield: Sheffield Phoenix Press, 2023), vii–xvi.

Monotheism, violent scriptural texts, eschatology: none of these things is a sufficient cause for violent action, but they might be a partial cause, and therefore they raise questions that our survey of Scripture must address.

DESIRE AND THE SCAPEGOAT

René Girard was a French anthropologist whose work has been enormously influential and deserves thoughtful consideration in any study of violence. Girard identified a phenomenon he considered to be universal to all societies and present in all sorts of contexts.[69] This he terms *mimesis*. Mimesis describes the tendency for rivals to match one another in their desires. Consider two toddlers in a playroom. One picks up a toy that has not hitherto proved interesting to the other. Immediately it becomes an object of desire by both. Girard would say that the desirability of the object has been mediated to the second toddler by means of the first's possession of it.

More than this, the very *being* of humans, that is, their self-understanding, is conditioned by desire.

> Once his basic needs are satisfied . . . man [sic] is subject to intense desires, though he may not know precisely for what. The reason is that he desires *being*, something he himself lacks and which some other person seems to suggest.[70]

The next step as the mimetic rivalry intensifies is the development of mimetic violence. In the playroom this may involve one child bopping the other one on the head, but in the adult world it is far more sinister. Each act of violence is perceived to be a genuine and reasonable response to an aggressive act by the other party, and in this sense there is no true "first crime." (Girard traces it back to what he terms the "founding murder" of Abel by Cain.) Frequently the violence takes the form of, or at least begins with, posturing and threats. A classic example could be seen in the news a few years ago when Donald Trump and Kim Jong Un got into a bragging war about their nuclear buttons. Trump tweeted:

> North Korean Leader Kim Jong Un just stated that the "Nuclear Button is on his desk at all times." Will someone from his depleted and food starved regime please inform him that I too have a Nuclear Button, but it is a much bigger & more powerful one than his, and my Button works![71]

---

69. A helpful summary of Girard's complex thought is given by James Williams in his foreword to René Girard, *I Saw Satan Fall like Lightning*, trans. James Williams (Maryknoll, NY: Orbis, 2011), ix–xxiii.

70. René Girard, *Violence and the Sacred*, trans. Patrick Gregory (Baltimore: John Hopkins University Press, 1972), 146 (emphasis original).

71. Tweeted on January 2, 2018 and reported by Lauren Gambino, "Donald Trump Boasts That His Nuclear Button Is Bigger Than Kim Jong-un's," *The Guardian*, January 3, 2018, www.theguardian.com/us-news/2018/jan/03/donald-trump-boasts-nuclear-button-bigger-kim-jong-un.

Left to itself, violence would heap upon violence until the two parties destroy one another, and so in order to avoid this crisis a "scapegoat" is chosen. An individual or group is identified who bears similarity to both parties, but also bears a difference. They might have a physical disability, a different religion or skin color, be believed to be a witch, or have any one of a number of other markers of difference. This scapegoat then becomes the object of all-against-one violence. In this way, the violence is expended upon a third party, and "peace" is restored. A typical example of this is found in the Gospel of Luke, when Pilate and Herod colluded in Jesus's humiliation and murder: "That day Herod and Pilate became friends—before this they had been enemies" (Luke 23:12). In our own time we are familiar with the way that certain organizations or nations have intermittent "bloodletting" in order to restore unity.

Critical to the scapegoating action "working"—that is, in order for the sacrifice to succeed in deflecting the violence—is the belief that the scapegoat is guilty. They only got their just desserts.

> In order to be genuine, in order to exist as a social reality, as a stabilized viewpoint on some act of collective violence, scapegoating must remain nonconscious. The persecutors do not realize that they chose their victim for inadequate reasons, or perhaps for no reason at all, more or less at random.[72]

Thus, in the witch trials of the seventeenth century, the people had to believe that the witch was truly casting spells to blight their crops or cause women to miscarry. In the blood libel that has bedeviled Jews for centuries, it was important to justify the accusation that the Jews drank the blood of Christian children. And so on. This belief in the victim's guilt Girard terms the "scapegoat myth," and it is this that he considers to be the foundation of culture.[73] In this view, societies are all without exception founded on a primal act of violence and supported by the unswerving belief in the guilt of the victim. They are all founded on a lie.

Girard was a Catholic, and although he is critical of the ways that the church has historically associated itself with sacred violence,[74] he is highly positive about what he considers to be the true message of Christianity. In particular, he is interested in the way that the Bible has subverted the myth of the guilty victim. Whereas most literary texts perpetuate the myth of the scapegoat, in the Old Testament certain psalms, the book of Job, and Isaiah's great Servant Song (52:13–53:12) are exceptions, because they express empathy for victims and start to explore the possibility of their innocence. In this way, he considers that the Old Testament moves toward unveiling the lie. But this is an imperfect revelation; the Old Testament is "a text in travail."[75]

---

72. René Girard, "Generative Scapegoating," in *Violent Origins*, ed. Robert Hamerton Kelly (Stanford: Stanford University Press, 1987), 78.

73. Girard, "Generative Scapegoating," 106.

74. René Girard, *Things Hidden since the Foundation of the World*, trans. Stephen Bann and Michael Metteer (Stanford: Stanford University Press, 1987), 225–27.

75. Girard, "Generative Scapegoating," 141.

The revelation is climactically achieved in the teaching (e.g., Matt 5:38–40) and the death of Jesus Christ. Most particularly, the Gospels reveal Jesus to be the *innocent* victim, who goes willingly to his death. And this revelation has power beyond itself. In the revelation of *Jesus* as the innocent victim, the possibility of innocence for *all* victims becomes apparent, and the scapegoat mechanism has lost its power.

We will consider these texts more thoroughly in the middle portion of this book, but Caiaphas's words in John 11:50 would certainly seem to bear out a scapegoating purpose to Jesus's death: "It is better for you that one man die for the people than that the whole nation perish."

Girard's work has spawned a whole field of academic study, and this is not surprising. His arguments have a powerful explanatory effect, both in the consideration of ancient and premodern societies as well as in its ability to explain behavior in the twentieth and twenty-first centuries. He could, however, be accused of circularity in his arguments at times. This is particularly true in his appraisal of texts. He is keen to point out places where texts *expose* the scapegoat myth, but in places where they do not—even if it is the same text—he takes this as evidence of the power of the lie, which has deceived the writer. In this way, his argument is unfalsifiable.

Conservative readers of Scripture might be dissatisfied with much of Girard's work. He views Satan as the process of accusation that results in scapegoating.[76] Some will object that there is no room in his model for a personal fallen angel, but on the other hand he does take the presence of evil in the world far more seriously than some of his contemporaries. Likewise, and importantly, in Girard's understanding sacrifice achieves something on the "horizontal" plane (that is, within society) rather than having a "vertical" effect in propitiating a deity. This, of course, means that he firmly rejects a propitiatory view of the crucifixion.[77] God is most certainly at work here, but not in the way that traditional evangelical readings would suggest.

What of Girard's anthropology? For him, the defining characteristic of humans is desire.[78] All human culture is based on violence, with humanity effectively *coming into being* through the symbolic thought that emerges at the founding murder. This is a rather pessimistic interpretation of the biblical account of the nature and purpose of our creation. Nonetheless, in his argument that Jesus alone fulfills the true human destiny, his anthropology seems to be much richer than this.

> Jesus is the only man who achieves the goal God has set for all mankind, the only man who has nothing to do with violence and its works. The epithet "Son of Man" also corresponds, quite clearly, to the fact that Jesus alone has fulfilled a calling that belongs to all mankind.[79]

---

76. Girard, *Scapegoat*, 32–48.
77. Girard, *Things Hidden*, 180.

78. Girard, *I Saw Satan Fall*, x.
79. Girard, *Things Hidden*, 213.

Finally, Girard is adamant throughout this writing that the true God is utterly nonviolent. For instance, he continues the paragraph quoted above:

> If the fulfilment, on earth, passes inevitably through the death of Jesus, this is not because the Father demands this death, for strange sacrificial motives. Neither the son nor the Father should be questioned about the cause of this event, but all mankind, and mankind alone. . . . According to [the contrary] argument, the Father of Jesus is still a God of violence, despite what Jesus explicitly says.[80]

Girard makes some bold claims in his work, and we may not wish to follow him all the way (although this comment somewhat preempts our biblical survey). However, his work deserves serious consideration. In particular, his arguments on desire, on mimetic violence, and on society's tendency to scapegoat have enormous explanatory power and deserve careful theological scrutiny.

CONCLUSION

For many—but not all—readers of this book, violence is something "out there"; something that we read about but have not experienced and do not feel unduly threatened by. For other readers, and for many more in the world today, violence, or the very real threat of it, is a normal part of life. Those of us who fall into the first category must bear in mind that our experience is unusual. It is unusual in global terms, and it is unusual in historical terms. All of our reading, thinking, and praying must be held within this context.

In this chapter we have examined some of the prominent theories offered by scholars from a variety of fields, including sociology, psychology, and anthropology. This has not been an exhaustive survey. A textbook on theories of violence could easily fill all the pages of this book and still be incomplete. But the theorists who have been chosen are ones that seem to me to open up interesting dialogues with Scripture. They have invited us to ask the following questions of Scripture:

- What is the root cause of human violence?
- What drives individual humans to commit violent acts? Can human violence be overcome, or is it hardwired into us? Is it true that human societies are structured around violence, and if so what hope is there for a nonviolent world?
- Is Christianity inherently violent? How should we reckon with scriptural texts that speak of the scarcity of divine blessing, that command violence, and that seem to speak of eschatological violence?

---

80. Girard, *Things Hidden*, 213.

- What resources does the Bible offer us to help with our inclination to depersonalize the enemy? How can it arrest our tendency to brutalization? What role does forgiveness play in breaking cycles of violence?
- Is God nonviolent? Is the cross an act of human or divine violence?

One feature that each of these theories holds in common, although expressed in different ways, is the universal human tendency toward violence. This is one of the first questions that the Bible addresses in its opening chapters, and it is there that we will begin our biblical survey. First, however, we need to ask some questions about how we use the Bible, and this is the subject of our next chapter.

RELEVANT QUESTIONS

1. What experience have you had of violence in your own close circles or more broadly? What presuppositions do you bring to our study of violence?
2. We defined violence as *the use of force or coercion in a way that causes harm to another*. Did this challenge or expand your understanding of what it might encompass?
3. The violence theorists surveyed in this chapter were unanimous that violence is a universal human problem. Jesus tells us that the seeds of violence lie within our own hearts (Matt 5:21–22). How do you respond to this, personally?

CHAPTER 2

SCRIPTURE AS AN ETHICAL GUIDE

In the previous chapter we identified some important questions about the causes of violence and the ways our human condition can lead us to employ or collude with it. These are important questions that we will carry forward to our deep study of the scriptural witness, which begins in the following chapter. But there is another big question, which many readers will consider the most obvious one of all.

To what extent—if at all—are we permitted to use violence, and if we ever are, under what circumstances?

But before we can begin to address this question, we will need to consider two more:

How do we make moral choices?
And how can Scripture help us to do this?

This is far less straightforward than is implied by the bumper sticker-type slogan that says, "It's in the Bible, therefore God said it, therefore I do it."

Christian ethicist Oliver O'Donovan paints this picture to illustrate the point.

Imagine walking quietly down the street and hearing a voice mysteriously borne to you through the air: "Present arms!" What are you to do? Probably, you think, you have overheard something from a nearby barracks not intended for your ears. Alternatively, you may think that it was the voice of an angel sent to warn or command you in some way—although, you'll have to give your mind very seriously to interpreting what the angel meant by it. The one thing that you cannot possibly do is simply present arms. You do not have any arms, only an umbrella.[1]

In this thought experiment O'Donovan elegantly illustrates one of the chief problems facing the reader of Christian Scripture who wants to discern how to live God's way: *it was not addressed to us*. More than this, it is often expressed in a language that is alien to us (and that's still true even after we have translated it from

---

1. Oliver O'Donovan, "The Moral Authority of Scripture," in *Scripture's Doctrine and Theology's Bible: How the New Testament* *Shapes Christian Dogmatics*, ed. Markus Bockmuehl and Alan J. Torrance (Grand Rapids: Baker, 2008), 170.

the Hebrew, Aramaic, and Greek). At least we know approximately what "present arms!" means. If the drill sergeant had barked out, "Forward march and half!" many of us would be even more in the dark. And so it is for us when we read the stories, the proverbs, the polemics, and the letters of ancient people. They are other people's writing, to other people, and although we certainly can hear from God to us as we read and study them, there is a gap that must be overcome first.

In one sense this is simply illustrative of the need for good interpretive skills—an argument that has been made a thousand times and does not need to be expanded here. More than this, however, the questions the Bible is answering can never be direct answers to many of the questions that we ask because we live in different worlds. The Bible has nothing (directly) to say about guns, bombs, and drone technology. It never speaks (directly) about domestic abuse. It is written in a world that seems to presuppose slavery. And so on.

So is it therefore irrelevant to our modern age? Of course not. God does not change, his purposes are enduring, and at heart humans share the same fundamental temptations and weaknesses across all generations.

But how can we find the right way to live in our own morally complex age? And how can the Bible help us with that? In this chapter we will seek to lay out some parameters to help us as we move forward. First, we will briefly survey the classical ways that people have attempted to shape their ethical thinking, whether with or without appeal to a god, gods, or God.

ETHICAL SYSTEMS

There are three classical ways of approaching ethical decision-making. Some have their roots in Greek philosophy, and others in Enlightenment thought. We will take a brief look at each of them.

Rule-Based Ethics

Deontics is a system of ethics where conduct choices are based on laws or duties. A classic example is Immanuel Kant's (1724–1804) well-known categorical imperative, which he considers to form the bedrock of all moral conduct. "I ought never to act, except in such a way that I can also will that my maxim should become a universal law."[2]

God is a God who commands our obedience, but it is a typical misconception that Christianity has a rule-based system of ethics, founded on the Ten Commandments. Rather, as we shall see in a moment, the Old Testament Law[3] functions in quite a different way. There are several problems with this approach to ethics.

---

2. Immanuel Kant, *Groundwork of the Metaphysics of Morals*, trans. H. J. Paton (New York: Harper & Row, 1964), 70.

3. From here on, the capitalized word "Law" will be used to refer to the Old Testament law found in the Pentateuch.

First, there are theological objections. Even within the Old Testament, the Law did not operate in a purely deontic way. The Israelites' conduct was to be in imitation of God as much as in obedience to the Law.[4] The Law was intended to grow virtue in the people, to make them like God. Thus the prophets were able to chide Israel for keeping the letter but breaking the spirit of the Law (e.g., Isa 58:3–4).

"The law was our guardian until Christ came" (Gal 3:24), Paul writes to the Christians in Galatia. It is well-known that the Greek word here translated "guardian" is *paidagōgos*, a trusted slave who escorted children to and from school. But in the Roman world that Paul inhabited, the *paidagōgos* had a bigger role than this: Plutarch described him as a moral guide who assisted the young in their first steps toward virtue.[5] This is the role that the Law played prior to the coming of Christ, at least in Paul's perspective as he looks back on his Jewish upbringing.[6] We will consider the role of the Law for Christians a little later in this chapter, but here we simply note Paul's emphasis on freedom in guiding the moral development of the Galatian Christians (Gal 5).

There are pragmatic objections to a deontic ethical system too. One of the most significant for those seeking to apply biblical law is that it was written for a people who are very different from us. Their laws relate to life in the ancient Near East, not (for instance) to twenty-first century urban living. Since I do not own a field, does the prohibition on harvesting to the very edge of the field (Lev 23:22) have nothing to say to me?

The second pragmatic objection relates to the common human tendency to take shortcuts, to do only the minimum. This is the accusation that Jesus leveled at hypocrites: "You give a tenth of your spices—mint, dill and cumin. But you have neglected the more important matters of the law—justice, mercy and faithfulness" (Matt 23:23). We, too, will tend in the same direction if we attempt to model our conduct by obedience to a set of rules.[7]

Rules have an important role to play, but they should not be used as a platform for deontic ethics in the Christian worldview.

Consequentialist Ethics

The second type of ethical system we will briefly consider is termed *consequentialism*. As its name suggests, this pays attention to the consequences of an action. These might be determined in the moment ("Out of my options here, which will offer the optimal consequence in this instance?"), in which case it is termed *Act Consequentialism*. Alternatively, one might form a set of guidelines that are formed

---

4. John Barton, "Understanding Old Testament Ethics," *JSOT* 3.9 (1978): 61.

5. Norman H. Young, "Paidagogos: The Social Setting of a Pauline Metaphor," *NovT* 29.2 (1987): 158.

6. Of course, Paul never leaves Judaism but rather understood the coming of the Messiah to be its fulfilment.

7. N. T. Wright, *Virtue Reborn* (London: SPCK, 2010), 21.

on consequentialist grounds ("On the whole, this particular approach will tend to offer optimal consequences"); this is *Rule Consequentialism*. One of the great fathers of consequentialism was John Stuart Mill (1806–1873), who wrote these words:

> In the golden rule of Jesus of Nazareth, we read the complete spirit of the ethics of utility. To do as you would be done by, and to love your neighbour as yourself, constitute the ideal perfection of utilitarian morality.[8]

Utilitarianism received a more robust theological justification later, in the work of Joseph Fletcher (1905–1991). In Fletcher's system, the consequence to be pursued is love (*agape*). Fletcher quotes Paul in 2 Corinthians 3:6, "the letter kills, but the Spirit gives life," and Galatians 5:14, "the entire law is fulfilled in keeping this one command: 'Love your neighbor as yourself,'" before going on to write the following:

> *Christian* situation ethics has only one normal or principle or law . . . that is binding and unexceptionable, always good and right regardless of the circumstances. That is "love"—the *agapē* of the summary commandment to love God and the neighbour. Everything else without exception, all laws and rules and principles and ideals and norms, are only *contingent*, only valid if they happen to serve love in any situation.[9]

"Love first and in all circumstances" sounds attractive. And it can scarcely be denied that this approach might be pragmatically useful, and most of us instinctively use it from time to time. But once again there are significant pragmatic and theological objections with adopting consequentialism as a guiding principle.

One problem is the difficulty in evaluating what qualifies as a "good" outcome, and over what time period this should be gauged. What is the scope of the "situation"? Does it just encompass the actors and acted-upon in a particular situation? What of onlookers? What of the community? What of later, perhaps even generational, consequences? The approach takes an optimistic view of human wisdom—on our ability to discern the outcomes and benefits of our actions.

Further, utilitarian ethics might be described as a sort of ethical efficiency, and it is by no means clear that Jesus operated on such principles. His attention to the individual at the cost of the crowd, for instance, would seem to refute the idea that he was guided by this sort of moral calculus. In a similar manner, private virtuous actions that bring no clear or immediate benefit to anybody would be excluded on the basis that that time might be spent doing something more "beneficial."

Ultimately, probably the greatest objection to this approach is that it relativizes all actions in the pursuit of optimized outcomes. Actions possess no inherent ethical

---

8. John Stuart Mill, *Utilitarianism*, 2nd ed., with an introduction by George Sher (Indianapolis: Hackett, 2001), 17.

9. Joseph Fletcher, *Situation Ethics: The New Morality* (Louisville: Westminster, 1966), 30 (emphases original).

content, but should be evaluated by consideration of their consequences. By this calculus it would be acceptable to kill someone (for example) if a greater good could thereby be achieved. Few Christians would be comfortable with commending this approach wholeheartedly (though we may, in part, if we subscribe to just-war theory, which we will discuss later). The Ten Commandments do not form the total basis for our ethical systems, but nor are they expendable.[10]

With the role of the Ten Commandments and the rest of the Law still undefined, we will now turn to the third main ethical system, known as *virtue ethics*.

Virtue Ethics

One of the most ancient ethical systems, known as *virtue ethics*, was articulated by Aristotle (384–322 BCE) in his *Nicomachean Ethics*. Aristotle proposed that life should be oriented toward a virtuous goal (*telos*), which he identified as becoming a fully formed human: "being well and doing well in being well."[11] In order to reach that goal, certain habits, or virtues, should be cultivated. In his system, these cardinal virtues were courage, justice, prudence, and temperance. Aristotelian philosophy influenced both Augustine and Aquinas, and in the modern era a number of theologians have developed the ideas further, such as Alasdair MacIntyre in his magisterial book *After Virtue*.

For our purposes, however, Tom Wright's exploration of virtue will be more relevant, as it is more evidently based upon the worldview and teaching of Scripture.[12] He writes in opposition to the pervasive opinion that one should "act from the heart" and "be true to oneself." Christian character is formed within us by our faithful practice of the virtues—and the word *practice* is used intentionally. He gives the example of Chesley Sullenberger III, the pilot of the US Airways Flight 1549 on January 15, 2009, who successfully landed it in the Hudson River following a catastrophic bird strike.[13] What enabled Sullenberger to make the right decisions in the two or three minutes that he had was the endless repetition of good habits that had filled the decades preceding that moment. This, says Wright, is how virtue works. It is through conscious and deliberate practice that it starts to feel natural.

But how do we identify the correct habits to be practicing? We grow them from three roots: our *being* (who we are); our *history* (what our story is); and our *telos* (the goal toward which we are summoned).

---

10. The total disregard of the Old Testament law by Christians is known as *antinomianism* and can result in a variety of excessive and harmful behaviors.

11. Alasdair Macintyre, *After Virtue: A Study in Moral Theory*, 3rd ed. (Notre Dame: University of Notre Dame Press, 2007), 148.

12. Wright's book has been marketed differently on the two sides of the Atlantic. The North American version is titled *After You Believe: Why Christian Character Matters* (New York: HarperOne, 2012) and has a slightly different introduction and first chapter from the original UK publication. Reference here is made to the UK version title *Virtue Reborn* (London: SPCK, 2010).

13. Wright, *Virtue Reborn*, 7–10.

In Christian virtue ethics, our *being* fundamentally shapes our *doing*.[14] This is summed up in Paul's so-called indicative-imperative, which we could paraphrase as *be who you are*. For example:

> Since we live by the Spirit, let us keep in step with the Spirit. (Gal 5:25)

> Do you not know that your bodies are temples of the Holy Spirit, who is in you, whom you have received from God? You are not your own; you were bought at a price. Therefore honor God with your bodies. (1 Cor 6:19–20)[15]

This is not simply about trying harder to live up to some external standard. That would be a return to rule-based ethics. Fundamentally, our *being* is not simply *who* we are but *whose* we are. Like Israel of old, called to be holy because Yahweh is holy (e.g., Lev 11:44), we are called to the imitation of Christ (e.g., 1 Cor 11:1; 1 Pet 2:21). But even this is complex. We are not Jesus and are not able to—or even commanded to—make the same choices as he did. The simple application of the motif "What Would Jesus Do?" is wrongheaded because Jesus is in a "category of one."[16] Our task is, rather, to discover the pattern of humanity that Jesus demonstrated and then pattern ourselves accordingly.

> What the earliest Christians were struck by, and what they returned to again and again, was that in Jesus they had seen . . . a way of being human which nobody had ever imagined before. This was a way of generosity and forgiveness, a way of self-emptying and a determination to put everyone else's needs first.[17]

The second root for virtue is our *history*. This certainly includes the history of the church—we will briefly consider one or two moments in church history in a later chapter—but our history is deeper still. Our story is rooted in theologically rich memories, retold each time we break bread together. "Do this in remembrance of me," said Jesus, as he himself lived in and reinterpreted the theologically rich Passover story with his disciples (1 Cor 11:24).

The third root for the development of virtue is our *telos*, or goal. For Aristotle, the virtuous goal was to be a complete, flourishing human—no bad thing in itself. But for Christians, our goal is even bolder and more ambitious—nothing less than who we will become at the renewal of all things. We have already glimpsed what this is like in the life and teaching of Jesus. In our redemption, we have now stepped into the reality of this: "He chose to give us birth through the word of truth, that

14. Colin Gunton, "The Church as a School of Virtue? Human Formation in Trinitarian Framework," in *Faithfulness and Fortitude: In Conversation with the Theological Ethics of Stanley Hauerwas*, ed. M. T. Nation and S. Wells (Edinburgh: T&T Clark, 2000), 212; Joseph J. Kotva Jr., *The Christian Case for Virtue Ethics* (Washington: Georgetown University Press, 1996), 30.

15. Similarly, see Eph 4:1; Phil 2:12–13; Col 3:12.
16. Wright, *Virtue Reborn*, 113.
17. Wright, *Virtue Reborn*, 114.

we might be a kind of firstfruits of all he created" (Jas 1:18, cf. 2 Cor 5:17). As Tom Wright says, "The practise and habit of virtue . . . is all about learning in advance the language of God's new world."[18]

And this takes us right back to our history, our being, and our *telos*; in other words, to how we define what humanity truly is. It will be by the study of the whole of Scripture (including, but by no means limited to, the Law) that we will come to discover what these look like. It is through our apprehension of God's great story that we will come to orient our lives in that direction, and by our study of the true vocation for humanity that we can learn to shape ourselves in the same way, through the work of the Spirit.

THE CHALLENGE OF SCRIPTURAL DIVERSITY

Clearly, then, we need to read and study the whole of Scripture. But immediately as we try to do this, a new problem arises. This is the sheer diversity of the texts that we have in our Bibles. They are diverse in genre, historical setting, in style—*and in their theology*. They do not all speak with a single voice. So how can we discern the voice of God?

As an example, consider the question, "Is human violence against other humans ever acceptable?" Ask this question of the writer of Genesis. "Yes, in exceptional circumstances," he replies thoughtfully—"The shedding of human blood must be repaid by the shedding of human blood" (see Gen 9:6). Ask the question of the writer of Joshua. "Of *course*!" he says, without a moment's hesitation. "Aggressive war is *perfectly* acceptable, at least in certain circumstances." Ask the question of the speaker in Lamentations. "*How could you even ask*?" she[19] weeps, as she lies in her own vomit (Lam 2:11 NRSV). Ask the question of Jesus: "All who draw the sword will die by the sword" (Matt 26:52), he replies, as he is arrested by men wielding swords.

How are we to find our way out of this maze? The question of the diversity of Scripture has kept generations of theologians busy in fulfilling publishing contracts. Here we will briefly survey some of the possible approaches.

Smorgasbord

For the uninitiated, a smorgasbord is a Swedish buffet table; it is a delicious opportunity to fill your plate with anything from the lavish selection of dishes provided. This is how some people treat Scripture. In the face of the diversity of biblical responses to the test question I posed above, they will select the parts they prefer. Some will prioritize those words of Jesus (though in doing so they will have to take account

---

18. Wright, *Virtue Reborn*, 61–62.
19. Although it is likely that Lamentations was penned by a man, the female voice (daughter Zion) is prominent within it.

of—or write out—the part where he commends his disciples for having two swords [Luke 22:38]). Others will allow the retributive words of Genesis to take priority. As we saw in the previous chapter, some will quote Old Testament conquest texts to justify their own aggressive war.

There are (at least) two fundamental problems with this smorgasbord approach. The first is that if we pick the parts of Scripture that suit our purposes and reject the rest, we are effectively forming a canon-within-a-canon. Who gets to decide what is included and what isn't? On what basis? And perhaps most fundamentally, why did God even give us the other parts of Scripture?

The second problem with this approach is the way that it tends to use prooftexting. It operates by drawing *those* particular words of Jesus, *that* particular verse from Genesis, and so on, completely out of their original contexts. Again, Scripture was not written to us. We need to attend to the context (literary, historical, and so on) of every text we read in order to have any hope of discovering what it is really saying.

Some people have employed a particular version of this smorgasbord approach, and that is the rejection of the Old Testament from their Bibles. In this logic, the New Testament is full of love and peace, and the Old Testament is violent and regressive. In the days of the early church, a man called Marcion made such a proposal and was declared to be a heretic by the early church in 144 CE. His doctrine was vigorously rebutted by Tertullian (ca. 160–220 CE) in his treatise *Against Marcion*. In our own time, some seek to do something similar to Marcion by explicitly rejecting parts of the Old Testament, or by simply ignoring it.

There are at least three reasons why this is unwise and unhelpful. The first I have already alluded to. *If* we believe Scripture to be the word of God (and I realize that not everyone does, and that people will mean different things by the expression), then we do need to pay attention to all of it. I stand in that tradition, and so I am committed to taking the Bible seriously throughout, even—perhaps most particularly—when it is difficult.

The second problem with the rejection of parts or all of the Old Testament is that it is wrongheaded. A thoughtful reading of the New Testament will reveal quite as many difficult passages as the Old Testament offers. Jesus frequently speaks about judgment, sometimes using quite florid metaphors. The book of Revelation uses some frankly hair-raising images. It is illogical to reject the Old Testament (which abounds in affirmations of God's love, incidentally) and retain these parts of the New. And ultimately if we keep cutting out the parts of Scripture that don't appeal to us, in the end we will have a book that completely reflects our own opinions. Such a book will never challenge us and therefore is unlikely to transform us.

The third problem with rejecting the Old Testament is that such an approach fails to appreciate how much Jesus's words are dependent upon it. He rarely speaks without quoting, referring to, reprising, adapting, or even subverting something from the Old Testament. We cannot possibly hope to understand Jesus if we are ignorant of the Scriptures in which he was so steeped.

So if we are not going to treat Scripture as a smorgasbord, what other options are open to us as we are confronted by its diversity?

Developmental Approaches

Another common approach to the diversity of Scripture's perspectives on violence is to attempt to explain it by chronological or contextual factors. In its crudest form, the logic goes like this: *back in ancient times, the people were violent, but now we have learned a better way.* Typically the person then rejects some or all of the Old Testament. While there may be an element of truth to the statement that human ethics have improved, such an unnuanced assertion raises a number of problems for us. First, this approach underestimates the diversity of perspectives on violence that are contained within texts of similar provenance. As I have indicated above, and as our biblical studies will prove, violence is not confined to the older biblical texts. Conversely, the Old Testament contains many passages and themes that tend toward peace—remarkably progressive for those "unenlightened" peoples!

This brings us to the second problem, which is the sense of moral superiority that tends to lie behind such an explanation. Living as we do barely a century after the First World War, and well under a hundred years from the second, not to mention the many wars and conflicts that the world has seen since, we are in no position to lecture ancient peoples on *their* violence. What they did to tens and hundreds, we do to millions—we have perfected the art of killing one another. (Though no doubt even as I write, people are working on ways to refine the art even further.)

The third problem is perhaps the most substantive: this approach tends to explain away the difficult texts by arguing that—in one way or another—they are wrong. The people misunderstood God's intention, or, even more problematically, God has changed and become less violent. Effectively this has now returned us to the smorgasbord approach—we will select and prioritize the texts which seem to us to present the "best" ethic, and we will relativize the rest.

It is indeed important to remember that all Scripture is refracted through the contexts in which it was set or written. It has human authors as well as divine inspiration, and those human writers used language and metaphors that they knew and were familiar with. They spoke to situations of their day, sometimes engaging with them with passion and polemic. This presents the sort of interpretive problems we noted at the top of this chapter, and we will take note of these issues as we turn to our biblical study shortly. But it is a big leap from noting the *Sitz im Leben*[20] of a

---

20. *Sitz im Leben* means "situation in life" and is used to refer to the context within which a text is composed.

text to suggesting that this context has been determinative for its meaning. A better approach is to seek the divine voice by employing the best interpretive skills we have, which includes attending to its *Sitz im Leben*.

However, there is a more constructive version of the "development" argument, and this is the "redemptive movement" approach. It was first proposed by William Webb, and later applied by Webb and Oeste to the war texts of the Old Testament.[21] The redemptive movements that Webb identifies are places where the biblical text is moving the ethics of the people of the author's own day toward an ideal but not-yet-attained goal.

I am reminded of the once-popular slogan, "Be patient, God hasn't finished with me yet." In each era of God's dealings with humanity, at least those recorded in Scripture, God is gently tugging his people toward a better way, *but they (and we) have not yet attained it*. Each step is a small improvement on what would have otherwise been the undisputed norm. For example, Webb and Oeste write that "biblical war practices are hugely redemptive—at least in an incremental sense—relative to the horrific war atrocities of the day."[22]

I consider this redemptive movement approach to be a valuable approach to the diversity of Scripture's theology of violence, and we will return to it from time to time as we proceed. But it reshapes the problem rather than removing it altogether. So we will now turn to consider another approach.

Polyphony

Polyphony is a musical term which refers to a composition that contains two independent and equally important musical motifs that play simultaneously. The term was appropriated by the Russian literary critic, Mikhail Bakhtin, who uses the idea to explore dialogue within texts. In a polyphonic text there are multiple "voices" which dialogue with one another. Key to Bakhtin's concept is the idea that none of those voices has the final word. Rather, the voices are a literary device employed by the author, who allows ideas to be tested by the dialogue. For Bakhtin, as for Socrates, truth is discerned where voices clash.[23] Within Scripture, polyphony might be found within a text (we will find a good example of this in Joshua and Judges), or between texts.[24] The different voices need not reflect different sources but at times might do so, with a final editor who was skillful and subtle in bringing together, rather than attempting to resolve, the different strands of thought.[25]

21. William J. Webb, *Slaves, Women and Homosexuals: Exploring the Hermeneutics of Cultural Analysis* (Downers Grove, IL: InterVarsity Press, 2001); William J. Webb and Gordon K. Oeste, *Bloody, Brutal and Barbaric? Wrestling with Troubling War Texts* (Downers Grove, IL: InterVarsity Press, 2019).

22. Webb and Oeste, *Bloody, Brutal and Barbaric?*, 17.

23. See his work in Mikhail Bakhtin, *The Dialogic Imagination: Four Essays*, trans. C. Emerson and M. Holquist (Austin: University of Texas Press, 1981); and idem, *Speech Genres and Other Late Essays*, ed. C. Emerson and M. Holquist, trans. V. McGee (Austin: University of Texas Press, 1986).

24. For a discussion of the use of polyphony in biblical scholarship, see Helen Paynter, *Reduced Laughter: Seriocomic Features and Their Functions in the Book of Kings* (Leiden: Brill, 2016), 45–49.

25. Yairah Amit, *Hidden Polemics in Biblical Narrative*, trans. J. Chipman (Leiden: Brill, 2000), 33.

While polyphony cannot be invoked as an answer to every theological disagreement that we find in Scripture, it is a useful model to help us grapple with some of them. Consider, for example, the divergent voices of Proverbs and Job. While Proverbs itself is not monologic (see, e.g., the two proverbs in Prov 26:4–5), an important message that it promotes is that righteous living will result in a long and prosperous life. By contrast, the book of Job is an exploration of innocent suffering. Indeed, Job the character sometimes appears to take elements from Proverbs and Psalms and dispute them.[26] In the face of this apparent contradiction, Bakhtin would urge us not to try to find a middle ground between the two perspectives but to allow the tension to stand, and to notice the sparks that fly when they clash.

As we seek to take the Bible seriously in all its rich diversity, looking for polyphony can be a valuable implement in our toolbox, because in the end truth is often too complex to collapse into a simple assertion.

Yet, wherever possible, we are seeking coherence. So we will now turn to consider two approaches that seek to discover coherence within the Bible's diversity.

Description before Synthesis

In the light of the diversity of emphasis he finds within the New Testament, Richard Hays has developed a canonical approach to New Testament ethics.[27] This technique takes place in four stages.

First is the *descriptive*, or exegetical, task; to conduct a detailed analysis of the relevant theme within each biblical document *on its own terms*. This includes not simply the Scripture's didactic teaching on the subject but also "the stories, symbols, social structures and practices that shape the community's ethos."[28] This is an important point to bear in mind as we embark on our own, even more ambitious, study of both testaments. The ethical witness they offer is contained not only in law and direct teaching but may and must be discerned in all the genres, in ways that we will explore below.

Next comes the *synthetic* task: to attempt a synthesis of the biblical witness. For this to be possible, the distinct voices examined in the first stage now need to be located within an organizing framework, one which Scripture itself already provides. Hays's own approach prioritizes what he considers to be the three fundamental paradigms of the New Testament—cross, community, and new creation. This is not the only framework that could be used, however. Christopher Landau, for instance, suggests that Jesus's prioritization of the double love command would be a more justifiable framework for the synthetic task.[29]

26. Cf., e.g., Prov 16:4 with Job 21:30.

27. Richard Hays, *The Moral Vision of the New Testament: Community, Cross, New Creation: A Contemporary Introduction to New Testament Ethics* (San Francisco: HarperSanFrancisco, 1996).

28. Hays, *Moral Vision*, 4.

29. Christopher Landau, *A Theology of Disagreement: New Testament Ethics for Ecclesial Conflicts* (London: SCM, 2021), 191–93.

The third task is termed the *hermeneutical* task, which seeks to apply the principles that have been identified to the context of the reader's world. This requires "an integrative act of the imagination," which Hays likens to a blues rock band improvising within the constraints of time and key signature, and perhaps chord sequence.[30] We will return to this helpful metaphor in chapter 12. Related to this is the fourth step, the *pragmatic* task; tackling real-life issues in the real world.

Although Hays (confining his study to the New Testament) was attempting to discover ethical coherence within a more limited text than our own, his approach is helpful, and one which we will emulate to some extent. In our survey of Scripture that begins after this chapter, we will largely do the first, descriptive task. Chapter 12 will then attempt a synthesis of some of the themes we have identified. The work of hermeneutical and pragmatic application will be the task of the final part of this book.

Biblical Theology

A second way that we can detect coherence in the diverse testimony of Scripture is by seeking its biblical-theological trajectories. It will come as no surprise to readers of a book in the series *Biblical Theology for Life* that the author is a fan of biblical theology! But the term perhaps deserves some explanation, as it is used in different ways by different people. I quote here from Brian Rosner's helpful introduction to the *New Dictionary of Biblical Theology*.

> Biblical theology is principally concerned with the overall theological message of the whole Bible. It seeks to understand the parts in relation to the whole and, to achieve this, it must work with the mutual interaction of the literary, historical, and theological dimensions of the various corpora, and with the inter-relationships of these within the whole canon of Scripture. Only in this way do we take proper account of the fact that God has spoken to us in Scripture.[31]

It will be seen here that underlying Rosner's description of the task is a recognition of the diversity of genres, *Sitze im Leben*, and theological perspectives that Scripture contains. The biblical-theological task is neither nihilistic in the face of that diversity, nor naive about the challenges it presents. It seeks to discover *coherence within* and does not attempt to impose *uniformity upon* the text.

Biblical theology is therefore fundamentally a faith endeavor. It is predicated on the belief that God has spoken through his word, and so it is coherent. Nobody who approaches Scripture without this presupposition will be able to do it.

Such an approach will use some of the methodologies already discussed, along with other good exegetical techniques. It may well take account of redemptive

---

30. Hays, *Moral Vision*, 6.
31. Brian Rosner, "Biblical Theology," in *New Dictionary of*   *Biblical Theology*, ed. T. D. Alexander and B. S. Rosner (Downers Grove, IL: InterVarsity Press, 2000), 3.

trajectories in Scripture, as Webb and Oeste would urge. It will attend to Hays's descriptive task, although the synthesis it seeks to achieve might be framed differently. In particular, it will seek to identify patterns that recur through Scripture.[32] In order to do this, it will pay particular attention to the way texts employ other texts. Seeking intertextuality in this way allows us to identify the places where themes recur, or where existing ideas are being appropriated, developed, or even subverted by later writers.

Ultimately we hope to investigate the deep themes of Scripture, particularly those that touch upon the question of human violence. As we do this, we will discover that those which work best for our inquiry are not what we might consider the most obvious ones. Rather, as I have already hinted, it is the nature and purpose of humanity that will provide one of the most useful frameworks to help us make sense of the diversity. Perhaps this will not come as a shock; not only did this question emerge from our study of virtue ethics above, but it was also one of the most pressing issues from our survey of theories of violence from the previous chapter.

HOW DOES THE OLD TESTAMENT HELP?

Whether we are going to use a polyphonic reading of Scripture, seek to identify its theological trajectories, or attempt a canonical approach such as Hays proposes, we will need to reckon with the whole of the Bible. Most readers will immediately appreciate that certain portions will be more difficult to use than others. Here we will briefly consider two of the genres that present the greatest difficulty to us in this task. John Barton describes the problem like this:

> Old Testament writers are maddeningly unsystematic. Asked for a general statement of moral principle, they reply with a little rule about local legal procedures, a story about obscure people of dubious moral character, or by extolling some virtue in God with which human beings are supposed to somehow to conform. Knowledge of the good for humankind lies through the observation of particulars, if Old Testament writers are to be believed.[33]

While there is certainly plenty of debate about the ethical thrust of the New Testament—and we will consider elements of this in due course—the Old Testament is especially challenging in this regard. This is partly because of its antiquity; the worlds in which it was written are even further removed from our own world than the Greco-Roman culture of the New Testament, with which we have many enduring connections. It is also because of the very nature of the Old Testament in relation

---

32. Important biblical-theological patterns include the creation-de-creation-re-creation pattern, and the tripartite temple pattern. We will consider a number of these as we turn to study the Scriptures.

33. John Barton, *Ethics and the Old Testament: The 1997 Diocese of British Columbia John Albert Hall Lectures* (Harrisburg, PA: Trinity Press International, 1998), 15.

to the New. To what extent are they in direct continuity, and to what extent is there a radical discontinuity with the coming of Jesus? And finally, some of the genres used in the Old Testament present particular challenges. Most particularly, what is the ethical value of a story? How do we discover what (if anything) the writer is attempting to teach us?

These questions are most pressing for two particular genres of the Old Testament—Law and narrative. And, as we shall see, they are closely linked. Let us first consider what value the Law has for Christians today.

The Enduring Value of the Law

It is clear from the words of Jesus in the Sermon on the Mount that the Law has an enduring significance (Matt 5:17–20). Indeed, it would be nonsense, in gospel terms, to imagine otherwise. Waldemar Janzen writes:

> To ask whether Old Testament ethics can be abandoned once Jesus has manifested its climax is to ask whether . . . land is no longer to be tended responsibly once we know that an eternal home has been prepared for us. It is to ask whether father and mother should no longer be maintained in dignity once we know that we have new fathers and mothers and brothers and sisters from among those who do the will of God. To truncate God's story like this . . . was certainly not the gospel of Jesus.[34]

Yet at the same time the Law has ceased to be definitive with the coming of Christ. Earlier we considered how Paul described the role that the Law used to fulfill as a *paidagōgos*. Now, with the coming of Christ, that role is no longer needed. To continue the metaphor, the child has reached majority, and the *paidagōgos*'s role in shaping the youngster's moral development is now discharged.

So, what are Christians to do with the Law? Traditionally, we have often been taught that it falls into moral, civil, and ceremonial categories, and that the moral ones continue to be binding. However, there is no good evidence behind such an assertion, and the distinctions appear to be entirely arbitrary.[35] Consider the Sabbath laws, for example. Is it a moral law? It is predicated upon God's own rest, so it might fall into that category. On the other hand, it includes rest for one's servants and household, so it could be considered a civil law. But it also falls within the provision for festivals and holy days, so it might be better regarded as a ceremonial law.[36]

---

34. Waldemar Janzen, *Old Testament Ethics: A Paradigmatic Approach* (Louisville: Westminster John Knox, 1994), 210.

35. See, e.g., the discussion in David Dorsey, "The Law of Moses and the Christian: A Compromise," *JETS* 34.3 (1991): 321–34.

36. This example is from Hetty Lalleman, *Celebrating the Law? Rethinking Old Testament Ethics*, 2nd ed. (Carlisle: Paternoster, 2016), 44.

Shaping the People of God

Perhaps the most useful way of interpreting the Law for the Christian is to seek to understand what sort of people it is seeking to form. If we are trying to understand God's design and purpose for humanity, this will be a relevant part of that inquiry. Let us return to the example we briefly visited earlier, the prohibition on harvesting to the edge of a field. What sort of people is this law seeking to shape? The answer is the sort of person who is generous toward the less fortunate, who permits the poor the dignity of assisted self-sufficiency, who does not seek to extract every last drop of profit. Of course, this law does not stand in isolation; we would also need to interpret it within the context of many others which speak of care for the vulnerable, of the use of honest scales, and so on.

Clearly this principle is easier for us to apply to some parts of the Law than others. But, as we have discussed, woven throughout is the injunction to be holy as Yahweh is holy. We may struggle to understand how certain laws assist with that purpose, but the sort of people they are seeking to shape is clear enough—a holy people who resemble God himself.

Law in Relation to Narrative

It is also important to note that the Law was given in the context of Yahweh's covenant with newly redeemed Israel at Sinai. It is deeply embedded in the narrative of God's covenant people and is not intended to operate in isolation from that. Rather, the laws are embedded in narrative: "shorthand formulations of ethical values and imperatives emerging from a particular story."[37]

It is therefore unwise to drive a deep wedge between the Law and the historical (narrative) portions of the Old Testament. Indeed, some have argued that the narratives provide a set of worked examples based on the laws. Ashley Hibbard, for example, has shown that significant parallels exist between the stories found in Genesis 34–38 and the laws of Deuteronomy 22–25. She suggests that

> the law represents life as it could be with the worst of human action restrained and corrected, and Genesis shows life as it was without the worst of human action restrained and corrected by the guidance of legal *torah*. The narratives have instructive value by providing more vibrant examples of legal situations than are found in casuistic law, as well as demonstrating the need for the moral and ethical instruction that *torah* provides.[38]

---

37. Janzen, *Old Testament Ethics*, 58.
38. Ashley Hibbard, *Deep Calls to Deep: An Investigation into* *a Chain of Intertextualities between Some Genesis Narratives and Deuteronomic Laws* (PhD diss., Aberdeen University, 2020), 17.

In a similar way, Gordon Wenham suggests that the Law provides an ethical floor and needs the narratives of the Old Testament to flesh it out.[39] This might not surprise us if we consider the example of Jesus and his own use of story to illustrate a principle. Consider the parable of the Good Samaritan, for example (Luke 10:30–37). Jesus told this story in response to a question about the Law. Instead of getting into a legal squabble when he was asked, "Who is my neighbor?" (v. 29), he answered the question with a story. This may help illustrate the relationship between Law and narrative in the Old Testament.

None of this, of course, should be taken as an aspersion against the historicity of the biblical narratives. The ethical purpose of a story can only be more pressing if the story has a historical basis. Key to this is our understanding that history-telling is not a neutral endeavor. History is always told for a purpose.

History as Pedagogy

Of course the Gospels were written much later than the Old Testament narratives, and yet they do provide some clues which might help us understand what the Old Testament historians were doing. Luke begins his Gospel by explaining his purpose.

> Many have undertaken to draw up an account of the things that have been fulfilled among us, just as were handed down to us by those who from the first were eyewitnesses and servants of the word. With this in mind, since I myself have carefully investigated everything from the beginning, I too decided to write an orderly account for you, most excellent Theophilus, so that you may know the certainty of the things you have been taught. (Luke 1:1–4)

The writer of the Fourth Gospel says something similar.

> Jesus performed many other signs in the presence of his disciples, which are not recorded in this book. But these are written that you may believe that Jesus is the Messiah, the Son of God, and that by believing you may have life in his name. (John 20:30–31)

Two things are clear from these excerpts. First, the writers have selected what stories of Jesus to tell and which to omit, and they have presented them in an orderly fashion. Second, this has been done with a specific intention: "that you may know the certainty," "that you may believe." While the purpose of the gospel writers might not be identical to the Old Testament historians, these principles can reasonably be retrojected onto their compositions.

History-telling is never a neutral enterprise, and as we have seen the gospel writers made no pretenses otherwise. This is not the same thing as saying that they

---

39. Gordon Wenham, *Story as Torah: Reading the Old Testament Ethically* (Edinburgh: T&T Clark, 2000), 80.

have cynically omitted stories that would show Jesus in a poor light (for example). It is simply that they have come to believe in Jesus as the Messiah and to write their Gospels in order that others might do so also.

In a similar way, the writers of the Old Testament have a purpose in mind and have selected and arranged their materials accordingly. There is something (probably more than one thing) that they want to persuade the reader of. How can we discern what this is?

The Rhetorical Force of Narrative

In his book *Story as Torah*, Gordon Wenham warns against interpretations of Old Testament narratives that are "arbitrary and whimsical."[40] We probably all have encountered such readings in sermons or books (e.g., that David's five stones represent faith, courage, obedience, trust, and praise). In order to try to avoid such readings, Wenham proposes a dual methodology: reading a text within its historical setting, and reading it for its rhetorical force.[41] The historical setting will attend to (among other things) the social customs of the time, the likely expectations of the intended audience, and any relevant comparisons from other ancient Near Eastern texts. This will help to tether the text to its original purpose. Rhetorical criticism then seeks to uncover what the author is *doing* with his text. For example, is it demonstrating the inexplicable patience of God, deconstructing a warrior's reputation, or demonstrating a nation's culpability?

Discovering the rhetorical force of a text is a learned skill, and much has been published on this in the last few decades. Readers are directed to the works of Robert Alter and Meir Sternberg, among others.[42] Here we will consider just a few of the useful techniques that will help us dig deeper into narratives.

The first thing to say is that we should not expect the narrative to demonstrate normative conduct. In other words, they do not tend to show us how things *should be* but rather how they *were* (and perhaps still are). There are few narratives in the Old Testament where the protagonists cover themselves with glory. In the main, the people are flawed: deceitful (e.g., Gen 27:5–20), vengeful (e.g., 2 Sam 3:27), ambitious (e.g., 2 Sam 15:1–6), lustful (e.g., 2 Sam 13:1–2), or murderous (e.g., 2 Kgs 10:6–8). Perhaps the first thing we need to do when we read these familiar stories is lay down our Sunday school affection for the characters and prepare ourselves to approach them again with fresh questions.

Related to this is the principle that reported speech need not be considered reliable. This statement exerts no pressure at all on an evangelical reading of Scripture. This is perhaps best demonstrated with a fictional example from modern news reporting.

---

40. Wenham, *Story as Torah*, 1.
41. Wenham, *Story as Torah*, 3.
42. Robert Alter, *The Art of Biblical Narrative*, rev. ed. (New York: Basic Books, 2011); Meir Sternberg, *The Poetics of Biblical Narrative: Ideological Literature and the Drama of Reading* (Bloomington: Indiana University Press, 1987).

Imagine a news report that is describing a scandal—let us say a shortage of bread in a particular city. (We will assume that this news outlet is trustworthy.) The reporter tells you that this is because the mayor of that city has imposed a punitive tax on vehicles bringing in flour from the surrounding countryside. Now the reporter interviews the mayor. In the background is a long queue of people waiting outside a supermarket. "There's no problem," says the mayor. "There's plenty of bread. No shortage at all." What are you to make of this? You trust this reporter, and you can see the footage for yourself. Must you also believe the mayor's words? Of course not. You distinguish the reliable reportage from the unreliable direct speech of the mayor. More than that, the inclusion of his interview in the report allows you to learn something important about him. Measuring his claims against the truth of the situation, you are able to draw some conclusions about his character and his honesty.

We form this sort of evaluation intuitively in most situations, but when we come to read the Bible, many of us leave these critical faculties at home. And yet the narratives of the Old Testament are full of characters who dissemble (e.g., Gen 23:15, deceive (e.g., 2 Sam 16:1–4), change their mind (1 Kgs 2:8–9; cf. 2 Sam 16:11–12 and 19:22–23), or boast of exploits they have not performed (e.g., 2 Sam 1:8–10). The narrator expects to be believed, but when we hear direct speech, we are more likely to learn about the speaker's character than about the facts of the matter.

Techniques such as these will help us to start to discover the author's evaluation of situations and actions. While sometimes his comment is explicit (e.g., 2 Sam 11:27), more often it is less clear. But in these instances, we should not infer that he is morally neutral about what he is telling us. Sometimes if we are patient, we will discover that a character receives a reward or comeuppance much later. Sometimes we need to notice the narrator's use of irony or hyperbole to cast a sly insinuation. Or one narrative might employ another for subversive effect. (For example, note the similarities between the story of the "ideal king" David and Bathsheba and the archetypally wicked Ahab and his appropriation of Naboth's vineyard.) Sometimes we need to refer back to the Law—the narrator expects his readers to be familiar with it—to understand the illegitimacy of someone's actions.

It can be seen, then, that the Law may be illuminated by the narratives, and conversely the Law provides a framework for understanding the narratives. Reading and rereading can therefore take us deeper into the intention of the Scriptures. This is because we are changed as we read.

THE ROLE OF THE READER

This brings us to one final question to consider before we move on. This is the role of the reader in the interpretive process. What do we as readers contribute to a text?

That simple question encapsulates almost all the debates in the field of hermeneutics over the last thirty years. This is not the place to try to cash out those arguments, but I will set out the approach which I take, which I consider to be consistent with an evangelical approach to Scripture.

I believe that the reception of a text (how it is read) does matter, for three important reasons. First, it matters because people hear texts differently, and we need to understand that texts we find helpful, or neutral, can be troubling or disturbing for others. For example, someone who has struggled with infertility will probably respond to the stories of Sarah and Hannah quite differently from someone who hasn't. This is not to say that the text's essential *meaning* changes, but it is a warning to us about the way that Scripture can provoke very real, visceral responses. God's word is good, but in a bad world it may not always seem so. We need to be sensitive in our handling of it.

The second reason is related to the first. Just as the Bible might be received in such a way that it causes hurt, so it might be received in such a way that it causes harm. Ten minutes with an internet search engine (far less, really) will provide you with ample examples. Recently I watched an online recording of a sermon where the preacher said that homosexuals (I won't write out the word he used) should be shot—"Front of the head, back of the head, it doesn't matter. Because Leviticus says they should be stoned, and the bullet is the natural evolution of the stone." Either this man has begun with a deep homophobia and sought biblical prooftexts that seem to support it, or someone has taught him to read the Bible very badly indeed. Perhaps both are true. The reader plays an important role in the interpretation of Scripture, and sometimes their misreadings can be terribly harmful.

The third reason is illustrated by both these examples. This is that we engage with a text like we engage with a conversation partner. We always bring something of ourselves to that conversation, and therefore can always be changed by it. This should caution us against the idea that anyone can read the Bible objectively. We can try, but we will never wholly achieve it. Nor can anyone read it perfectly. There is always more that we can learn, and—importantly—there is always the possibility that we may need correction in our interpretation.

While this capacity for gaining a deeper and deeper understanding on repeated readings is true of any text, it is most true of the Bible because of its divine inspiration and because the Spirit is at work within us as we prayerfully read. We could diagram this journey of discovery like this, in what is known as the hermeneutical spiral.[43]

---

43. For a much fuller exploration of this, see Grant R. Osborne, *The Hermeneutical Spiral: A Comprehensive Introduction to Biblical Interpretation*, rev. ed. (Downers Grove, IL: IVP Academic, 2006).

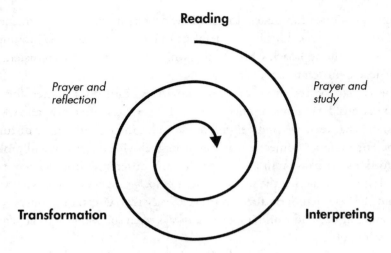

Reading

Prayer and reflection

Prayer and study

Transformation

Interpreting

Prayer and obedience

The point of the diagram is this. As we read, we become transformed, and this means that we read differently next time. Over time, and under the guidance of the Spirit, we gradually become better readers. This whole process depends upon the idea that there is an ideal interpretation of the Bible and that we are limited in our ability to apprehend this, but that we can get better and better as we study and pray.

It is my prayer that we will all engage in such a journey as we turn to our studies of the Bible in the next chapter.

CONCLUSION

In this chapter we have been laying the groundwork for our studies of the biblical testimony about human violence. We have considered different systems in which ethical decisions can be made and noticed the ways in which our *being*, our *history*, and our *telos* shape us in the virtues of Christlikeness. These can only be discovered by deep attention to the theologically rich history of God's dealings with his people.

We then turned our attention to the challenges that scriptural diversity presents as we attempt to discern answers to ethical questions. We noted several different approaches to this diversity, concluding that the whole of Scripture's testimony must be taken into account and offering some ways in which to attempt this.

This rich, complex, and sometimes disturbing text we call "Scripture" is, at heart, a great narrative. It is telling a big story—the story of God's dealings with his people. It is a story of redemption and covenant, of betrayal and steadfast love, of despair and hope, of punishment and forgiveness. It is a story which has not yet ended, although there are plenty of spoilers. It is a story which began with the first creative breath of God. And it is there that we will now begin.

RELEVANT QUESTIONS

1. Which type of ethical system tends to inform your moral decision making?
2. Are there portions of Scripture that you have rejected or functionally ignore?
3. Can you think of examples of the hermeneutical spiral in operation in your own experience?

PART 2

ARRIVING AT ANSWERS

CHAPTER 3

FROM OF OLD

The LORD is king, he is robed in majesty;
the LORD is robed, he is girded with strength.
He has established the world; it shall never be moved;
your throne is established from of old;
you are from everlasting.
Psalm 93:1–2 NRSV

So we turn to study what the Bible teaches us about violence.

There will be plenty of texts to consider. Partly this is because the Bible reflects the fact that it was written in a world where violence of all sorts was commonplace. For many of us, while violence has far from vanished from our world, it does not present itself intrusively into our lives. This was not the case for many people in the ancient world. Structural violence and military conflict would have been a routine part of life at many times in the biblical history.

But within the whole panoply of biblical texts that will preoccupy us for the next few chapters, none will prove more significant than the myths of Genesis 1–11. Although the word *myth* is often used pejoratively, perhaps synonymously with the somewhat dubious term *old wives' tale*, its proper meaning is much more positive than that. Without delving too far into the anthropological and philosophical issues that it raises, we might define a myth *as a sacred narrative which has explanatory power for a society*, and which is likely to shape both the society's identity and its sociopolitical reality.[1]

As far as we can tell, every ancient society had a creation myth, explaining its own origins, and cosmic origins, in ways that influenced their understanding of their own reality. In this regard, the Israelite nation was no different. They, too, had stories that explained to them how the world came into being, and these stories shaped their understanding of the meaning of the world. These have come down to us in Scripture, chiefly in Genesis 1–11, and as such they carry an authority for us modern believers in the God of whom they speak. As we begin our investigation into how the Bible views violence, these are foundational texts that help us to understand the answers to fundamental questions like these:

---

1. See, e.g., the discussion in Percy S. Cohen, "Theories of Myth," in *Man* 4. 3 (1969): 337–53.

- Is violence inherently part of the world we live in? In other words, was it there in the very beginning, or did it somehow become later woven into the fabric of this created order?
- Why does human nature tend toward vengeance? (This will be addressed in the following chapter.)
- On what basis do we assert the sanctity of human life?

Within this very significant scriptural opening, Genesis 1–2 has a privileged position; in fact, I would argue that the first two chapters of the Bible hold a unique role within the whole canon. This is because in Genesis 1 and 2 we see a representation of the world in an idealized form. We have a glimpse of God's intention for the whole created order, and for humanity within it. There is nothing yet which resists the will of God, and therefore what we are seeing is something that we might understand as exemplary, that is, how the world might look if it were perfect. After this, every other text in Scripture, until we get to the very last two chapters of Revelation,[2] is operating within a world where God's will is resisted. In this sense, once we get past Genesis 1 and 2, we are experiencing something—mediated through the text—which is less than ideal.

BLOOD, GUTS, AND A BRAVE NEW WORLD?

In order to understand the biblical myths, it is important first to place them in the context of the other myths that were in circulation at around the same time. The people of Israel did not live in a hermetically sealed environment. They were part of the world we refer to as the ancient Near East,[3] living alongside many other people groups. In its early years, the nation was in a perpetual flux between conflict and trade, suzerainty and vassalage, with other people groups such as the Philistines, the Moabites, and the Egyptians.[4] Later in its history it came under Mesopotamian control and was in vassalage to, and then conquered by, Assyria and Babylonia. Much of the Old Testament came into its final form during the Babylonian exile, and the prevalent ideas of the wider culture shaped the way the stories and myths were told.

This is not to suggest that the ancient biblical writers uncritically adopted pagan ideas and incorporated them into Scripture. They may not even have read the pagan myths that we will be considering.[5] Rather, the writers were operating within a milieu

---

2. Arguably one might also include other biblical texts that provide a glimpse of God's promised future.

3. This is an imprecise term to refer to civilizations located in the approximate area of the modern Middle East. It includes ancient Egypt, Iran, the Levant, Assyria, and Babylonia.

4. See, e.g., Israel's relations with the Moabites: on good enough terms for international travel and intermarriage during the premonarchy (Ruth), in conflict with Saul (1 Sam 14:47), conquered

by David (2 Sam 8:2), providing women for Solomon's harem (1 Kgs 11:1–8), and paying heavy tribute by the time of Ahab (2 Kgs 3). Extrabiblical evidence for some of this is found in the Mesha Stela, currently housed in the Louvre Museum.

5. Gordon Wenham suggests that this is rather like our current generation being aware of the ideas in Darwin's *Origin of Species* without actually having read it (*Rethinking Genesis 1–11: Gateway to the Bible* [Eugene: Cascade, 2015], 51).

which was infused with these theologies and ideologies. While the worldviews within the region and over the long Old Testament time frame were not homogeneous, they carried strong common themes, described by John Walton as a "cultural river":

> The ancient cultural river had among their shared ideas currents that are totally foreign to us. Included in the list we would find fundamental concepts such as community identity, the comprehensive and ubiquitous control of the gods, the role of kingship, divination, the centrality of the temple, the mediatory role of images, and the reality of the spirit world and magic. . . . When we read the Old Testament, we may find reason to believe that the Israelites were supposed to resist some of the currents in their cultural river. Be that as it may (and the nuances are not always easy to work with), they remain in that ancient cultural river.[6]

This river, to continue with Walton's image for a moment, shaped the cognitive environment of the biblical writers. It is the same for us today, of course. I might speak of the principal of my theological college making a "State of the Union address," using a phrase and a concept that is familiar to me as I describe the nature of his speech at our annual alumni celebration. But using such a phrase does not carry any implication of whether I endorse or deprecate the current occupant of the White House. So, to reiterate the point, saying that the biblical writers are operating in this ancient Near Eastern milieu does not mean that the Bible is indistinguishable from other ancient Near Eastern texts or uncritical of their worldviews. Quite the contrary; it often makes its point by means of contrast.[7]

This is an important idea, and we will linger here a moment longer. Difference matters and should be identified, because it is frequently by means of difference that important things are communicated. Consider the well-known story in Luke 10:25–37. Jesus tells his listeners a story about a man who falls among thieves. In many regards the parable starts in an unremarkable way; Jesus's hearers would be very familiar with the bandit-ridden road between Jerusalem and Jericho. There may have been a frisson of surprise when the well-respected Pharisee and Levite walked past the man. But the real moment of communication—the punch in the gut—comes when the audience is utterly astonished by the appearance and conduct of a "good Samaritan." From this, the parable derives its shock and impact. In the same way, the biblical writers sometimes used contrast with prevailing ideas for strong polemical purpose.

On the other hand, sometimes they used the prevailing imagery as a way to communicate their own ideas. We all adopt the linguistic conventions of those we interact with—this is how language acquisition works. We can see the same process

---

6. John Walton, *Ancient Near Eastern Thought and the Old Testament: Introducing the Conceptual World of the Hebrew Bible*, 2nd ed. (Grand Rapids: Baker Academic, 2018), 5.

7. Walton, *Ancient Near Eastern Thought*, 10.

at work today. When a minister says to a member of their congregation, "See you on Thursday," they are not consciously invoking or endorsing the pagan mythology that gave the name of the god Thor to the day of the week.

So it is important to read the myths of ancient Israel because they have foundational and enduring relevance for our inquiry into the biblical perspective on violence. And it is important to read the parallel ancient Near Eastern myths in order to help us understand the biblical ones. It is there, then, that we shall start. As we read, we will attend in particular to the *way* the deities create, *why* they create, and *what* the role of humanity is within their new world.

Ancient Near Eastern Creation Themes

From the study of these and many similar ancient texts, John Walton has identified a number of common steps which—in the ancient Near Eastern mind—a god had to fulfill in order to create the world.[8] I will set them out here, giving just one example from the ancient literature to illustrate each.

- Before the god acts, there is primordial *chaos*; disordered, nonfunctional, unnamed, and undifferentiated. Note how in this example, from the Akkadian creation myth *Enuma Elish*, the monster Tiamat is identified with this watery chaos:

  > When on high no name was given to heaven,
  > Nor below was the netherworld called by name,
  > Primeval Apsu was their progenitor,
  > And matrix—Tiamat was she who bore them all,
  > They were mingling their waters together,
  > No cane brake was intertwined nor thicket matted close.
  > When no gods at all had been brought forth,
  > None called by names, none destinies ordained . . . [9]

- This chaos principally included the heavens, the earth, and the seas, all merged in this primordial state, and the god's first task was to *separate* them. Here is an example from the Sumerian text, the "Song of the Hoe":

  > Not only did the lord who never changes his promises for the future make the world appear in its correct form . . .
  >   not only did he hasten to separate heaven from earth, and earth from heaven. . . . [10]

---

8. Walton, *Ancient Near Eastern Thought*, 188–91.

9. W. W. Hallo and K. L. Younger, *The Context of Scripture, Volume One: Canonical Compositions from the Biblical World* (Leiden: Brill, 1997), 391.

10. Hallo and Younger, *Canonical Compositions*, 511.

- Having separated chaos from order, chaos must now be *maintained within its bounds*. This is an excerpt from the Hittite text, "Crossing of the Taurus."

  > Who holds all the lands? Don't I fix in place the rivers, mountains and seas? I fix the mountain in place, so that it cannot move from its place. I fix the sea in place, so that it cannot flow back.[11]

- The god must then *assign roles* to the things he has created, and give them names. A good example is found in the Egyptian text called the *Papyrus Insinger*, dated to the second or third century BCE. Here, the god's creation of things is for their functional role. For example:

  > He created sleep to end weariness, waking for looking after food,
  > He created remedies to end illness, wine to end affliction,
  > He created the dream to show the way to the dreamer.[12]

- If all of this might be considered as an operational approach to the act of creation, it can alternatively be viewed as an epic battle, frequently termed Chaoskampf ("struggle against chaos"); in fact, as we have already seen, the two approaches are often mingled. In Chaoskampf, the primordial chaos is represented as the sea, or a monster which must be slain, or at least contained. Examples abound in ancient Near Eastern imagery of monsters—often seven-headed, dragon-like—being killed by the gods. These monsters are often given names in the literature. We have encountered Tiamat, who is closely associated with salt water and the sea. The sea is sometimes personified as Yamm (*yam* is "sea" in several Semitic languages). So, for example, in a Canaanite text known as the Baal epic, Baal slaughters Yammu:

  > Kôṯaru prepares two maces and proclaims their names:
  > You, your name is 'Ayyamurru;
  > 'Ayyamurru, expel Yammu,
  > expel Yammu from his throne,
  > Naharu from his seat of sovereignty. . . .
  > So the mace whirls in Baʿlu's hand,
  > like a hawk in his fingers,
  > Strikes Prince Yammu on the head.[13]

  Another important monster of the ancient Near East was called Lotan, who also features in the Baal epic:

11. Hallo and Younger, *Canonical Compositions*, 184.
12. Quoted in John Walton, *The Lost World of Genesis One: Ancient Cosmology and the Origins Debate* (Downers Grove, IL: InterVarsity Press, 2009), 33.

13. Hallo and Younger, *Canonical Compositions*, 248–49.

> When you smite Lôtan, the fleeing serpent,
> finish off the twisting serpent,
> the close-coiling one with seven heads. . . . [14]

So, in summary, in the ancient Near East, creation could be described in a number of ways, which in practice were often mingled:

Divine acts	*Chaoskampf* images
Naming Separation Assigning function	Conquest of monster Subduing the sea

Another point of similarity shared by many of the Mesopotamian creation myths was the purpose of human creation. Here are two excerpts from the Akkadian Atrahasis epic:

> [The gods] did forced labor, they bore drudgery.
> Great indeed was the drudgery of the gods. . . .
> [They were compl]aining, denouncing,
> [Mut]tering down in the ditch . . .
> "Create a human being that he bear the yoke,
> Let him bear the yoke, the task of Enlil,
> Let man assume the drudgery of god."[15]

Richard Middleton has pointed out that certain elements of these myths lent legitimacy to Assyrian and Babylonian structures of hierarchy, notably the temple apparatus and the institution of kingship.

> Beyond providing legitimation for the forcible suppression of external chaos in the form of the enemies of the Babylonian or Assyrian empire, the *Chaoskampf* could also serve to reinforce the hierarchical class structure by which the chaos internal to Mesopotamian society was suppressed and held in check. The ideological division between the masses created for menial service to the gods and the privileged elites who controlled access to the gods as mediators of blessing constitutes an oppositional dualism that looks very much like an internal version of the chaos cosmos scheme.[16]

This will be explored further in a later chapter.

14. Hallo and Younger, *Canonical Compositions*, 265.
15. Hallo and Younger, *Canonical Compositions*, 450–51.
16. J. Richard Middleton, *The Liberating Image: The Imago Dei in Genesis 1* (Grand Rapids: Brazos, 2005), 180.

Genesis among the Epics

It will probably be apparent by now that the biblical stories of creation have important points of similarity and dissimilarity with their ancient Near Eastern equivalents.

The Mesopotamian idea of precreational *chaos* is hinted at in Genesis 1:2, in the Hebrew words commonly translated "without form and void" (KJV) or "formless and empty" (NIV). In Hebrew it is beautifully assonant, and almost seems to be onomatopoeic of the echoing void: *tohu va-bohu*. The first of these words is used in the Hebrew Bible to convey desolation and emptiness, often in reference to the wilderness. See, for example, the haunting words from Deuteronomy 32:10:

> He found him in a desert land,
>> and in the howling waste [*tohu*] of the wilderness. (ESV)

The second of these words, *bohu*, only occurs in conjunction with *tohu* and is found just three times in the Hebrew Bible. It is used by Jeremiah (4:23), when he is explicitly evoking the creation account. The other time the pair of words are used is in this discomfiting passage by Isaiah (34:11), where the prophet is clearly attempting to convey the idea of a desolating return to precreational chaos:

> The desert owl and screech owl will possess it;
>> the great owl and the raven will nest there.
> God will stretch out over Edom
>> the measuring line of chaos [*tohu*]
>> and the plumb line of desolation [*bohu*].

In combination with this compelling pair of words, we also have an image in Genesis 1:2 of the wild, almost bottomless sea, tossed by a howling wind. While Genesis 1:2 is sometimes soothingly translated "darkness was over the surface of the deep, and the Spirit of God was hovering over the waters" (NIV), the image may rather be one of terrifying desolation. It could equally be rendered, "the abyss was wreathed in darkness, and a mighty wind[17] was whipping across the waters." The word I have rendered "abyss" is *tehom* and is used many times in the Hebrew Bible to evoke something quite primal and often terrifying. It also occurs with hints of personification. For example:

---

17. The Hebrew is *ruakh elohim*. *Ruakh* can be translated "spirit" (or "Spirit"), "breath," or "wind." While *elohim* is most commonly used to mean "God" or "gods," it can also be used as an intensifier: "great" or "mighty." One example of this is in Jonah 3:3, where Nineveh is probably best described as a "great city" (D. Winton Thomas, "A Consideration of Some Unusual Ways of Expressing the Superlative in Hebrew," *Vetus Testamentum* 3.1 [1953]: 209–24). However, it is not clear whether this is the best translation of *ruakh elohim*. Richard Middleton argues that the similarities between the creation account and the creation of the tabernacle in Exodus 31 imply that the *ruakh* is indeed the Spirit of God, "holding his breath" before the act of creation (Middleton, *Liberating Image*, 88).

> Blessings of heaven above,
>> blessings of the deep [*tehom*] that crouches beneath.
>> (Gen 49:25 ESV)

> The mountains saw you and writhed;
>> the raging waters swept on;
> the deep [*tehom*] gave forth its voice;
>> it lifted its hands on high. (Hab 3:10 ESV)

When I make you a city laid waste, like the cities that are not inhabited, when I bring up the deep [*tehom*] over you, and the great waters cover you. . . . (Ezek 26:19 ESV)

This combination of imagery and the particular vocabulary selected suggest that the opening verses of the Bible are intended to evoke an image of primal chaos. But as we shall discuss below, it is tamed by the divine command alone. Incidentally, it is hardly coincidental that the gospel accounts of the calming of the storm[18] show Jesus stilling it simply by the power of his voice.

There are further points of similarity with the pagan myths. In particular, the themes of naming, separating, and assigning function are quite evident. Note here, in the first three days, the three acts of separation.

And God said, "Let there be light," and there was light. God saw that the light was good, and he separated the light from the darkness. . . .

And God said, "Let there be a vault between the waters to separate water from water." So God made the vault and separated the water under the vault from the water above it. And it was so. . . .

And God said, "Let the water under the sky be gathered to one place, and let dry ground appear." And it was so. (Gen 1:3–9)

God is also active in naming things:

God called the light "day," and the darkness he called "night." . . . God called the vault "sky." . . . God called the dry ground "land," and the gathered waters he called "seas." (Gen 1:5–10)

He also assigns them functions, seen most clearly on day four.

God said, "Let there be lights in the vault of the sky to separate the day from the night, and let them serve as signs to mark sacred times, and days and years, and let them be lights in the vault of the sky to give light on the earth." And it was so. God made two great lights—the greater light to govern the day and

---

18. Matt 8:23–27; Mark 4:35–41; Luke 8:22–25.

the lesser light to govern the night. He also made the stars. God set them in the vault of the sky to give light on the earth, to govern the day and the night, and to separate light from darkness. (Gen 1:14–18)

A Gentle Creation

Notwithstanding the similarities between the Genesis account and its Mesopotamian parallels, the differences are striking, and for the reasons discussed above, particularly important to notice.

One of the most obvious and important contrasts between the Genesis account of creation and the pagan ones is that only one God is involved in the action, rather than a pantheon. Perhaps related to this, then, is the means by which creation is brought about. Most, if not all, of the other creation myths are violent; the gods are fighting among themselves or with creatures of chaos. By contrast, the God who speaks at the beginning of Genesis 1 has nothing to prove. He is king. He has no rival, is engaged in no combat, and simply speaks creation into being.

While, as we have seen, there may be traces of precreational chaos in Genesis 1:2, it makes no act of resistance. It is passive; there is nothing of the monster here. In fact, as Richard Middleton has pointed out, the two elements that are redolent of chaos are demythologized in the text. The sea is no threat, and the great sea creatures (*tanninim*, see the discussion in the next chapter) are part of the created order (v. 21).[19]

Those of us who have grown up with these stories may fail to notice the wonder of this moment, or we may allow ourselves to become distracted by asking scientific questions of the ancient text. Here, at the beginning of all things, there is no violence but rather a calm command.

God said, "Let there be light," and there was light. (Gen 1:3)

In fact, though God's word clearly carries authority, it is not the dictate of a tyrant. The Hebrew grammatical form used here, "let there be," is called a jussive; something that we don't really have in English. The closest that we would have are the slightly wishful utterances, "May s/he rest in peace," or "May the king/queen live for ever." It doesn't quite carry the force of an imperative. As Eugene Roop says, "Creation comes by divine direction, not by a dictator's demand."[20]

Indeed, the creation account in Genesis is remarkable for its collaborative nature. For God's creative activity in Genesis 1 is not his action alone. After the "gentle cadence"[21] of the divine fiat in verses 2, 6, and 14 (let there be light; let there be a vault, let there be lights), God appears to address what he has already made,[22] bringing

---

19. Middleton, *Liberating Image*, 264.

20. Eugene F. Roop, *Genesis*, Believers Church Bible Commentary (Scottdale, PA: Herald Press, 1987), 27.

21. Middleton, *Liberating Image*, 265.

22. Terence Fretheim, *God and World in the Old Testament: A Relational Theology of Creation* (Nashville: Abingdon, 2005), 38.

what is already created into a power-sharing relationship. So, on the third day, he involves the land, and on the fifth day, the waters and the land again:

> Let the land produce. . . . (Gen 1:11)

> Let the water teem. . . . Let the land produce. . . . (Gen 1:20, 24)

As Middleton puts it, "They are invited . . . to exercise their God-given fertility and thus to imitate God's own creative actions in filling the world with living things."[23] This is a gentle act of creation, exercised by relational means, even before the creation of humanity. Other biblical writers who meditate on creation reflect this by using unabashedly covenantal terms:[24]

> God said to Noah and to his sons with him: "I now establish my covenant with you and with your descendants after you and with every living creature that was with you—the birds, the livestock and all the wild animals, all those that came out of the ark with you—every living creature on earth." (Gen 9:8–10)

> This is what the LORD says: "If you can break my covenant with the day and my covenant with the night, so that day and night no longer come at their appointed time. . . ."
> This is what the LORD says: "If I have not made my covenant with day and night and established the laws of heaven and earth, then I will reject the descendants of Jacob." (Jer 33:20, 25–26)

Further, the work of creation is a divine act of hospitality. We saw above how the other Mesopotamian myths had humans created to be the slaves of the gods. Here the creation of the man and the woman is motivated not from frustration and in order to create slaves who will fashion a home for the deity. Rather, God first creates a lush, fructiferous garden for them to live in, and at each stage in the process he evaluates it and declares it "good." This is an act of divine hospitality, with creation set up for the benefit of humanity. John Walton compares it to a modern company whose employees are stakeholders rather than simply workers on the machine line, which is a model closer to the pagan creation myths.[25]

In 2016 our family left England for a three-week holiday of a lifetime in the southwestern USA. It was on that trip that I had an experience which has shaped my understanding of the garden of Eden imagery used in Genesis.

---

23. Middleton, *Liberating Image*, 288.

24. For further examples, see Job 38:33; Ps 148:6; Jer 31:36.

25. Walton, *Lost World of Genesis One*, 69.

The dry heat that we experienced in Death Valley was quite unlike any previous experiences we had had. Most of the family stayed in the air-conditioned car rather than risk the brutal heat that was dangerous on even the shortest foray to the salt flats.

Our next stop was Yosemite, and it was as if we had crossed into a different world. Our hotel was a complex of cabins nestling under tall conifers. The cool beneath them was of a different quality to the shade of a concrete building. I could almost taste the fragrance of tree resin. And there was life! Ground squirrels flitted from tree to tree below, and birds did the same overhead. After the desert, it felt like paradise.

As indeed it should have. Coming from England, where we seldom pass more than a few days without rain, I am spoiled with a thousand shades of green. And our temperatures are rarely fierce enough for me to *need* the shade of trees. So perhaps I have rather underestimated the value of gardens. But that first night in Yosemite, I felt a new appreciation for the divine hospitality in creation:

> The LORD God made all kinds of trees grow out of the ground—trees that were pleasing to the eye and good for food. . . . A river watering the garden flowed from Eden. . . . (The gold of that land is good; aromatic resin and onyx are also there.) . . .The LORD God took the man and put him in the Garden of Eden. . . . And the LORD God commanded the man, "You are free to eat." (Gen 2:9–16)

Clearly the language of human service to God is not absent from the Old Testament; the servant language in Isaiah (e.g., Isa 41:8) would be a classic example, and we should not forget that the Hebrew word being employed, *ebed*, can be translated either "servant" or "slave." But here, in this foundational creation account, the idea of slavery is notable for its absence. Richard Middleton comments:

> The rhetoric of the text, both by what it explicitly says and by its omissions, highlights the radical distinction between oppressive Mesopotamian notions of human purpose (bond servants to the gods) and a liberating alternative vision of humanity as the royal-priestly image of God.[26]

This brings us to a key element of the creation account. After God has made humanity, his first words to them are of blessing (Gen 1:28), and their—our—purpose is spelled out. Far from being slaves, humanity is charged to multiply, to fill the earth

---

26. Middleton, *Liberating Image*, 210.

with image bearers, and to *reign*. In fact, this language of governance is directly coupled with the language of "image."

HUMAN VOCATION, PART ONE

The symbol of humanity as the image of God has been interpreted in a multitude of ways over the generations, so much so that the theologian Hendrikus Berkhof dryly commented that "systematic theologies have poured meaning into Genesis 1:26."[27] But if we draw out the clues in the passage itself, and those from the ancient Near Eastern cognitive background, then we see that the principal significance of the image motif relates to *kingship*. Within the context of the divine kingship, the image declaration is embedded in a section of the text which is all about governance.

> Then God said, "Let us make humankind in our image, in our likeness, so that they may rule over the fish in the sea and the birds in the sky, over the livestock and all the wild animals, and over all the creatures that move along the ground."[28]
>
> So God created humankind in his own image,
>> in the image of God he created them;
>> male and female he created them.[29]
>
> God blessed them and said to them, "Be fruitful and increase in number; fill the earth and subdue it. Rule over the fish in the sea and the birds in the sky and over every living creature that moves on the ground."
> Then God said, "I give you every seed-bearing plant on the face of the whole earth and every tree that has fruit with seed in it. They will be yours for food. And to all the beasts of the earth and all the birds in the sky and all the creatures that move along the ground—everything that has the breath of life in it—I give every green plant for food. (Gen 1:26–30)

It is worth taking a moment to consider some elements of the Hebrew used here.

- The word translated "rule" in verses 26 and 28 is *radah*, a word commonly used to express authority and often royal reign. So the psalmist writes, "May [the king] rule [*radah*] from sea to sea" (Ps 72:8).
- The word translated "subdue" in Genesis 1:28 is sometimes misunderstood. It is true that it is sometimes used elsewhere in the Old Testament to refer to violent action (e.g., Josh 18:1: "The country was brought under their control"). However, these uses are always found in the context of interhuman conflict.

27. Hendrikus Berkhof, *Christian Faith: An Introduction to the Study of the Faith*, trans. S. Woudstra, rev. ed. (Grand Rapids: Eerdmans, 1986), 184.

28. NIV amended.
29. NIV amended.

Here, where no conflict is in view, it seems to refer to the cultivation of the earth and therefore to reflect the divine creative action of imposing order upon chaos.[30]

This is significant, because inherent to the idea of "image" is (obviously) the notion of similarity to that which is imaged. If the task of the image bearer is to rule, the manner of that rule is to reflect God's own kingship. This is what Richard Middleton refers to as both the *representative* (standing for) and the *representational* (being like) elements of image bearers as rulers.[31]

The metaphor of priesthood is also operative here. Both the ancient Near East texts and Genesis 1 view the creation of the cosmos as temple-building.[32] Within this metaphor, in the biblical account, humanity is placed in the temple as priests to serve within it.[33] The linkage of these twin vocations to be kings and priests finds resonance in Exodus 19:6, and on into the New Testament (1 Pet 2:9; Rev 1:6; 5:10).

These first divine words to humanity have in their rich layers a number of theologically important consequences. It is to these that we now turn our focus.

Male and Female

First, we should notice that male and female are created as equals. There is no hierarchy here. Neither sex can claim exclusive possession of the divine image, as the triplet in verse 27 draws out:

> God created humankind in his own image,
> in the image of God he created them;
> male and female he created them.

In Genesis 1, then, God's plan for humankind involves cooperation and mutuality between men and women. However, some have regarded the following chapter as offering a counterpoint to this. While the discussion of gender relations might be considered somewhat beyond the scope of this book, so much violence is exercised in a gendered way (whether physical and sexual violence, or structural violence against women) that a brief foray into this subject is necessary.

Briefly put, the case for a gender-hierarchical interpretation of Genesis 2 is as follows. The man stands alone in the garden, and God decides to create a helper for him, to allow him to populate the earth and to assist him in his duties. In order to do this, God creates a woman out of an offcut from the man, and Adam exerts his authority over his new wife by naming her, just as he had done to the animals.

30. Fretheim, *God and World*, 52.
31. Middleton, *Liberating Image*, 88.
32. Walton, *Ancient Near Eastern Thought*, 147–70.
33. It is striking that the twin verbs describing God's charge to humanity in Genesis 2:15 (*abad* and *shamar*, which the NIV translates "work" and "take care of") are the same two verbs used of the priestly role in Numbers 3:7; 8:26; and 18:7. They do not appear as a pair anywhere else in Scripture.

When the biblical narrative is described like this, we might well concur with the scurrilous epithet quoted (not approvingly) by Calvin, that women are a "necessary evil."[34]

This is badly to misunderstand the thrust of the text, however. While it does indeed dwell upon the "fit" between the man and the woman (v. 23), the emphasis is upon mutuality rather than dominance; male and female being one flesh (and consequently the man having to make considerable accommodation for his wife, v. 24). The act of naming is by no means a universal code for the assertion of authority—see Genesis 16 where Hagar names God![35] The Hebrew word translated "helper" (*ezer*, vv. 18, 20) does not describe a passive handmaiden, whom we might imagine mopping the great man's forehead while he does his important work. Rather, it is the word used to describe military assistance (e.g., 1 Chr 12:1) or frequently of God himself (e.g., Ps 70:6). And, as some early rabbis described,[36] the "rib" (*tsela'*), from which Eve was made, might better be translated "side," as it is the word used for half of a boat or half of a building. So it is not so much that the woman is grown from the man's "spare rib," but rather that a primitive, ungendered creature (better translated as "the human" rather than "Adam" at this point) is cloven in half to create a man and a woman.[37] This provides a much better explanation for why the act of sexual union causes the man and the woman to become "one flesh" again (v. 24).

In summary, Genesis 2 should not be regarded as a text unfavourable to women. Gordon Wenham puts it like this:

> Here the ideal of marriage as it was understood in ancient Israel is being portrayed, a relationship characterized by harmony and intimacy between the partners.[38]

I will not expand further on this theme here, but I trust that it is evident that Genesis 2 in no way undermines what Genesis 1 has made explicit: man and woman comprise the image of God, and God's blessing, his declaration of human vocation, and the charge to humanity apply equally to both sexes. There is no hierarchy, no dominion of one human over another, or one sex over the other taught here in Genesis 1–2.

Democratization of Image Bearing

Recalling that this ancient text was written in a time of undeniable patriarchy, it is unexpected that the woman should be represented as coequal with the man

34. Quoted in Jean Calvin, *Commentary on the First Book of Moses Called Genesis*, trans. J. King (Bellingham: Logos Bible Software, 1847 [2010]), 1:129.

35. G. W. Ramsey, "Is Name-Giving an Act of Domination in Genesis 2:23 and Elsewhere?," *CBQ* 50.1 (1988): 24–35.

36. See, e.g., Rabbi Shmuel bar Nachmani, in *Bereshit Rabbah* 8.1, which can be found here www.sefaria.org/sheets/179959 .9?lang=bi&p2=Bereshit_Rabbah.8.1&lang2=bi.

37. Walton, *Lost World of Adam and Eve*, 70–81.

38. Gordon J. Wenham, *Genesis 1–15*, WBC 1 (Dallas: Word, 1987), 69.

in these chapters. There is no equivalent, as far as I am aware, in Mesopotamian creation mythology. In the pagan texts, we are far more likely to encounter the female personified in the chaos agent that requires violent suppression—remember Tiamat in the *Enuma Elish*. We should not overlook the surprise—scandal, even—that the Genesis account ought to present.

But this "democratization" of the image of God does not operate upon gender alone. In the ancient Near Eastern parallels, it is the *king* who is the image of God. But in Genesis, this role is accorded to humanity as a whole. This is emphasized further by noting where "image" recurs later in Genesis. In Genesis 5:1–3, we read how the image of God is transmitted to Adam's descendants:

> When God created humankind, he made them in the likeness of God. He created them male and female and blessed them. And when they were created, he called them "humankind." When Adam had lived 130 years, he had a son in his own likeness, in his own image; and he named him Seth.

There is an ancient Sumerian document, known as the Sumerian King list, which provides an account of the royal line of the house of Sumer and, in particular, connects the royal family with the gods by describing them as having been lowered from heaven. This Sumerian King list has striking points of similarity with Genesis 5–9, even including a brief flood account. When the two documents are compared, however, something interesting becomes apparent. The two places after Genesis 1 where the "image" language is used correlate to two specific moments in the Sumerian King list—the moments when the kingship descends from heaven.

Genesis	Sumerian King List
Adam in the image of God (Gen 5:1)	Line 1, "kingship descended from heaven"
Human genealogy	Royal genealogy
Flood	Flood
Humans in image of God (Gen 9:6)	Line 41, "kingship descended from heaven"

The first person to identify this parallel was J. Maxwell Miller. Writing in 1972 (and therefore using rather unhelpful "man" rather than "human" language), he wrote:

> [The] writer [of Genesis] seems to have affirmed the order of primeval events presupposed by the Mesopotamian myths, and may have even patterned his own account after a Mesopotamian prototype. Yet he radically modified the basic concepts and motifs reflected in the Mesopotamian myths and substituted details from his own Hebrew heritage. His dual emphasis upon man's creation

in the "likeness" of God and man's royal status among the creatures is to be understood in this light.[39]

In other words, the writer of Genesis is democratizing the image of God. It is humanity that occupies this royal role in the world.[40]

There is so much more that could be said of these two marvelous chapters at the beginning of our Bibles. But with our focus on questions of violence, we have probably drawn out the main ones. Foremost of all, the *goodness* of God is primordial; violence is not. The earth is not founded, as the pagan myths of Mesopotamia asserted, upon the tenuous control that fickle and fallible gods manage to exert over ever-erupting chaos. Rather, it is founded on the goodness and faithfulness of God, who surveys the world he has created, with humanity as its pinnacle, and declares it "very good" (Gen 1:31). Violence, when we encounter it in the story, will come as an aberration.

Moreover—and this will prove to be particularly relevant when we consider structural violence in later chapters—while humanity is charged with the responsibility to govern on God's behalf, there is at this stage an entirely flat power structure. All of humanity, male and female, is represented within the figures of Adam and Eve. Humans (male and female) are kings, not slaves; they are recipients of divine generosity and blessing, not subjects of divine instrumentalization. The language of the image of God speaks to the dignity and value of all human life and will be the basis, as we shall see shortly, for the prohibition of murder.

As the great C. S. Lewis put it in his allegorical novel *Prince Caspian*:

> "You come of the Lord Adam and the Lady Eve," said Aslan. "And that is both honour enough to erect the head of the poorest beggar, and shame enough to bow the shoulders of the greatest emperor on earth."[41]

We turn next to the shame.

CONCLUSION

The creation account in Genesis stands in contrast to the creation myths of the other nations that lived near Israel in the ancient world. While it bears similarity to those myths at some points, the biblical account of creation shows the world coming into being by God's calm, authoritative fiat and created as an act of hospitality rather than conquest. This means that violence is not ontological; it is not a primordial reality.

39. J. M. Miller, "In the 'Image' and 'Likeness' of God," *JBL* 91.3 (1972): 303–4.

40. Middleton, *Liberating Image*, 214.

41. C. S. Lewis, *Prince Caspian* (Harmondsworth: Penguin, 1951), 185.

Within this newly minted world, humans—male and female—are created in the image of God with the charge to govern as his representatives, acting as vice-regents and priests. There is no hierarchy between them, and the traditional kingly language of "image of God" is democratized by being applied to all humans.

RELEVANT QUESTIONS

1. If Scripture shows that there is a flat structure of human power before the fall, how might that influence our approach to gender relations and other power imbalances?
2. What difference does it make to us if we understand that goodness and peace are primordial and ontological, but violence is not?

CHAPTER 4

THINGS FALL APART

Things fall apart; the centre cannot hold;
Mere anarchy is loosed upon the world,
The blood-dimmed tide is loosed, and everywhere
The ceremony of innocence is drowned.
—W. B. Yeats, "The Second Coming"

In Genesis 3, things begin to unravel, as the man and the woman disobey God and eat from the forbidden tree. The chapter is the link between the Edenic narratives and the stories that follow; it provides the vital bridge which takes the reader from the nonviolent, hospitable world we have been discussing to the ever-intensifying horrors that provide such a contrast in the later chapters.

What is the primal sin of Genesis 3? Is it disobedience, lack of faith, ambition, disordered desire, untruth? It is perhaps hard to tease out just one of these. God's instruction not to eat is clearly relayed, even intensified, by the woman (v. 3), so disobedience is in the frame. One could argue for a lack of faith in God: Was his word considered untrustworthy, perhaps? Or was his good intent toward humanity in doubt? The woman certainly seems attracted by the idea of being "like God" (v. 5), which would be ambition. Is it disordered desire (v. 6)? And the serpent certainly peddles half-truths, which the woman is willing to believe.

Some commentators consider that "the fall"—a theologically rich and complex idea, whose extent lies far beyond the Genesis text itself—is not so much a fall from perfection as a failure to cooperate with God in the ongoing process of wresting order out of chaos. It is our ancestors "pulling out of the program" prematurely, as John Walton puts it:[1]

> Genesis 3 is more about the encroachment of disorder into a world in the process of being ordered than it is about the first sin. It is about how humanity lost access to the presence of God when its representatives tragically declared their independence from their Creator.[2]

---

1. Walton, *Lost World of Adam and Eve*, 145.   2. Walton, *Lost World of Adam and Eve*, 147.

In response to Adam and Eve's choice to position themselves as the centers of order and the source of wisdom, God speaks words of judgment to them (Gen 3:14–19). (Note that the language of "curse" is applied to the snake [v. 14] and the ground [v. 17], but *not* to humanity.) The consequences God describes are expressed in direct reference to the creation mandate of Genesis 1:27–28. From now on, both the exercise of dominion (vv. 17–19) and populating the earth (v. 16) will be hard and painful. And the relationship between the sexes will be one of competition and the mutual desire to dominate, rather than of cooperation (v. 16).

It is important that we understand God's words here as descriptive, not prescriptive; in other words, they describe to the humans the consequences of their actions rather than commanding how things must be from then on. The testimony of the remainder of Scripture, as we shall see, is that God's heart is set on a trajectory that will restore the lost order. It seems inconceivable that he would here establish with authoritative force a system which conclusively contradicts such a trajectory.

"Some Bible interpreters argue that this curse of inequality is prescriptive for all times—that we dare not tamper with it. But the curse on the ground that meant Adam would be tilling the soil snarled with thorns and thistles has been largely reversed. Even as inventions of machinery and fertilizers have relieved the backbreaking work of agriculture, so have legal statutes mitigated the effects of gender inequality."[3]

THE INVENTION OF VIOLENCE

The effects are immediately and disastrously apparent; the man and the woman do not physically die that same day, as God had seemed to imply (2:17), but the change they experience is perhaps even more appalling: not only physical decay but alienation, toil, and bondage.[4]

Physical death is not far behind, however, and the genealogy of chapter 5 with its repeated refrain "and he died" hammers the point home effectively. But in particular, what we encounter now is a series of stories exposing the rapid spiraling of human violence. Fratricide (4:2–16) gives way to multiplicative vengeance[5] (vv. 23–24) and then the whole earth filled with violence (6:11).

3. Ruth Tucker, *Black and White Bible, Black and Blue Wife: My Story of Finding Hope after Domestic Abuse* (Grand Rapids: Zondervan, 2016), 47.

4. David J. Atkinson, *The Message of Genesis 1–11: The Dawn of Creation* (Nottingham: Inter-Varsity Press, 1990), 96–97.

5. Lamech's threat to repay violence done to him seventy-sevenfold in response to Cain's sevenfold punishment is probably echoed—and subverted—in Jesus's conversation with Simon Peter about forgiveness (Matt 18:21–22).

> While the tower of Babel has traditionally been understood to be a ziggurat, more recent scholarship suggests that it more closely resembles a great tower built for civic or imperial function rather than for religious purpose.
>
> The Assyrian king Ashurbanipal II claimed that he "made the totality of all peoples/people speak one speech" and that "through his sovereign approach [he] made the unruly and ruthless kings speak one speech from the rising of the sun to its setting."[6]
>
> It seems likely that the Babel story is told in opposition to this sort of imperial and cultural hegemony. Richard Middleton writes, "While confusion is certainly the initial result of multiplying the languages of Babel, in the context of the primeval history this is fundamentally a restorative move, reversing an unhealthy, monolithic movement toward imposed homogeneity."[7]

We might also add the structural violence of polygamy (Gen 4:19), the emergence of warriors (10:8), and the hegemonic oppression being critiqued in the tower of Babel story (11:1–9). These early chapters set out the "invention" of violence, which takes place alongside the explosion of human culture in building (4:17), farming (v. 20), music (v. 21), and metalwork (v. 22):

> What becomes clear from the first primeval history, then, is that the cultural achievements of the human race testify not only to a God-given human power and agency, but also to the possibility of using that power/agency to accomplish evil. Specifically, the culture that humans develop is profoundly intertwined with violence.[8]

The significance of violence in Genesis 3–11 becomes even more evident if we consider what alternatives the narrator might have chosen to highlight the corrupting effects of the fall. It is striking that idolatry makes no appearance this early in the narrative. It is not this which the text highlights as the first symptom of human disobedience. Alternatively, unlike the apocryphal book of Sirach (for example), it does not focus on male control of female sexuality. The Genesis narrator could likewise have chosen stories of wayward women to make his point, but he doesn't. Or there could have been a focus on deviant sexual practice; but there isn't.[9] Or, thinking of Ezra's determined purification of the exilic returnees much later in the

---

6. Quoted in David Smith, "What Hope after Babel? Diversity and Community in Gen. 11:1–9; Exod. 1:1–14; Zeph. 3:1–13 and Acts 2:1–3," *Horizons in Biblical Theology* 18.1 (1996): 173.

7. Middleton, *Liberating Image*, 225.

8. Middleton, *Liberating Image*, 119–20.

9. It is true that the beginning of Genesis 6 gives a mythic and mysterious account of angels interbreeding with women, but this is not "human" sin in the same way that the other actions in Genesis 4–11 are. In Genesis 9, Ham's actions against his father Noah probably reflect an act of violent incest, but this is a late event, coming after the stories of Cain and Abel and the flood being narrated in these chapters.

story, the writer of Genesis could have characterized exogamy or even miscegenation as primal sins; but he doesn't.

What the narrator does highlight is violence. But he is not exclusively focused on violence that is *experienced*. Rather, the evils of violence *committed* are the focus of the text. As we shall see, Abel's subjection to violence certainly gets its share of attention. But the focus upon Cain is striking, as God preemptively warns him against the temptation to commit sin (Gen 4:6–7). It is not human experience of violence that is emphasized in Genesis 6 but rather human complicity in it. This is not, of course, to suggest that God is uninterested in the experience of violence by its victims. We will discuss this at length in chapter 7. Rather, I am suggesting that the unarticulated assumption of the text here is that the most tragic thing that can happen to humanity is that they *become* violent.

THE DOOR TO THE FUTURE LEFT AJAR[10]

In response to these cycles of violence, we see God repeatedly stepping in. His actions are different on each occasion but reveal an unchanging purpose of directing humanity and the created order toward the good.

As we have seen, when Cain is entertaining murderous thoughts toward his brother, God steps in to warn him. Here, in the very first recorded crime, we see three key elements of God's dealings within humanity: he forbids and warns but does not coerce; he attends to the victim and condemns the violence committed against them; he punishes but has mercy on the perpetrator—in particular, taking action to prevent the unlimited spiraling of reciprocal violence (Gen 4:6–15).

For many, God's actions in causing the flood call into question his goodness and good intention toward humanity. It is not possible here to offer a full theodicy, but there are several things that should draw our attention to God's good purposes. First, the evil and violence that have enveloped the world is expressed in terms of the disruption of the creation blessing and mandate.

> God blessed them and said to them, "Be fruitful and increase [*rabah*] in number, fill [*mala'*] the earth." (Gen 1:28)

> The LORD saw that the wickedness of humankind had increased [*rabah*] upon the earth . . . and the earth was full [*mala'*] of violence. (Gen 6:5, 11)[11]

Rather than the earth being full of image bearers, it is now full of violence, because wickedness has multiplied as the people have multiplied. (In chapter 7, we

---

10. This lovely metaphor for God's unfailing patience with his fallen creatures is taken from David Smith, "What Hope after Babel?," 171.

11. Both these verses are my own translation, to bring out the verbal similarities.

will see a similar challenge to the creation ordinance when Pharaoh speaks at the beginning of the book of Exodus.) This is no ordinary petty crime; it is a direct threat to the goodness of the created order. It is as if an evil anti-creation is building itself parasitically upon God's good world. What is a creator to do when such a threat presents itself?

What God chooses to do is often misunderstood, based upon our translations, as an act of petty spite, of holocaust-like destruction. But the Hebrew could be rendered more accurately, though woodenly, like this translation offered by Daniel Hawk:

> Yahweh looked at the earth. Look! It was ruined [niphal of *shachat*], for all flesh had ruined [hiphil of *shachat*] its way on the earth. God said to Noah, "The end of all flesh has arrived right in front of me, for the earth is saturated with violence before them. Look! I'm going to ruin [hiphil of *shachat*] them with the earth. . . . I am bringing a flood of water to ruin [piel of *shachat*] all flesh." (Gen 6:12–13, 17)[12]

God's actions can therefore be viewed not as a vengeful act of punishment but as a preempting of the ruinous trajectory that the earth was already set upon:

> We are left with the sense that God is not so much sending the flood to punish the world as facilitating, through the flood, the inevitable descent into chaos caused by human destructiveness and violence. God ruins an already ruined creation, and in so doing creates the conditions for a reordering and a renewal to take place. . . . The narrator relates *no action* on the part of Yahweh other than seeing (vv. 5, 12) and saying (vv. 7, 13). God *says* a lot about the flood, but, at least the way the narrator tells it, God doesn't *do* much. . . . Aside from a note that Yahweh closed the hatch for Noah (7:16), God remains out of the picture when the action takes place. God only reenters the narrative after the flood has done its work.[13]

This idea of God giving humanity over to the consequences of its actions is echoed again and again in Scripture. Perhaps one of the most explicit places is in the language used by Paul in Romans 1:

> Therefore God gave them over in the sinful desires of their hearts to sexual impurity (v. 24). . . . God gave them over to shameful lusts (v. 26). . . . God gave them over to a depraved mind, so that they do what ought not to be done. (v. 28)

---

12. L. Daniel Hawk, *The Violence of the Biblical God: Canonical Narrative and Christian Faith* (Grand Rapids: Eerdmans, 2019), 32 (transliterations added).

13. Hawk, *Violence of the Biblical God*, 33 (emphasis original).

If Hawk's interpretation of God's involvement in the flood is correct, we should focus on the lifesaving actions of God in commissioning the ark and providing for both humans and animal preservation in the face of impending catastrophe.

This is highlighted when the Genesis account is compared with the other ancient flood myths, particularly the Atrahasis epic. In the pagan accounts, the gods are frustrated by the noise of mankind:

> Twelve hundred years had not yet passed
> when the land extended and the peoples multiplied.
> The land was bellowing like a bull.
> The gods were disturbed with their uproar.
> Enlil heard their noise and addressed the great gods.
> "The noise of mankind has become too intense for me
> with their uproar I am deprived of sleep."[14]

In response to this nuisance, the gods send first a plague to control the human population, then a drought, then a famine. Then, with the flood, they unveil the ultimate solution. Their plan is thwarted when one god, Enki, whispers of the forthcoming catastrophe to a man called Atrahasis and urges him to build a boat. After the inundation, the gods realize that they do need humans after all (who will do the work, if they are all destroyed?), but they take active and horrible steps to limit human population growth in the future.

> In addition, let there be a third category among the peoples,
> Among the peoples women who bear and women who do not bear.
> Let there be among the peoples the Pagittu-demon to snatch the
>   baby from the lap of her who bore it.
> Establish Ugbabtu-women, Entu-women, and Igisitu-women and
>   let them be taboo and so stop childbirth.[15]

In the Genesis account, as we have seen, it is the evil of humanity, and in particular its violence, which causes God to permit the flood. And afterward, far from seeking to control the population, God actively promotes human flourishing. In Genesis 9:12–17 he sets his rainbow in the sky as a sign of the covenant between himself and his created order (including but not limited to humanity). Whether the rainbow represents a huge divine war bow turned aside in reconciliation, or a boundary to hold in place the waters of the firmament,[16] it signifies a promise that

---

14. This excerpt from the Atrahasis epic is quoted in Tikva Frymer-Kensky, "The Atrahasis Epic and Its Significance for Our Understanding of Genesis 1–9," *The Biblical Archaeologist* 40.4 (1977): 149.

15. Quoted in Frymer-Kensky, "Atrahasis Epic," 149.

16. Laurence A. Turner, "The Rainbow as the Sign of the Covenant in Genesis IX 11–13," *Vetus Testamentum* 43.1 (1993): 119–24.

the earth will never again be destroyed in this way. But first, God makes another statement to Noah that is profound in its affirmation of human life, both in relation to human fertility as well as in establishing the sanctity of human life in the first biblical homicide law, rooted in the divine image:

> Then God blessed Noah and his sons, saying to them, "Be fruitful and increase in number and fill the earth. . . . And for your lifeblood I will surely demand an accounting. I will demand an accounting from every animal. And from each human being, too, I will demand an accounting for the life of another human being.
>
> "Whoever sheds human blood,
>   by human beings shall their blood be shed;
> for in the image of God
>   has God made mankind.
>
> As for you, be fruitful and increase in number; multiply on the earth and increase upon it." (Gen 9:1–7)

The contrast between the biblical account and the pagan one could not be more striking. As Jeremy Cohen puts it,

> Even beyond the question of crime and punishment, the Babylonian epic measures the value of human life in terms of the immediate, physical gratification of the gods. In the Bible . . . the words of Gen. 1.28 epitomize the blessing of God, investing human life and the means for its perpetuation with the spiritual worth that withstands the evil of Noah's generation and the cataclysm of the flood.[17]

This excerpt from Genesis 9 contains the roots of several themes that will prove important in later parts of Scripture. In particular, it is the canonical first expression of the law of talion (commonly referred to as "an eye for an eye"). We will discuss this further in chapter 6. Equally important, however, is its reference to the significance of blood, which we have already seen in the Cain and Abel story. Let us turn to consider this in more detail.

THE POWER OF SPILLED BLOOD

We have encountered two very important sayings about blood in Genesis 1–11. Add Leviticus 17 to these two sayings, and these three texts probably express the basic

---

17. Jeremy Cohen, *Be Fertile and Increase, Fill the Earth and Master It: The Ancient and Medieval Career of a Biblical Text* (Ithaca: Cornell, 1989), 43.

ideas behind much of the Old Testament's use of the language of blood. The first is from the Cain and Abel story, the second is spoken by God to Noah after the flood, and the third is part of the Levitical law concerning sacrifice in the tabernacle:

> The LORD said, "What have you done? Listen! Your brother's blood cries out to me from the ground. Now you are under a curse and driven from the ground, which opened its mouth to receive your brother's blood from your hand. When you work the ground, it will no longer yield its crops for you." (Gen 4:10–12)

> You must not eat meat that has its lifeblood still in it. And for your lifeblood I will surely demand an accounting. I will demand an accounting from every animal. And from each human being, too, I will demand an accounting for the life of another human being.
>
> > Whoever sheds human blood,
> >   by human beings shall their blood be shed;
> > for in the image of God
> >   has God made mankind. (Gen 9:4–6)

> I will set my face against any Israelite or any foreigner residing among them who eats blood, and I will cut them off from their people. For the life of a creature is in the blood, and I have given it to you to make atonement for yourselves on the altar; it is the blood that makes atonement for one's life. Therefore I say to the Israelites, "None of you may eat blood, nor may any foreigner residing among you eat blood." (Lev 17:10–12)

This is a complex issue, as I will sketch out below, but one thing seems very clear: there is something special about blood in the biblical worldview. There is no similar set of instructions related to the disposal of cut hair or toenails, for example, although dead bodies and semen do get special treatment, probably for a related reason, as we shall see.

In the Old Testament, the word "blood" (*dam*, also sometimes used in the plural, *damim*) stands for more than simply the red stuff that oozes out of a cut. However, the symbolism is complex. There is a range, sometimes an apparent contradiction, of ideas which *dam* can signify, as in this diagram:

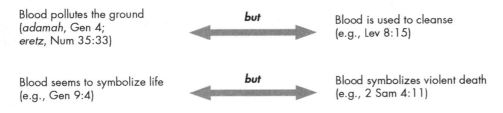

Blood pollutes the ground (*adamah*, Gen 4; *eretz*, Num 35:33)   *but*   Blood is used to cleanse (e.g., Lev 8:15)

Blood seems to symbolize life (e.g., Gen 9:4)   *but*   Blood symbolizes violent death (e.g., 2 Sam 4:11)

There is therefore a variety of functions that blood can perform. This might be represented in the following diagram:

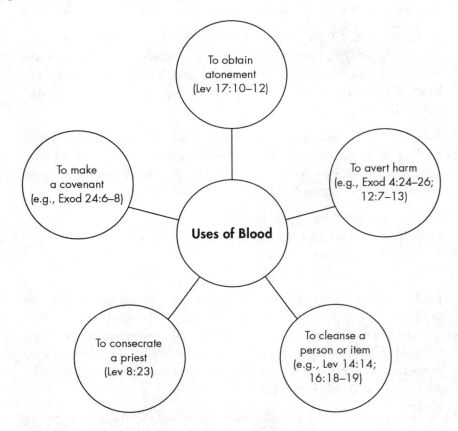

Blood appears to connote a confusing range of symbols and to fulfill a broad range of functions. How can this be?

Before we attempt to tease this out, it is important that we do not try to flatten the whole canon, or even just the Old Testament, into a single text as if it were all written by the same author at the same time and for the same purpose. Words and theological ideas change over time, and symbols are used to different effect by different authors. Nonetheless, there are some important common threads which seem to bind these ideas together, and these can shed light on the most perplexing and apparently contradictory examples above.

As a way into the topic, we should note the careful work of the anthropologist Mary Douglas, whose studies of taboos and laws in the Old Testament have shed a

18. Mary Douglas, *Leviticus as Literature* (Oxford: Oxford University Press, 1999), 178.

great deal of light in recent years. For instance, she identifies similarities between the taboos on menstrual blood and semen, as they both imply a failure of fertility. Semen spilled is not producing life; menstrual blood implies the failure of conception.[18]

Douglas's insight links to the key idea that underlies the blood prohibition. There is something powerful about blood; something that has great capacity to bring about good; something life-giving. But because of this power, it is not to be trifled with. It is not to be eaten. And, as we have seen, it is not to be spilled lightly.

When we speak of "power" in blood, we must remember that we are speaking in metaphorical terms. We should not start thinking about white blood cells or oxygen transport—these are far from the ancient mind. Rather, we need to understand that it is charged with potency to make it the dominant metaphor for violence. This highlights the significance of life, and not merely human life but animal life too. But it is for human life that Genesis urges the greatest respect. The spilling of blood requires an accounting because life is in the blood. The spilling of human blood requires a great accounting because humans are in the image of God.

Here is the sanctity of human life spelled out, right at the beginning of the story. Spilled blood cries out from the ground, and God answers it.

ENTER THE MONSTER

It is curious that medieval religious art developed such a florid style for representing Satan and his minions—from horns and tails, to the gleeful employment of pitchforks—when Scripture itself gives a different and far more graphic image for the archenemy of God. While the concept of Satan as employed by much of the church today is a largely New Testament phenomenon,[19] the Old Testament is replete with references to the enemies of God, often employing mythic imagery of the chaos monster.

In Genesis 3, we encounter an enemy described as a serpent (*nakhash*). While this word can be used of a classifiable animal (see, e.g., Ps 58:4 [58:5 MT]; Amos 5:19; Mic 7:17), the symbol is often used in ways that intersect with the ideas of the monsters of chaos found in Babylonian, Egyptian, and Canaanite mythology. Here, serpents appear in images and texts to represent forces that oppose the gods, guard the underworld, and are agents of chaos.[20] In the Hebrew Bible, too, the ideas of the many-headed monster Leviathan, the *tannin*[21]—variously translated "monster" (NIV), "sea creature" (ESV; NRSV), or "dragon" (ESV), the *nakhash* (serpent), and the sea (a symbol of primordial chaos) often overlap. The following table gives some examples of where the terms are used as if synonymous.

19. C. Breytenbach and P. L. Day, "Satan," *DDD* 729.
20. R. S. Hendel, "Serpent," *DDD* 744–48.

21. *Tannin* is the singular form; the plural is *tanninim*.

	nakhash	sea	Leviathan	*tannin*
Amos 9:3	x	x		
Isaiah 27:1	x	x	x	x
Psalm 104:25–26		x	x	
Psalm 74:13–14		x	x	x
Job 7:12		x		x
Exodus 7:8–15;* cf. 4:2–5	x			x

* *Tannin* is found in Exod 7:8–12, but in v. 15 the serpent is a *nakhash*.

With this cognitive field in play when the writer of Genesis 3 is writing and when his intended readers are reading, the serpent who introduces doubt into the mind of Eve and Adam should clearly be understood as an anti-creational force. God has created a cosmos distinguished by order; the serpent introduces the first elements of chaos.

HUMAN VOCATION, PART TWO[22]

It is then that we encounter one of the most significant biblical statements about the human vocation. In response to the disobedience of the man and the woman, God says this to the serpent:

> I will put enmity
>> between you and the woman,
>> and between your offspring and hers;
> he will crush[23] your head,
>> and you will strike his heel. (Gen 3:15)

This verse is sometimes called the *protevangelium*; the first statement of the gospel in Scripture, looking ahead to Jesus's victory over Satan on the cross. But to project it immediately onto Jesus is to miss what it says about God's call upon humanity. God has previously spoken words of dominion and kingship to the man and the woman (1:28), and he here charges them and their offspring with the responsibility of striking the head of the serpent. This is what a true human will do.

These verses in Genesis 1 and 3 form a sort of job description for humanity. It is

---

22. "Human Vocation, Part One" was in the previous chapter.
23. The NIV has "crush," but the same Hebrew verb is operative in both halves of this couplet.

a role that every human who comes later—whether evaluated individually (Adam, Cain, Abraham), corporately (Israel), or as an individual who represents the nation (Saul, David)—fails to live up to. Only the one true human will achieve it, and in this respect it does point ahead to Jesus. But throughout the Old Testament it is held up as a goal, and the clue to identifying this is to note the thread of head-crushing that runs through Scripture. When we see this language emerge, usually in relation to enemies rather than to serpents *per se*, we should recall the divine instructions in the garden.

Often the language is explicitly reminiscent of this verse, but sometimes it is rather obscured. So, for example, Jacob's dying prophecy and blessing to his sons identifies Judah as the son who will reign (Gen 49:10; the Davidic line is in the tribe of Judah) and who will place his hand upon the neck of his enemies (v. 8).

This is taken up by Balaam, who gives an oracle that speaks of a future king of Israel who will fulfill this charge:

> A star will come out of Jacob;
>> a scepter will rise out of Israel.
> He will crush the foreheads of Moab,
>> the skulls of all the people of Sheth. (Num 24:17)

Joshua symbolically crushes the necks of the five defeated kings of Canaan (Josh 10:24–25). It is Saul's failure to complete this task that led to his loss of the kingship, narrated in 1 Samuel 15. Saul is not being punished for failing to kill every last Amalekite but for failing to destroy the "head" of the monster—the king. In preserving the king of Amalek, he had failed in his primary kingly responsibility.[24]

By contrast, when David faces Goliath, there are many allusions to the divine charge which amount to a positive evaluation of David. We should note that, like a serpent, Goliath is clad in scales (1 Sam 17:5). The text's description as being monstrously large (vv. 4–7) and, somewhat deformed,[25] represents him as a monster. Further, his blustering words to the gathered armies of Israel (v. 10, cf. vv. 26, 45) that challenge the reliability of Yahweh echo the serpent's slur upon God's truthfulness: "Did God really say . . . ?" (Gen 3:1). As is well-known to most Sunday school children, David kills this creature by smashing a stone into his forehead (v. 49), and then cutting off his head (v. 51), to drive the point home to both Goliath and future readers alike. As William Dempster writes:

> The seed of the woman has arrived, and in David's first action as king he is a warrior, an anointed one who conquers and beheads a monstrous giant, whose speech echoes the serpent's voice.[26]

---

24. William J. Webb and Gordon K. Oeste, *Bloody, Brutal and Barbaric? Wrestling with Troubling War Texts* (Downers Grove, IL: InterVarsity Press, 2019), 217.

25. See an alternative rendering of this story in 2 Sam 21:20.

26. Stephen G. Dempster, *Dominion and Dynasty: A Biblical Theology of the Hebrew Bible*, NSBT 15 (Downers Grove, IL: InterVarsity Press, 2003), 140.

In a later chapter we will consider how this theme is picked up by the writer of Revelation, but for now we note that Genesis 3 contains a sort of addendum to the divine charge of Genesis 1:28: the task of the true human will be to destroy the enemy of God. How Jesus fulfills this task, and what this means for his followers today, will be subjects to consider in later chapters.

YOUR DESIRE SHALL BE . . .

We should also note the role of shame in these very early texts, and how it quickly turns to violence. While the man and the woman were once naked and without shame (Gen 2:25), shame quickly follows the fall. First Adam and Eve cover their nakedness with fig leaves because of their shame before the divine gaze (3:7–10). But the divine gaze is also desirable; the fact that God turns to look with favor upon Abel's offering, not Cain's, shames him (4:5). As Judith Rossall writes, "Just as God turned her [sic] face toward Abel's sacrifice, now Cain turns his face away. This, I suggest, is his instinctive fig-leaf. . . . He no longer looks his brother in the eye."[27]

Cain's homicidal attempt to preserve his honor is rapidly adopted and accentuated within four generations. It is his great, great grandson Lamech who boasts of returning seventy-sevenfold vengeance upon one who has injured him (4:23–24). These associations of violence and shame are similar to the links picked up by the psychologist James Gilligan, which we discussed in chapter one. It might seem that Genesis 1–11 is a game of two halves: the peaceful half and the violent half. While Genesis 3 represents an enormous disruption between the prelapsarian and postlapsarian[28] states of the world, it is possible to overstate the gulf. The first reason for this is because God graciously does not wash his hands of the world when its first rulers fail at their appointed task, nor when the earth is filled with violence to such an extent that it threatens to destroy itself. He is continually active in these chapters, working for good: warning Cain, and then protecting him from the effects of his own murderous nature; saving the nucleus of a new world out of the turmoil of the flood; instituting life-promoting regulations; nudging humanity into fulfilling his command to spread out and fill the earth with image bearers. Genesis 3–11 is very clear on this matter: God does not leave the world to its own self-destructive devices.

But there is a second way that the two halves of the myth are linked, and this can be traced through the following sequence of excerpts:

Be fruitful and increase in number; fill the earth and subdue it. (Gen 1:28)

27. Judith Rossall, *Forbidden Fruit and Fig Leaves: Reading the Bible with the Shamed* (London: SCM, 2020), 13.

28. These terms relate to the fall: *prelapsarian* means before the fall, and *postlapsarian*, after it.

When the woman saw that the fruit of the tree was good for food and pleasing to the eye, and also desirable [*ta'vah*] for gaining wisdom, she took some and ate it. (Gen 3:6)

Your desire [*teshuqah*] will be for your husband, and he will rule over you. (Gen 3:16)

The key idea here is desire. Take another look at Genesis 1:28 above, part of the creation mandate. There is no sense of stasis here. The vocation given to humanity, even before the fall, is to progress, to develop, to strive. They are to increase in number and populate the earth, and they are to subdue it. We discussed the meaning of this earlier, linking it with the divine work of imposing order out of chaos. This is not a passive task. Anyone who has done any gardening, for instance, will be able to imagine that even before the advent of thorns and thistles (3:18) it is still a vigorous, physical activity. There is earth to be turned, there are holes to be dug. Humans are to strive upward, as it were; they are to desire something better than the present.

But at the taking of the fruit, desire becomes distorted. The woman's desire for illegitimate, godlike wisdom—or indeed for God's very *being* (3:6)—leads her to take the fruit. As a consequence, both she and her husband will seek to dominate the other (3:16)—desire has twisted away from its proper object. In Genesis 4 we see Cain and Abel both desiring divine approval for their sacrifice, as though God's blessing were a zero-sum gain. We discussed the ideas of René Girard in chapter 1; here in these earliest moments of the human story we watch mimetic desire and violence begin.[29]

What this suggests is that the urge that leads us to violence may yet be, at root, something God-given. While distorted desire has led to murder, sexual violence, and wars, there is still within humanity an urge to impose order that has at its heart something of the divine charge about it. Before the fall, humans use this urge for the godly governance of creation, but afterward they abuse that same urge to pursue their own, corrupted desires. This has led one writer to describe this cooperation with the divine maker in ruling the cosmos as "proto-violence," because it is that same urge to tame and improve and strive that will shortly become corrupted into the desire to conquer and dominate and control.[30] Maybe it is no mere coincidence that early Israelite swords were curved like sickles, but with the sharp blade on the outer curve.[31] Swords and ploughshares are perhaps not so far apart as we might imagine:

29. This was well understood by James, brother of Jesus: "Each person is tempted when they are dragged away by their own evil desire and enticed. Then, after desire has conceived, it gives birth to sin; and sin, when it is full-grown, gives birth to death" (Jas 1:14–15); "What causes fights and quarrels among you? Don't they come from your desires that battle within you? You desire but do not have, so you kill. You covet but you cannot get what you want, so you quarrel and fight" (Jas 4:1–2).

30. Stephen Finamore, "Violence and Covetousness: 'Nor Anything Else That Belongs to Thy Neighbour,'" in *Expecting Justice but Seeing Bloodshed: Some Baptist Contributions to Following Jesus in a Violent World*, ed. Anthony Clarke (Oxford: Regents Part College, 2004), 15.

31. Boyd Seevers, *Warfare in the Old Testament: The Organization, Weapons, and Tactics of Ancient Near Eastern Armies* (Grand Rapids: Kregel, 2013), 58.

> They will beat their swords into plowshares
>> and their spears into pruning hooks. (Isa 2:4)

> Beat your plowshares into swords
>> and your pruning hooks into spears. (Joel 3:10)

If only our distorted desires didn't keep corrupting us!

CONCLUSION

The good world that God has made is quickly ruined through the disordered desire of humanity. The result is a disruption of all of the creational blessings. Dominion is now a power struggle that encompasses the entire created order and afflicts the relationship between the sexes; the filling of the earth is fraught with pain; the beautiful innocence of humans occupying their identity as image bearers gives way to humans who cower away from the divine gaze or strive to attain it. One of the first and most fundamental ruins brought upon the world by this catastrophe is the invention and multiplication of violence.

But amid this ruin God is not inactive. Rather, by warning and direct action, he steps in to contain evil and to punish evildoers. Yet even his judgment is tempered by mercy, demonstrated toward Cain, and to the whole of humanity in the provision of the ark.

Most particularly, God adds a new dimension to the human vocation given in Genesis 1. In addition to ruling well and wisely and to bearing the image of God, humanity is charged to crush the head of the serpent. The true human will do this. As Genesis closes, the true human is still awaited.

RELEVANT QUESTIONS

1. In the early chapters of Genesis, we see God continually stepping in to nudge humanity toward a more peaceful, ordered existence. What traces of this divine activity do you detect later in Scripture? And what do you see in the world today?
2. What do God's responses to the spilled blood of Abel and to the violent ruin of his world reveal of his character?
3. Where do you see the problems of shame and disordered desire driving violence today?

CHAPTER 5

VIOLENCE IN WARTIME

Deliver me from the workers of iniquity,
and save me from bloody men.
Psalm 59:2 KJV

In chapter 1 we considered Hannah Arendt's term "the banality of evil." It will be recalled that she used the term following the trial of Adolf Eichmann in Jerusalem in 1961. By its use she was referring to the routineness—the ordinariness—of astonishing evil. It is present in a thousand ways within society, and many of the actors in these egregious instances are themselves just small cogs within a machine. In this chapter and the one that follows, we will consider the "banality of violence"—the way the biblical narrative both assumes and represents the presence of violence at every level in society, and in every conceivable form.

The Bible is set in violent worlds.[1] The people of God are surrounded by those who commit violence. Sometimes they are subject to that violence. Sometimes they express violence themselves. The Bible unflinchingly demonstrates this.

Violence can take a wide variety of forms: international or intertribal military action, mob violence, judicial violence, physical violence between individuals, sexual violence, structural violence, and verbal violence. All of these can be found within the pages of Scripture. It will not be possible here to offer an exhaustive account of every instance of every type of violence in these chapters; rather, my aim is to provide a representative survey.

In this chapter we will begin our tour of biblical violence by considering the conduct of military action in the Old Testament: the violence of wartime.

---

1. I use the plural because there is a huge difference between the culture at the time of the patriarchs and life under the tyranny of the Babylonian Empire, or the context of the Roman Empire.

A SURVEY OF MILITARY VIOLENCE
IN THE OLD TESTAMENT

At the top of this chapter, I quoted Psalm 59:2: "Deliver me from the workers of iniquity, and save me from bloody men." These words, found in the King James Version, have been chillingly set to music in Karl Jenkins's choral work "The Armed Man," subtitled "A Mass for Peace." In just a few seconds, they convey something visceral about the consequences of warfare in a way far more powerful than written words on a page can manage. I commend it to the reader.

At the beginning of the David-Bathsheba account in 2 Samuel 11, there is a telling phrase, often overlooked as readers rush through to the well-known part of the story. "In the spring, at the time when kings go off to war . . ." (v. 1).

To some extent, there is a pragmatism about this statement. Spring refers to the time when the first harvest is over, and there is a long dry spell before the autumn harvest. In the absence of a large standing army, spring was the season when men could most easily be spared from agricultural work.[2] Yet the phrase also sounds a note of grim inevitability: springtime = wartime. We see a similar idea in 1 Kings 20:22, "Strengthen your position and see what must be done, because next spring the king of Aram will attack you again."

The reference to "kings going to war" is immediately followed by the statement that David did not go but rather stayed at home. Coupled with his indolence in the next verse—lounging about in bed in the daytime and wandering on the palace roof with no better thing to do than ogle the local women—this amounts to a critique of his character. The role of a king was to lead the people into battle (e.g., 1 Sam 8:20).

Such normalization of military action is seen in many places in the unfolding story. There are local skirmishes in Genesis between the patriarchs and their neighbors (e.g., Gen 14). Newly escaped from Egypt, Israel is attacked by a number of armies, most notably the fearsome Sihon and Og (Num 21:21–35; Deut 3:1–11), and the Amalekites, who attack the people at the trailing, weak rear (Exod 17:8–16; Deut 25:17–18).

Eventually the people enter the land of Canaan through a series of conquests (see esp. Joshua 6–11), beginning with Jericho. At this point it is starting to become

---

2. Seevers, *Warfare in the Old Testament*, 68.

apparent that Israel does not possess a lucky charm that guarantees them victory in every military conflict. In particular, disobedience to God is likely to result in defeat (Josh 7:15; cf. Num 14:39–45).

This pattern continues in the book of Judges, where the partially dispossessed nations attempt to reclaim their territory. The book contains several cycles, not arranged chronologically,[3] that follow this pattern: disobedience—defeat—raising up of a judge—obedience—victory. This is summarized in Judges 2:

> The Israelites did evil in the eyes of the LORD and served the Baals. . . . In his anger against Israel the LORD gave them into the hands of raiders who plundered them. . . . Whenever Israel went out to fight, the hand of the LORD was against them to defeat them, just as he had sworn to them. They were in great distress.
>
> Then the LORD raised up judges, who saved them out of the hands of these raiders. . . . Whenever the LORD raised up a judge for them, he was with the judge and saved them out of the hands of their enemies as long as the judge lived; for the LORD relented because of their groaning under those who oppressed and afflicted them. (Judg 2:11–18)

The project of the conquest and defense of the land was a profoundly theological one. God had promised the land to Abraham (e.g., Gen 12:7), and he was the divine commander who determined when the people were to go to battle and when they were to remain at home (e.g., 1 Sam 30:7–8). The soldiers were to be consecrated before battle (Deut 23:9–10). Often the ark would precede the people into battle (e.g., Josh 6:1–15). Victory was granted or withheld by the Lord (1 Kgs 20:13); in fact, sometimes the Lord intervened directly (Josh 10:9–14). The conclusion of many battles was the dedication of the spoils to the Lord (e.g., Josh 6:17). (We will discuss this element in much more detail in chapter 8.)

In 1 Samuel 4 we encounter a flagrant attempt by Eli's sons, Hophni and Phinehas, to manipulate God into granting them victory. The people had suffered a military defeat by the Philistines for an undisclosed reason (although the clue may be that the battle had not been sanctioned by God), suffering four-thousand battle casualties. In response, Hophni and Phinehas led the people back against the Philistines, this time preceded by the ark of the covenant. The outcome was disastrous: thirty-thousand men were killed, including Hophni and Phinehas. But most catastrophic of all, the ark itself was captured by the enemy. The God of Israel would not be treated as a talisman.

---

3. One of the strongest pieces of evidence that Judges is not arranged chronologically is the appearance of Aaron's grandson Phinehas at the end of the book (Judg 20:28).

The time of the kings was marked by frequent military engagement, as we saw earlier. It is now no longer an infallible pattern that obedience resulted in victory, and disobedience in defeat. The reforming king Josiah, for example, dies in battle against the Egyptians (2 Kgs 23:29; 2 Chr 35:20–27). Nevertheless, in the large storyline the final defeat of Israel by Assyria and Judah by Babylon are firmly attributed to the nation's covenantal unfaithfulness (2 Kgs 17; 21:10–16).

Military action is not confined to internation conflict. The Old Testament speaks of at least three full-blown civil wars. One followed the appalling gang rape, murder, and dismemberment of the Levite's wife, described in Judges 19–21. The crime was conducted by Benjamites, and the outrage provoked the rest of Israel to muster against Benjamin, with catastrophic consequences. The second was centered around the attempt by David's son Absalom to displace him from his throne (2 Sam 15–18). The third took place on the death of Solomon, when his son Rehoboam rejected the people's plea for leniency (1 Kgs 12:1–24). The factional group was led by a former military general named Jeroboam, and the conflict resulted in the permanent division of the nation, with the northern half, Israel, taking Jeroboam as its first king. Rehoboam remained king of the southern nation, Judah, which retained the Davidic kingship thereafter.

> Relations between Israel and Judah were alternately hostile and amicable. For example, in 1 Kings 21, the kings of the two nations form a military alliance against Syria (Aram in some Bibles). In contrast, as we read in Isaiah 7 (cf. 2 Kgs 16:5), king Ahaz of Judah was warned by God not to be alarmed by the saber-rattling of the king of Israel, who had made an alliance with Syria against him.

Weaponry

Early in the story, Israel was poorly armed compared to its neighbors. When they first came out of Egypt, they probably would not have been well-equipped. In the early days of the conquest, they are clearly portrayed as being the inferior in military strength. The Philistines, for example, had iron-smelting technology, which Israel lacked (1 Sam 13:19–22). Horses and chariots were the crack military equipment of the day, and when we read of them (e.g., Exod 14:9), a shiver of fear should run down our spines, particularly in the earlier parts of the story when Israel did not possess such equipment.

That the Old Testament is by no means unambiguously in favor of militarism is something we will explore in chapter 8. At this point, however, it might be helpful to identify how the conduct of war, as viewed in the Bible, is quite different from the conduct of other ancient Near Eastern cultures.

CONDUCT OF WAR BY ISRAEL AND ITS NEIGHBORS

So how did Israel and its ancient Near Eastern neighbors conduct war? It is slightly risky to generalize, because we are talking about a range of societies with a wide geographic and chronological spread, but essentially war in the ancient Near East was brutal and violent. However, the weight of evidence suggests that Israel was, by statute and in practice, more restrained that its neighbors. Very helpful work has been done on this topic by William Webb and Gordon Oeste. They argue that the Old Testament shows God continually nudging his people forward in a series of what they term "redemptive movements." The ethics within a text should be compared with what they would have been without the divine limitation. When such a technique is applied, it can be seen that God is constantly moving his people onward.

> OT war texts should be understood within an incremental, redemptive-movement ethic, an understanding that acknowledges elements of the ugly and the beautiful. The ethical problems in the war texts are real, not just apparent. While saddened by the degree to which God must bend down to act in coagency endeavors within our fallen world, we recognize also a wonderful, positive side that ought to be celebrated—the redemptive movement happening in the biblical war texts when understood within the ANE context and/or canonical setting. That which is incrementally redemptive awakens our hope of complete redemption.[4]

We will look briefly at a range of examples in military conduct.

Terror as a Weapon

The Assyrians conducted what might be called psychological warfare or an "ideology of terror" in order to assert their dominance in a region.[5] They were deliberately brutal in their treatment of captives, as we shall see below. The Bible represents the psychological element of Assyrian warfare when King Sennacherib's emissary comes to besiege Jerusalem (2 Kgs 18:17–37). The Rabshakeh, as he was termed, sought to undermine morale in the city by making public threats and an assertion of superior military strength. Mindful of the effect of his words, the Judean officers ask him to speak in Aramaic, which was not widely spoken in Judah at the time. In response, the Rabshakeh redoubles his threats in the vernacular Hebrew.

> Was it only to your master and you that my master sent me to say these things, and not to the people sitting on the wall—who, like you, will have to eat their

own excrement and drink their own urine?" Then the commander stood and called out in Hebrew, "Hear the word of the great king, the king of Assyria! This is what the king says: Do not let Hezekiah deceive you. He cannot deliver you from my hand. Do not let Hezekiah persuade you to trust in the LORD. (2 Kgs 18:27–30)

The people of Israel would have had good reason to be scared. The Assyrians were notorious for the brutality of their treatment of their captives.

Treatment of Captives

An Assyrian frieze of the aftermath of the conquest of Lachish can be found in the British Museum in London. It represents some of the atrocities they perpetrated against their captives, here described by Boyd Seevers:

> They impaled some captives on poles, killed or dismembered others, apparently flayed still others, and deported the surviving inhabitants before looting and burning the city. . . . They also blinded; decapitated; removed noses, ears, and extremities; and created piles of bodies or body parts in front of targeted cities.[6]

The binding of captives was often cruel, too. With reference to Egyptian tomb art, Mark Janzen describes how captives are portrayed. Of one, for example:

> His arms are pinned behind his back in a manner that is disturbing to behold and physically impossible to duplicate without injury. His shoulders are forced back far enough to allow his elbows to meet at his spine. His arms are then bent back, making an X-shape, with his left and right hands aligning vertically with their respective shoulders. He is bound precisely at the elbow joints, which are bent back in severe fashion. Such a binding would have caused severe damage to the joints and muscles of the shoulders and chests (deltoids and pectorals, respectively), including dislocation of the shoulder, while cruelly injuring his elbows, perhaps shattering them.[7]

In the early chapters of Amos, the prophet gives a prolonged invective against the pagan nations, which is largely oriented toward war crimes they have committed. These include the use of iron sledges to kill captives (1:3), the enslavement and sale of people (1:6, 9), attacks against women (1:11, 13), and the desecration of corpses (2:1).[8]

The Old Testament histories record a number of instances of such mutilation committed *against* Israelites in order to shame them (Judg 16:21; 1 Sam 10:27–11:11;

---

6. Seevers, *Warfare in the Old Testament*, 239.
7. Mark D. Janzen, *The Iconography of Humiliation: The Depiction and Treatment of Bound Foreigners in New Kingdom Egypt* (Memphis: The University of Memphis, 2013), 61.

8. Non-burial, or the disrespectful treatment of a corpse, was appalling in the ancient mind.

2 Sam 10; 2 Kgs 25:1–7).[9] However, there is little to suggest that such conduct was standard practice in Israel. An exception is found in Judges 1 where the men cut off the great toes and thumbs of the conquered king Adoni-Bezek. Surprisingly, he seems to accept his fate phlegmatically, as fitting recompense for the way that he himself had had seventy thumbless and toeless kings scrabbling about beneath his table for scraps (1:7).

With regard to a number of the other practices we have considered above, William Webb and Gordon Oeste consider Israel to be significantly more humane than their pagan neighbors.[10] The practice of stripping captives naked to shame them was not an approved practice for Israelite warriors. Nor is there evidence that body-binding torture was practiced in Israel. The practice of selling conquered communities into slavery, as we have seen, invited severe opprobrium. It was not Israelite practices to dig up the graves of their enemies and scatter their bones. Ripping open pregnant women was viewed as deplorable (e.g., 2 Kgs 15:16). The impaling and displaying of captives was not conducted routinely, and it only appears to have been practiced against dead captives and for a few hours (see, e.g., Josh 10:26).

Ecological Effects

The ecological effects of war are also clear in the ancient Near Eastern literature. Here is a fairly representative example from an Assyrian inscription:

> The strong walls, together with 87 towns of their neighborhood I destroyed; I leveled to the ground. I set on fire the houses within them; and their roof beams I left in flames. I opened up their well-filled granaries. And food beyond counting I let my army devour. Their orchards I cut down; and their forests I felled. All their tree trunks I gathered; and I set on fire.[11]

By contrast, the book of Deuteronomy prohibits the felling of fruit trees in times of war:

> When you lay siege to a city for a long time, fighting against it to capture it, do not destroy its trees by putting an ax to them, because you can eat their fruit. Do not cut them down. Are the trees people, that you should besiege them? However, you may cut down trees that you know are not fruit trees and use them to build siege works until the city at war with you falls. (Deut 20:19–20)

Law does not necessarily control conduct, of course. The book of Judges records the actions of the would-be king Abimelech, who salted a city to render it uncultivable (Judg 9:45).

9. Tracy M. Lemos, "Shame and Mutilation of Enemies in the Hebrew Bible," *JBL* 125.2 (2006): 225–41.

10. Webb and Oeste, *Bloody, Brutal and Barbaric?*, 263–87.

11. Excerpt from "Sargon's Letter to the God," translated by and quoted in Younger, *Ancient Conquest Accounts*, 117–18.

War Rape

War rape was another horrific consequence of war that was considered normal in the ancient Near East. We see a hint of this in the song of Deborah, where she is envisioning what the mother of the slain Canaanite commander Sisera will be imagining. (Note that she is not describing Israelite practice but an Israelite perspective on Canaanite conduct.)

> Through the window peered Sisera's mother;
>> behind the lattice she cried out,
> "Why is his chariot so long in coming?
>> Why is the clatter of his chariots delayed?" . . .
> "Are they not finding and dividing the spoils:
>> a womb or two for each man." (Judg 5:28–30)[12]

War rape was the archetypal demonstration of victory. As William Webb and Gordon Oeste put it:

> Ancient male warriors celebrated victory with the ultimate "we beat them" ritual that expressed their success in battle and the complete possession and humiliation of their enemies—by phallic penetration, thrusting, and ejaculation within the most protected "territory" of the enemy. . . . Rape enacted defeat at a far deeper psychological level than mere killing on the battlefield; it took from the opponents the most prized persons and property they had failed to protect. Sexual violation of the enemy's beloved daughters and wives offered a ritualized climax to the killing frenzy on the battlefield.[13]

Israel's attitude to war rape is a little more ambiguous. Certainly, there was provision for a man to marry a female captive (Deut 21:10–14), with no suggestion that her consent should be sought. However, William Webb and Gordon Oeste make a convincing argument that the conduct of battle by the Israelites in this regard also would have been distinctive from that of the nations around them.[14] First, there are a number of pieces of evidence to suggest that battlefield rape was unacceptable. Because war was viewed as a holy action, conducted with the sanction of the deity, worship practices (which, in Israel, absolutely prohibited cultic prostitution) appear to have influenced battlefield conduct. In 1 Samuel 21:2–5, David protests to Ahimelech that his soldiers have not been sexually active for days. Moreover, war rape is not represented in Israel's literature or artwork, unlike, for example, the art and literature of Mesopotamia, Greece, and Rome, in all of which it is prominent and emphatic.

12. Translation slightly modified to represent the coarseness of the underlying Hebrew. The NIV's "a woman or two" is more precisely rendered "a womb or two."

13. Webb and Oeste, *Bloody, Brutal and Barbaric?*, 101.
14. Webb and Oeste, *Bloody, Brutal and Barbaric?*, 99–127.

In contrast, Deuteronomy 21:10–14 sets out in some detail how a captured woman, taken in battle and brought into the home of an Israelite soldier, was to be treated. First, there was a month-long waiting period to permit her to grieve for her parents. Within the ancient world this would have been regarded as quite a long period of mourning. Second, there was a set of assimilation rituals involving the removal of the woman's hair, the trimming of her nails, and the changing of her clothes. These were mourning customs, and this provision conveys the idea that the woman's grief was not to be overlooked. Third, no sexual activity was to take place until the woman had been bound to the man by a marriage covenant, as suggested by the words "then you may go to her and be her husband and she shall be your wife" (v. 13). Fourth, the woman was not to be sold as a slave. If the man chose to divorce her, she was free to go where she pleased. Finally, concern is expressed within the text for the woman's honor: "You must not sell her or treat her as a slave, since you have dishonored her" (v. 14). Webb and Oeste conclude, "That the biblical authors would care at all about the honor of a divorced female war captive is nothing short of amazing."[15]

Naturally we feel unsettled when we read of the forced marriage of female captives, but Webb and Oeste's argument is that we *should* feel such discomfort. In its day it represents a significant move along what they term the "redemptive trajectory," but thankfully we have moved further in the same direction toward God's ultimate goal.

The Ban

In many ancient societies, war was concluded by a ritualized destruction of the conquered territory and its peoples. This is often referred to as "the ban"; the ancient term for it, with slight variations across the ancient Near Eastern languages, was *ḥerem*. It involved great destruction—the firing of cities and the putting of at least some of their inhabitants to the sword—and was viewed as a quasi-sacrificial activity where the conquered people and spoils were given over to the deity. For example, on a stone inscription known as the Mesha Stela, the king of Moab describes how he performed the ban (here translated "I devoted them") to his god Kemosh:

> Kemosh said to me, "Go, seize Nebo from Israel," So I went at night and I attacked it from the break of dawn until noon when I seized it and I slew everybody—seven thousand men, boys, ladies, girls, and maidens—for to the warrior Kemosh I devoted them.[16]

---

15. Webb and Oeste, *Bloody, Brutal and Barbaric?*, 125.

16. Translation in Philip Stern, *The Biblical Herem: A Window on Israel's Religious Experience* (Atlanta: Scholars Press, 1991), 55–56.

In company with the other ancient Near Eastern nations, Israel also sometimes conducted the ban against its enemies. For Israel, the ban was to be performed, by divine command, upon seven people groups who were inhabiting Canaan: the Hittites, Girgashites, Amorites, Canaanites, Perizzites, Hivites, and Jebusites (Deut 7:1–6). It was not to be used indiscriminately; the Philistines, for example, were not subject to the ban.

This will be discussed much more extensively in later chapters, where we will consider the theological rationale for Israel's actions. For now, we note that there is archaeological evidence for the burning of Hazor, described in Joshua 11:10–13.[17] However, it is likely that by the time the cities were conquered (and by "cities," we mean something more like a medieval town), they would have been populated largely by soldiers. Common sense would suggest that women and children would have been sent away, and there is evidence from 1 Samuel 15:4–6 that it was customary for noncombatants to retreat before an advancing army. The numbers of dead may not be as great as we imagine.

WAR IN THE NEW TESTAMENT

Where warfare is normal and even normative in the Old Testament, it is not so in the New. The way that the people of God are to organize themselves is wholly different in the two testaments. In the Old Testament, they form a theopolitical entity, a nation with (at least in theory) autonomous existence with a set of laws to govern them, which is administered by a king who is guided by the priests and prophets. In the New Testament there is never any attempt by the early church to organize themselves in such a way. Here, the rule of God is expressed in terms of citizenship of his kingdom while continuing to operate as subjects of Rome. This makes a huge difference to the ways that violence might be experienced or wielded by the two expressions of the covenant people.

The Old Testament expresses a much wider range of violence than the New. This is not because the cultures within which ancient Israel found itself were inherently more violent than the Greco-Roman world. Far from it. But the concerns of the Old Testament are broader. It spends more time in what we might call "social" stories, and its concerns embrace the whole range of the human experience. By contrast, the New Testament narratives are limited to three years in the life of Jesus and a few years in the time of the early church. Moreover, the epistles are focused on the early church and a narrow range of pastoral issues they were facing. Violence is ever present behind the New Testament text. For instance, consider the ways that the

17. Amnon Ben-Tor, "Who Destroyed Canaanite Hazor?," *Biblical Archaeology Review* 39.4 (2013): 26–36, 58.

Jewish leaders are repeatedly plotting Jesus's death, or Paul's frequent references to the persecution of the early church. But explicit violence only bubbles to the surface infrequently—at the martyrdoms of John the Baptist and Stephen, for example, and—supremely—at the cross. We will consider this in later chapters.

CONCLUSION

In this chapter we have considered the ubiquity and ubiquitous brutality of warfare in Israel and across the ancient world. We had read frankly stomach-churning accounts of the weaponization of terror, the brutal treatment of captives, especially captive women, damage to agriculture, and the wholesale destruction of communities. Nevertheless, there are some glimmers of difference between Israel and her neighbors. Ancient Israel appears to have conducted herself with more restraint, both on the battlefield and afterward, than her pagan neighbors did. This is evidenced both in laws and historical records (biblical and extrabiblical).

With regard to our tour of violence in the Bible, however, we have barely scratched the surface. In the following chapter we will consider violence that manifests within communities and between individuals in peacetime.

RELEVANT QUESTIONS

1. Does it surprise you that an Old Testament prophet decries war crimes? What might we learn from Amos 1 and 2?
2. Does knowing that ancient Israel conducted itself in warfare more humanely than the surrounding nations help to resolve some of the discomfort caused by the biblical description of Israel's military actions?
3. To what extent is your view of militarization conditioned by the prevailing attitudes in our society, and by the international scene?

CHAPTER 6

VIOLENCE IN PEACETIME

I am the best friend you ever had in all your life. But I will tell you; I cannot help punishing people when they do wrong. I like it no more than they do; I am often very, very sorry for them, poor things: but I cannot help it. If I tried not to do it, I should do it all the same.

—Mrs. Bedonebyasyoudid, in Charles Kingsley's *The Water Babies*

In the previous chapter, we began to look at the ways in which violence permeates every level of society and every culture that is described in the Bible. There, we focused on Old Testament military conflict and its aftermath. But violence goes far beyond this. In this chapter we will look at some of the many examples of interpersonal and community violence that are represented in the Old Testament.

INTERPERSONAL VIOLENCE
Power Grabs

In the previous chapter we considered some of the great civil wars of Israel, one of which permanently divided the nation. These are by no means the only intertribal or community conflicts, however. There are many instances of more localized power grabs. For example, in Judges 9 there is a bloody battle for supremacy between the sons of Gideon, which spills over into community violence and only ends when the chief antagonist is killed by a woman dropping an upper millstone on his head from the walls of a city he is attacking.

The northern nation Israel is particularly troubled, experiencing coup after coup. First Kings 15:25–16:16 gives a summary of their turbulent history, full of coups, murders, and palace intrigues. Life in Israel in those days must have been terrifying, as it always is when violent and ambitious people are able to act in an unrestrained manner.

Getting Even

Hunger for power is not the only reason for violence in the biblical narrative, of course. Violence is often exercised in revenge for an injury, large or small. Samson is a good example. While he invokes the law of "an eye for an eye" ("I merely did to [the Philistines] what they did to me"; Judg 15:11), his actions by no means demonstrate the relevant qualities of reciprocity, equivalence, and enactment under the authority of the elders. Rather, he escalates the violence on every occasion and usually projects it beyond the initial conflict, too, such as the time he responds to the Philistines who cheat him by killing thirty *other* Philistines (Judg 14).[1]

Another example is Joab, David's henchman, who conducted all sorts of dirty deeds in the dark to give the king plausible deniability. He also became entangled in a deadly vendetta with Abner, who slew his brother Asahel (2 Sam 2:23), and whom he knifed in retribution (2 Sam 3:27). To be fair, Joab was not wholly without legal warrant for his actions. In the case of a person killed intentionally, the responsibility for punishing their crime belonged to their nearest relative, the so-called "avenger of blood" (Num 35). In the days before a police force and prisons, this provided a mechanism whereby murder was punished by death. In order to protect those who had been the accidental cause of someone's death, six cities of refuge were provided (Exod 23:13–14; Num 35:6–34; Deut 4:41–43; 19:1–13; see also Josh 20:1–9). The killer could flee to one of these cities and put his case before the congregation. If he were judged to have been innocent of intent to kill, he could remain safe by staying within the city for the lifetime of the high priest.

Violence to Make a Point

Violence often has a public purpose: to threaten, subdue, or in some other way to assert power. There are a number of places where we see this in the Old Testament. A good example is during the rebellion of Absalom. When David was (temporarily, as it turns out) displaced from Jerusalem by his rebellious son, he left ten secondary wives or concubines to take care of the palace (2 Sam 15:16). On Absalom's occupation of the palace a little later, he publicly raped them as a way of consolidating his power (2 Sam 16:21–22).

Another example of public violence is seen when the Gibeonites sought vengeance for Saul's attempt to annihilate them when he was king. (The Gibeonites were supposed to have protected status within the nation of Israel; Josh 9:15.) When David, now king, inquired what would satisfy them for the wrong done, they requested the execution of seven of Saul's descendants (2 Sam 21:6). David acceded to their request, resulting in one of the most pathetic scenes in Scripture:

> The king took Armoni and Mephibosheth, the two sons of Aiah's daughter Rizpah, whom she had borne to Saul, together with the five sons of Saul's daughter Merab. . . . He handed them over to the Gibeonites, who killed them and exposed their bodies on a hill before the LORD. . . .

---

1. Helen Paynter, "'Revenge for My Two Eyes': Talion and Mimesis in the Samson Narrative," *Biblical Interpretation* 26.2 (2018): 133–57.

Rizpah daughter of Aiah took sackcloth and spread it out for herself on a rock. From the beginning of the harvest till the rain poured down from the heavens on the bodies, she did not let the birds touch them by day or the wild animals by night. (2 Sam 21:8–10)

Both of these examples of violence had to be public in order to achieve their intended effect. For Absalom, the purpose was to shore up his power base against his father. For the Gibeonites it was to obtain public vindication and publicly shame the house of Saul, not just by public execution but also by the scandalous non-burial of their bodies.

The exposure of the bodies of Saul's family is also one of the great moments of female resistance in the Hebrew Bible. As Christine Jeske has shown, Rizpah's actions inverts the effect of the scandal.

> She has one ability: the power to make people look. She does this by enacting a rite of public mourning that turns the meaning of these deaths from disgrace to honor. She leaves the bodies of the murdered on the mountainside in plain sight and places sackcloth on a rock to sleep there beside them. Then she refuses to leave. . . . It's impossible to know her precise motives, but by shooing away scavengers, she ensures that the bodies remain—intact, visible, and undeniable in all their terror—for public mourning.[2]

Violence against the Other

Violence against the stranger is common, even though the law strongly commanded care for the sojourner (e.g., Lev 19:33–34). One of the best-known examples has given us the term *shibboleth* because of the way that the word was used to distinguish between the Gileadites and the Ephraimites, both members of Israel, but rivals:

The Gileadites captured the fords of the Jordan leading to Ephraim, and whenever a survivor of Ephraim said, "Let me cross over," the men of Gilead asked him, "Are you an Ephraimite?" If he replied, "No," they said, "All right, say 'Shibboleth.'" If he said, "Sibboleth," because he could not pronounce the word correctly, they seized him and killed him at the fords of the Jordan. (Judg 12:5–6)

Another egregious example is found in the books of Ezra and Nehemiah, which are set in Jerusalem at the time of the return from exile. Some of the returnees had

---

2. Christine Jeske, "Stop Looking Away: What an Obscure Bible Character Shows Us about George Floyd's Death," Cateclesia Institute, July 1, 2020, https://cateclesia.com/2020/07/01/stop -looking-away-what-an-obscure-bible-character-shows-us-about -george-floyds-death/.

married foreign women, and when Ezra discovered the matter he sent them and their children away (Ezra 9–10). Ezra does this after fasting and praying, but there is no record that his actions were ordered by God. It is interesting to compare this with the much later, but somewhat comparable situation that the apostle Paul addresses, when one person out of a married couple becomes a Christian:

> If any brother has a wife who is not a believer and she is willing to live with him,
> he must not divorce her. And if a woman has a husband who is not a believer
> and he is willing to live with her, she must not divorce him. (1 Cor 7:12–13)

It is clear that Paul has substantially advanced the ethic that Ezra and his contemporaries had adopted so willingly.

Sexual Violence

In Genesis 19 and Judges 19 we read a pair of stories with many similarities, both containing the severe threat of stranger violence. In both stories, some travelers come to a foreign town and are given hospitality by a foreigner in that town. As night falls, the men of the town surround the house and demand that the visiting men be turned out to them for them to gang rape. What happens next in Judges is truly appalling. The visitor takes his wife and puts her out to the men in his stead. She is raped all night, eventually crawling back to the threshold of the house, where she lay with her hands on the lintel. In the morning, her master takes her home and dismembers her body to evoke indignation and action in Israel.

The parallel Genesis story is set in Sodom, and the conclusion is happier. The visitors are angels, and they rescue the patriarch Lot and his family before the town is destroyed with fire and brimstone.

It is important that we do not make the mistakes of many interpreters when reading these stories.[3] Some have overemphasized the "homosexual" aspect of the story, failing to realize that rape is an act of power and humiliation, not of sexual desire. This is a serious misunderstanding.[4] Some have even suggested that the rape of the woman is a better outcome than the threatened "homosexual" rape. But homosexuality is not the focus of this story. As the prophet Ezekiel makes clear, the primary sin for which Sodom is punished is its supreme inhospitality:

> Now this was the sin of your sister Sodom: She and her daughters were arrogant,
> overfed and unconcerned; they did not help the poor and needy. (Ezek 16:49)

Another mistake that interpreters sometimes make when reading the Judges story is to blame the woman for what happened to her (why had she left her husband?),

---

3. A survey of the range of interpretive approaches to this story is offered in Helen Paynter, *Telling Terror in Judges 19: Rape and Reparation for the Levite's Wife* (Abingdon: Routledge, 2020), 8–23.

4. Chris Greenough, *The Bible and Sexual Violence against Men* (Abingdon: Routledge, 2020), 21.

and even to cast her violent death as divine judgment. Such interpretations have led many feminist critics to view the story as profoundly misogynistic.[5]

However, the story should be read as part of Israel's downward spiral of violence, which Judges depicts to show the consequence of a nation where there is no king, and "every man did what was right in his own eyes" (Judg 17:6; 21:25; my translation). When viewed in this way, the narrator is seen to separate himself from the misogyny of the actors in the narrative.[6]

Sexual violence against women is not uncommon in the Old Testament. In addition to the incidents above, we have the rapes of Dinah (Gen 34:1–31) and Tamar (2 Sam 13:1–22). There are, in addition, a number of stories where wives, who are failing to conceive, give their maidservants to their husbands to bear children in their stead (Gen 16:1–4; 30:3–13). By modern standards, this too is rape. We should also notice the terrible story of Esther, who is sex trafficked for the pleasure of the king of Persia (Esth 2). This is no beauty pageant or love story, as it is sometimes described.

Men, too, are subject to sexual violence. In addition to the attempted male rapes of Genesis 19 and Judges 19, there is Potiphar's wife's sexual assault and the subsequent false allegation against Joseph (Gen 39). There are also plausible implications of sexual violence in a number of other narratives, notably Ham against Noah (Gen 9:20–27), Ehud against Eglon (Judg 3:12–30), Jael against Sisera (Judg 4), and Delilah and the Philistines against Samson (Judg 16). In addition, David Tombs has recently written of the nakedness of Jesus and the sexual assault that this implies.[7] We will consider this in chapter 9.

STRUCTURAL VIOLENCE

However, not all violence is conducted with a raised fist or with a weapon. There are systems of violence that operate equally harmfully and that are sustained by the threat of or the execution of physical violence. Here, we will briefly consider three such systems that are expressed in Scripture: the structural violence of the monarchy, slavery, and institutionalized poverty.

Monarchy

When the people approach Samuel for a king, he gives them a scathing list of reasons why they should not desire one.

> He will take your sons and make them serve with his chariots and horses. . . .
> He will take your daughters to be perfumers and cooks and bakers. He will

---

5. See, e.g., Cheryl Exum's essay "Raped by the Pen," in her book *Fragmented Women: Feminist (Sub)versions of Biblical Narratives*, JSOTSup 163 (Sheffield: Sheffield Academic Press, 1993).

6. Paynter, *Telling Terror in Judges 19*, 71–77.

7. David Tombs, "Crucifixion, State Terror, and Sexual Abuse," *Union Seminary Quarterly Review* 53 (1999): 80–109.

take the best of your fields and vineyards and olive groves and give them to his attendants. He will take a tenth of your grain and of your vintage and give it to his officials and attendants. . . . He will take a tenth of your flocks, and you yourselves will become his slaves. (1 Sam 8:11–17)

The kings certainly did act abusively. Consider the similar incidents of the "theft" of Bathsheba by David and the theft of Naboth's vineyard by Ahab, for example (2 Sam 11; 1 Kgs 21). And as Samuel had warned, by the time of the third king, Solomon, there was a harsh and efficient system of taxation and forced labor in order to sustain his building projects and the phenomenal appetites of his court (1 Kgs 4:7–28; 9:15–21). Prosperous as the kingdom was in Solomon's day, it was probably not a very good place to live if you were a peasant or a resident alien.

Of course, Solomon is just one example of such excessive living. We could look to the empires of Egypt, Assyria, or Babylon for at least equally egregious structural violence. Several hundred years later, the early church was established during the time of the Roman Empire, an even more stratified society, with even more extreme abuses of power at the higher levels.

Slavery

This brings us to the question of slavery, which is found in both testaments. We must not imagine that all slavery within the Bible is the same, however, or that it bore much resemblance to the years of the transatlantic slave trade, with which readers are probably familiar.

In the ancient Near East, both chattel slavery and forced labor of tenant farmers appear to have been common, and this is reflected in the early part of the story of Israel.[8] Abraham and his grandsons all had concubines, and Joseph was trafficked into slavery in Egypt by his own brothers, after which the entire family of Abraham became enslaved there. Following the exodus event, which is frequently characterized as redemption from slavery (e.g., Lev 25:55), there were strict laws on the matter.

In contrast to the ways that the surrounding nations treated their slaves, the law of Moses was—for its time—relatively humane. For instance, foreign male slaves were to be circumcised, which effectively meant that they were integrated into the household and permitted to participate in the Passover (Exod 12:44; cf. Gen 17:13). Slaves were to be given rest on the Sabbath (Exod 20:10). Slaves who had fled from their owners were not to be handed over to them (Deut 23:15–16). Slaves who suffered personal injury at the hands of their masters were to be set free (Exod 21:20–27). Women who were taken into slavery were not to be cut loose when their masters were tired of them (Deut 21:10–14).

---

8. For a thorough discussion of Old Testament slavery, see G. H. Haas, "Slave, Slavery," in *Dictionary of the Old Testament:* *Pentateuch*, ed. T. D. Alexander and D. W. Baker (Downers Grove, IL: InterVarsity Press, 2003), 778–83.

In addition, kidnapping someone to sell them into slavery was strictly prohibited by the law (Exod 21:16), although the earlier trafficking of Joseph by his brothers forms a key part of the patriarchal story. As we have seen, the trafficking of conquered peoples appears to have been common in the ancient Near East and is the subject of round condemnation by the prophet Amos. Much later, Esther was one of many women trafficked to the palace of the king of Persia for him to use sexually.

Within the community of Israel itself, "slavery" is probably the wrong term to describe the bonded labor that effectively served as a primitive sort of social security. People who fell into poverty, after they had exhausted other options, including selling their land, could sell themselves as bonded labor to a more prosperous neighbor. They would effectively be taken within the household of that neighbor and provided for while they worked for them. They could be redeemed at any time, either by a member of the family or by themselves, if they acquired enough wealth to do it. In the Sabbath year, which would be a maximum of seven years later, they would be released (Exod 21:2; Deut 15:12), with an abundance of gifts (Deut 15:13–14). Sometimes there was sufficient affection between the bonded servant and their master that the bonded servant would choose not to go free (Deut 15:16–17). In this situation the bonded laborer would serve the master for life.

New Testament slavery was different again.[9] Roman slavery was chattel slavery, mainly of people taken in battle, though some were born into it or committed to slavery as punishment for a serious crime. Some slaves were highly educated and held positions rather like civil servants. Many more were skilled and worked as artisans. A great number were used for hard manual labor, particularly in agricultural work and in mining. For them, conditions were particularly brutal. While many slaves were manumitted (legally freed) by their masters, runaway slaves were treated with great brutality, and crucifixion was generally regarded as the slave's punishment. Slavery was the bottom tier of a highly stratified social structure and an integral part of the Roman Empire. It appears that few Jews in Palestine owned slaves in New Testament times. But overall in the empire, there were probably four or five times as many slaves as citizens, and it would have been inconceivable for people of the day to imagine taking that structure apart. We will discuss the apostle Paul's treatment of the subject of slavery in chapter 11.

Poverty

> For three sins of Israel,
>   even for four, I will not relent.

---

9. For a fuller discussion of New Testament slavery, see J. A. Harrill, "Slavery," in *Dictionary of New Testament Background: A Compendium of Contemporary Biblical Scholarship*, ed. C. A. Evans and S. E. Porter (Downers Grove, IL: InterVarsity Press, 2000): 1124–27; and Ben Witherington III, *Conflict and Community in Corinth: A Socio-Rhetorical Commentary on 1 and 2 Corinthians* (Grand Rapids: Eerdmans, 1995), 181–85.

They sell the innocent for silver,
> and the needy for a pair of sandals.
They trample on the heads of the poor
> as on the dust of the ground
> and deny justice to the oppressed. (Amos 2:6–7)

The Israel of Amos's day was a highly stratified society. At the top were the superrich who lived in excessive luxury, with summer and winter houses decorated with ivory and other luxurious materials. But most were at the other end of the economic scale. These were subsistence farmers, for whom natural hardships such as poor rainfall or soil quality were compounded by human factors: warfare, taxation, and abusive practice by their rich neighbors.[10]

Societal conditions in Amos's Samaria are relatively well understood, due in part to Amos's own critique of them, and also to recent excavations that have uncovered some of the homes of the wealthy. Poverty, however, for all the reasons outlined above, was a constant threat in ancient agrarian cultures such as those of ancient Israel and Judah.

One of the central concerns of the law of Israel is the protection of those who lived in such precarity, especially those who were marginalized even further by dint of their status as widow, orphan, or foreigner. In addition to the system of bonded labor and the seven-year cycle of release described above, the law of Moses provided a complex system to protect the poorest in society. For example, the law of Leviticus says:

> When you reap the harvest of your land, do not reap to the very edges of your field or gather the gleanings of your harvest. Do not go over your vineyard a second time or pick up the grapes that have fallen. Leave them for the poor and the foreigner. I am the LORD your God. (Lev 19:9–10)

Further, the law of Jubilee was intended to protect the poor by ensuring that all ancestral land reverted to its original owners every fifty years (Lev 25:14–17). In theory, Jubilee provided a reset for the whole of society and prevented the rich from continually enriching themselves and widening the gap between them and the poorest. However, it is unclear whether this was ever practiced. Instead, we read these words in Isaiah, condemning what is now known as latifundialization—the process of land acquisition by the wealthy at the expense of the peasantry:[11]

> Woe to you who add house to house
> > and join field to field

---

10. R. M. Daniel Carroll, *The Book of Amos*, NICOT (Grand Rapids: Eerdmans, 2020), 17.

11. Devadasan N. Premnath, "Latifundialization and Isaiah 5.8–10," *JSOT* 13.40 (1988): 49–60.

> till no space is left
>
> and you live alone in the land. (Isa 5:8)

The book of Job is a rich exploration of the question of innocent suffering. But as part of Job's complaint, he describes the situation of the poor in very powerful terms. Chapter 24 (esp. vv. 5, 8–12) describes a number of situations of structural violence: "structural" because, as David Clines points out,

> People do not get up in the middle of the night and move a neighbor's boundary stone, to the consternation of the landholder the next morning. When landmarks are moved, there is at least a tacit approval by the community, and those responsible believe they are within their rights in so doing.[12]

The treatment of the poor described here involved transgression of the boundary law of Deuteronomy 19:14, and coats taken as collateral not being returned at night, as ordered in Deuteronomy 24:12–13. Children were taken as bonded slaves in payment for a debt (cf. 2 Kgs 4:1). And, in what Marx would have referred to as "alienation," agricultural workers were not permitted to enjoy the fruits of what they labor to produce. This, as Gustavo Gutierrez argues, is violence:

> The poverty described is not the result of destiny or inexplicable causes; those responsible for it are named without pity. Job is describing a state of affairs caused by the wickedness of those who exploit and rob the poor. . . . The daily life of the poor is a dying says the Bible. The oppressors of the poor are therefore called murderers.[13]

It is clear that Israel did not succeed in avoiding structural violence, even though various prohibitions were in existence to prevent or attenuate it. This brings us to the final question for our current chapter: In what ways was violence curbed by the use of violent practice?

USING VIOLENCE TO LIMIT VIOLENCE

In chapter 3 we saw how the creation act establishes God as king, with humans as his vice-regents. The kingship that characterizes God is, among other superlative attributes, supremely righteous. In both his activity and his decrees, God is utterly just. The giving of the law is predicated upon his very self. For example, the phrase "I am the LORD" is found many times in Exodus and Leviticus, often in association with his acts of judgment or decrees.

---

12. David J. A. Clines, *Job 21–37*, WBC 18A (Nashville: Thomas Nelson, 2006), 602.

13. Gustavo Gutiérrez, *On Job: God-Talk and the Suffering of the Innocent*, trans. Matthew J. O'Connell (Maryknoll, NY: Orbis, 1987), 33.

I will bring judgment on all the gods of Egypt. I am the LORD. (Exod 12:12)

I am the LORD your God; consecrate yourselves and be holy, because I am holy. (Lev 11:44)

I am the LORD your God. Keep my decrees and laws. (Lev 18:4–5).

As we will see in chapter 10, God's righteousness is demonstrated in his acts of re-creation, where he reimposes right order on a disordered cosmos. But in addition, he calls for justice in all the created order. For example, Psalm 82 shows him rebuking the heavenly beings for their failure to act justly. And he expects justice in his people. During the time of the monarchy, the enactment of justice was most particularly the responsibility of the king, as Psalm 72, probably a coronation prayer, suggests.

> Endow the king with your justice, O God,
>   the royal son with your righteousness. (Ps 72:1)

The Old Testament demonstrates a number of ways by which violence or other forms of evil action were punished or contained. Some of these are what we might call direct divine action, where God takes matters into his own hands.

Direct Divine Action

This would include instances where God's power is encountered in unmediated ways, such as the fire that consumed Nadab and Abihu because they approached God in an impermissible fashion. As God's words explain, this is because they had treated his holy presence lightly (Lev 10:3).

Similar accounts are found in the striking of seventy[14] inhabitants of Beth-Shemesh, who looked into the ark (1 Sam 6:19), or Uzzah, who was struck down for touching it (2 Sam 6:6–7). Our narrator is entirely unembarrassed about these events. If we are, perhaps this is because we have not really begun to appreciate the utter and terrifying holiness of God.

At other times God's direct action occurs as a result of transgression, disobedience, or rebellion. This is enacted both against God's covenant people and also at times against their enemies. Key examples would be the striking of the firstborn of Egypt (Exod 12:29) and the earthquake that consumed the rebellious Korah and his family (Num 16:31–33).

It is not the task of this book to address divine violence in detail. However, it is important to notice these events because of their relevance to the present-day conversation about whether God is wholly nonviolent. The Old Testament witness (and, indeed, a few New Testament texts, such as Acts 5:1–11) is that God retains the prerogative to act in violent judgment toward his creatures.

---

14. Some manuscripts have a rather less plausible 50,700 dead.

However, most punishment or judgment in the Old Testament is enacted through human mediation, mainly through the judicial system. Like every society, ancient Israel needed to find ways to control interpersonal violence. And like every society of any size, it was unable to do this without using violence, or the threat of it.

Divinely Sanctioned Retribution

The Mosaic law[15] contains two principal types of legislation: apodictic law ("thou shalt not"; e.g., "You shall have no other gods before me," Exod 20:3), and casuistic law ("in this case . . ."; e.g., "Anyone who beats their male or female slave with a rod must be punished if the slave dies," Exod 21:20). The law thereby covers a wider range of circumstances and uses violence (principally stoning) as a punishment for many offenses.

The language of punishment and retribution in the Old Testament is complex, full of overlapping terms and ideas. The verb *shaphat* and its related noun *mishpat* generally refer to the making of a judicial decision, often in a formal setting such as a court. The word often translated "avenge" (*naqam*) carries more of a sense of legal recompense than personal vendetta.[16] *Shub*, whose core meaning is "to return," is used in the sense of repaying judgment or turning evil back upon its perpetrator. Similarly, the root *shalam* generally refers to the giving of compensation and connotes either positive reward or negative retribution, with the root idea of completeness, linking the word with its better-known relation *shalom*.

These terms have overlapping meanings, as suggested by the way that they are often used in conjunction with one another (e.g., Deut 32:35; Isa 34:8). Indeed, all four are found in the Lord's words in Deuteronomy 32:41:

> When I sharpen my flashing sword
> > and my hand grasps it in judgment [*mishpat*],
> I will take vengeance [*shub* and *naqam*] on my adversaries
> > and repay [*shalam*] those who hate me.

Another motif is that of "doubling" of a punishment, which is sometimes misunderstood to indicate the application of a double measure of retribution:

> I will repay them double for their wickedness and their sin. (Jer 16:18; see also Isa 40:2; Jer 17:18)

However, a better translation for the word translated "double" above would be "matching" or "equivalent" punishment—*the* double.[17] This clearly relates to the so-called *lex talionis* or law of talion ("an eye for an eye").

---

15. That is, the law given by (or to) Moses.

16. George E. Mendenhall, *The Tenth Generation: The Origins of the Biblical Tradition* (Baltimore: John Hopkins University Press, 1973), 76–77.

17. Meredith G. Kline, "Double Trouble," *JETS* 32.2 (1989): 169–79.

Lex Talionis

This law is given three times in the Old Testament, each one covering slightly different circumstances, and all apparently relating to its more general statement in Genesis 9:6. In Exodus 21:22–25, the law is to be applied to a fighting man who causes accidental harm to a pregnant woman. Leviticus 24:17–22 relates to personal injury of anyone within the community. And Deuteronomy 19:16–21 applies the principle to harm that was intended but not accomplished.

In practice, this law was probably largely interpreted as an imperative for retributive equivalence in interhuman matters.[18] However, this principle of equivalent punishment being visited upon the perpetrator (rather than, as in some other ancient societies, their families) became paradigmatic for the way that the people of Israel viewed divine justice. Thus we read prayers for retribution against individuals or nations and other descriptions of divine justice, patterned on the law of talion, often using some of the vocabulary identified above, for example, Lamentations 3:64 and Obadiah 1:15b, which both use *shub*.

Sometimes the retributive equivalence seems to refer to a comeuppance that results from the person's own actions rather than by divine intervention (e.g., Job 18:7; Esth 7:9–10). Sometimes the writer seems content to refer simultaneously to both divine judgment and the consequence of one's misdeeds rebounding (e.g., Pss 7:12–16; 9:15–16; Jer 50:15).

In summary, the Old Testament uses a matrix of words and ideas to express divine punishment and judgment. The well-known law of talion (equivalent punishment visited upon the original perpetrator) is also frequently caught up within this matrix, and it is often used within the Old Testament as a paradigm for what true justice should be.

But in the end, in ancient Israel as in every society, the limitation of violence must be performed by violence, or at least force. The creation accounts have shown us that this is not the intended paradigm, but at the close of the Old Testament, no alternative has yet been revealed.

CONCLUSION

Consider the words of Isaiah as he describes the kingdom of the Prince of Peace:

> Of the greatness of his government and peace
>   there will be no end.
> He will reign on David's throne

---

18. A. T. Nissel, "Equality or Equivalence: A Very Brief Survey of *Lex Talionis* as a Concept of Justice in the Bible," *International Law: Routledge Critical Concepts*, ed. J. Weiler and A. T. Nissel, vol. 6 (London: Routledge, 2010), 111–45; Jonathan Burnside, "Imagining Biblical Law," *University of Queensland Law Journal* 30 (2011): 225–34.

> and over his kingdom,
> establishing and upholding it
> with justice and righteousness
> from that time on and forever. (Isa 9:7)

The words are probably very familiar. But take a moment to examine the converse. If the kingdom of peace will be established and upheld with righteousness and justice, then in a violent world society will both establish itself with violence and uphold itself with violent systems. This is exactly what we have been describing in this chapter.

We have explored the Old Testament representation of a wide range of violent actions that are conducted within society, including private vendettas, power grabs, and ethnic violence. We have also considered some of the many instances of sexual violence in the Old Testament. But the description of violence by the narrator does not equate to endorsement of that violence. We need to be careful readers who seek to identify the purpose of the perpetrator of violence and distinguish that from the purpose of the narrator in telling us of it.

Next, we considered examples of structural violence, looking particularly at the case studies of monarchy, slavery, and poverty. We saw that Israel's law offered various approaches to ameliorate structural injustice, but they were not eliminated altogether from society due to the disobedience of the people.

Finally, we went on to look at the ways that violence and other forms of evil were punished. In addition to direct divine action, God sought to limit interpersonal violence through the Law of Moses. In particular, we considered the law of talion (an eye for an eye), which proves to be very significant in shaping the thought patterns of Old and New Testament writers, as we shall see.

RELEVANT QUESTIONS

1. The Old Testament does not shy away from describing violence. Why not?
2. Under what circumstances, if any, is it appropriate for Christians to watch violence portrayed on their screens? Is your answer affected by whether the violence is "real" or not?
3. Are there instances of violence in the Bible that you have previously thought the writer endorsed, but now wish to reevaluate? How would you respond if someone said to you that if it is in Scripture it must be "okay"?
4. What systems of structural violence do you see in the world today? Where might you be complicit with them?

CHAPTER 7

VIOLENCE SEEN FROM THE UNDERSIDE

*[The LORD] looked for justice [*mishpat*], but saw bloodshed
[*mispakh*];
for righteousness [*tzedaqah*], but heard cries of distress
[*tse'aqah*].*
Isaiah 5:7

Ancient Near Eastern history writing was generally sponsored by the king and served to bolster his reputation. The Old Testament has its share of such "propaganda" (a term which need not have a negative connotation), such as the bold declaration of Solomon's supreme wisdom and surpassing wealth (1 Kgs 4:20–34). However, it also contains satire and subversion against the kings, the prophets, and others.[1] Indeed, Walter Brueggemann has argued that it is often those passages that appear to be bolstering the king's reputation that contain the seeds of subversion against him.[2] The king may have attempted to sponsor the writing of Israel's history, but he was not wholly successful.

In fact, two of the most striking things about the Old Testament are the way that it represents the voices of the weak, the marginalized, and the victim, as well as the fact that it expresses self-criticism (that is, it reflects critically on its own history) on almost every page. In this chapter we will notice both of these as we turn our attention to the way that the Old Testament represents violence from the underside. We will first do this by listening to the voices it contains—in particular, the voices of lament, of outcry, and of criticism. We will then consider some of the resistance movements that the story shows.

---

1. This is explored in detail in Helen Paynter, *Reduced Laughter: Seriocomic Features and Their Functions in the Book of Kings* (Leiden: Brill, 2016). A much-abbreviated summary of some of the ideas can be found in Helen Paynter, *The Strange World of Elijah and Elisha* (Cambridge: Grove, 2019).

2. Walter Brueggemann, *The Prophetic Imagination*, 40th anniversary ed. (Minneapolis: Fortress, 2018), 21–38.

VOICES OF GRIEF AND PROTEST

Lament

In this section, we will consider, by means of a test case, some of the ways in which the grief of the Babylonian exile is expressed in the Hebrew Bible. Anyone who has watched the news in the last few years will be readily able to recall images of ruined cities. Perhaps the devastation of Aleppo or Mariupol come to mind. And, of course, the infrastructural damage is simply the visible marker in the concrete of the trauma that is borne by a whole people in their bodies and minds—whether the trauma be that of mass rape, the tearing apart of families, the witnessing of violence death, or physical injury from air assault or chemical weapons.[3] The weapons of war may be different, but the lived experience of these unfortunate people is very similar to the traumas that would have been endured in Jerusalem at the time of the Babylonian exile when Nebuchadnezzar's armies slew, looted, sacked, and raped.

Of course, we cannot shy away from the fact that the Hebrew Bible explicitly views this defeat as divine punishment for breach of covenant by the nation of Judah. These consequences had been spelled out in advance (e.g., Deut 28:49–68) and warned about repeatedly by the prophets (e.g., Isa 39:5–7; Jer 20:1–6). But, as we shall see in a moment, God was far from insouciant about these events.

A number of the psalms appear to be referring to the events of the exile in their laments. Psalm 79, for example, speaks graphically of the dead lying unburied in the streets, a horror that captures not only the multiplicity of corpses but also the most egregious wrong of denying them burial (vv. 1–3).

But perhaps nothing captures the raw grief that came in the wake of the Babylonian army as well as the book of Lamentations, commonly—but probably incorrectly—attributed to the prophet Jeremiah. The book is comprised of five poems, the first four of which are alphabetic acrostics, providing, as it were, the A–Z of grief. In this book, the rawest of emotion is processed. The poet speaks through a number of voices in order to accomplish this.[4] First, there is the voice of an onlooker, a journalist in modern terms, who describes the silence of the streets:

> How deserted lies the city,
> > once so full of people! (Lam 1:1a)

Then Jerusalem herself takes up the lament, speaking as a raped woman (cf. v. 10):

> Is it nothing to you, all you who pass by?
> > Look around and see.
> Is any suffering like my suffering . . . ? (Lam 1:12a).

---

3. See, e.g., Christina Lamb, *Our Bodies Their Battlefield: What War Does to Women* (London: Harper Collins, 2020).

4. William F. Lanahan, "The Speaking Voice in the Book of Lamentations," *JBL* 93.1 (1974): 41–49.

In Lamentations 3 we encounter the voice of a broken, vanquished soldier who complains, "I am the man who has seen affliction by the rod of the LORD's wrath" (v. 1), and he proceeds to offer a litany of his woes and injuries (e.g., Lam 3:13, 16).

In Lamentations 5 the rigid structure of the acrostic breaks down, perhaps reflecting the chaos of war. Now a community voice takes up the lament and calls upon God to attend to their affliction:

> Remember, LORD, what has happened to us;
> look, and see our disgrace. (Lam 5:1)

The extreme grief given voice in Lamentations provides articulation for the many woes in our own world. As Kelly Wilson writes,

"It is difficult to read about intense famine (Lam. 1.11; 2.12), the rape of women (1.12), the removal of people from their homes (1.3), personal belongings taken away (1.10), and people fainting in the streets (2.11, 19, 21) while the perpetrators of these sufferings cheer and mock (1.7; 2.15), without thinking of the Holocaust. It is difficult to read about enemies hissing and gnashing their teeth, crying "We have devoured her! Ah, this is the day we longed for; at last we have seen it!" (2.16) without thinking of Hitler's *Endlösung*—the plan to exterminate the Jews."[5]

Such lament is also expressed by a number of the prophets, most notably Jeremiah. But here, God himself takes up the lament, summoning the mourning women to express his distress:[6]

> Since my people are crushed, I am crushed;
> I mourn, and horror grips me. (Jer 8:21; see also Jer 9)

God intensely shares in the grief of his people. As Juliana Claassens says, "God feels the devastation of war in God's own self."[7]

---

5. Kelly Wilson, "Daughter Zion Speaks in Auschwitz: A Post-Holocaust Reading of Lamentations," *JSOT* 37.1 (2012): 93–108.

6. Juliana Claassens, *Mourner, Mother, Midwife: Reimagining God's Delivering Presence in the Old Testament* (Louisville: Westminster John Knox, 2012). On initial impression it may seem that the prophet is speaking in his own voice here. However, Claassens points out that 9:3 contains the words "says the Lord" and enlists the support of Walter Brueggemann who claims that "my people" is generally used in direct divine discourse. Claassens concludes that "the prophet's tears merge with the tears of God, who ultimately functions as the principal speaker in the poem 8:22–9:3" (23).

7. Juliana Claassens, *Mourner, Mother, Midwife*, 20.

Outcry

Violence in the biblical text evokes an outcry that rises to God.[8] This is a metaphor based upon an ancient Near Eastern custom. An individual who had a complaint of violence to make, either because they had suffered it directly or because they were speaking on behalf of another, voiced their distress to the king or the judge, as an *outcry*. This functioned at once as a protest, a legal accusation, and an appeal for justice. So, for example, Tamar made her outcry after Amnon, her half-brother, had raped her (2 Sam 13:19). Tragically in Tamar's case, her father the king had no interest in pursuing justice for her as the victim.

Another individual who embodies the outcry very powerfully is Rizpah, King Saul's secondary wife (sometimes referred to as his concubine). Almost certainly a victim of rape by the powerful Abner (2 Sam 3:7), her trauma is later horrifically compounded by Saul's successor David in the story we referred to in the previous chapter. After the murder of her sons, Rizpah embodies the outcry with the sustained fury of a woman who has nothing more to lose (2 Sam 21:10). Her outcry is heard by David, who is finally shamed into burying the bodies. Wilda Gafney writes powerfully of the way Rizpah speaks truth to power like a prophet:

> Rizpah bat Aiah watches the corpses of her sons stiffen, soften, swell, and sink into the stench of decay. . . . Rizpah fights with winged, clawed, and toothed scavengers night and day. She is there from the spring harvest until the fall rains, as many as six months . . . sleeping, eating, toileting, protecting, and bearing witness.[9]

As we eavesdrop upon these ancient articulations of grief, we should note the attention the text pays to the voice of victims, and the tenderness with which it holds them.

But the outcry was not simply a social phenomenon whereby an individual sought redress from the king. It is also a common metaphor for the way God attends to human violence. The first such instance is found in Genesis 4, where murdered Abel's blood is spilled upon the earth. God then says to Cain, "Listen! Your brother's blood cries out to me from the ground" (v. 10). Within this metaphor, the outcry is not made directly *to* God but rises before him, and when he hears it he cannot but respond to it, here by directly addressing the human cause of the bloodshed.

A few chapters later, another outcry *goes up* to God, this time because of the wickedness of Sodom and Gomorrah (Gen 18:20–21). On this occasion, God responds by *coming down* to investigate it. And the investigation does indeed demonstrate that Sodom is a city of great violence.

---

8. Matthew Lynch, *Portraying Violence in the Hebrew Bible: A Literary and Cultural Study* (Cambridge: Cambridge University Press, 2020), 147–66.

9. Wilda C. Gafney, *Womanist Midrash: A Reintroduction to the Women of the Torah and the Throne* (Louisville: Westminster John Knox, 2017), 200–201.

Entering Sodom confronts the divine messengers with a litany of injustices, including failure to show hospitality, attempted gang rape, willingness to deliver one's daughters to rapists, and an effort to harm Lot by breaking down his door. All of these instances confirm the severity of the initial outcry, and suggest that such behaviour was representative, and not anomalous.[10]

One of the greatest events in the Old Testament—the exodus from Egypt—is triggered by the outcry of the enslaved Hebrews reaching God. In fact, the outcry is mentioned twice, first by the narrator (Exod 2:23b–24a), and then in God's speech to Moses from the burning bush (3:7–8). Note that once again, the *rising* of the outcry results in God *coming down* to intervene. The God of the Hebrews is concerned about the oppressed and traumatized; he is "God of slaves."[11]

The writing prophets take up the outcry on behalf of the victim in a number of places. One of the starkest is Jeremiah's protest:

> Whenever I speak, I cry out
> proclaiming violence and destruction. (Jer 20:8a)

In what Lissa Wray Beal has called a "multivalent" cry, Jeremiah expressed not only the trauma of the military conquest that he is witnessing but also his own personal trauma:

> In the embodied and representative ministry of Jeremiah, [the people of Judah] find reflected their own experience as Yahweh's called people. Caught in the agonizing effects of trauma, Jeremiah's words of violence and destruction provide words for their own lament and pain.[12]

Jeremiah is embodying the grief of his people, something that the prophets are called to do quite regularly. Consider Ezekiel, whose wife's death (Ezek 24:15–27) reflects the suffering of the people. Or, most famously, the suffering servant of Isaiah 53.

This pair of words, *khamas* and *shōd* ("violence" and "destruction"), is used a number of times in the prophets (e.g., Jer 6:6–7; Ezek 45:9; Amos 3:10; Hab 1:3) to indicate the outcry arising from violent death and oppression. The outcry is also taken up by Isaiah, in his charge to the people to serve as advocates for the victim (Isa 1:17).

---

10. Matthew Lynch, *Portraying Violence in the Hebrew Bible*, 155.
11. L. Daniel Hawk, *The Violence of the Biblical God: Canonical Narrative and Christian Faith* (Grand Rapids: Eerdmans, 2019), 71.
12. Lissa Wray Beal, "Prophetic Ministry in Jeremiah 20.7–18: 'Violence and Destruction,' and Paradoxical Hope for a Shattered Community," in *Violent Biblical Texts: New Approaches*, ed. T. Laurence and H. Paynter (Sheffield: Sheffield Phoenix, 2022), 164–81.

In a similar vein, the letter of James in the New Testament picks up the metaphor of the outcry that reaches God, as James rebukes rich oppressors:

> Look! The wages you failed to pay the workers who mowed your fields are crying out against you. The cries of the harvesters have reached the ears of the Lord Almighty. (Jas 5:4)

In both testaments, the implication of this metaphor is that violence itself instigates the outcry. Those who are violated may not be able to voice anything other than the most inarticulate, primal of cries,[13] and sometimes they are no longer alive to express their outcry. But as Genesis 4 shows us, even then the blood cries out, and God hears it.

Criticism

We have already considered the role of the prophet in embodying the grief and expressing the outcry of the people. Now we turn to another vital element of the prophetic calling: the articulation of criticism. One of the strikingly distinctive things about biblical prophecy compared to its ancient Near Eastern equivalents is its bold criticism of the king.[14] Indeed, the prophetic calling must have been a rather miserable one to receive, given that so many of the prophets received harsh treatment, even martyrdom, because of the message they were charged to deliver.

In 1 Kings 22:1–28, we see a remarkable comparison of faithful and unfaithful prophecy. The kings of Israel and Judah are contemplating a military campaign and realize that they need to consult God before they do so. The king of Israel has four hundred court prophets, who are very quick to affirm his certain victory (v. 6). We see them acting in the typically ecstatic attitude of certain types of ancient Near Eastern prophecy (vv. 10–11). But the king of Judah insists that a more authentic voice should be sought, and accordingly Micaiah is summoned (vv. 7–9). Note that he is not already present; he is not a court prophet and presumably not in the pay of the king. Indeed, the king of Israel is quite petulant about Micaiah: "I hate him because he never prophesies anything good about me, but always bad" (v. 8). Micaiah is warned by the messenger who summons him that his words should align with those of the other prophets. But he is adamant, "As surely as the LORD lives, I can tell him only what the LORD tells me" (v. 14). Micaiah is the true prophet who speaks truth to power, and he is able to do so, in part, because of his independence from the king.

13. Elaine Scarry, *The Body in Pain: The Making and Unmaking of the World* (Oxford: Oxford University Press, 1985), 366.
14. J. Stökl, "Ancient Near-Eastern Prophecy," in *Dictionary of the Old Testament Prophets*, ed. M. J. Boda and J. G. McConville (Downers Grove, IL: InterVarsity Press, 2012), 16–24.

One example of a prophet with an unwelcome message is Nathan, instructed by God to confront King David with his sin in his adultery with (or rape of) Bathsheba and murder of Uriah. In view of the danger, Nathan employs the shrewd technique of telling the king a fictional story with parallels to David's own wrongdoing. The king only realizes this after he has roundly condemned the actions of the man in the story—an effective opportunity for the prophet's rebuke: "You are the man!" (2 Sam 12:7).

Nathan is bold in condemning the king's violence, fatefully foretelling that violence will from now on be endemic to the house of David. This does indeed prove to be the case, as rape and murder become a recurrent pattern in the family. To avenge the rape of his sister (and David's daughter) Tamar (2 Sam 13:1–22), Absalom murders his brother Amnon (vv. 23–39). Ironically, Absalom later leads a civil war against David his father, and he himself rapes the king's concubines (16:20–22). After Absalom's murder by David's henchman Joab (18:9–15), Solomon succeeds David as king and begins his reign by murdering another brother to shore up his grip on the throne (1 Kgs 2:22–25). And so it continues. Perhaps Jesus had these words of Nathan in his mind when he rebukes Peter: "All who draw the sword will die by the sword" (Matt 26:52).

The prophets do not simply address the kings acting in their private capacity, of course. They also speak to the wider society that he governs and to the power structures that maintain it. We considered the prophecy of Amos in a previous chapter, but his words are worth revisiting here, as he sharply condemns the people of Israel for their oppressive practices, in a word that encompasses both men and women in the society:

> Father and son use the same girl
> and so profane my holy name. (Amos 2:7)

> Hear this word, you cows of Bashan on Mount Samaria,
> you women who oppress the poor and crush the needy . . .
> (Amos 4:1)

So far in this chapter we have seen how the Old Testament gives voice to the victims of violence in a number of ways. It provides space for their lament, promotes their outcry, and records the prophetic protest. But preeminently the Old Testament bears witness that God himself is attentive to the outcry, inspires the prophetic protest, and participates in the lament. God shares his people's tears—and their rage.

Before we move on, let us consider this idea of anger in a little more detail.

Anger

A heart that is filled with violence will express itself violently. In his letter to the early church, James describes how the disordered desire of the heart spills over into conflict:

> What causes fights and quarrels among you? Don't they come from your desires that battle within you? You desire but do not have, so you kill. You covet but you cannot get what you want, so you quarrel and fight. (Jas 4:1–2)

James's letter is deeply steeped in dominical[15] words. He probably has this saying of Jesus in his mind:

> A good man brings good things out of the good stored up in his heart, and an evil man brings evil things out of the evil stored up in his heart. For the mouth speaks what the heart is full of. (Luke 6:45)

Jesus takes this idea even further in the Sermon on the Mount. No one who has unrighteous anger in their heart can congratulate themselves on not being a murderer (Matt 5:21–22).

How do we know that Jesus is speaking of *unrighteous* anger rather than all anger? It is interesting that some of the ancient manuscripts have sought to "clarify" Jesus's words, modifying them to "anyone who is angry . . . without cause." While these attempts to be helpful are probably later additions, the intention behind them seems reasonable. On a number of occasions in the Gospels Jesus himself demonstrates anger. See, for example, his diatribe against the religious leaders in Matthew 23, or his anger (*orgē*) in Mark 3:5.

Jesus's words are similar to the rhetoric of the Old Testament prophets, who employ invective in their condemnation of both the covenant people (especially the leaders) and the other nations around. For example, consider the way Jeremiah likens the people of Judah to a camel in heat (Jer 2:23–24).[16] The prophet uses powerful rhetoric to reflect his message of divine anger.

The anger of God is an unfashionable notion these days. However, as we have seen, God is a righteous king whose commitment to justice is reliable. His judgment is enacted by means of divine anger, which is not so much an emotion[17] as an implacable opposition to evil. The wicked shrink from God's wrath (e.g., Hos 10:8), but the righteous (and, in the New Testament, this is clearly those who have been *declared* righteous) welcome God's judgment as good news. For instance, the twenty-four elders in John's vision sing in celebration of the coming judgment (Rev 11:17–18).

---

15. The term *dominical* is related to the Latin word *dominus*, which means "master." A dominical saying, then, is one that can be traced back to Jesus himself.

16. The image of the nation as a sexually frenzied she-donkey probably seems offensive to us, but in fact the offense is deeper that we might imagine, because the primary target of Jeremiah's invective was *men*. Jeremiah is shaming his audience by the comparison because he considers that it is merited by the offense of Judah's unfaithfulness to their covenant with God. See the related discussion in Helen Paynter, "'Redeeming the Prostitute': Babylon and Her Fate in Revelation," in *Violent Biblical Texts: New Approaches*, ed. T. Laurence and H. Paynter (Sheffield: Sheffield Phoenix, 2022), 248–74.

17. However, we do encounter the metaphor of God's anger flaring up (cf. Ps 2:12). In the divine self-revelation on Sinai, God says that he is "slow to anger" (Exod 34:6). This is the difficulty with complex metaphors.

Unlike the human tendency, God's love and his wrath are not antithetical to each other. D. A. Carson writes:

> Our problem, in part, is that in human experience wrath and love normally abide in mutually exclusive compartments. Love drives wrath out, or wrath drives love out. We come closest to bringing them together, perhaps, in our responses to a wayward act by one of our children, but normally we do not think that a wrathful person is loving. But this is not the way it is with God. God's wrath is not an implacable, blind rage. However emotional it may be, it is an entirely reasonable and willed response to offenses against his holiness.[18]

Clearly, the angry word plays an important part in Scripture. While the word can be a weapon that harms (e.g., Pss 55:21; 64:3), the same metaphor is also used in a much more positive way to represent the power of the word of God in the mouth of the obedient servant of the Lord (e.g., Isa 49:2; Eph 6:17; Heb 4:12). The seeds of murder lie within us all, as Jesus has clearly shown. But not all anger and harsh words are evil. Some reflect God's own righteous rage.

Therefore Paul tells the church in Ephesus, quoting Psalm 4:4, "In your anger do not sin" (Eph 4:26). Indeed, both the Old and New Testament versions of this could be translated, "Be angry and do not sin."[19] The key questions are what is causing the anger, and from what springs the words are flowing.

Now we turn our attention to a different way in which the Bible encourages the viewing of violence from the underside. We will look at the ways in which the Old Testament testifies to the resistance offered by victims of violence against their oppressors. We will see examples of passive and active resistance, of peacefulness and violence. We should not automatically assume that any one of these approaches offers a paradigm for contemporary behavior, but we will trace out the threads here, with the aim of reflecting on their relevance in the closing chapters of this book.

RESISTANCE

Memory as Resistance

Holocaust survivor Elie Wiesel, whose father was taken to the Buchenwald crematorium while Elie slept by his side, is said to have declared, "I can tolerate the memory of silence, but not the silence of memory."[20] His memory of evil was less traumatic to him than its deliberate suppression. The story should be told and retold. To lose it is to compound the trauma.

---

18. D. A. Carson, *The Difficult Doctrine of the Love of God* (Wheaton: Crossway, 2000), 69.

19. Paul is quoting from the Greek version of the Old Testament (the Septuagint). The Hebrew version has "tremble and do not sin."

20. These words are often quoted, but the exact reference is hard to obtain. Wiesel says something similar in his 1986 Nobel Prize acceptance speech, "Hope, Despair and Memory," The Nobel Prize, Nobel lecture given December 11, 1986, nobelprize.org/nobel _prizes/peace/laureates/1986/wiesel-lecture.html.

In the ancient Near Eastern mindset, the importance of memory was even more marked than in our own. This is frequently expressed as the loss or perpetuation of *name*, which is tied up with the idea of descendants. We might recall the command against the hated Amalekites that their memory be blotted out—an injunction ironically subverted by its perpetuation in our text and paradoxically contradicted by the instruction to remember to forget (Deut 25:19b).

The threat of one's name being lost was quite common. It is made, for example, against any Israelites contemplating idol worship (Deut 29:20), against the prophet Jeremiah (Jer 11:19), and against oppressive Nineveh, the capital of Assyria (Nah 1:14). Fear of this fate motivated, among others, the daughters of Zelophehad (Num 27:4), Joshua (Josh 7:9), Saul (1 Sam 24:21), and the woman of Tekoa (2 Sam 14:7). It is therefore a particularly precious promise that Isaiah makes to faithful eunuchs.

> To them I will give within my temple and its walls
>> a memorial and a name
>> better than sons and daughters;
> I will give them an everlasting name
>> that will endure forever. (Isa 56:5)

The Hebrew phrase here translated "a memorial and a name" is *yad vashem*, the name given in modern times to the World Holocaust Remembrance Centre, located just outside Jerusalem. This is motivated by the same impulse: to ensure that those whose lives were stolen from them are not lost to remembrance as well. "The names of more than one million of those who were murdered remain unknown—and time is running out. It is our collective moral imperative to persist in our efforts to recover their names and restore their identities."[21]

For these reasons, choosing to remember, or being remembered, may be viewed as an act of resistance. So, for example, the exiled Jews in Babylon, taunted by their captors, sang of their refusal to forget Jerusalem (Ps 137:5–6).

A stubborn refusal to "die" in the memory is a means by which the Bible portrays the resistance of the oppressed and their value to God. Juliana Claassens says that survival after rape is the ultimate form of resistance; it is an obstinacy that will not allow the rapist to win.[22] Claassens sees this in Tamar's refusal to die after

---

21. "The Central Database of Shoah Victims' Names," Yad Vashem: The World Holocaust Remembrance Centre, https://yvng.yadvashem.org/.

22. L. Juliana M. Claassens, *Claiming Her Dignity: Female Resistance in the Old Testament* (Collegeville, MN: Liturgical Press, 2016), 50.

being abused by her half-brother Amnon, as well as in Absalom's choice to name his daughter after her aunt (2 Sam 14:27).

Not every biblical victim of rape or other violence in the Bible is able to hold to life with such tenacity, however. But in these cases, it is not the refusal to die but the refusal to die in the memory that constitutes the act of resistance. Perhaps a prime example is the Levite's wife in Judges 19, which we discussed in chapter 6. Strikingly, the narrator refuses to allow the victim—a low-status *woman*—to be forgotten. In this way, the text stands in anamnestic solidarity with her.[23] It stubbornly testifies about her and thereby testifies about the suffering of all victims of sexual violence who have come after.[24]

Refusal to forget is the first act of resistance against a violent oppressor. The second is civil disobedience.

Civil Disobedience
Five Women in Egypt

One of the great examples of civil resistance is found in the opening chapter of the book of Exodus, where the midwives Shiphrah and Puah disobey the Pharaoh's orders. The role of women in these chapters is very prominent. In 1:10 the Pharaoh uses an unexpected female plural verb, probably best rendered "lest the women wage war. . . ."[25] How might the women wage war? By bearing children; the fecundity of the women is a major theme in these verses and evidently perceived by the Pharaoh as a threat:

> The children of Israel were *fruitful* and *multiplied* and *became many* and they were *very, very numerous* and *the land was filled with them*. And a new king arose over Egypt, who did not know Joseph. And he said to his people, "Look the people of the children of Israel are *greater* and *more numerous* than we are. Come let us deal shrewdly with them, lest they become *numerous*; if the women wage war, they will *augment* our enemies and will fight against us and will escape from the land." (Exod 1:7–10, my translation and emphases)

We should not forget that the divine command to Adam and Eve in the garden was to be fruitful and to multiply and fill the earth (the Hebrew word, *eretz*, can be translated "earth" or "land" and is the same noun used in the excerpt quoted above). Despite their circumstances, the people of Israel were flourishing in the way

23. *Anamnesis* is a term employed by Walter Benjamin, a Jew who fled the holocaust. Walter Benjamin, *The Arcades Project*, trans. Howard Eiland and Kevin McLaughlin (Cambridge: Harvard University Press, 1999).

24. I explore this further in *Telling Terror in Judges 19: Rape and Reparation for the Levite's Wife* (Abingdon: Routledge, 2020).

25. Jacqueline E. Lapsley, *Whispering the Word: Hearing Women's Stories in the Old Testament* (Louisville: Westminster John Knox, 2005), 71.

that God wants humans to flourish, and Pharaoh is represented as an anti-creational force who tries to oppose the primal purpose of God for humanity.

The first step of Pharaoh's plan is to try to work the people into decline (v. 11), presumably hoping to induce miscarriage in the women through forced labor.[26] When this fails (v. 12), his next plan is to exterminate the male babies at birth. Jacqueline Lapsley suggests that this was a crucial miscalculation; pragmatically this is so because in the next generation it will only take a few of those male infants, escaped and grown up, to father a lot of babies, but more fundamentally because Pharaoh has underestimated the female capacity for resistance. He is afraid of the men who might take arms against him, but he should have feared the women who are stubbornly continuing to bear children.[27] "Pharaoh fatally underestimates the power of God to work deliverance through the vulnerable—and seemingly powerless—on behalf of the vulnerable."[28]

Into this charged situation step five courageous women. The names of Shiphrah and Puah, midwives for the Hebrews are—remarkably—preserved in the text, perhaps a signifier of the honor in which they were held. Their lie to the Pharaoh, "Hebrew women are not like Egyptian women; they are vigorous and give birth before the midwives arrive" (Exod 1:19), is the first in an honorable line of women misdirecting men in order to preserve life (see also Josh 2:4–6; 1 Sam 19:14; 2 Sam 17:20). Their deceit is quickly followed by Moses's mother's concealment of her child (Exod 2:2), the princess's willingness to defy her father (v. 6), and Miriam's ingenuity in offering Moses's own mother as his wet-nurse (vv. 7–8). The opening two chapters of Exodus are a study in feminine civil disobedience.

Four Men in Babylon

Two further examples of civil disobedience are offered in the book of Daniel. The story of Daniel in the lions' den is probably well-known to most readers, so we will focus on the other one, which involves Daniel's three friends, Hananiah, Mishael, and Azariah, better known as Shadrach, Meshach, and Abednego. The violence that these Jewish men have experienced is hinted very early in the book, where their renaming by the king of Babylon is recounted (Dan 1:6–7). Renaming is an act of imperial power; here, Nebuchadnezzar has obliterated the identities of these conquered subjects, and in particular has overwritten their theophoric (God-bearing) names. Hananiah means "Yahweh has been gracious"; Mishael, "Who is what God is?"; and Azariah, "Yahweh has helped."[29]

The first challenge that the young men face tests the extent to which they will

---

26. Lapsley, *Whispering the Word*, 72.
27. Lapsley, *Whispering the Word*, 73.
28. Lapsley, *Whispering the Word*, 74.

29. Ernest C. Lucas, *Daniel*, Apollos Old Testament Commentary (Downers Grove, IL: IVP Academic; Leicester: Apollos, 2002), 53.

assimilate with local custom at the expense of their identity as Jews. Along with Daniel, they take a stand and get away with it (Dan 1:11–16). So far, so good. But this is only the beginning of their difficulties. Soon they have a stark choice to make: bow down in worship to the statue of the king or face punishment by death (3:1–30). The narrative bristles with hyperbole and ironic overlay. The statue is enormous, only slightly smaller than the Colossus at Rhodes. The amount of gold that it would have contained would have been astronomical—or was it hollow? The careful choreography of the musicians and all the people who are bowing down takes on an almost comedic tone.[30] But for the young Jewish men, the situation is anything but funny. The king's ire is ignited, and things quickly become very dangerous.

The passage is fraught with the emotion of the king. He is initially furious with rage (v. 13), then in verse nineteen his fury leads him to order the furnace heated to seven times its normal temperature (whatever that means), so that it kills the men who obey his orders. In verse twenty-four the king leaps to his feet in amazement; then (v. 26) he approaches the opening of the blazing furnace and bellows into the opening in a display of *lèse-majesté*. Ultimately, he makes another ludicrous and hyperbolic order: anyone of any nation or language who says anything against the God of Shadrach, Meshach, and Abednego will be cut into pieces, and their houses turned into piles of rubble (v. 28). There are no half-measures with this tyrant.

In the middle of this perfect storm of imperial emotion, Shadrach, Meshach, and Abednego are the calm eye. They do not bluster, but nor do they dissemble. They don't try to conceal their disobedience, but neither do they attempt to resist the king's officers. For me, this is one of the most glorious moments in Scripture. They simply stand before the king, and quietly defy him.

But they are not, they cannot be, confident that God will rescue them. The text of Daniel is believed by many to have been written during the time of the Greeks, under whom the Jews suffered fierce persecution. No such reader of this narrative could imagine that obedience to God was a "get out of jail free" card.[31] But for Shadrach, Meshach, and Abednego, obedience is not conditional upon divine deliverance from evil. And so they look the king in the eye and calmly say that whether God saves them or not, they will not betray him by bowing down to an idol (v. 18).

Puah and Shiphrah, Pharaoh's daughter, Jochebed,[32] Miriam, Hananiah, Mishael, and Azariah are the foremothers and forefathers of all who have exercised civil resistance since.

---

30. Lucas, *Daniel*, 87.

31. Even if the book was written in the sixth century BC, as others claim, the Jewish experience of life under Persian rule was hardly benign. For a discussion on the dating of the book, see Tremper Longman III, *Daniel*, NIVAC (Grand Rapids: Zondervan, 1999), 21–24. For a discussion of the barbarities of the Persians, see Peter Hatton, "No Condemnation? The Old Testament's Puzzling Treatment of Persian Violence," in *The Bible on Violence: A Thick Description*, ed. H. Paynter and M. Spalione (Sheffield, Sheffield Phoenix, 2020), 157–67.

32. Moses's mother is named in Exod 6:20.

> Jonathan Augustine has written of the close links between the action of Shadrach, Meshach, and Abednego and the civil rights activists under Martin Luther King Jr.:
>
> > The Hebrews fully understood the potentially fatal consequences of their civil disobedience by refusing to participate in the immorality of idolatry. Indeed, regardless of potentially life-ending consequences, the Hebrews were not detoured, much in the way the Movement's activists were not detoured from their acts of civil disobedience, fully appreciating their potentially life-ending consequences. Consequently, the Hebrews' rejection of Nebuchadnezzar's order is a form of civil disobedience, with an understood anticipation of what was presumed to be certain death, that sets a theological foundation for the Freedom Rides of 1961, the Bloody Sunday March across the Edmund Pettus Bridge in 1965, and King's obvious willingness to accept the potentially fatal threat of being incarcerated in Birmingham in 1963.[33]

Verbal Resistance

Situations of power imbalance tend to result in both an official discourse (laws, court records, official histories) and in "hidden transcripts" (semi-concealed actions and words that allow the underclass to express their contempt for their masters).[34] Thus there is an Ethiopian proverb which states, "When the great lord passes, the wise peasant bows deeply—and silently farts."[35]

Mass Hallucinations and Chariots of Fire

Such hidden transcripts are found in parts of the Old Testament and constitute acts of resistance directed toward those who held power, particularly those who held oppressive power. A good example is found in 2 Kings 6:8–7:20. A subversive interpretation has been offered by LaBarbera, who views it as a peasant narrative that satirizes the militarism of the king and his warriors, "a folk narrative in which the military elite utterly fail to do what they so proudly claim to be the best at doing, demonstrating military expertise."[36]

The text constitutes part of the anti-militarism thread that we will consider in the following chapter, but in brief it contains a story full of unexpected twists

---

33. Jonathan C. Augustine, "The Fiery Furnace, Civil Disobedience, and the Civil Rights Movement: A Biblical Exegesis on Daniel 3 & the Letter from a Birmingham Jail," *Richmond Public Interest Law Review* 21 (2017): 243–62.

34. James Scott, *Domination and the Arts of Resistance: Hidden Transcripts* (New Haven: Yale University Press, 1990), xii.

35. Quoted in Scott, *Domination and the Arts of Resistance*, title page.

36. Robert LaBarbera, "The Man of War and the Man of God: Social Satire in 2 Kings 6:8–7:20," *CBQ* 46.4 (1984): 651.

and bizarre characterizations. A posse of soldiers is duped by the prophet they are seeking to capture. A king and his officer are utterly bewildered—the officer is later trampled to death by the common people. A siege is lifted through a divinely sent auditory hallucination, but nobody notices it has been lifted until four lepers happen upon the abandoned camp—and even then, not until they have first fed well on the discarded spoils. It is humorous, but this is humor with a purpose—to critique human powers, particularly as they set themselves up in defiance of God:[37] "There is not one military person in the passage, be he soldier, adjutant, or king, who succeeds. Instead, it is the prophet Elisha who is victorious—Elisha, with his horses and chariots of fire."[38]

Esther as Comedy

Another example of subversive resistance can be found in the book of Esther, set in the time when the Jewish people were subject to their Persian overlords. The book has a comedic plot, full of improbable situations and coincidences and peopled with farcical characters. The Persian king is a buffoon, who blindly follows the advice of his advisers, and can be wrapped around Esther's little finger. Haman is an arch-baddie, seemingly straight off the stage of a pantomime. The language is hyperbolic and the situations at times hilariously inflated. "A woman says 'No' to her husband and suddenly an entire kingdom is under threat."[39]

But this is not frivolous comedy, existing for a cheap laugh. Humor can be a truth-seeking device, challenging oppressive hierarchies.[40] Texts such as this are satirizing the regime, cutting down to size the pomp of the governing power. In an era of brutal oppression by a foreign occupying force, how is one to express one's resistance? By telling stories such as that of Esther and her fool of an emperor-husband.

Physical Resistance

We have considered an escalating scale of resistance against oppressive power: memory, civil disobedience, and hidden transcripts that satirize and mock. The final form of resistance to consider is direct physical action. We will begin by continuing the story of Esther.

Exodus and Esther

The story of Esther then takes a darker turn, as the queen responds to the uncovering of Haman's plot against the Jewish people by requesting time for them to slaughter their non-Jewish neighbors.

---

37. Paynter, *Reduced Laughter*, 84–89.
38. LaBarbera, "Man of War and the Man of God," 651.
39. Melissa Jackson, *Comedy and Feminist Interpretation of the*

Hebrew Bible: A Subversive Collaboration (Oxford: Oxford University Press, 2012), 209.
40. Paynter, *Reduced Laughter*, 4.

It is instructive to compare the responses of the Hebrews under Moses (book of Exodus) with the exilic Jews of Susa (book of Esther) in response to the threats of genocide that they both faced. In the book of Exodus, the people place themselves entirely in God's hand (e.g., Exod 14:13–14). They do accept financial gifts (restitution, perhaps) from the Egyptians on their way out of Egypt (12:35–36), but they do not take any action themselves against their erstwhile oppressors. Indeed, it is a "mixed multitude" that comes out of Egypt (v. 38), implying that some Egyptians were in their number.

This is in striking contrast with the actions of the Jews in Susa and beyond in the time of Esther. Following the admittedly horrific threat of annihilation plotted by Haman, their response when the tables are turned is to inflict the violence that was intended for them against their enemies. In fact, the response is so disturbing, amounting to two days of unmitigated violence (Esth 9:5–16), that some have considered this to be dark comedy.[41] It is Esther who takes the lead here, petitioning the king for an extra day for the killing spree. There is no suggestion that God has endorsed this; it is perhaps better viewed as evidence that all of God's chosen leaders have a dark side.[42] It is a clear example of the mimetic violence highlighted by Girard,[43] and perhaps, too, a reflection that hurt people often hurt others. It is not hard to imagine that the trauma of Esther's early life might render her brittle and vindictive.[44]

Ehud

The book of Judges has a number of examples of direct action against oppressors. In this pre-monarchical period, the nation of Israel (though it is deeply fragmented and can scarcely be called a nation at this point) is intermittently in a state of vassalage to the nations around. These include Moab (Judg 3:12), Midian (6:1), and the Philistines and Ammonites (10:7–8). The story of Ehud (Judg 3:12–30) is set during the vassalage to the Moabites and is rich with humor and trickery.

Left-handed Ehud is the one chosen to deliver the tribute to Eglon, king of Moab. The word *eglon* means "calf," and the king is indeed suggestively represented as a fattened animal ready for sacrifice. After eighteen years of demanding tribute, he is obese on the profits. Sunday-school children everywhere can gleefully relate

---

41. For example, Brandon Hurlbert has compared the concluding scenes of Esther to a Quentin Tarantino film and thereby argues that the violence contains its own contradictions: "Even though the story seems to relish in the violence . . . its underlying goal is to counteract this violence. The story functions as a mirror that reveals the chaotic horror of real-world violence that occurs in the present. Readers then condemn such violence . . . wherever [it] is mimicked in the real world" (Brandon Hurlbert, "Once upon a Time in Persia: The Ethics of Violence in the Book of Esther and Quentin Tarantino's *Once Upon a Time in Hollywood*," in *Map or Compass? The Bible on Violence*, ed. M. Spalione and H. Paynter [Sheffield: Sheffield Phoenix, 2022], 175–92).

42. Karen H. Jobes, *Esther*, NIVAC (Grand Rapids: Zondervan, 1999), 201.

43. See chapter 1.

44. Erika S. Dunbar, "For Such a Time as This? #UsToo: Representations of Sexual Trafficking, Collective Trauma, and Horror in the Book of Esther," *Bible and Critical Theory* 15.1 (2019): 29–48.

the next part of the story; left-handed Ehud draws his concealed blade and strikes Eglon in the stomach. The fat closes over the hilt. The assassin makes his getaway while Eglon's servants are too embarrassed to enter the locked chamber.

In actual fact, "left-handed" is a rather loose translation of the Hebrew, which would be better rendered "restricted of right hand." Perhaps Ehud has a disability of some sort; if so, this could explain why it was he who was chosen to deliver the tribute.[45] He could hardly be a threat if his right hand is out of action—could he? The theme of God acting in weakness (if indeed this is how we should interpret Ehud's left-handedness) is an important one that we encounter again and again, especially in Judges. Recall Gideon, for instance, fearfully threshing indoors and yet addressed by the angel as "mighty warrior" (Judg 6:11–12). Gideon is later instructed to send most of his army home because they are "too many" (Judg 7:2, 4).

However, there are problematic moments in the Ehud story. It is not until he reaches the "stone images near Gilgal" (Judg 3:19) that he turns back for his murderous encounter with the king. Were his actions inspired by God or by the false gods of the land? Further, his claim that he has a "word of God" for the king (v. 20, author's translation) proves to be a double-mouthed (deceitful) promise, like his "double-mouthed" sword (v. 16).

This Ehud-Eglon encounter can be compared with the Moses-Pharaoh confrontation of the book of Exodus. Whereas Eglon commands silence and rises to receive the word of the Lord (vv. 19–20),[46] the Pharaoh hardens his heart against God. Although Moses initially attempts to resist by means of assassination (Exod 2:12), this results in forty years of exile, and ultimately it is by his impartation of the word of the Lord that the people are delivered. By this standard, Ehud could be considered to have failed in the prophetic task: "What is shocking . . . is that Ehud does not speak to Eglon. He offers divine revelation, but instead of proclaiming that promised word, he murders him."[47]

Like other judges of Israel, Ehud may not be a clean-cut hero after all. Is God behind his direct action? Or are we to view this act as rather more morally ambiguous?

Jael

Sunday-school children everywhere will probably be familiar with the actions of Jael in Judges 4. This time the people of Israel are under the thumb of the Canaanites, most particularly Jabin's commander Sisera, who oppresses them for twenty years

45. Barry G. Webb, *The Book of Judges*, NICOT (Grand Rapids: Eerdmans, 2012), 171.

46. The early rabbis considered Eglon to have acted honorably before God in this regard and wrote that in reward he was written into King David's family line by fathering Ruth (Rabbah 2, available here: www.sefaria.org/Ruth_Rabbah.2. See comment on Ruth 1.4).

47. Brandon Hurlbert, "Will the Real Ehud Please Stand Up? Toward a Negative Reading of Judges 3:12–30," paper presented at the annual conference of the Society for Biblical Literature, November 2020. I am indebted to Dr. Hurlbert for allowing me to read the script of his paper. I am drawing on his ideas throughout this section on Ehud.

with an astronomical nine hundred chariots of iron (Judg 4:3). An iron chariot represents cutting-edge military technology; Israel did not have chariots in those days (Judg 1:19) and were reliant on bronze weaponry (1 Sam 13:19–22). So our narrator is laying it on thick as he describes the power imbalance between the two peoples.

If a warrior's *capacity* to act has been disparaged by the Ehud and the Gideon narratives, this narrative disparages a warrior's *willingness*. Deborah, prophetess of Israel, instructs Barak to muster an army and confront Sisera. Barak, however, seems far from keen: "If you go with me, I will go; but if you don't go with me, I won't go" (Judg 4:8). In response, Deborah tells him, "Because of the course you are taking, the honor will not be yours, for the LORD will deliver Sisera into the hands of a woman" (v. 9). And so it proves to be; Barak routs the Moabite army, but Sisera himself meets his nemesis in the person of Jael, a women in whose tent he has taken refuge. Having been narrated in prose in Judges 4, the incident is then celebrated poetically in the following chapter.

The view the text takes of this is disputed. Some commentators celebrate the power of the women in these two chapters.[48] Others decry the failure of male leadership that made the unwomanly actions of Deborah and Jael necessary.[49] Instead of weighing in too heavily in this gender debate, there are certain features of the story that should catch our attention. First, this is yet another story of victory-through-weakness. We will pick this theme up in the following chapter.

We should not allow the graphic nature of Sisera's assassination to distract us from the dangerous dynamics at play here. In her song, Deborah envisions the Canaanite women salaciously conjecturing about Sisera's post-victory activities: "Are they not finding and dividing the spoils: a woman or two for each man?" (Judg 5:30). It is clear that an Israelite woman could expect to be raped by a Canaanite warrior, should he come across her unprotected. In fact, the Hebrew is coarser than this translation suggests; even the ESV's "a womb or two for every man" might still be euphemistic.[50] Sisera may be a warrior in flight, but he is still a warrior, and Jael is alone. In biblical literature, a man's entry into a woman's tent is by definition a sexually charged situation.[51] In this context Jael's composure and resourcefulness is striking; she puts the man at ease, and when he is asleep strikes him dead with the closest thing to a weapon that she possesses. It is an act of self-defense.

48. J. Cheryl Exum and Letty M. Russell, "'Mother in Israel': A Familiar Story Reconsidered," in *Feminist Interpretation of the Bible*, ed. Letty M. Russell (Louisville: Westminster John Knox, 1985), 73–85.

49. John Piper and Wayne Grudem, "An Overview of Central Concerns: Question and Answers," in *Recovering Biblical Manhood and Womanhood: A Response to Evangelical Feminism*, ed. John Piper and Wayne Grudem (Wheaton: Crossway, 1991), 84.

50. Adrien Janis Bledstein, "Is Judges a Woman's Satire on Men Who Play God?," in *Feminist Companion to Judges*, ed. Athalya Brenner (Sheffield: JSOT Press, 1993), 41.

51. Danna Nolan Fewell and David M. Gunn, "Controlling Perspectives: Women, Men, and the Authority of Violence in Judges 4 & 5," *Journal of the American Academy of Religion* 58.3 (1990): 392.

Scholars who debate Jael's motivation for killing Sisera are usually writing from the privileged position of being male, have never lived in a postwar situation, have never been displaced from the safety of a lockable front door into a tent, or all three. In chapter 5 we discussed the frequency of battlefield rape in ancient times and still today. But Jael's predicament also calls to mind a precarity experienced by many displaced people. While for Jael and her husband Heber tent-living was normal, the story draws to our attention the precarity of living without a lockable front door.

Such are the living circumstances of millions of people worldwide, who have been displaced from their homes by natural disaster, war, climate change, or fear. For instance, a whole year after the Haiti earthquake of 2010, the BBC reported that rape in the camp of people still awaiting rehousing had reached epidemic levels: "They often come armed with knives and pistols. In darkness, they slit open tents and rape the women inside."[52]

It is hard to find in this text the sort of ambiguity that lingers over Eglon's assassination. The victory that results from Jael's bold and decisive action is celebrated at length in the poem that follows. Honors are shared by Deborah and Barak (vv. 7, 12, 15), with Jael getting a whole stanza in her honor (vv. 24–27). Noteworthy in the poem is the commendation of willing volunteers (vv. 2, 9), the indictment of those who stayed away from the battle (vv. 15b–17, 23), and praise heaped upon those who showed up. In a fragmenting nation without a standing army, victory is (humanly) impossible without a mass response to the military muster. But we should not overlook the theophany of verses 4–5. What is the rumbling of nine hundred chariots compared to the earth shaking and the mountain quaking at the arrival of the Lord? As is so frequently seen in accounts of military engagement, human endeavor and divine intervention are both considered instrumental, with no contradiction evinced.

MOVING INTO THE NEW TESTAMENT

In future chapters we will consider the New Testament's radical call for enemy love and passive resistance and how that might be lived out today. Interestingly, the New Testament contains little reference to what we might term armed resistance, although it was a constant feature of life under the Romans. But close to the heart of the most central narrative of all there is an intriguing detail, where Jesus's life is traded for

52. Sima Kotecha, "Rape at 'Crisis' Levels in Haiti Camps," BBC News, Jan 13, 2011, www.bbc.co.uk/news/newsbeat-12171443.

Barabbas's, who was almost certainly an armed resistance fighter. For Pope Benedict, this is a reflection of the third temptation offered to Jesus at the beginning of his ministry, the temptation to achieve the good goals of God by illegitimate—here, violent—means:

> Barabbas was a messianic figure. The choice of Jesus versus Barabbas is not accidental; two messiah figures, two forms of messianic belief stand in opposition. . . . Up until the third century, many manuscripts of the Gospels referred to the man in question here as "Jesus Barabbas"—"Jesus son of the father." Barabbas figures here as a sort of alter ego of Jesus, who makes the same claim but understands it in a completely different way. So the choice is between a Messiah who leads an armed struggle, promises freedom and a kingdom of one's own, and this mysterious Jesus who proclaims that losing oneself is the way to life. Is it any wonder that the crowds prefer Barabbas?[53]

But Jesus resists the temptation in the desert (Matt 4:8–9) and the temptation to escape the cross (26:53). For he knows that good cannot be served with evil and that violence cannot cast out violence. And as the prophet had foretold (Isa 53:7), Jesus embraced the status of every victim and did not resist the evil men (cf. Matt 5:39).

This is no masochistic glorification of suffering but the culmination of a thread that has run through the Scriptures to this point—the gradual dismantling of justification for violent systems and structures. This is the subject of our next chapter.

CONCLUSION

Unusually for ancient literature, the Old Testament pays acute attention to the weak, the conquered, and the violated. Their voices are preserved and represented in our text as lament, outcry, criticism, and rage. Human dignity is cherished, and the divine voice joins the sad song, for God is implacably opposed to the wicked. But the Bible also contains stories of resistance by such people, who refuse to be consigned to the category of eternal victim. Some resist by surviving—or by being commemorated in our text. Others resist by disobedience, by a stubborn refusal to comply with the immoral instructions of their masters. Still others resist by writing stories of disgrace into the sacred text, mocking and subverting pomp and power. Finally, and not unambiguously, there are stories of physical resistance—celebrated but also at times undermined with quiet subversion.

---

53. Benedict XVI, *Jesus of Nazareth*, trans. Adrian J Walker (London: Bloomsbury, 2007), 66.

RELEVANT QUESTIONS

1. With attention to the voices that we identified in the first part of the chapter (lament, outcry, criticism, rage), where is the divine presence in relation to each one? How do we see these lived out in the life of Jesus?

2. What are the practices of remembrance that we observe in church, home, or wider society? Who is remembered? Who is forgotten?

3. Can you identify other examples of civil resistance in Scripture? What do these teach us today?

4. Should Christians get angry? If so, when and how?

CHAPTER 8

REDEMPTIVE TRAJECTORIES BEFORE THE CROSS

A collection of antiwar or subversive war texts in Scripture . . . present Yahweh as an uneasy/highly reluctant war God.
—William J. Webb and Gordon K. Oeste, *Bloody, Brutal and Barbaric? Wrestling with Troubling War Texts*

It is easy—and common—to characterize the Old Testament as full of violence and the New Testament as bringing the word of peace. This is unfair. The cross is, among other things, the apotheosis of nonviolence, but it does not arrive "out of the blue." It is the culmination of many deep themes and grand trajectories in the Old Testament. Among them are the devalorization of warfare, the gradual subversion of vengeance, and the emergence of the idea of the innocent sufferer. In this chapter we will consider each of these, and then in the following chapter we will turn to the cross itself, the place where all human violence is absorbed.

DEVALORIZATION OF WARFARE

The gods of the ancient Near East were aggressive warriors. Consider this excerpt from an Assyrian inscription, where the monarch's excessive violence is understood to originate from the deity.

> I brought upon them an inundation. I fell upon them like a blazing fire, and I put to the sword 1,616 of their troops. Furthermore, I removed the hands and lower lips of 80 of their troops; and I let them go free to [spread the news of my] glory. . . . I inflicted this defeat by the power of Šamaš and Marduk, Adad and Apla-Adad, the great gods.[1]

By contrast, and contrary to popular opinion, the God who is revealed in the Old Testament sends his people to war only reluctantly, and the text is riddled with places where warfare is devalorized. But before we can discover this, we need to take

---

1. Abbreviated from K. Lawson Younger's translation of the Ninurta-kudurrī-uṣur-Suḫu annals, in W. W. Hallo and K. L. Younger, *Context of Scripture*, vol. 2 (Leiden; Boston: Brill, 2000), 115B, 280.

a closer look at some of the elements in the conquest of Canaan as described in the first half of the book of Joshua.

The Book of Joshua

The conquest of Canaan (hereafter simply "the conquest") is a problem with which many Christians struggle. How could God command the indiscriminate destruction of whole cities in the pursuit of giving his people the promised land? It is not the intention here to rehearse all of the many arguments offered in apology for this issue. The concerned reader is directed to some of the excellent work that has been published in recent years in an attempt to grapple with it.[2] Essentially, however, the answers that have been offered do not amount to a full explanation. I regard them as forming something like an incomplete jigsaw puzzle where many of the pieces are still missing. Some of the key ideas are offered here, in brief, but no attempt is made to provide a full apologia.

First, as we have discussed in several of the preceding chapters, God retains the prerogative of judging, even violently, his creatures. We have seen him do this by direct action on a number of occasions. Our modern and sometimes rather narcissistic concept of "rights" is both anachronistic in that the ancient writers would not have thought in such categories, and theologically flawed in that we are all by nature under the righteous wrath of a holy God and have no rights before him.[3] Consider Paul's words, written for a different but not dissimilar purpose:

> Who are you, O man, to answer back to God? Will what is molded say to its molder, "Why have you made me like this?" Has the potter no right over the clay, to make out of the same lump one vessel for honorable use and another for dishonorable use?
>
> What if God, desiring to show his wrath and to make known his power, has endured with much patience vessels of wrath prepared for destruction, in order to make known the riches of his glory for vessels of mercy. (Rom 9:20–23 ESV)

---

2. Of the recent work on the Canaanite conquest that I consider to be most useful, I would highlight the following. In my opinion, the best approach published in recent years is the redemptive hermeneutic applied by William J. Webb and Gordon K. Oeste, *Bloody, Brutal and Barbaric? Wrestling with Troubling War Texts* (Downers Grove, IL: InterVarsity Press, 2019). John and Harvey Walton also offer an excellent analysis of the problem by allowing other ancient Near Eastern writings to shed light upon the thought-world of the biblical writers in *The Lost World of the Israelite Conquest: Covenant, Retribution, and the Fate of the Canaanites* (Downers Grove, IL: InterVarsity Press, 2017). Also very helpful is Daniel L. Hawk, *The Violence of the Biblical God: Canonical Narrative and Christian Faith* (Grand Rapids: Eerdmans, 2019). Paul Copan and Matthew Flannagan take a very careful, forensic look at the question in *Did God Really Command Genocide?: Coming to Terms with the Justice of God* (Grand Rapids: Baker, 2014). I have found chapter two of R. Walter L. Moberly's *Old Testament Theology: Reading the Hebrew Bible as Christian Scripture* (Grand Rapids: Baker Academic, 2013) to be helpful. And my own modest attempt to address the issue at a relatively accessible level is found in Helen Paynter, *God of Violence Yesterday, God of Love Today? Wrestling Honestly with the Old Testament* (Abingdon: Bible Reading Fellowship, 2019).

3. This is entirely separate from the human-rights question in terms of how we humans treat one another.

Without wishing to get into a discussion of predestination (the hot potato of the conquest is quite sufficient for me!), Paul's argument has a bearing upon our understanding of the conquest. God is entitled to do as he wishes with his creatures. The wonder is not that some are destroyed but that any are preserved.

Certain elements of the biblical account (e.g., Deut 9:4–5; 12:29–31) mark the Canaanites out for righteous judgment, a judgment that God delays in his mercy. As he says to Abraham of his descendants, "they shall come back here [to Canaan] in the fourth generation, for the iniquity of the Amorites is not yet complete" (Gen 15:16).

For some commentators, this is enough. God does as he pleases, and we humans would do well to be pleased with it too. The actions of God through Joshua can never be repeated,[4] as they have a very specific role in God's unfolding purposes, but they stand as a template for the eschatological battle.[5]

But reading the events of the book of Joshua continues to make many of us squirm—or weep. The good news is that Scripture permits, even invites, the sort of faithful wrestling exercised by the psalmists, the prophets, and Job. The good news is also that the biblical text itself demonstrates discomfort toward these events, and—remarkably—*so does God*. In fact, the overarching command to exterminate the Canaanites is tempered in multiple ways, as we shall set out below. As Webb and Oeste point out, in the quotation with which I began this chapter, God is a highly reluctant war God.

In order to understand this, we first need to consider the underlying meaning of one of the most important warfare words, *ḥerem*,[6] sometimes translated as "the ban," which we began discussing in chapter 5. As we shall see, despite the implication offered by some Bible translations, it does not equate to "slaughter."

What Does Ḥerem Mean?

While there are a number of words used for the conquest of Canaan, the word *ḥerem* is widely regarded as the most problematic, as it appears to validate the indiscriminate slaughter of men, women, and children. The issue can perhaps be exemplified with just two texts that are representative of the wider issue. The first is from Deuteronomy, which provides a setting for Moses's final instructions to the people of Israel as he reaches the end of his life:

> When the LORD your God brings you into the land you are entering to possess
> and drives out before you many nations—the Hittites, Girgashites, Amorites,

---

4. See the arguments in Matthew Rowley, "On the Impossibility of Imitating Biblical Violence," in Paynter and Spalione, *Bible on Violence*, 42–61; and Copan and Flannagan, *Did God Really Command Genocide?*, 53–60.

5. For an example of such a perspective, see Eugene Merrill,

"The Case for Moderate Discontinuity," in C. S. Cowles, Eugene H. Merrill, Daniel L. Gard, and Tremper Longman III, *Show Them No Mercy: Four Views on God and Canaanite Genocide* (Grand Rapids, Zondervan, 2003), 91.

6. The word is sometimes written *cherem* or *herem*.

Canaanites, Perizzites, Hivites and Jebusites, seven nations larger and stronger than you—and when the LORD your God has delivered them over to you and you have defeated them, *then you must destroy them totally*. Make no treaty with them, and show them no mercy. (Deut 7:1–6, emphasis added)

The second typical text is taken from the book of Joshua, where Joshua is shown to be obeying these instructions:

At that time Joshua went and destroyed the Anakites from the hill country: from Hebron, Debir and Anab, from all the hill country of Judah, and from all the hill country of Israel. Joshua *totally destroyed* them and their towns. No Anakites were left in Israelite territory; only in Gaza, Gath and Ashdod did any survive. (Josh 11:21–22; emphasis added)

In the excerpts given above, *ḥerem* was translated in terms of total destruction and marked in italics. It is a technical word that has links with the modern English word *harem* and an Arabic word that may be familiar to readers, *haram* ("forbidden"). The underlying idea is not destruction but removal of the object or person from normal life. When in the biblical text the action is committed against an object, it may imply destruction, but it may equally be accomplished by bringing that object intact into the sanctuary.

When the action is committed against a people group, it probably means removing that people group from existence.[7] This is not the same as killing every member of that people group but necessitates the killing of the king[8] and the scattering or absorption of that people group so that they are blotted out from memory (cf. Exod 17:14). Clearly the action did not exclude killing, and there are other verbs that imply death within the narratives, but *ḥerem* is probably the most theologically significant word in the lexicon of the conquest, and it does not equate to "massacre," as is often believed.

Additionally, pragmatic reasoning suggests that the individuals Joshua encountered at the various cities he conquered are unlikely to have been whole families. In Joshua 2:9–11, Rahab describes the fear that went ahead of Joshua's army, and while she herself had clearly not fled, it is not unreasonable to assume that many men would have sent their families away. We see something similar in 1 Samuel 15:6, where the Kenites clear out in advance of Saul's army. But we also need to notice the presence of symbolism and hyperbolic representation in the text.

---

7. Walton and Walton, *Lost World of the Israelite Conquest*, 169–229.

8. Webb and Oeste, *Bloody, Brutal and Barbaric?*, 204–30.

Rhetoric and Hyperbole

The war rhetoric of the book of Joshua is told in a very stylized way. Note the repeated patterns of seven in the Jericho account (Josh 6:4–16). It was seven nations that were designated for *ḥerem* in Deuteronomy 7, and there is a very stylized way of describing what Joshua does. As Nicholas Wolterstorff writes:

> The first time one reads that Joshua struck down all the inhabitants of a city with the edge of the sword, namely, in the story of the conquest of Jericho (6:21), one makes nothing of it. But the phrasing—or close variants thereupon— gets repeated, seven times in close succession in chapter 10, two more times in chapter 11, and several times in other chapters. The repetition makes it unmistakable that we are dealing here with a formulaic literary convention.[9]

Furthermore, the seven nations designated for *ḥerem* in Deuteronomy probably no longer existed at the time that the text reached its final form. (Deuteronomy is widely regarded to have been written quite late in Israel's history.) This suggests that the instruction, at least as conveyed in that text, is to be regarded in a symbolic sense rather than a literal one.[10]

In other words, the intention of the text may not be so much about mortality figures but rather about making an ideo-theological claim upon the land. This is further supported by the archaeological data.

Archaeology

It is important that we do not consider archaeology to "trump" the textual accounts. Excavated artifacts require interpretation just as much as texts do, and the archaeological enterprise can be every bit as ideologically driven as biblical study. However, archaeology can help us to understand the biblical background and can shed helpful light upon the text.

The excavations at Hazor support (but do not "prove") the biblical account in Joshua 11:13. There is an intense burn layer from approximately the right date.[11] However, the overall impression from the archaeological evidence is that the conquest was a rather more gradual affair than a cursory reading of Joshua might imply. Unusually, this is something about which conservative and skeptical biblical historians broadly agree. Maximalist[12] scholar Kenneth Kitchen describes the conquest as "an entry into Canaan, initial raids and slow settlement,"[13] while minimalist historian

---

9. Nicholas Wolterstorff, "Reading Joshua," in *Divine Evil? The Moral Character of the God of Abraham*, ed. Michael Bergman, Michael J. Murray, and Michael C. Rea (Oxford: Oxford University Press, 2010), 251.

10. Moberly, *Old Testament Theology*, 59.

11. Amnon Ben-Tor, "Who Destroyed Canaanite Hazor?," *Biblical Archaeology Review* 39.4 (2013): 26–36, 58.

12. The terms *maximalism* and *minimalism* refer to biblical historians who view the biblical storyline as a highly accurate historical account or an unreliable historical account, respectively.

13. Kenneth Kitchen, *On the Reliability of the Old Testament* (Grand Rapids: Eerdmans, 2003), 239.

Philip Davies says that "the archaeologist does not see here a vital or dramatic moment in Palestine's history when everything changes as 'Israel' enters the scene."[14]

So the theological lexicon, the literary genre, and the archaeology all cast doubt on the idea that Joshua scorched his way into Canaan, slaughtering all in his path. But alongside all of this, there is another voice within the text of Joshua itself, and here we begin to discover the devalorization of militarism.

Countercurrents in Joshua

Alongside the militant narrative in Joshua, there is another voice that appears to be in contention with it. This, which I term a countercurrent, is expressed in a number of ways.

Twisting God's Arm?

First, there are a number of people in the narrative who manage to buck the trend of native extermination/Israelite victory. Rahab of Jericho is saved from the destruction of her city on the basis of her expression of faith and consequent actions (Josh 2), whereas Achan, an Israelite, becomes subject to *ḥerem* for his disobedience (Josh 7). Rather like Rahab are the Gibeonites, who use trickery to make peace with Joshua rather than suffer *ḥerem*, again on the basis of their faith in God (Josh 9). From these narratives we are led to the conclusion that membership of the nation, or destruction by it, depends more upon faith than it does upon bloodlines.

But we do not get the sense that these individuals have twisted God's arm in negotiating their survival. Rahab is brought into the heart (lit. the "innards," Josh 6:25) of the nation and finds her way into David's family line, as Matthew's genealogy makes clear (Matt 1:5). She even appears in the book of Hebrews, with her salvation out of conquest paralleled with the conquest element of the Jericho account (Heb 11:30–31).

The Gibeonites likewise become so integrated into the nation that they serve at the temple (Josh 9:23, 27), and Joshua keeps his *covenant* with them (note this theologically charged term, vv. 16–17) to the extent of going to war to defend them (Josh 10). Much later, the Gibeonites are so integrated that they help Nehemiah with the rebuilding of the walls of Jerusalem (Neh 3:7; 7:25). God's willingness to allow even more people than Rahab and the Gibeonites to escape death and become incorporated in this way is hinted at in Joshua 11:19: "Except for the Hivites living in Gibeon, not one city made a treaty of peace with the Israelites, who took them all in battle."

---

14. Philip Davies, *The History of Ancient Israel: A Guide for the Perplexed* (London: Bloomsbury, 2015), 112–13.

Incomplete Conquest

The second element of the countercurrent in Joshua is the question of how total the conquest was. While we encounter what I term a "totalizing voice" that makes grand claims of total conquest, alongside it there is a more moderate one. Perhaps the most striking example is found in Joshua 10:20, where the two halves of the verse appear to contradict one another:[15]

> When Joshua and the sons of Israel had finished striking them with a great blow until *they were wiped out*, and when *the remnant that remained of them* had entered into the fortified cities. . . . (ESV; emphases added)

We also encounter different accounts of how complete the conquest was in terms of territory taken. Near the end of the book of Joshua, we read a summary account implying that the whole territory is subdued:

> So the LORD gave Israel all the land he had sworn to give their ancestors, and they took possession of it and settled there. The LORD gave them rest on every side, just as he had sworn to their ancestors. Not one of their enemies withstood them; the LORD gave all their enemies into their hands. (Josh 21:43–44)

But at the beginning of Judges, it is clear that there is still territory to be taken. For example, the opening words of the book are:

> After the death of Joshua, the Israelites asked the LORD, "Who of us is to go up first to fight against the Canaanites?"
>
> The LORD answered, "Judah shall go up; I have given the land into their hands."
>
> The men of Judah then said to the Simeonites their fellow Israelites, "Come up with us into the territory allotted to us, to fight against the Canaanites." (Judg 1:1–3)

Opinions vary about the cause of such an apparent contradiction. Rejecting the inclination of those who would simply appeal to the text being compiled from a number of historical traditions, Brevard Childs puts it down to the "unique theological perspective of the Deuteronomic editor,"[16] who is entirely unembarrassed by the tension, using it to emphasize both the "ideal" situation when Israel is obedient and the consequences of disobedience.[17] In other words, the writer(s) have different theological perspectives. An alternate proposal is provided by K. Lawson Younger, who suggests that understanding the extent of the hyperbole in the Joshua account

---

15. Many more examples are given in Copan and Flannagan, *Did God Really Command Genocide?*, 86–87.

16. The "Deuteronomic editor" is not the editor of Deuteronomy, but of the Deuteronomic writings, broadly Judges to 2 Kings.

17. Brevard Childs, *Introduction to the Old Testament as Scripture* (London: SCM, 1979), 249.

removes the problem: "It is not meant to be interpreted in a wooden, literal sense."[18] There is, Lawson insists, no reason to interpret the Joshua text as claiming total conquest.

It does not seem to me that these two explanations are necessarily at variance with one another. The use of hyperbole in the Joshua account of the conquest is entirely consistent with a vigorous theological claim to the land. Alongside this is the more cautious, perhaps more historically tethered voice, both within Joshua itself and also in Judges. In any case, we need to notice the tension and that the narrative of "total war" is contested within the text itself.

Whose Side Is God On?

Another element of the countercurrent comes in the unexpected moment when Joshua encounters a man with a drawn sword as he is contemplating the attack on Jericho:

> Now when Joshua was near Jericho, he looked up and saw a man standing in front of him with a drawn sword in his hand. Joshua went up to him and asked, "Are you for us or for our enemies?"
>
> "Neither," he replied, "but as commander of the army of the LORD I have now come." (Josh 5:13–14)

Until this point in the story, Joshua has never had any cause to doubt God's unequivo- cal commitment to Israel. Joshua has witnessed the plagues against Egypt, the parting of the Red Sea, and the destruction of Pharaoh's army; he has been miraculously fed and watered in the desert; and he has stood at the foot of Mount Sinai as it shook and smoked with the presence of the covenant-making God. But the answer from the man—who turns out be commander of the heavenly host—is astonishing. *Are you for us or for our enemies? Neither.* God has allegiance to no nation. He will lend his support where he wills, but he is the ruler, and they are the subjects. I would argue that this little narrative, often overlooked by readers, should be a controlling text as we move through the remainder of the book of Joshua.

A Developing Story

Another piece of the puzzle is offered by William Webb and Gordon Oeste,[19] who draw on many of the ideas outlined above to argue that, while God does command some violence at the point of the conquest, the idea that he commanded a general massacre to the extent of genocide is to fail to understand the hyperbolic and rhetorical purpose of the text. Their core argument is that, troubling as the

---

18. K. Lawson Younger, *Ancient Conquest Accounts: A Study in Ancient Near Eastern and Biblical History Writing*, JSOTSup 98 (Sheffield: Sheffield Academic, 1990), 247.

19. Webb and Oeste, *Bloody, Brutal and Barbaric?*.

story continues to be, it is in itself a substantial move forward from the ancient Near Eastern alternatives—a redemptive movement. Nor is it the end of the story. It needs to be viewed as a step on the way to the final subversion of the war machine, to the self-sacrificing, nonviolent messiah, and to the eschatological goal of shalom in the new heavens and the new earth.

Incomplete as all of these answers are, Webb and Oeste's comments, in conjunction with the other counternarratives we have identified, position us well to view the conquest narratives within the overall biblical witness on the subject of violence.[20] We now turn our attention to some other significant redemptive moves.

Victory in Weakness

We will remain with the conquest of Canaan for a little longer. One of the key themes from the exodus through to the conclusion of the conquest is that the battle is God's rather than Israel's.[21] On the borders of the Red Sea, Moses instructs the people, "Stand firm and you will see the deliverance the Lord will bring you today" (Exod 14:13).

In the lead-up to the battle of Jericho, this is made very clear. Boyd Seevers points out the apparently ludicrous geography and timing of the circumcision that Joshua orders. The new generation of Israelites had not been circumcised in the desert. And yet immediately after they have entered the land, Joshua orders them circumcised *en masse* and Passover to be celebrated. Seevers suggests that it would be far wiser for them to have done these things on the far side of the Jordan.[22] But instead, they cross the river, move up to Gilgal, which is a very short distance from Jericho, and are circumcised virtually within sight of the city. This would have made them extremely vulnerable for several days.

Their vulnerability would have been compounded by the fact that they may have been underequipped. Spears are not mentioned at all in the book of Joshua, and Judges 5:8 explicitly states that they did not possess them. With this in mind, the instruction not to keep any weapons or metals as plunder after Jericho fell (Josh 6:19) must have felt like lunacy.[23]

The "lunacy" continues into the book of Judges, where God calls Gideon—a lad so timid that he is threshing in a winepress (Judg 6:11)—to deliver Israel from the Midianites. The conversation that Gideon has with God makes repeated, sometimes sardonic, reference to his weakness:

20. Whatever mitigation we accord to the conquest narratives along the lines of the suggestions above, we need to understand that they are *sui generis*; that is, they are "in a class of their own." They are positioned at a unique point in the history of God's dealings with humanity, and this point can never be repeated.

21. Indeed, the theme continues beyond the end of the conquest; e.g., see 2 Chr 20:15. The difference is that some of the battles

undertaken later in Israel's history are in disobedience, or at least indifference, to the will of God.

22. Boyd Seevers, *Warfare in the Old Testament: The Organization, Weapons, and Tactics of Ancient Near Eastern Armies* (Grand Rapids: Kregel, 2013), 24.

23. Seevers, *Warfare in the Old Testament*, 34, 60.

> The LORD turned to him and said, "Go *in the strength you have* and save Israel out of Midian's hand. Am I not sending you?"
>
> "Pardon me, my lord," Gideon replied, "but how can I save Israel? *My clan is the weakest* in Manasseh, and *I am the least* in my family."
>
> The LORD answered, "I will be with you, and you will strike down all the Midianites." (Judg 6:14–16, emphases added)

Once Gideon has mustered his army, God twice tells him he has *too many* men (Judg 7:2, 4), sequentially whittling down his army from thirty-two thousand men to ten thousand and then to just three hundred. This is despite the enemy being encamped as "thick as locusts," with camels that "could no more be counted than the sand on the seashore" (v. 12). Only then, and with an odd weaponry set that largely relied on trumpets, torches, and clay pots (vv. 16–20), does Gideon engage the enemy and win. Note that the men might have shouted about swords, but their hands were encumbered with other things:

> The three companies blew the trumpets and smashed the jars. Grasping the *torches in their left hands* and holding *in their right hands the trumpets* they were to blow, they shouted, "A sword for the LORD and for Gideon!" (v. 20)

The theme of God assisting the people to victory despite their weakness is a common one. The story of David and Goliath would be another good example, where the utterly underequipped shepherd lad faces the giant bristling with aggressive and defensive arms, and defies him, before proceeding to prove his words true:

> You come against me with sword and spear and javelin, but I come against you in the name of the LORD Almighty, the God of the armies of Israel, whom you have defied. (1 Sam 17:45)

This leads us to the consideration of another way in which God involves himself in battles—by supernaturally averting them.

Divine Aversion to Warfare

Probably the most striking example of such divine intervention is in 2 Kings 6–7. This tells a bizarre, comedic[24] story that begins with the king of Aram[25] sending a unit of soldiers to try to capture Elisha, who seems to be supernaturally spying upon him. The soldiers surround Dothan, where Elisha is staying, with their horses and chariots; but unbeknown to them, *they* become encircled by divine horses and

---

24. Robert LaBarbera, "The Man of War and the Man of God: Social Satire in 2 Kings 6:8–7:20," *CBQ* 46.4 (1984): 637–51.

25. In some translations "Aram" is rendered "Syria."

chariots of fire (6:15–17). As the men come down toward the prophet, they are struck blind. This may be the blindness of confusion rather than physical blindness, like the blindness that struck Lot's would-be attackers in Sodom (Gen 19:11). In either case, they trustingly follow Elisha, and he leads them directly into the court of the king of Israel, who is somewhat perplexed. He asks Elisha if he should kill the men that the prophet has served up on a plate. Elisha's reply is astonishing:

> "Do not kill them," he answered. "Would you kill those you have captured with your own sword or bow? Set food and water before them so that they may eat and drink and then go back to their master." So he prepared a great feast for them, and after they had finished eating and drinking, he sent them away, and they returned to their master. (2 Kgs 6:22–23)

Disarmed by Israel's charm offensive, the soldiers of Aram return home, and for a while there is peace: "So the bands from Aram stopped raiding Israel's territory" (v. 23).

This is not the end of the story, however. The king of Aram soon tries again to engage Israel in combat. On this occasion, the king sends his entire army to besiege Samaria, and the siege is indeed harsh and prolonged (2 Kgs 6:24–25). But God has a different trick up his sleeve this time. Previously he made seeing eyes blind (particularly to the reality of the heavenly army that was present) and sent soldiers away well-fed. This time, the Arameans' spiritually deaf ears hear the attack of an army that is not human (7:6), and in their flight they abandon their camp and supplies (v. 7), presumably returning home hungry. The military provisions serve instead as a rich banquet for the four hungry lepers who lift the siege without lifting a finger (v. 8). Perhaps this reappropriation of campaign food into a feast for beggars is the equivalent of the prophetic promise that swords will be beaten into ploughshares (Isa 2:4; Mic 4:3).

Ambivalence toward Militarization
The King's Army

It was not until the time of David that Israel began to acquire a standing army. Prior to that, leaders were largely dependent upon a military muster, an army temporarily assembled for a particular exigency (e.g., Judg 20:1–2; 1 Sam 11:6–8). Indeed, there are indications that a standing army was contrary to God's intention for kingship. In Deuteronomy a king was not to be characterized by the size of his chariot force:

> The king, moreover, must not acquire great numbers of horses for himself or make the people return to Egypt to get more of them, for the LORD has told you, "You are not to go back that way again." (Deut 17:16)

This emphasis against cavalry and chariot technology[26] is emphasized again in Joshua 11, where captured horses are to be hamstrung, that is, put out of action for military use. Walter Brueggemann views this as a radical policy, intended to prevent endless expansionism:

> All the real action . . . is to be done by Israelites, who are to sabotage and immobilise the imperial weapons of war. Yahweh undertakes no direct action. We should note that in this direct command, the only object of violence is horses and chariots, i.e., weapons. There is nothing here about burning cities, killing kings or people, or seizing war booty. Yahweh's is a very lean mandate that addresses the simple, most important issue, the military threat of monarchal power against this alternative community lacking in military technology.[27]

Accordingly, Samuel tries to dissuade the people from appointing a king, warning them that he will build his army at their expense:

> This is what the king who will reign over you will claim as his rights: He will take your sons and make them serve with his chariots and horses, and they will run in front of his chariots. Some he will assign to be commanders of thousands and commanders of fifties . . . and still others to make weapons of war and equipment for his chariots. (1 Sam 8:11–12)

This is indeed what happens. In 1 Kings 10, a chapter which sets out the excess (one might say obscenity) of Solomon's wealth, we read this:

> Solomon accumulated chariots and horses; he had fourteen hundred chariots and twelve thousand horses, which he kept in the chariot cities and also with him in Jerusalem. (1 Kgs 10:26)

Thus, the military project was closely tied up with a negative evaluation of kingship.

David's Census

Another striking moment when militarization is devalorized is found in 1 Chronicles 21.[28] King David decides that he wishes to conduct a census. His adviser and second-in-command, Joab, counsels against such an action. But David

---

26. Allusion to horses here probably relates to chariots, as Israel does not appear to have used cavalry until quite late (Seevers, *Warfare in the Old Testament*, 50–51).

27. Walter Brueggemann, *Divine Presence amid Violence: Contextualising the Book of Joshua* (Milton Keynes: Paternoster, 2009), 22.

28. The parallel passage of 2 Sam 24 contains some differences, most notably concerning who incited David to conduct the census. Consideration of this matter is outside the scope of the present discussion.

will have his way. So Joab does as he is bid (more or less; see v. 6) and reports back with the numbers. At this point we start perhaps to understand the nature of David's intention. He is not counting the people to ensure that there is sufficient food for them all in a dry season. He is not even counting them for the purposes of taxation. What he is counting are fighting men: "In all Israel there were one million one hundred thousand men drawing the sword, and in Judah four hundred and seventy thousand drawing the sword" (v. 5, author's translation). David is wishing to make a tally of his military might. This is driven by one of two motives, it seems. Either David wishes to glory in his military strength, or he feels insecure and wants to reassure himself. Either way, his confidence in God is being replaced by confidence in the sword.

God is displeased with David's actions and offers him the option between three different modes of punishment, any one of which will significantly reduce the population David has just tallied. Within the second and third options, note again the sword motif:

> Take your choice: three years of famine, three months of being swept away before your enemies, with their swords overtaking you, or three days of the sword of the Lord—days of plague in the land." (1 Chr 21:11b–12a)

David emphatically rejects three months of war as too terrible to contemplate: "Let me fall into the hands of the Lord, for his mercy is very great, but do not let me fall into human hands" (v. 13). There is an important lesson here about the brutality of human warfare. So David chooses plague, and his intuition proves correct. Although the angel of the Lord is revealed "standing between heaven and earth, with a *drawn sword* in his hand extended over Jerusalem" (v. 16), God's mercy intervenes before the capital city is touched.

The passage poses a number of theological questions that lie beyond the scope of this discussion. However, it does function as a sharp critique of David's confidence in military power and as a commentary on the relative tenderness of the divine warrior. We might compare God's mercy here with David's lack of it, in the victory song that he sings at the end of his life:

> I pursued my enemies and crushed them;
> > I did not turn back till they were destroyed.
> I crushed them completely, and they could not rise;
> > they fell beneath my feet. (2 Sam 22:38–39)

God relented, but David did not.

Temple-Building

There is another moment in the life of David that is instructive for our inquiry. This is his desire to build a temple for God, and God's rejection of the offer. The story is related in 2 Samuel 7 and 1 Chronicles 17, but it is elsewhere in Chronicles that we discover the reason for God's refusal. David publicly explains why:

> God said to me, "You may not build a house for my name, for you are a man of war and have shed blood." (1 Chr 28:3 ESV)

It was standard practice in the ancient Near East that a victorious warrior would construct a temple for his deity.[29] In other words, temple-building was inherently bound up with warfare. But this was not to be the case in Israel. David was a "man of war"; he had killed his "tens of thousands" (1 Sam 18:7), and as a consequence he was *unfit* to build. That task would be handed down to his son Solomon, whose name means "peace." This wordplay is evident when David charges his son with the task:

> This word of the LORD came to me: "You have shed much blood and have fought many wars. You are not to build a house for my Name, because you have shed much blood on the earth in my sight. But you will have a son who will be a man of peace and rest. . . . His name will be Solomon [*Shelomoh*], and I will grant Israel peace [*shalom*] and quiet during his reign." (1 Chr 22:8–9)

Before we move on, there is one more strand in the theme of devalorization of the military, and this relates to the motif of foolish warriors.

Foolish Warriors and Valorous Women

Naaman

There are a number of places in the Old Testament where warriors, "mighty men," are represented as foolish, blundering thugs. We have already seen the example of these soldiers of Aram in our discussion of 2 Kings 6–7 above. To this we might add the characterization of Naaman in the preceding chapter. Our author begins by heaping up the epithets. Naaman is "commander of the army of the king of Aram," a "great man," "highly regarded," a "valiant soldier" (2 Kgs 5:1). After such a buildup, it is an anticlimax to discover that he has leprosy—which would disqualify him from military command and from serving in the king's presence. However, it is not Naaman's leprosy that is his chief problem but rather his pride. To his credit, he does pay heed to the word of the "little lass"[30] from Israel who serves his wife and sets out for Israel to seek healing from their God. But he travels there in great pomp, with a letter of authorization (command, even) from his king and with rich gifts with which to buy the favor of the Israelite God. He goes first to the king of Israel, and then in all his pomp to Elisha (vv. 5–6, 9). Elisha will have none of it. In fact, he will not even dignify Naaman by going out to meet him. Instead, he sends the dismissive word that Naaman is to bathe seven times in the Jordan (v. 10).

---

29. This is explored in more detail in Webb and Oeste, *Bloody, Brutal and Barbaric?*, 297–303.

30. Verse 2, author's translation.

Again, Naaman's pride almost gets in the way. He wants the man of God to treat him with dignity, to perform a ritual. Why should he bathe in the muddy Jordan River when there are far more acceptable rivers back at home? However, he allows himself to be persuaded by his servants and is healed. Tellingly, when he comes up out of the water on the seventh occasion, his skin is like that of a "young lad" (v. 14, author's translation), the counterpart to the "young lass" who gave him the advice in the first place. This is a story where humility triumphs, and neither pride nor power and wealth can avail. The great military man is at once humbled in his pride and vindicated in his humility.

Samson

The book of Judges contains a number of instances where mighty military men are depicted as foolish. The great Samson is characterized as gorilla-like throughout, unable to speak with common courtesy or even a decent grasp of Hebrew syntax. He resorts to thuggish behavior at the least provocation. He only prays twice in the entire narrative, both are times when his life is at stake. On at least the first of those occasions, his prayer sounds more like an ultimatum than a humble request (Judg 15:18). Overall, as I have argued elsewhere,[31] his presentation in Judges is far from positive and casts a critical eye on his claimed mighty acts.

Three Warrior Women

But it is in the striking actions of three valorous women that perhaps the most surprising subversion of masculine militarism is found. We briefly considered the story of Deborah and Barak in the previous chapter. Barak, commander of the army, is too fearful to go to battle unless Deborah comes with him (Judg 4:8). Because of this timidity, or faithlessness, or lack of leadership, the victory is given into the hands of a woman (v. 9). The woman in question, of course, is not Deborah but Jael, who initially shelters the fleeing enemy captain before murdering him. In a nice piece of satire by our author, the fleeing Sisera tells Jael to inform anyone seeking to search the tent that "no man" is present (v. 20). This proves to be true, for by the time they come looking, there is no living man to be found. But it additionally highlights for us one of the key themes of the text. There is no real "man" in the story. Sisera, and through him Barak, has been unmanned by Jael.[32] The victory goes to a woman, and, moreover, one who uses a domestic implement rather than a weapon of war.

This is not the only place where a woman kills a man in Judges. In a less well-known passage we meet ambitious Abimelech, who murders his seventy brothers

31. Helen Paynter, "'Revenge for My Two Eyes': Talion and Mimesis in the Samson Narrative," *BibInt* 26.2 (2018): 133–57.

32. "Sisera the commander was defined by his chariots.... To dismount from his chariot... is the dishonorable act *par excellence*: the man is forced to give up the very sign of his superiority, hence, of his identity based upon it" (Mieke Bal, *Murder and Difference: Gender, Genre, and Scholarship on Sisera's Death*, trans. Matthew Gumbert [Bloomington: Indiana University Press, 1988], 120).

(9:5) in his attempt to be declared king. A few years later, as he is fighting off a coup attempt, he burns the fortress of Shechem along with the one thousand men and women who were sheltering there (v. 49). When he attempts to do the same to Thebez, a woman drops an upper millstone on his head as he approaches the fortress wall (v. 53). Once again, it is a woman's victory, using whatever domestic implement she has to hand. Further, the poetic justice is heightened by the inverse symmetry of seventy brothers murdered "on one stone" (v. 5) and Abimelech meeting his end when one stone is dropped on him.

Honor and shame were a fundamental part of the society that produced the Old Testament, and nowhere do we see these themes more clearly than in the book of Judges. It is honor that causes Samson to indulge in many of his violent vendettas (e.g., Judg 14:18–19), and indeed it seems to be shame that motivates his final revenge in the temple of Baal (16:28). It is fear of shame that drives Jephthah to keep the vow against his daughter that he should never have made in the first place (11:30–35).[33] Within this worldview, the ways that these "mighty warriors" are represented as bumbling buffoons, upstaged by women who have nothing more to hand than domestic implements, is a shaming device. This serves further to subvert the militarism of these societies, and of the men in them.

We have considered a number of ways in which militarism is devalorized by the Bible. The second great redemptive theme is the invalidation of vengeance.

INVALIDATION OF VENGEANCE
Human Tendency to Avenge

In chapter 4 we looked at the human tendency to vengeance. We saw how violence enters the human story in Genesis 4 with the original fratricide and then escalates later in the same chapter with Lamech taking seventyfold vengeance for an act of violence against him. Thus begins the descent into mimetic violence, so ably described by René Girard, as we saw in chapter 1 above. There are many, many examples of violent vengeance in Scripture.

David's house was particularly riddled with such rivalries. After his daughter Tamar was raped by their half-brother Amnon (2 Sam 13:1–22), Tamar's full brother Absalom took his time but eventually murdered his brother for the evil he had done (vv. 23–29). Another brother, Adonijah, died on the instructions of Solomon because he had the temerity to make a bid for the crown (1 Kgs 1:1–2:25).

We saw in chapter 6 how David's chief mighty man Joab exacted vengeance

---

33. Compare this with Saul's climbdown in similar circumstances (1 Sam 14:26–46). Ashley Hibbard points out that the significant difference between these two narratives is that Jonathan has people to advocate for him (1 Sam 14:45), but there is nobody to speak for Jephthah's daughter (Ashley Hibbard, "Jonathan and Jephthah's Daughter," Centre for the Study of Bible & Violence, April 27, 2021, www.csbvbristol.org.uk/2021/04/27/jonathan-and-jephthahs-daughter/).

against Abner for his brother's battle-killing (2 Sam 3:27). For Joab's actions, David instructed Solomon to bring revenge upon this brutal but loyal henchman after David's death. "Do not let his gray head go down to Sheol in peace" (1 Kgs 2:6 ESV).

Nor is this the most disturbing act of vengeance that David commanded on his deathbed. Shimei was a character whose only offense against David was to mock him loudly and to throw dirt and stones at him as David was leaving Jerusalem during Absalom's rebellion (2 Sam 16:5–13). In his lifetime, David appeared to show great restraint toward him when urged to have him put to death (19:22–23). But the matter was far from forgotten, as we discover on David's deathbed. "Bring his gray head down to the grave in blood" (1 Kgs 2:8–9). David's very last recorded words show that he died a bitter man.

Judicial Restraint of Vengeance

Because of the human tendency to excessive and unrestrained vengeance, shown so clearly in these and other narratives, the law of the Torah sought to limit that vengeance in two particular ways. As we have discussed, the *lex talionis* ("an eye for an eye") limited appropriate vengeance to that which was reciprocal, commensurate, and exercised under the aegis of the elders. Second, just as God had extended mercy to the first manslayer in Genesis 4, there were instructions for the provision of cities of refuge (Num 35:9–24; Deut 4:41–43), which sheltered someone who had inadvertently killed another person from the legitimate pursuit of the "avenger of blood."

The life and death of Jesus as the culmination of the great redemptive themes we are identifying will be the focus of the next chapter. But it might be helpful here to consider Jesus's words in regard to the law of talion.

> You have heard that it was said, "Eye for eye, and tooth for tooth." But I tell you, do not resist an evil person. If anyone slaps you on the right cheek, turn to them the other cheek also. (Matt 5:38–39)

In the light of the Sermon on the Mount, the *lex talionis* receives bad press from many modern writers. Gregory Boyd, for example, describes this as Jesus *repudiating* the law.[34] In support of this claim, Boyd comments that the *lex talionis* is often not expressed in terms of a limit but a prescription. "Show no pity: life for life, eye for eye, tooth for tooth, hand for hand, foot for foot" (Deut 19:21).

But it is important to remember the stratified society within which this law was operative, particularly by the time the later formulation in Deuteronomy was codified. In a society where wealth and influence can buy impunity, a law that not only limits punishment, but also prescribes it, surely has merit. We see the lack of

---

34. Gregory Boyd, *Crucifixion of the Warrior God: Interpreting the Old Testament's Violent Portraits of God in Light of the Cross*, 2 vols. (Minneapolis: Fortress, 2017), 1:71.

such legal impartiality in the account of the rape of Tamar, for instance (2 Sam 13). Amnon, the king's eldest son and the crown prince, receives no official sanction for his appalling actions against his half-sister. A similar example of royal impunity might be seen in the later account of Ahab's theft of Naboth's vineyard by means of judicial murder (1 Kgs 21). It is only because of the intervention of the prophet Elijah that Ahab receives any punishment. It seems clear that by this point in Israel's history the king and his family are functionally above the law. In this context, then, the instruction to "show no pity" would seem to be good news for those at risk of abuse by their more powerful neighbors.

In recent years, news stories from many parts of the world have shown the contemporary relevance of this principle that powerful people should not have impunity for their actions. By way of examples, we could name the casting couch of Harvey Weinstein,[35] the apparent implication of a crown prince of Saudi Arabia in the murder of the journalist Jamal Khashoggi,[36] and the seeming impunity that a senior member of the British royal family enjoys despite credible allegations of his involvement in Jeffrey Epstein's underage sex parties.[37]

Jesus's call to nonresistance and enemy love is something that few individuals and no societies have attained. Therefore, most interpreters read from a position on the ethical scale somewhere between the harsh but impartial justice of *lex talionis* and the ideal that Jesus sets out. The tendency of the modern interpreter then, is to look backward, as it were, to the law of talion, and forward to Jesus's ideal. This then leads interpreters to view the two as antithetical, pulling in opposite directions.[38]

Talion   Us   Turn the other cheek

But the idea that Jesus is repudiating the law of talion fails to take account of the significant benefit that the law brought in its day. A more helpful perspective is to see

35. Jan Ransom, "Harvey Weinstein's Stunning Downfall: 23 Years in Prison," *New York Times*, March 11, 2020, www.nytimes.com/2020/03/11/nyregion/harvey-weinstein-sentencing.html

36. Ben Hubbard, "Saudi Arabia Seeks Death Penalty for 5 Suspects in Khashoggi Killing," *New York Times*, January 3, 2019, www.nytimes.com/2019/01/03/world/middleeast/saudi-arabia-khashoggi-death-penalty.html.

37. Matthew Weaver, "Prince Andrew Refuses to Deny He Stayed in Jeffrey Epstein Mansion," *Guardian*, December 14, 2020, www.theguardian.com/uk-news/2020/dec/14/prince-andrew-refuses-to-deny-he-stayed-in-jeffrey-epstein-mansion.

38. These diagrams were first published in Paynter, *God of Violence Yesterday, God of Love Today?*, 114–15.

how the law of talion has limited vengeance and progressed the ethic in a direction of nonviolence, which Jesus considerably extends in the Sermon on the Mount.

Jesus's words, then, are not repudiation but intensification of the nonviolent imperative. We will consider how he works this out in practice in the following chapter. First, however, we turn to the third redemptive move that the Old Testament makes: the shift to the innocence of the victim.

THE INNOCENT VICTIM

Casual readers of the Old Testament find it easy to identify prooftexts that God blesses those who are obedient, whether this is with health, wealth, or military success. A key text in this theme is Deuteronomy 28, which lists the blessings and curses of the covenant. If Israel is obedient to the covenant, the chapter says, they will be blessed in many ways. The land will bear plentiful harvests, they will have many children, and their enemies will flee before them. On the other hand, if Israel is unfaithful to the covenant commands, the converse will be true. The land will fail to yield a harvest, there will be a fall in the fertility rate, and there will be military defeat.

There are at least two important misunderstandings that can arise from such texts. The first of them, which we will only touch on briefly, is to assume that such words can be directly applied to modern nations. They were not spoken to twenty-first century America (for example); they were addressed to Israel, God's covenant people. Any conclusions that we wish to draw need to be derived from a careful and thoughtful consideration of who the covenant people of God are today and what relationship (if any) they have with particular geopolitical entities.[39] The second misunderstanding is to imagine that this is the only word that Scripture has to offer about prosperity and suffering. This is the mistake made by the proponents of the so-called "prosperity gospel," which collapse Scripture's subtle testimony about suffering into a mechanistic formula: God blesses the righteous.

It is also the mistake made by Job's friends in the extended investigation of the question of innocent suffering that the eponymous book comprises. While there is much about the book that remains mysterious, Job's innocence is clear (1:1–2:9; 42:8). He is not guilty of any significant wrongdoing, and the severe suffering that comes upon him is not caused by his own sin. His friends who, to their credit, come

39. I explore this further in Helen Paynter, "Porous Borders and Textual Ambiguity: Why Old Testament Israel is No Model for Modern Nationalism," *Journal of European Baptist Studies* 20.1 (2020): 117–30.

and sit in solidarity with him are unable to imagine such a deviation from the divine economy that they have in mind. Repeatedly they insist that Job must search his heart, identify his wrongdoing, repent of it, and thereby restore his good fortune (e.g., 4:7–8; 5:8). Repeatedly Job asserts his innocence (e.g., 31:5–35). This complex story gives the lie to a simple tit-for-tat theology where God guarantees that those who are righteous will be impervious to harm.

So alongside the theological strand that asserts that God rewards the righteous, we see another lying alongside it. Perhaps we can say that there is a dialogue between texts that assert that righteousness results in blessing and wickedness with a curse, and the texts that declare that sometimes the wicked prosper and the innocent suffer. Walter Brueggemann calls this *testimony and counter-testimony*:[40]

There are many such instances in the psalms. Compare these two examples:

Testimony

> The righteous person may have many troubles,
>> but the Lord delivers him from them all. . . .
> Evil will slay the wicked;
>> the foes of the righteous will be condemned. (Ps 34:19–21)

Counter-testimony

> This is what the wicked are like—
>> always free of care, they go on amassing wealth.
>
> Surely in vain I have kept my heart pure
>> and have washed my hands in innocence.
> All day long I have been afflicted,
>> and every morning brings new punishments. (Ps 73:12–14)

We see a similar counter-testimony in the servant song of Isaiah 52:13–53:12, where the faithful servant of the Lord is afflicted by the violence of his fellow human beings despite his innocence:

> See, my servant will act wisely. . . .
> . . . he was pierced for our transgressions,
>> he was crushed for our iniquities;
> the punishment that brought us peace was on him,
>> and by his wounds we are healed.
> We all, like sheep, have gone astray,
>> each of us has turned to our own way;

---

40. Walter Brueggemann, *Theology of the Old Testament: Testimony, Dispute, Advocacy* (Minneapolis: Fortress, 2005), 317.

and the LORD has laid on him
the iniquity of us all.
. . . though he had done no violence,
nor was any deceit in his mouth. (52:13; 53:5–6, 9)

The question of whether Isaiah has Jesus directly in view as he writes or whether he is writing about a contemporary situation relating to the exile, lies outside our current purview.[41] What is clear, however, is that Isaiah sets out unambiguously the possibility that a righteous person can suffer, and thus enters into dialogue with the texts that seem to equate righteousness with an exemption from the woes of life. We will track this theme into the New Testament in the following chapter.

CONCLUSION

In this chapter we have been considering three different redemptive strands where apparently well-established themes of violence within the Old Testament are subverted by the text itself. We have touched on some New Testament texts where these strands are continued, but we will develop these much more fully in future chapters.

First, we looked at a number of ways in which warfare is devalorized by the Old Testament. We considered the theological case for the conquest of Canaan and God's prerogative to act in judgment toward any of his creatures. Surprisingly, then, there is evidence of textual, and even divine, discomfort with totalizing war. We identified countercurrents in Joshua: where unexpected people escape from Joshua's conquest and find themselves included in the people of God, where God is revealed as being on nobody's side, and where a voice of restraint counterbalances the voice of total victory. More generally, we noticed a number of places where Scripture appears deeply ambivalent toward militarism. This includes warnings against army building and expansionism and God's deep hostility toward David's census of fighting men. We also noted God's direct intervention at times to avert war and his refusal to allow David, a man of blood, to build his temple. Finally, we identified a number of places where warriors are critiqued and mocked by the text, as their actions and characters are subverted and shamed by women.

The second redemptive strand that runs through the text is the progressive invalidation of vengeance. We noted how the human tendency to exercise violent vengeance is limited by Old Testament law, both through provision of cities of

---

41. For a christological reading of the servant, see, e.g., J. Alec Motyer, *The Prophecy of Isaiah: An Introduction and Commentary* (Downers Grove, IL: InterVarsity Press, 1993), 424–44. As an example of a different point of view, Zerubbabel is proposed as the suffering servant in John D. W. Watts, *Isaiah 34–66*, WBC 25 (Nashville: Thomas Nelson, 2005), 783–86. A third possibility is offered by Jonathan Lunde, who argues that the righteous servant of Isaiah refers to the righteous remnant of Israel, who suffer alongside those deserving the exilic punishment and thus points to Jesus in a typological way (Jonathan Lunde, *Following Jesus, the Servant King: A Biblical Theology of Covenantal Discipleship* [Grand Rapids, Zondervan, 2010], 232–35).

refuge and most particularly through the law of talion—"an eye for an eye." We then tracked this strand into the New Testament and considered how Jesus extends the anti-vengeance imperative, in his instruction to his followers to turn the other cheek and to love their enemies.

The third strand that we identified was the gradual development of a theology of innocent suffering, which lies alongside and in dialogue with the theology that God will vindicate the righteous. The possibility of an innocent sufferer establishes important theological precedence in order for us to understand the cross of Jesus Christ. It is to this that we will turn in our next chapter.

RELEVANT QUESTIONS

1. How well is the Old Testament's devalorization of militarism reflected in the teaching—and the children's curriculum—of your church?
2. How do we balance the disputing voices that Scripture contains on a number of themes, especially in our preaching and church teaching?
3. Does the Bible's emphasis on the possibility of innocent victims challenge the way we respond to those who make allegations of abuse?

CHAPTER 9

REDEMPTIVE TRAJECTORIES AT THE CROSS

When they hurled their insults at him, he did not retaliate; when he suffered, he made no threats.

1 Peter 2:23

All the great themes of Scripture that run through the Old Testament into the New find their supreme expression at the cross of Jesus Christ. In this chapter, we will pick up the three redemptive threads we began to examine in the previous chapter: the devalorization of violence, the invalidation of vengeance, and the emergence of the innocent victim. What we will discover is that the cross is the great moment where violence is revealed, shamed, subverted, and ultimately undone. First, however, we need to briefly survey the debate around the nature of the violence that is present in the atonement.

DIVINE VIOLENCE AT THE CROSS?

The cross is a violent event, there is no doubt about it. But where was God in relation to that violence? Here we enter the difficult territory of models of the atonement. By what means is God saving the world through his Son on Golgotha?

God as the Source of Violence

Broadly, atonement models fall into three categories. Proponents of the satisfaction models, which include propitiatory atonement, believe that human sin incurs God's righteous judgment.[1] God's wrath is directed toward humans on account of their sin, and he cannot simply overlook it because that would deny his holy nature. On the cross, Jesus is the recipient of God's righteous wrath and thereby diverts it from his people.

The problem with this model, as some see it, is that God is the author of the violence at the cross. The human violence of crown and nails is simply a visible

---

1. One of the first theologians to articulate a satisfaction model was Anselm (1033–1109 CE). See St. Anslem, *Cur Deus Homo* in *Proslogium; Monologium; An Appendix, In Behalf of the Fool by Gaunilon; and Cur Deus Homo*, trans. Sidney Norton Deane (Chicago: Open Court, 1939), 177–275.

manifestation of the divine violence that must be expressed toward Jesus in order for him to save the world. They therefore consider such a model incompatible with the idea of a nonviolent God who calls for nonviolence in his followers.[2]

> Reflecting on Black surrogacy, where White women hired "mammies" to care for their children, forcing them to accept low rates of pay and to neglect their own children, womanist theologian Delores Williams sees parallels with the substitutionary model of the cross:
>
> > Jesus represents the ultimate surrogate figure; he stands in the place of someone else: sinful humankind. Surrogacy, attached to this divine personage, thus takes on an aura of the sacred. It is therefore fitting and proper for black women to ask whether the image of a surrogate-God has salvific power for black women or whether this image supports and reinforces the exploitation that has accompanied their experience with surrogacy.[3]

For many Christian pacifists, this is a circle that can only be squared by denying the possibility of a substitutionary atonement and reading Scripture differently. However, this is often a retrograde action, whereby the interpreter's preconceptions are knowingly read back into their interpretation of Scripture.[4] Commonly allusion is made to an exploded "myth of redemptive violence"—a term we will consider more fully in chapters 10 and 14. By this logic, any punitive action by the Father upon the Son buys into the myth that violence can solve violence. A typical comment to this effect is this from a blog post by Richard Rohr.

> As long as we employ any retributive notion of God's offended justice (required punishment for wrongdoing), we trade our distinctive Christian message for the cold, hard justice that has prevailed in many cultures throughout history. We offer no redemptive alternative, but actually sanctify the very "powers and principalities" that Paul says unduly control the world (Ephesians 3:9–10; 6:12). We stay inside the small "myth of redemptive violence"—which might just be

2. For an overview of the relationship between atonement theologies and stances on nonviolence, see Jeffrey McPherson, "Violence and the Cross: The Affinity between Theories of Atonement and Christian Attitudes Toward War and Peace," in *The (De)Legitimization of Violence in Sacred and Human Contexts*, ed. Muhammad Shafiq and Thomas Donlin-Smith (New York: Palgrave Macmillan, 2021), 7–26.

3. Delores Williams, *Sisters in the Wilderness: The Challenge of Womanist God-Talk* (Maryknoll, NY: Orbis, 2013), 127.

4. As we discussed in ch. 2, readers always come to Scripture with preconceptions that shape their interpretation. This is why interpretations are always provisional and subject to the hermeneutical circle under the guidance of the Holy Spirit and within the community of disciples. However, when a stance is so fixed that it is itself a hermeneutical tool, the danger of misinterpretation is far higher.

the dominant story line of history. I think the punishment model is buried deep in most peoples' brain stem.[5]

However, as pacifist theologian Ron Sider argues, there is no contradiction per se in a God who acts in violent judgment and yet calls his disciples to live nonviolently:

> [Are we] involved in a logical contradiction and a heretical doctrine of the Trinity if we say both that Jesus taught nonviolence and God willed Jesus's death? This would be a logical contradiction only if Jesus condemns violence in precisely the same way that God uses violence at the cross. But that is not the case. The action of an infinite God substituting Godself for sinful persons at the cross is not identical with the action of finite persons using violence against other persons.[6]

As Sider suggests, in logical terms it is reasonable to reject human violence while accepting the possibility of divine violence, since certain actions are valid for God but not for humans. However, it would be illogical to make the opposite move. If "redemptive" violence by humans is ever considered acceptable, then it should certainly be permissible for God to exercise such violence. Those who reject penal substitutionary atonement on the basis of rejecting the myth of redemptive violence, then, should necessarily be pacifist.

In fact, faced squarely, there has been scant evidence thus far in our study of the Bible that God is wholly nonviolent. We will consider this further in the next chapter, where we look at eschatological violence, of which Jesus speaks a good deal.

God Absorbing Human Violence

Another model of the atonement, also with ancient roots, is known as *Christus Victor*.[7] In this metaphor, the fundamental achievement of the cross is not the satisfaction of an angry God but the defeat of the powers of Satan (or of a demythologized "forces of evil"). The cross represents a cosmic victory. There are a number of variations of this model. The "classic" version of this model is both described and defended by Gustav Aulen, in his book of the same name. Here, God in Christ is *waging war* against Satan and the evil powers of this world.[8]

This may seem an inherently violent image, but some have mounted a pacifist argument on the basis of a modified version of this model where God is entirely the recipient of violence, never its perpetrator. One theologian who does this is

5. Richard Rohr, https://acireland.ie/richard-rohr-jesus-and-the-cross/.

6. Ronald Sider, *If Jesus Is Lord: Loving Our Enemies in an Age of Violence* (Grand Rapids: Baker, 2019), 156.

7. An early articulation of the *Christus Victor* model is found in the writings of Gregory of Nyssa (ca. 335–395 CE). See, e.g., Gregory of Nyssa, "The Great Catechism," in *Gregory of Nyssa:*

Dogmatic Treatises, vol. 5 of *Nicene and Post-Nicene Fathers, Series II*, ed. P. Schaff and H. Wace, trans. W. Moore (New York: Christian Literature Company, 1893).

8. Gustav Aulen, *Christus Victor: An Historical Study of the Three Main Types of the Idea of the Atonement*, trans. A. G. Herbert (London: SPCK, 1970), 4.

J. Denny Weaver. Weaver offers what he calls a *narrative Christus Victor* model. Weaver acknowledges that his nonviolent stance influences his exegesis, but argues in mitigation that the satisfaction model has likewise been read back into the text, in its case from a starting point that accepts violence.[9]

Weaver's approach to the atonement places a larger emphasis on Jesus's life and ministry than traditional models. Jesus was killed because he was visibly manifesting the kingdom of God and thus represented a threat and challenge to the principalities and powers of the world:

> Narrative Christus Victor . . . portrays sin as bondage to the forces of evil, whose earthly representatives include the structures of imperial Rome, which had ultimate authority for Jesus' death; the structures of holiness code, to which Jesus posed reforming alternatives; and the mob and the disciples in their several roles. . . . Salvation is to begin to be free from those evil forces, and to be transformed by the reign of God.[10]

In this model, then, Jesus's death was inevitable, not because God required it of him but because faithful obedience inevitably led to it.[11]

Moral Influence

The third broad model for the atonement states that, unlike the two previous models, nothing decisive and ontological takes place at the cross. Rather, Jesus's self-giving love is the supreme example for humanity to follow. One of the first theologians to express this perspective was Clement of Alexandria, in the third century: "For each of us he laid down his life, the life which was worth the whole universe, and he requires in return that we should do the same for each other."[12] The model was later set out more fully by Peter Abelard and then gained influence during the Enlightenment because of its "demythologizing" approach to the cross.[13] It is easy to see that this atonement model lends itself well to a wholly nonviolent interpretation of God's character and a pacifist ethic.

Proponents of each of these models are wont to make their favored approach the only valid interpretation and often marginalize or reinterpret biblical evidence that seems to support the alternatives. Others, however, have argued that these models are not necessarily mutually exclusive.[14] Indeed, there is scriptural support for each of these; consider the following examples, all from the same epistle (emphases added):

9. J. Denny Weaver, *The Nonviolent Atonement* (Grand Rapids: Eerdmans, 2011), 7.

10. Weaver, *Nonviolent Atonement*, 46.

11. Weaver, *Nonviolent Atonement*, 89.

12. Clement of Alexandria, exposition on Mark 10:17–31, in *The Christian Theology Reader*, ed. Alister E. McGrath, 3rd ed. (Oxford: Blackwell, 2007), 345.

13. Alister McGrath, *Christian Theology: An Introduction*, 3rd ed. (Oxford: Blackwell, 2001), 427.

14. See, e.g., the work of Henri Blocher, who argues for

[Jesus Christ] is the *atoning sacrifice* for our sins, and not only for ours but also for the sins of the whole world. (1 John 2:2)

The one who does what is sinful is of the devil, because the devil has been sinning from the beginning. The reason the Son of God appeared was *to destroy the devil's work*. (1 John 3:8)

This is how we know *what love is: Jesus Christ laid down his life for us*. And we ought to lay down our lives for our brothers and sisters. (1 John 3:16)

In my view, the atonement is a mystery so deep that it defies reductive explanations. Each of the models given above is just that—a model—and can add to our understanding of the mystery if we allow it to enrich our interpretation. Where the metaphors appear to contradict one another (e.g., whether God "sent" Jesus to the cross or not) serves to remind us of the richness of the mystery and should lead us into worship in fresh humility. Nonetheless, the rejection of penal models of the atonement on the basis of a nonviolent God cannot be sustained by the reading of Scripture as we have set it out in the preceding chapters. The violence of God in judgment is clear at many points in the biblical storyline, while being tempered by the very mercy that provides the impulse for the cross.

As we now consider the ways in which the cross proves to be the culmination of the great redemptive moves that we began to trace out in the previous chapter, we will see elements that relate to each of these atonement models.

DEVALORIZATION OF VIOLENCE

In the previous chapter we noted one of the key moments in the book of Joshua—the place where Joshua meets with the commander of the armies of the Lord and is told that God is on neither side. This marks a real turning point in the story of Israel. As I commented, until this point Joshua has had little reason to doubt that God is unequivocally on Israel's side. But from here on, it is clear that God's support for Israel can by no means be taken for granted. Immediately after the battle of Jericho, disobedience in the camp causes God to abandon Israel at their very next battle (Josh 7). Ultimately, in accordance with the warnings of Deuteronomy 28, when the people of Israel broke the covenant God turned against them and released enemy armies upon them (e.g., 2 Kgs 17). This marks a significant and surprising development. God will not be co-opted by any human agenda.

coherence between the penal and victor models of the atonement (Henri Blocher, "Agnus Victor: The Atonement as Victory and Vicarious Punishment," in *What Does It Mean to Be Saved? Broad-* *ening Evangelical Horizons of Salvation*, ed. John Stackhouse Jr. [Grand Rapids: Baker, 2002], 67–91).

As we move into the New Testament, this theme is developed even further. Whereas the writer of Exodus has spoken of God as a "man of war" (Exod 15:3 ESV) who uses violence to achieve a laudable end, this is completely inverted at the cross.[15]

What Kind of King?

While the life of Jesus has again and again been marked by his refusal of violence, this theme becomes more intense in holy week, and will culminate in his rejection of Peter's violent defense in the garden (Matt 26:52). The week begins, of course, with Jesus's entrance to Jerusalem on a donkey, an action that was richly symbolic on a number of levels. Hundreds of years previously, the prophet Zechariah had prophesied of the coming of Zion's (i.e., Jerusalem's) king (Zech 9:9). So by entering to great acclaim on a donkey rather than simply walking in on foot or entering in some other private way, Jesus was making an explicit, public claim to be the rightful king of Israel. But this kingship was to be unusual, as the prophet goes on to show:

> I will take away the chariots from Ephraim
> and the warhorses from Jerusalem,
> and the battle bow will be broken.
> He will proclaim peace to the nations.
> His rule will extend from sea to sea
> and from the River to the ends of the earth. (Zech 9:10)

The familiar trappings of kingship from the surrounding nations and Israel's own history were the accoutrements of the war machine. Riding on a donkey was an explicit rejection of such a notion of kingship.[16]

The other symbol that would have been in people's minds as Jesus entered Jerusalem on a donkey comes from several events of the previous few centuries in the history of the city of Jerusalem.[17] In 332 BCE, the great conqueror of the world Alexander the Great rode into Jerusalem on his mighty horse Bucephalus to (orchestrated) public acclaim, and went directly to the temple.[18] In 164 BCE, when Judas Maccabeus had prevailed in the armed rebellion against the brutal oppression of the Seleucids, he too rode into the city "with a chorus of praise and the waving of palm branches" (1 Macc 13:51) and went directly to the temple. When Pompey, the greatest general of the day, conquered Jerusalem for the Roman Empire in 63 BCE,

---

15. The canonical development of the "warrior God" theme is explored in Tremper Longman III, "Warfare," in *New Dictionary of Biblical Theology*, ed. T. D. Alexander and B. S. Rosner (Downers Grove, IL: InterVarsity Press, 2000), 835–39.

16. It should be noted that Zech 9 contains violent elements, but these are arguably eschatological. See, e.g., Mark J. Boda, *The Book of Zechariah*, NICOT (Grand Rapids: Eerdmans, 2016), 570–74. We will discuss eschatological violence in ch. 10.

17. I am grateful to Stephen Finamore for drawing my attention to these historical parallels.

18. Josephus, *Antiquities* 11.7, §5, in *The Works of Josephus: Complete and Unabridged*, trans. W. Whiston (Peabody: Hendrickson, 1987), 306–7.

he also entered in grand procession and proceeded right into the holy of holies in the temple.[19]

The similarity of Jesus's entrance to Jerusalem to these stories would have resonated in the minds of the onlookers and the first gospel readers. The differences were very telling. Time and again, Jesus had refused satanic and human offers of kingship (e.g., Matt 4:8–10; John 6:14–15), with all their abusive connotations. Rather, he taught the humility that characterizes his rule (e.g., Luke 22:25–29).

And as he enters Jerusalem on Sunday, he knows that in just a few days he would be demonstrating it in an astonishing way:

> Jesus knew that the Father had put all things under his power, and that he had come from God and was returning to God; so he got up from the meal, took off his outer clothing, and wrapped a towel around his waist. After that, he poured water into a basin and began to wash his disciples' feet, drying them with the towel that was wrapped around him. (John 13:3–5)

So as Jesus enters the city on Palm Sunday, he is—ironically—claiming kingship and simultaneously subverting it.

Indeed, the last days of Jesus's life are fraught with ironies. The people who hail him as king on Sunday have rejected him as king by Friday. His enemies deny his kingship ("we have no king but Caesar," John 19:15), and yet use it as a tool for his downfall (Luke 23:2). By the end of the week, Jesus will be choking to death beneath a sign that declares in three languages, "The King of the Jews" (John 19:19–20), though nobody believes its claim—least of all the man who ordered it written. And the deepest irony of all is that at that moment, when Jesus is to all appearances least dignified and regal and utterly powerless, he is in fact most kingly, most glorious, and achieving a victory of cosmic significance.

Victory through Suffering

As the apostles wrestle to describe this victory, they draw on military language. Like Saul or David of old, Jesus Christ is revealed as the conquering hero. The New Testament has no anxiety about using military language for his triumph; Colossians 2 describes the victory of the cross using an image borrowed from a victory parade of triumphant Roman generals.[20]

> Having disarmed the powers and authorities, he made a public spectacle of them, triumphing over them by the cross. (Col 2:15)

19. Josephus, *Antiquities* 14.4, §4, in *Works of Josephus*, 370.
20. Douglas Moo, *The Letters to the Colossians and to Philemon*, Pillar New Testament Commentary (Grand Rapids: Eerdmans, 2008), 214.

However, the means by which the victory is achieved is quite different. It is not achieved by the exercise of violence against the enemy but by the absorption of the enemy's violence. But what is the enemy that the New Testament has in view? In this part of Colossians, Paul is speaking in terms of "powers and authorities," spiritual forces that conspired against Jesus, manifested in the systems and structures that took him to the cross.[21] These spiritual enemies were conquered, "triumphed over."

But that was not the only form of enemy being addressed at the cross. In a very real sense, it was we ordinary humans, whose sins (including our violence) were the direct cause of his death. As Peter puts it in his Pentecost sermon:

> Jesus of Nazareth was a man accredited by God to you by miracles, wonders and signs, which God did among you through him, as you yourselves know. This man was handed over to you by God's deliberate plan and foreknowledge; and you, with the help of wicked men, put him to death by nailing him to the cross. (Acts 2:22–23)

In this sense, we are the enemy—language that Paul explicitly uses in Romans 5:10. But unlike the principalities and powers, we are not "conquered" by the cross. Rather, in the truest fulfillment of his own instructions to love one's enemy (Matt 5:44), Jesus gives himself to us for our redemption:

> You see, at just the right time, when we were still powerless, Christ died for the ungodly. Very rarely will anyone die for a righteous person, though for a good person someone might possibly dare to die. But God demonstrates his own love for us in this: While we were still sinners, Christ died for us. (Rom 5:6–8)

In this respect, the cross—rather than being a conquest—is a peacemaking mission. Those who were alienated from God have now been reconciled (Col 1:19–22).

In response, then, to the hostile enemy that is the human race, Jesus comes to give himself to us, to love us, and to forge reconciliation with us. By so doing, he achieves victory over the spiritual forces that have disrupted the order of the cosmos. The myth of militarism has been totally subverted.

INVALIDATION OF VENGEANCE

We come now to the second great redemptive theme that we began to trace out in the previous chapter, the invalidation of vengeance. We saw how Jesus calls for an

---

21. Here I draw on Walter Wink's groundbreaking work on the interpretation of the "principalities and powers," particularly as set out in the first two of his books on the powers: Walter Wink, *Naming the Powers: The Language of Power in the New Testament* (Philadelphia: Fortress, 1984), and *Unmasking the Powers: The Invisible Forces that Determine Human Existence* (Philadelphia: Fortress, 1986). I find Wink's work on the spiritual forces at work in human institutions to be deeply insightful, although I have reservations about his exegesis of Paul's use of the term.

intensification of the limitation of personal vengeance that the law of talion initiates, involving turning the other cheek and not resisting an evil person (Matt 5:38–39).

Do Not Resist an Evil Person

What is the nature of the nonresistance that Jesus is demanding? This has been the subject of much debate over the years. At one extreme we find the approach taken by the Russian novelist Leo Tolstoy, whose plain—and devoted—reading of the text led him to conclude that "Christ forbids all human institutions of justice . . . he could mean nothing else."[22] Such an opinion is clearly an outlier and is not sustained by careful reflection on the broader biblical witness.

An entirely different reading is offered by Walter Wink, who suggests that Jesus's words offer a third way to people who feel trapped between the appalling alternatives of violent resistance or passive acceptance of evil. Wink points out that the Greek word *antistēnai*, commonly translated "resist," is generally used in the Greek Old Testament to refer to forcible, violent resistance (e.g., Judg 2:14).[23] So Jesus appears to be forbidding violent resistance. To suggest that Jesus is forbidding all resistance against evil would be absurd, Wink insists.[24]

Wink also notes that it is the *right* cheek that is being struck in Jesus's hypothetical scenario, as told in Matthew's Gospel. For a right-handed person to strike someone facing them on the right cheek, they have not thrown a punch, but have delivered a backhanded slap; an assault aimed at a subordinate rather than an equal. Turning the other cheek, then, is neither a passive acceptance of everything that the assailant offers nor is it entering into a fistfight. It is an invitation to the assailant to strike again, but this time as an equal:

> The person who turns the other cheek is saying, in effect, "Try again. Your first blow failed to achieve its intended effect. I deny you the power to humiliate me. I am a human being just like you. Your status does not alter that fact. You cannot demean me."[25]

Wink sees a similar dynamic being played out in Jesus's further instructions to offer the inner garment when a creditor illegitimately demands one's coat (Matt 5:40, cf. Deut 24:10–13, 17), and to insist on carrying a soldier's pack a second mile after the statutory mile that the soldier could legally demand (v. 41).[26]

Wink's suggestion that Jesus is offering a third way, which includes humor, is tantalizing, and we will return to it in chapter 14. However, I am not wholly persuaded that he has fully accounted for the nuances of implication in Jesus's words

22. Leo Tolstoy, *What I Believe*, trans. Constantine Popoff (New York: William S. Gottsberger, 1886), 9.
23. Walter Wink, *Jesus and Non-Violence: A Third Way* (Minneapolis: Fortress, 2013), 13, 107.
24. Wink, *Jesus and Non-Violence*, 10.
25. Wink, *Jesus and Non-Violence*, 16.
26. Wink, *Jesus and Non-Violence*, 25.

here. One problem is that Luke's version of the pericope (Luke 6:28–31) is quite as radical as Matthew's, but does not lend itself to Wink's argument nearly so well since it does not name the *right* cheek, which is an important plank in his argument.

Jesus and the Third Way

The proof of the pudding, as they say, is in the eating. In what ways did Jesus's life demonstrate the intention that lay behind these words? Was he advocating a creative third way, or a total submission to the malign forces of violence? We do see the sort of creative, humorous engagement with those who wished him harm on a number of occasions. We might put his burlesque suggestion of fishing for a four-drachma piece to pay the temple tax into that category (Matt 17:24–27).

Moreover, there is nothing of the cringing victim in Jesus as his enemies close in. In each of the gospel accounts, we see similar quiet courage and dignity in his demeanor at his arrest and trials. Despite his evident power to escape from the situation or to turn the tables on his opponents, he chooses not to do so. When he is quite literally struck on the cheek (Matt 26:67), he offers no resistance but rather permits himself to be struck "again and again" (Matt 27:30). Nowhere is this meek submission better summarized than in Philippians 2:

> he made himself nothing
>> by taking the very nature of a servant . . .
>> he humbled himself
>> by becoming obedient to death—even death on a cross!
>>> (Phil 2:7–8)

Jesus began his ministry by urging his followers to pray for their persecutors, turn the other cheek when struck, and love their enemies. He ended it by praying for his persecutors, turning his other cheek, and loving his enemies.

Resurrection Vengeance?

But we have not yet exhausted the non-vengeful development that Jesus exemplifies. He meets his end apparently utterly defeated, gasping out his final words on a Roman cross, mocked and reviled by his enemies. Three days later he has the opportunity to wreak a lasting vengeance upon them. Perhaps our familiarity with the resurrection accounts causes us to miss the astonishing nature of what happens on Resurrection Sunday. Jesus does not visit his disciples like Hamlet's ghost, demanding that they take vengeance upon his murderers.

> If thou didst ever thy dear father love . . .
> Revenge his foul and most unnatural murder.[27]

---

27. William Shakespeare, *Hamlet*, act 1, scene 5.

Nor does he visit Pilate or Caiaphas in their bedrooms to taunt or harm them. In fact, he has no words at all about his persecutors. Read the resurrection accounts with this question in mind, and it is hard to escape the impression that the Jewish leaders and Roman officials who had conspired to bring about his death were now irrelevant to him. He prayed for their forgiveness at his crucifixion, but now his words are all for his disciples and about the new thing that God has begun.

We have not yet considered the question of whether the ascended Jesus seeks vengeance upon his enemies in the apocalyptic literature, and we will look at this in the following chapter. For now, we will continue our investigation of Jesus's life and death as the culmination of the great redemptive themes, as we turn to the third of them.

JESUS, THE INNOCENT VICTIM
Did Not the Messiah Have to Suffer?

We saw in the previous chapter that the Hebrew Bible contains a gradually developing theme of the innocence of the victim—or rather, that victims of violence *could* be innocent. This seems to have been only imperfectly understood in the first century. When Jesus starts to warn his disciples about his forthcoming passion, Peter is appalled and rebukes him. Jesus's reply indicates that Peter fundamentally misunderstands the way that God is at work: "You do not have in mind the concerns of God, but merely human concerns" (Mark 8:33).

A similar conversation appears to have taken place on Resurrection Sunday, on the road to Emmaus (Luke 24:13–35). In response to the disciples' bewilderment, Jesus shows them the inevitability of the suffering of the Messiah from Old Testament texts.

Revealing the Lie

The gospel writers are clear that Jesus does not deserve his fate. He is declared innocent by Judas Iscariot (Matt 27:4), Pilate and Herod Antipas (Luke 23:14–15), the dying thief (23:41), and by other Romans (Matt 27:19; Luke 23:47). The epistles similarly pick up the theme. To the church in Corinth, Paul writes, "God made him who had no sin to be sin for us" (2 Cor 5:21). Similar themes show up in Hebrews 4:15 and 7:26 and in 1 John 3:5.

The servant song of Isaiah 52:13–53:12, which is a key moment in the development of the Old Testament's theology of innocent suffering, has many New Testament echoes and resonances.[28] This text was clearly part of Jesus's self-understanding as he quoted from it in relation to himself (Luke 22:37), and the writer of the Fourth

---

28. For a fuller examination of the echoes of Isaiah 53 in the New Testament, see D. A. Carson and G. K. Beale, eds., *Commen-tary on the New Testament Use of the Old Testament* (Grand Rapids: Baker Academic, 2007).

Gospel explicitly quotes it in connection with Jesus (John 12:38). It is Isaiah 53 that the Ethiopian eunuch is reading in his chariot prior to his conversion (Acts 8:32–33). The apostle Paul refers to it twice in Romans (10:16; 15:21). Perhaps most clearly of all, Peter quotes it in his first letter as part of his discourse on innocent suffering (1 Pet 2:20–23).

René Girard, whose thought we looked at in chapter 1, considers that the gospel demonstration of the innocence of Jesus is the great turning point in the history of violence and the great achievement of the cross. The monstrous and universal lie that underlies what he calls the "texts of persecution" (written by the persecutors to account for collective violence) is that the victims were harmful to society and needed to be expelled or murdered.[29] Girard argues that the Old Testament is gradually coming to terms with the possibility that the victim might not be guilty. Yet at the cross of Jesus, his innocence is made plain. In this way, the lie is exposed and no longer has power.[30]

The cross, then, as the judicial murder of the exemplary victim, invites us to be attentive to victims, and to read from the underside.

In his magnum opus *The Better Angels of Our Nature*, Steven Pinker argues that one of the prime reasons for the decline in human violence around the time of the Enlightenment was the widespread availability of printed literature, which activated the human imagination and enabled readers to inhabit the minds of others.[31] This empathy, Pinker argues, enhances the regard for human life. While he has little sympathy for the Bible,[32] the principle of innocent victimhood that the cross exemplifies is indeed a monumental step in the redemptive trajectory that shifts our attention toward those who suffer violence.

For Girard, "he himself bore our sins in his body on the cross" (1 Pet 2:24, also referencing Isa 53) refers to an absorption of the effects of others' sin rather than a taking on of the tariff for sin. Some will find Girard's perspective on the cross deficient for this reason, since the salvific event is the narrative *telling* of the innocence of Jesus rather than the crucifixion itself. Nonetheless, Girard's insights are helpful in drawing our attention to one of the striking features of the cross: Jesus was the innocent victim of mob violence, and as such he stands in solidarity with all those who also experience violence at the hands of others.

29. René Girard, *The Scapegoat*, trans. Yvonne Freccero (Baltimore: Johns Hopkins University Press, 1986), 15.

30. René Girard, "Generative Scapegoating," in *Violent Origins*, ed. Robert Hamerton Kelly (Stanford: Stanford University Press, 1987), 141.

31. Steven Pinker, *The Better Angels of Our Nature: Why Violence has Declined* (London: Penguin, 2011), 175–77.

32. Pinker, *Better Angels of Our Nature*, 6–17.

Solidarity with the Victim

With this solidarity in mind, Black theologian James Cone argues in his groundbreaking work *The Cross and the Lynching Tree* that much of the significance of the cross has escaped White readers. For enslaved Black people in America or those living under Jim Crow, the parallels between the crucified man and the lynched man were inescapable:

> Black ministers preached about Jesus' death more than any other theme because they saw in Jesus' suffering and persecution a parallel to their own encounter with slavery, segregation, and the lynching tree.[33]

As Cone points out, "lynching" can take a huge number of manifestations, and it is sometimes conducted within the rule of law.[34] He draws connections not simply with the familiar image of a Black body hanging from a tree but also with a criminal justice system in America—a system stacked against Black men. We might add the murder of George Floyd as another example, among many more. Cone believes that the cross and the lynching tree interpret each other. Though he writes in the American context, the point is more widely applicable:

> The lynching tree frees the cross from the false pieties of well-meaning Christians. . . . The cross needs the lynching tree to remind Americans of the reality of suffering—to keep the cross from becoming a symbol of abstract sentimental piety. Before the spectacle of this cross we are called to more than contemplation and adoration. We are faced with a clear challenge. . . . Yet the lynching tree also needs the cross, without which it becomes simply an abomination. It is the cross that points in the direction of hope, the confidence that there is a dimension to life beyond the reach of the oppressor.[35]

The cross, then, presents a challenge to structures of violence because of its focus on the innocent victim. But this is by no means the same as valorizing the suffering of Jesus for its own sake.

Valorization of Suffering?

Jürgen Moltmann rightly criticizes what he calls the "mysticism of suffering":

> Here the crucified Christ was seen less as the sacrifice which God creates to reconcile the world to himself, and more as the exemplary path trodden by a righteous man suffering unjustly, leading to salvation. . . . the way to glory leads through personal suffering.[36]

---

33. James H. Cone, *The Cross and the Lynching Tree* (Maryknoll, NY: Orbis, 2011), 75.

34. Cone, *Cross and the Lynching Tree*, 163–66.

35. Cone, *Cross and the Lynching Tree*, 161.

36. Jürgen Moltmann, *The Crucified God: The Cross of Christ as the Foundation and Criticism of Christian Theology*, trans. R. A. Wilson and John Bowden (Minneapolis: Fortress, 1974), 45.

The valorization of the sufferings of Jesus is highly problematic because of the risk that it will be used to validate human suffering or to view it as somehow redemptive. For example, in the 1980s Audrey Santo, who was put into a persistent vegetative state in a swimming accident, became the focus of Catholic attention when various miracles appeared to take place around her bed. A local priest made the disturbing comment, "Audrey Santo is a tremendous treasure to our church in this time in history. We need more victim souls, and she is serving [us] so perfectly in her silent way."[37]

Indeed, many people who have experienced abuse within a church setting testify that such a theology has been employed against them in an attempt to keep them silent or compliant. Let me cite two examples. The first comes from the experience of "Dina," an ex-nun who experienced abuse while part of her order:

> Jesus' suffering was seen as heroic, and he was seen as accepting it and suffering in silence. This suggested that Dina should also suffer in silence. She said: "The only feeling that I could allow is to bury it and not complain."[38]

The second depicts the suffering of a survivor of child abuse in a Protestant setting:

> Elizabeth was a vulnerable child being violated by a parent. Her church taught her a good child honors her father as Jesus honored his when he consented to die at his father's request. At the same time it taught her to see herself as a sinner whose internal sense of resistance to abuse threatened the life of her father. By keeping silent she protected her father from "being crucified." Her silence "saved him" and trapped her in ongoing violation.[39]

But this is utterly to misunderstand the nature of our relationship with Jesus's sufferings, for at least three reasons. First, the suffering and death of Jesus is uniquely redemptive (1 Pet 3:18; Heb 10:10). Second, while Christians are sometimes called to suffer persecution in order to maintain a faithful Christian witness (see, e.g., the letters to the seven churches in Rev 2–3), there is never any suggestion that all suffering must simply be endured. For example, Paul says to slaves, "If you can gain your freedom, do so" (1 Cor 7:21). Similarly, Peter and Paul both accept release from prison when it is offered (e.g., Acts 12:9; 16:35–40), and Paul claims the privileges of his Roman citizenship to avoid a flogging (Acts 22:25). The apostles clearly understand Jesus's call to his disciples to take up their crosses daily and follow him (Luke 9:23–27) as a call to radical discipleship (which may well entail suffering), rather than a call to accept suffering for its own sake.

---

37. George Joyce, quoted in Paula M. Kane, "'She Offered Herself Up': The Victim Soul and Victim Spirituality in Catholicism," *Church History* 71.1 (2002): 83.

38. Rocío Figueroa and David Tombs, "Seeing His Innocence, I See My Innocence," in *When Did We See You Naked? Jesus as Victim of Sexual Abuse*, ed. Jayme Reaves, David Tombs, and Rocío Figueroa (London: SCM, 2021), 292.

39. Rita Nakashima Brock and Rebecca Ann Parker, *Proverbs of Ashes: Violence, Redemptive Suffering, and the Search for What Saves Us* (Boston: Beacon, 2002), 28.

Additionally, whenever the New Testament calls for the patient endurance of suffering, it does so through the words of someone who is in extreme peril himself. For example, Jesus, who is eventually crucified, summons his disciples to place their own lives under the threat of that most heinous of deaths (Matt 16:24). James, who eventually is probably thrown from the top of the temple and stoned, invites his readers to consider "trials" to be "pure joy" (Jas 1:2). Peter, whose means of death is described in church tradition as an upside-down crucifixion, calls on his readers to consider their innocent suffering as rendering them "blessed" (1 Pet 3:13–15). And, Paul, a victim of beheading under Nero's regime, calls on his young protégé to join with him in suffering for the Lord Jesus (2 Tim 2:1, 3). The use of the sufferings of Jesus by *abusers* to try to force compliance in their victims is evil.

It could be argued that Colossians 1:24 is a counterexample to the quotations from 1 Peter and Hebrews: "Now I rejoice in what I am suffering for you, and I fill up in my flesh what is still lacking in regard to Christ's afflictions, for the sake of his body, which is the church." Of these rather enigmatic words of Paul's, Douglas Moo argues that as an apostle, Paul is peculiarly called to share in the suffering of Jesus.

> Because Paul's apostolic ministry is an "extension" of Christ's work in the world, Paul identifies his own sufferings very closely with Christ's. These sufferings have no redemptive benefit for the church, but they are the inevitable accompaniment of Paul's "commission" to proclaim the end-time revelation of God's mystery (vv. 25–27).[40]

With such misapplications of the cross in mind, Arnfríður Guðmundsdóttir argues that the cross of Jesus Christ, especially once it is viewed in the light of the resurrection, is liberative for all victims:

> What is bad is still bad, evil and suffering are still there. But because of who God is, and because God is with us in the midst of our suffering, we are able, in retrospect, to see God bringing life out of death, transforming evil into something good, making the victim into a survivor, which indeed is a powerful symbol of God's compassion poured out *pro nos*. Evil, indeed, does not have the last word.[41]

The suffering of Jesus must be seen as good news, not bad news.

---

40. Moo, *Letters to the Colossians and to Philemon*, 152–53.
41. Arnfríður Guðmundsdóttir, "Abusive or Abused?," *Journal of the European Society of Women in Theological Research* 15 (2007): 37–54.

CONCLUSION

In this chapter we have considered how the three great redemptive themes from the Old Testament, considered in the previous chapter, come into focus at the cross and resurrection of Jesus Christ. The gradual devalorization of militarism, which we detected in many parts of the Old Testament, is intensified by Jesus's rejection of human kingship and all its abusive trappings. The theme then finds fulfillment in Jesus's conquest through self-surrender. Second, the gradual invalidation of vengeance is brought to a poignant climax in the teaching and actions of Jesus, particularly at the cross. Here, Jesus loves his human enemies and dies in order to achieve reconciliation with them. Jesus's dying words are a prayer for forgiveness for those who are persecuting him, and after his resurrection there is not even a hint of vengeance toward those who were instrumental in his murder. The third theme, the innocence of the victim, is apparent both in the gospel trial accounts of Jesus and in the apostolic testimony. The New Testament's use of Isaiah 53 firmly links the cross to this theme.

We began the chapter by considering three broad types of atonement theology and their relationship with the ethics of violence. Elements of each of these models has been evident through the remainder of the chapter. The uniqueness of the suffering of Jesus is an essential part of satisfaction models. *Christus Victor* was obvious in the military subversion of conquest. And although caution is needed in the application of this, it is evident that the cross of Jesus Christ forms a paradigm for the way that his followers are to serve and love others.

This chapter has considered the gospel accounts and some of the apostolic witness contained in the epistles. However, a significant challenge to some of the statements made here is found in the book of Revelation. We will therefore now turn to one of the key questions it raises: Does the Bible instrumentalize violence as a means to ultimate good?

RELEVANT QUESTIONS

1. Do you tend to see the cross as a conquest or a peacemaking mission? Might your vision be expanded to encompass a broader perspective?
2. Do you see evidence of the valorization of suffering in your own tradition? Are there ways in which you need to respond to that?
3. How do you respond to Wink's proposal of Jesus and a third way? Can you identify further examples in biblical or more contemporary narratives?

CHAPTER 10

THE END FROM THE BEGINNING[1]

Who overcomes
By force, hath overcome but half his foe.
—John Milton, *Paradise Lost*

God makes all things new. Voltaire may presumptuously have considered God's job description to be forgiving sinners,[2] but I would argue that it is better to say that God is in the business of re-creation. "See, I am doing a new thing!" God says through Isaiah (43:19).[3] Later in the book (65:18–25) the prophet speaks of new heavens and a new earth—imagery that is picked up by the writer of Revelation, who echoes and intensifies this promise of renewal:

> Then I saw a new heaven and a new earth, for the first heaven and the first earth had passed away. . . . He who was seated on the throne said, "I am making everything new!" (Rev 21:1, 5)

There is a certain periodicity, or cyclicity, in the way that time is narrated in the Bible.[4] We see this in small ways in, for example, the book of Judges, which has multiple recurrences of the same plot: the people of Israel lapse into disobedience and fall under the power of their enemies, they cry out to God, God raises up a deliverer, and the enemies are subdued. But we also see this in the great stories of the Hebrew Bible: flood, exodus, and exile. Each of these catastrophes and recoveries is told in explicitly creational language.[5] Each of them can be viewed paradigmatically as a movement from order to disorder to order, or from creation to de-creation to

---

1. I am indebted to Dr. Jesse Nickel, whose book *The Things That Make for Peace: Jesus and Eschatological Violence* (Berlin: de Gruyter, 2021), helped shape my thinking as I developed my argument for this chapter. The chapter also benefited from the critical eye of Dr. Stephen Finamore.

2. Voltaire is credited, perhaps incorrectly, with the words, "Le bon Dieu me pardonnera. C'est son métier" ("The good God will forgive me. That's his job.")

3. This theme is announced in the previous chapter, at Isa 42:9–10, and revisited in Isa 48:6–7.

4. For a useful discussion of cyclical and teleological time in the Bible, see Marc Brettler, "Cyclical and Teleological Time in the Hebrew Bible," in *Time and Temporality in the Ancient World*, ed. Ralph M. Rosen (Philadelphia: University of Pennsylvania Museum of Archaeology and Anthropology, 2004), 111–28.

5. More than this, John Walton argues that—as the ancient writer tells it—the role of *sustaining* creation is fundamentally a *creative* act of God. There is "both continuity and a dynamic aspect in God's work as Creator, because he continues to sustain the functions moment by moment. . . . Creation language is used more in the Bible for God's sustaining work (i.e., his ongoing work as Creator) than it is for his originating work" (John Walton, *The Lost World of Genesis One: Ancient Cosmology and the Origins Debate* [Downers Grove, IL: InterVarsity Press, 2009], 120).

re-creation. And so can the event of the cross, which is what leads the apostle Paul to say, "If anyone is in Christ, there is a new creation: everything old has passed away; see, everything has become new!" (2 Cor 5:17 NRSV).

But the Bible is not wholly cyclical, of course. It is directed toward a goal, the eschaton, when the cycles will cease. But even this final iteration of the process shares with the previous ones the pattern of order–disorder–order, or of creation–de-creation–re-creation.

It is the second half of that pattern that concerns us in this chapter, and there are two, related questions which we must address. First, to what extent does *God* use violence to bring about the new, better thing that he is doing? And second, most pertinently for the purposes of our present inquiry, to what extent does God employ *human* violence as he brings about the "new creation," whether that new creation is temporary and cyclical, or ultimate and eschatological? To put these questions another way: To what extent is the myth of redemptive violence a core part of the biblical worldview?

The Myth of Redemptive Violence

Walter Wink has argued that there is a recurrent and pervasive pattern of violence conquering violence in contemporary society, identifying it in media as diverse as children's cartoons, spy thrillers, and Westerns. He terms this *the myth of redemptive violence*: "the belief that violence saves, that war brings peace, that might makes right."[6] The myth is found beyond fiction too. He claims that it is both totalizing and addictive, socializing children—especially boys—into its norms and emerging in a range of situations, from nationalism to vigilante justice.

The idea of a false myth of redemptive violence has become very popular in certain Christian circles today, especially being employed in rejection of the penal substitutionary model of atonement.[7] We have touched on this question in the previous chapter, and further discussion is beyond the scope of this book. However, it is unnecessary to reject divine violence at the cross in order to view with suspicion the narrative of human violence solving human violence. Although the two ideas are related, they are not intrinsically dependent upon one another.

In order to consider these questions, we will first return briefly to the great plot movements of the Old Testament, to consider how the cycles are represented

6. Walter Wink, *The Powers That Be: Theology for a New Millennium* (New York: Doubleday, 1998), 42.

7. See, e.g., Gregory A. Boyd, *Cross Vision: How the Crucifixion of Jesus Makes Sense of Old Testament Violence* (Minneapolis: Fortress, 2017), 138–39.

there. Then we will turn our attention to the eschatological writings. How is the inauguration of God's endless reign represented in the Old Testament and in the extrabiblical writings of the Second Temple period? And how does the New Testament build upon these? In particular, how does Jesus speak of eschatological violence? And, finally, what about the book of Revelation? Does it portray a violent God? And does it provide license for humans to use violence in order that good may result?

CHAOSKÄMPFE[8] IN THE OLD TESTAMENT

We began the Arriving at Answers section of this book, the part where we give close attention to the biblical witness on violence, by looking at the Genesis creation accounts. We noticed how they contained elements of similarity to the other ancient Near Eastern creation accounts, but they also evinced important distinctions. In particular, we noticed how they subverted the *Chaoskampf* (struggle against chaos) that characterizes the Babylonian and Akkadian myths. Creation is not an act of violence.

But the chaos that God clears in Genesis 1 continually threatens to push back in again to overwhelm God's good creation. Each time, God responds in re-creative ways. And apparently, in this postlapsarian world, violence is employed or permitted to that end.

Flood

The first cycle of creation–de-creation–re-creation is found in the flood narrative. We looked at this in some detail in chapter 4, so here we will simply content ourselves to notice that the flood is told in terms that draw on the language of Genesis 1.

First, the flood event is described as a reversal of creation. Whereas God's assessment of his creation was that it was "good" or "very good" (Gen 1:10, 12, 18, 21, 25, 31), by chapter 6 God sees that it is corrupt (6:12). So the water above that God had separated from the waters below (1:6–7) is permitted once more to return upon the earth (7:11). The lower waters, which had been gathered together so that dry land appeared (1:9) now swell mightily on the earth so that the land is engulfed (7:19).

Then, after the storm, Noah steps out of the ark into what sounds very much like a brand-new world. The similarity of language between Genesis 1 and 8–9 is perhaps best represented in a table (see on the following page).

The flood, then, is the first cycle where God (here catastrophically) permits violent chaos to push back in, then reasserts his sovereignty over it once again. The next one occurs in the book of Exodus.

---

8. *Chaoskämpfe* is the plural of *Chaoskampf*, a term we introduced in ch. 3.

Earth, waters, wind / spirit, the deep	1:2	8:1b–2
Waters divided and gathered	1:6–10	8:5
Emerging of dry ground	1:9	8:11
Winged creatures	1:20–23	8:6–12, 17
Living creatures called forth	1:24–25	8:17–19
Image of God	1:26–28	8:16; 9:6
Blessing, feeding, command to rule	1:28	9:1–2

Exodus

At the very beginning of Exodus the people of Israel, grown into a nation while in Egypt, are shown to be fulfilling the creation mandate of Genesis 1:28.[9] The text is emphatically creational in its language here, the verbs of Exodus 1:7 having strong resonances with the creation narratives:[10]

they were exceedingly fruitful	be fruitful (Gen 1:28)
they multiplied greatly	to Noah: multiply on the earth (Gen 9:7)
they increased in numbers	increase in numbers (Gen 1:28)
they became numerous	this verb is etymologically linked with "bone" (Gen 2:23)
the land (*eretz*) was filled	fill the earth (*eretz*) (Gen 1:28)*

* The word *eretz* can be translated "earth" or "land."

This population explosion is perceived by the Pharaoh as a threat (Exod 1:8), and he actively seeks to inhibit it. Oppression with forced labour (v. 10) soon becomes an explicit attempt to annihilate them altogether by male infanticide (vv. 16, 22). Pharaoh is being positioned by the text as an anti-creational force.

In response, God's dealings with the Pharaoh have a strongly de-creational flavor. His serpent that swallows the serpents of the magicians (7:10) is described using the term *tannin*, often reserved for the monsters of chaos (cf. Isa 27:1). The plagues that follow dismantle, in representative terms, much of the work of creation. Water that should give life is the bearer of death. Animals created to swarm and creep and teem on the earth no longer respect their bounds and destroy cattle, crops, and human bodies like a living cancer—"creation gone berserk."[11] Finally, the sun

---

9. Terence E. Fretheim, *Exodus*, Interpretation Bible Commentary (Louisville: John Knox, 1991), 25.

10. T. Desmond Alexander, *Exodus*, Apollos Old Testament Commentary (London: Apollos, 2017), 42.

11. Terence E. Fretheim, *God and World in the Old Testament: A Relational Theology of Creation* (Nashville: Abingdon, 2005), 120.

itself is darkened and life is extinguished. God has given Pharoah up to the forces of de-creation that he has embraced.

Phoenix from the Ashes

In many, perhaps all, cultures, the myth of catastrophe and renewal is to be found. Rome was said to be founded when Aeneas snatched his father Anchises from burning Troy. In Greek mythology, the phoenix was a bird that rose with new life from its own funeral pyre.

These myths reflect the human appetite for restoration after catastrophe, an appetite that has never been fully satisfied by the many imperfect and temporary human attempts to make the world over again. (Consider the establishment of the League of Nations after the "war to end all wars.")

In the Hebrew Bible, this hunger for renewal is framed theologically. Re-creation is not something that humanity can achieve—at least not alone. Rather, humanity is invited to partner with God in his *métier*, re-creation. In this chapter and the ones that follow, we explore what that does and does not mean.

But the story is not yet over. Pharaoh has not yet acknowledged God's supremacy. So he pursues the people to the shore of the Reed Sea.[12] And here, at last, the chaos he has embraced engulfs him (Exod 14:27–28; 15:4). Just as we saw in the flood account, waters that have been divided once more coalesce. The parted sea is no longer held back, and the Pharaoh is consigned to the abyss. But the de-creation event is not the end of the matter. As Daniel Hawk writes:

> The end of Egyptian power, manifested by its forces being swallowed up by the sea, becomes at the same time *the event that creates* a new people through whom Yahweh's order will be reestablished on the earth.[13]

Just as the flood resulted in a new world, so too this destructive act is creative; it is constitutive of the people of God. The pattern is next renewed at the conquest of Canaan.

Conquest

Hitherto, the *Chaoskampf* has been God's action alone. There is no human involvement when the floodwaters subside and the earth is reborn. The triumph over the

---

12. Although it is often referred to as the "Red Sea," a better translation of the Hebrew *Yam Suph* is "Reed Sea."

13. L. Daniel Hawk, *The Violence of the Biblical God: Canonical Narrative and Christian Faith* (Grand Rapids: Eerdmans, 2019), 88 (emphasis added).

Egyptians is explicitly his work alone (Exod 14:13–14), although Moses functions as a mediator of divine instruction. By the time of the conquest of Canaan, however, the *Chaoskampf* is framed less in supernatural and more in historical terms, and this means human involvement. Mythic language is not wholly absent, however.[14] As the spies report to Moses:

> We saw the Nephilim there (the descendants of Anak come from the Nephilim).
> We seemed like grasshoppers in our own eyes, and we looked the same to them.
> (Num 13:33; see also Deut 2:11, 20)

In common with many ancient societies, the Israelites viewed the people living just beyond the bounds of their order as monstrous semi-humans.[15] Many of the descriptions of the Canaanites refer to uncouth and barbaric practices befitting such demiurges. So for example, Leviticus 18 describes them indulging in incest, child murder, and bestiality, and Deuteronomy 18:12 describes such practices as contrary to order, that is, as chaotic (*to'eba*; NIV: detestable).[16] Anthropological study has indicated that even today in traditional societies the act of conquering such a people is regarded as a creative act (a cosmogony).[17]

This also appears to have been the perspective of societies in the ancient Near East. The ninth-century BCE Moabite inscription shows that battle and cosmogony were linked in Moabite thought.[18]

A final clue that the conquest is being regarded as a *Chaoskampf* is its frequent coupling with the hope of rest. Just as God rested on the seventh day after the work of creation (Gen 2:2–3), so too the Israelites rested after their cosmogonic activities of conquest (e.g., Josh 11:23).

What of human involvement in this *Chaoskampf*? God does not consign the task wholly to human armies. The conquest is one of a number of "holy wars" that the Old Testament narrates. The term is used by commentators who have noted the presence of religious elements within military accounts. These include sacrifices on the eve of battle (e.g., 1 Sam 13:5–10), the consecration of the combatants (e.g., Josh 3:5), divine oracles (e.g., Judg 4:6–7), and—vitally—assurances that the battle is God's (Josh 10:14, 42).[19]

That the war, and therefore the victory, was primarily God's action is emphasized

---

14. Neither the terms "mythic" or "historical" should be understood as a comment upon the factuality or otherwise of the events. It is a description of genre.

15. This is discussed in much more detail in John H. Walton and J. Harvey Walton, *The Lost World of the Israelite Conquest: Covenant, Retribution and the Fate of the Canaanites* (Downers Grove, IL: InterVarsity Press, 2017), 137–50.

16. Cf. Gen 46:34, where shepherds are viewed as *to'eba* by the Egyptians.

17. Mircea Eliade, *The Sacred and the Profane: The Nature of Religion*, trans. Willard R. Trask (San Diego: Harcourt Brace Jovanovich, 1959), 31–32.

18. Philip Stern, *The Biblical Herem: A Window on Israel's Religious Experience* (Atlanta: Scholars Press, 1991), 41–42.

19. Roland de Vaux, *Ancient Israel: Its Life and Institutions*, trans. John McHugh (Grand Rapids: Eerdmans, 1961), 262–63.

in a number of ways: the use of natural (e.g., Josh 10:11) and supernatural (e.g., 10:12–14) phenomena; God throwing the enemy into confusion (e.g., Judg 7:22) or filling them with divine terror (e.g., 1 Sam 14:15); and frequent assertions that the battle is the Lord's, as discussed above.

So although the biblical descriptions of the wars of Israel's history clearly include human participation, the human warriors are secondary to the divine project. There does appear to be a *Chaoskampf* in the mind of the combatants, or at least of the narrators. The primary warrior is God himself.

Exile and Eschatology in Isaiah

For our purposes, the next great plot moves of the Old Testament are the Assyrian and Babylonian exiles, followed by the subsequent return of some Jews from Babylonia. As we turn to consider these, we will find ourselves drawn into consideration of the eschatological vision found in Isaiah, and then beyond.

God's redemption of his people from their Babylonian exile is one of the great themes of Isaiah. It is promised in terms that resonate both with the exodus and with creation. This is perhaps best seen in chapters 42–43. Here, the God who created the heavens and the earth (42:5), and Israel in particular (43:1), declares that he will redeem his people. He will achieve this by making a path in the sea and inundating chariots and horses (vv. 16–17), just as he did in the first exodus. Violence and newness are coupled: God's actions are likened both to a man of war (42:13) and to a woman in labor (v. 14).

But Isaiah may have something more in mind than the physical return of the original generation of exiles. Indeed, as N. T. Wright argues, the Jews of Jesus's day did not consider that they ever had fully returned from exile:

> Would any serious thinking first-century Jew claim that the promises of Isaiah 40–66 . . . had been fulfilled? That the power and domination of paganism had been broken? That YHWH had already returned to Zion? That the covenant had been renewed, and Israel's sins forgiven? That the long-awaited new exodus had happened?[20]

Isaiah appears to be borrowing the imagery of the exodus to describe an event which far exceeds a reversal of the exile catastrophe. Indeed, the language of de-creation and new creation is sometimes quite explicit. For example, one of the recurring motifs of Isaiah's judgment oracles is that the cities under condemnation will be overrun by wild animals. So, for instance, the oracle against Edom in Isaiah 34:8–17 shows the place given over utterly to chaos, as all sorts of wild animals and unclean birds

---

20. N. T. Wright, *Jesus and the Victory of God* (London: SPCK, 1996), xvii–xviii.

overrun the place and thorns and weeds encroach (cf. the "creation gone berserk" of the Egyptian plagues, discussed above).[21] This anti-creational move is then countered in a set of oracles that reverse the image with visions of a restored creation. Perhaps best known are these words from chapter 65, where the verb "create" (*bara'*) has just been used of God's activity (v. 18):

> The wolf and the lamb will feed together,
>> and the lion will eat straw like the ox.
>> (Isa 65:25; cf. Isa 11:6–9; 35:8–9)

How is this eschatological vision to be realized? As Isaiah foresees it, by a sovereign act of God alone, just as creation was in the first place. The personal pronoun "I"[22] is used emphatically three times in these words from Isaiah 65:17–18:

> See, I will create
>> new heavens and a new earth.
> The former things will not be remembered,
>> nor will they come to mind.
> But be glad and rejoice forever
>> in what I will create,
> for I will create Jerusalem to be a delight
>> and its people a joy. (cf. Isa 66:22)

Not only is the eschatological goal global peace (e.g., Isa 2:4), but there is little evidence that human violence has any role to play in bringing this to birth. While God has clearly been shown to employ the violence of humans with regard to Babylon's action against Israel (Isa 47:5–6), and Babylon's own punishment in turn (Isa 13), the role of humans becomes progressively muted as the eschatological project comes into view.

CHAOSKÄMPFE IN THE JEWISH APOCALYPSES

In order to continue our examination of eschatological violence, we now turn to the apocalypses. The genre of apocalyptic writing emerged among the Jewish people around 200 BCE and continued for around three hundred years. The earliest Jewish apocalypse is Daniel 7–12, but there are many extrabiblical examples. The Greek word *apokalypsis* translates into English as "revelation," and the apocalyptic genre

---

21. More specifically, the encroachment of the wild animals probably represents a failure of human dominion, a breach of the creation mandate of Genesis 1:28. See David H. Wenkel, "Wild Beasts in the Prophecy of Isaiah: The Loss of Dominion and Its Renewal through Israel as the New Humanity," *Journal of Theological Interpretation* 5.2 (2011): 251–63.

22. As freestanding pronoun *ani* and the pronominal suffix.

has been described as "revelatory literature with a narrative framework,"[23] where eschatological salvation is foretold and an unseen supernatural world is revealed. Apocalypses are marked by a number of features. They are typically pseudonymous and involve the description of visions experienced by an individual, visions which are interpreted to the individual by an angel. The genre is marked by number speculation, dualism, and typically contains frequent allusions to Old Testament texts. It is a genre born in persecution.[24]

The context of affliction and preoccupation with eschatology would seem to make this genre highly susceptible to promoting a myth of redemptive violence. With this question in mind, we will first consider the apocalyptic portions of Daniel, and then for comparison two of the intertestamental apocalypses, before we proceed to the New Testament.

Daniel

The prophecy of Daniel is often considered a book of two halves. The much better-known half contains the well-loved stories of the lions' den and the fiery furnace. The second half is much more mysterious and difficult to interpret. It is full of apocalyptic imagery and appears to relate to world events that we can sometimes only dimly reconstruct. It is undeniably violent. It also contains very clear references to cosmic conflict.[25]

The particular period of world history to which Daniel 11 refers is probably the time from Alexander the Great (almost certainly the military king of vv. 3–4), through the skirmishes between the Seleucids and the Ptolemies (referred to as the kings of the north and the south, first mentioned in vv. 5–6), up until the emergence of the Seleucid king Antiochus IV, who reigned over a large territory that included Palestine from 175 to 164 BCE.[26] The prophet speaks of him in scathing terms:

> In his place shall arise a contemptible person to whom royal majesty has not been given. He shall come in without warning and obtain the kingdom by flatteries. Armies shall be utterly swept away before him and broken. (Dan 11:21–22 ESV)

Under Antiochus, the Jews faced a time of intense persecution. They were forbidden from all religious practice including Sabbath observance, keeping the food laws, and circumcising their sons.[27] The responses to this oppression were varied. This was the time of the Maccabean revolt, which eventually succeeded in throwing off the Greek yoke and establishing home rule for a short time. According to the deuterocanonical

23. J. J. Collins, "Introduction: Toward the Morphology of a Genre," in *Apocalypse: The Morphology of a Genre*, ed. J. J. Collins, Semeia 14 (Missoula: SBL, 1979), 9.

24. Collins, "Introduction," 9; David Aune, *Revelation 1–5*, WBC 52A (Dallas: Word, 1997), lxxvii.

25. See, e.g., the angel's words to Daniel in 10:12–14, 20.

26. Ernest C. Lucas, *Daniel*, Apollos Old Testament Commentary (Downers Grove, IL: IVP Academic; Leicester: Apollos, 2002), 278–96.

27. B. E. Kelle, "Israelite History," in *Dictionary of the Old Testament Prophets*, ed. Mark J. Boda and J. Gordon McConville (Downers Grove, IL: InterVarsity Press, 2012), 419.

book of 1 Maccabees, this was viewed as a holy war in the tradition that we have already considered (1 Macc 3:17–22).

But not all Jews were interested in armed rebellion. Some of the priests were willing to collaborate with Antiochus and participated in a syncretic cult based in the temple.[28] There was also a third way, pursued by those who resisted the oppressive regime as much as possible by nonviolent means, mainly by noncooperation.[29] The book of Daniel appears to sit within this middle tradition.

The book is forthright about the violence of God's enemies (the rebellious kingdoms of ch. 2; the beast of ch. 7; the little horn of ch. 8; the kings of ch. 11) in florid terms. The kingdom will "crush and break" (2:40); there will be "astounding devastation" (8:24); and the faithful will suffer a "time of distress" (12:1). Like the book of Maccabees, the book of Daniel applies the motif of cosmic battle to these situations. But, unlike Maccabees, human involvement in this cosmic battle is very limited. It is true that the rock cut out of a mountain that destroys the statue (2:34–35; 44–45) is described as a "kingdom," and this probably has implications in the earthly realm as well as the spiritual one. But later in the book any human involvement retreats. For example, at the end of Daniel 11, the devastation wreaked by the king is brought to an almost anticlimactic conclusion, which amounts to a sort of divine passive:[30]

> [The king] will set out in a great rage to destroy and annihilate many. . . . Yet
> he will come to his end, and no one will help him. (Dan 11:44–45)

Divine violence is portrayed in far less florid terms than the violence of the evil powers.[31] A key theme is that enemies will be brought low, "but not by human hands" (Dan 2:34, 45; 8:25). There is an apparent critique of "those who are violent among your own people" in 11:14. And in the final words of the book, God's people are urged to exercise faithful expectancy (12:12), rather than taking matters into their own hands.[32]

Intertestamental Apocalypses

Now we will consider two of the extrabiblical apocalypses, with attention to the same question as before: To what extent do they endorse and promote the myth of redemptive violence? We will compare them with Daniel, and when we look at the book of Revelation later in this chapter, we will be able to draw further comparisons. The two apocalypses we will consider are 1 Enoch and the Qumran War Scroll.

---

28. P. M. Venter, "Violence and Non-Violence in Daniel," *Old Testament Essays* 14.2 (2001): 324.

29. Venter, "Violence and Non-Violence in Daniel," 326.

30. The verbs in the Hebrew and Greek versions of 11:45 are not passive, but the verse carries the same sense of speaking elliptically about God's involvement, which the classic divine passive exhibits.

31. Venter, "Violence and Non-Violence in Daniel," 327.

32. John E. Goldingay, *Daniel*, WBC 30 (Dallas: Word, 1989), 310.

These have been chosen because of the association that they make between violence and the eschatological enthronement.

At least some parts of the book of Enoch were probably also written with the Maccabean rebellion (167–160 BCE) in view.[33] It shares with other apocalypses a dualistic outlook and considers that the principal problem that must be resolved is that of human sin (with the issue of violence foregrounded).[34] In 1 Enoch 85–90, we have a section known as the "Animal Apocalypse," so-called because humans are portrayed as animals. Prominent among them are the sheep, representing the faithful and led at various times by rams, a sheep with a horn, and a shepherd. In the cosmic conflict that the apocalypse represents, human involvement in violence (though the humans are represented by animals) is explicit. For example:

> Then I saw that a great sword was given to the sheep; and the sheep proceeded against all the beasts of the field in order to kill them; and all the beasts and birds of heaven fled from before their face. (1 En. 90.19)[35]

The eschatological nature of this violence is clear. Immediately following this event, a throne is set up, the Lord takes his seat (90.20), and the wicked are condemned by being thrown into a fiery abyss (vv. 23–27). Thus human violence appears to be wholly bound up with the cosmic victory. In the following chapter, the righteous are again given a sword with which to participate in divine judgment. Again, this immediately results in enthronement:

> A sword shall be given to it in order that judgment shall be executed in righteousness on the oppressors, and sinners shall be delivered into the hands of the righteous. At its completion, they shall acquire great things through their righteousness. A house shall be built for the Great King in glory for evermore. (1 En. 91.11–12)

Once again, in this extrabiblical text, human violence appears integral to the eschaton.

Secondly, we turn to what is known as the War Scroll, or 1QM. Found in the Qumran caves on the banks of the Dead Sea, the types of military imagery that it uses probably date it to the late first century BCE or possibly the early first century CE.[36] It contains elements which appear to be based on Daniel 11–12, and has the common apocalyptic theme of a great cosmic conflict between the spirits of light and darkness.[37] Human involvement in eschatological conflict is evident in

---

33. G. W. E. Nickelsburg, *A Commentary on the Book of 1 Enoch: Chapters 1–36; 81–108* (Minneapolis: Fortress, 2001), 361.

34. Nickelsburg, *Commentary on the Book of 1 Enoch*, 356.

35. Translations of Enoch are by E. Isaac in *The Old Testament Pseudepigrapha*, ed. J. H. Charlesworth, vol. 1, ABRL (New York: Doubleday, 1983), 5–90.

36. Geza Vermes, *The Dead Sea Scrolls in English*, 4th ed. (Sheffield: Sheffield Academic Press, 1995), 124.

37. Vermes, *The Dead Sea Scrolls in English*, 124.

many places as the writer envisions the cosmic battle to come. Cosmic battle occurs right at the beginning:

> On the day when the Kittim[38] fall, there shall be battle and terrible carnage before the God of Israel, for that shall be the day appointed from ancient times for the battle of destruction of the sons of darkness. At that time, the assembly of gods and the hosts of men shall battle, causing great carnage; on the day of calamity, the sons of light shall battle with the company of darkness amid the shouts of a mighty multitude and the clamour of gods and men to (make manifest) the might of God. (1QM column 1)[39]

The manuscript calls humans to involve themselves in the cosmic conflict, while at the same time asserting that the victory is God's:

> Thou didst deliver Goliath of Gath, the mighty warrior, into the hands of David Thy servant, because in place of the sword and in place of the spear he put his trust in Thy great Name; for Thine is the battle. . . . Truly the battle is Thine and the power from Thee! It is not ours. Our strength and the power of our hands accomplish no mighty deeds except by Thy power and by the might of Thy great valour. (1QM column 11)[40]

In summary, the persecutions suffered by the Jews in the Second Temple period led to the emergence of a genre of literature that sought to help the suffering people make sense of what they were facing and what God was doing in it. This genre is marked by a coupling of eschatological battle and divine enthronement, with the marked tendency to divide the world in dualistic terms between the righteous who will be vindicated and the evil who will receive judgment. More diverse is the attitude to human violence that the texts demonstrate. The biblical book of Daniel appears to be at the more moderate end, where most of the eschatological violence takes place offstage and is attributed to the direct action of God. By contrast, the extracanonical Jewish apocalypses 1 Enoch and the War Scroll both incorporate human violence into the great cosmic battle.

We now attend to the apocalypse of the New Testament, that is, the book of Revelation.

A *CHAOSKAMPF* IN THE BOOK OF REVELATION?

The book of Revelation contains some of the most floridly violent imagery in Scripture. It is here that we read, for example, of the two witnesses who are given

---

38. This term appears to be a general one to designate wicked enemies of God's people.

39. Vermes, *Dead Sea Scrolls in English*, 125–26.
40. Vermes, *Dead Sea Scrolls in English*, 125–26.

the power to strike the earth with plagues as often as they wish (11:6), and of a river of blood as high as a horse's bridle that extends for around 180 miles (14:20). Such imagery has proved troubling or repellent to many. The Christian theologian Martin Luther wrote that Revelation is "neither apostolic nor prophetic. . . . Christ is neither taught nor known in it."[41] The atheist philosopher Friedrich Nietzsche reportedly described the book as "the most rabid outburst of vindictiveness in all recorded history."[42] Further, its readers have committed some terrible acts of violence. The leader of the Branch Davidian cult, David Koresh, was apparently inspired by the book of Revelation to heavily arm his Texas compound, beginning a series of events that culminated in seventy-six deaths in the Waco siege of 1993.[43]

But, bizarre and violent as much of the book is, it concludes with a picture of cosmic peace. The last two chapters show a new heaven and earth where there is no more mourning (21:1–4), where the river of the water of life also flows (22:1–2). In fact, there is explicit mirroring of themes from Genesis 1–3 in the seer's vision of the new heaven and earth (Rev 21:1, cf. Gen 1:1).[44] The waters of chaos were parted in the Genesis account (Gen 1:4–9); in the final age they are eliminated (Rev 22:1). Available once more will be the tree of life, which had been banned (Rev 22:2, cf. Gen 3:22), and there will no longer be a curse (Rev 22:3, cf. Gen 3:17).

Given that the re-creative events of the Hebrew Bible are often accomplished through violence, is Revelation doing the same? In other words, is it just another *Chaoskampf*? We will consider both the use and the subversion of violence in the book before drawing some tentative conclusions.

Violence of Divine Origin

Revelation arguably describes divine violence being exercised against three categories of beings: supernatural powers, structures, and individuals. We will briefly consider each in turn. First, Revelation presents what is sometimes referred to as a "satanic trinity" of the devil (often represented as a dragon), the beast from the sea, and the beast from the earth.[45] Their agenda is further promoted by the "false prophet" (16:13; some see the false prophet as the same as the second beast). These characters are, undoubtedly, the subject of divine violence in the text. Michael and his angels fight with the dragon, and he is thrown down to earth (12:7–12). The beast (the two creatures have collapsed into one here) and his false prophet are cast into the lake of fire (19:19–21), which is also the destination of the devil (10:10). And cosmic conflict is represented on multiple occasions.[46]

41. Quoted in Michael Gorman, *Reading Revelation Responsibly: Uncivil Worship and Witness: Following the Lamb into the New Creation* (Eugene: Cascade, 2011), 14.

42. Quoted in Richard Hays, *The Moral Vision of the New Testament: Community, Cross, New Creation: A Contemporary Introduction to New Testament Ethics* (San Francisco: HarperSanFrancisco, 1996), 169.

43. Koresh's use of Revelation is briefly discussed in Gorman, *Reading Revelation Responsibly*, 15.

44. I will refer to the writer of Revelation as "the seer."

45. Richard Bauckham, *Theology of the Book of Revelation*, NTT (Cambridge: Cambridge University Press, 1993), 89.

46. See 11:7; 12:7–17; 13:7; 16:12–14; 17:14; 19:11–16; 20:7–9.

Divine violence is also exercised against evil structures and systems. Indeed, the two beasts referred to above represent Rome and her systems of propaganda,[47] so it is not wholly possible to separate the first of our categories from the second. Indeed, one of the most striking places where violence is exercised against a structure is in chapter 17, where Rome is represented as the prostitute Babylon and subjected to the aggression of the beast. However, this treatment is clearly represented as being of divine origin (Rev 17:16–17), and this act is in response to the prostitute's own rampant violence, for she—Rome—is "drunk with the blood of the saints, the blood of the martyrs of Jesus" (17:6 ESV).[48]

For many modern readers the representation of Rome as a female prostitute, subjected to what might be viewed as sexualized violence (17:16; 18:21), is very disturbing.[49] However, it should be noted that cities were commonly—and not always negatively—personified in the Old Testament and that Rome was frequently self-represented as the woman Roma. The seer is drawing on both of these traditions as he constructs his imagery. Further, the image of the city as prostitute is mainly used in the Old Testament to point to the ungendered sins of pride and economic oppression, something which is certainly true of Rome and forms part of the seer's indictment against her (Rev 18:11–13). As Yarbro Collins writes,

> Besides idolatry, the qualities especially condemned in Rome are violence, oppression, arrogance, and pride. According to Revelation 17–18, the imperial system involves bloodshed (17:6; 18:24), slavery (18:13), and a false, overblown sense of self-sufficiency and power (18:7).[50]

Responsible handling of this passage will recognize that its critique of Roman power is sharpest toward the *men* who held most of that power.[51] As I have written elsewhere, "It is the weak and the vulnerable—often women—who suffer at the hands of abusive economic policies. The message of Revelation 17–18 is good news for them, and we should note this and proclaim it unabashedly."[52]

---

47. Bauckham, *Theology of the Book of Revelation*, 89.

48. Howard-Brook and Gwyther argue that Revelation employs language explicitly to challenge the myths (the foundational beliefs) that Rome propagated about herself: "In the empire's myth, military success and the quelling of dissent made for victory. Revelation's apocalyptic insight unveiled victory as the preparedness to lay down one's life in resistance to empire, and the willingness to live the way of God for the long haul" (Wes Howard-Brook and Anthony Gwyther, *Unveiling Empire: Reading Revelation Then and Now* [Maryknoll, NY: Orbis, 2006], 230).

49. Tina Pippin, *Death and Desire: The Rhetoric of Gender in the Apocalypse of John* (Louisville: John Knox, 1992), 105.

50. Adela Yarbro Collins, "Feminine Symbolism in the Book of Revelation," *BibInt* 1.1 (1993): 27.

51. Jonathan C. Groce, "Does It Help to Transgender the Whore of Babylon?" (Submitted for the Sixth Annual Fordham Theology Graduate Students Association Conference, 2016), 3.

52. Helen Paynter, "'Redeeming the Prostitute': Babylon and Her Fate in Revelation," in *Violent Biblical Texts: New Approaches*, ed. T. Laurence and H. Paynter (Sheffield: Sheffield Phoenix, 2022), 273.

Third, humans appear to be the object of divine violence in Revelation. No individual is singled out for violent attention, but certain groups of people, such as those who worship the beast and its image, receive violent judgment (e.g., Rev 14:9–10).

In summary, in Revelation the eschaton appears to be brought in by use of divine violence. But are humans co-opted to the project? As I will show, human involvement is far less evident.

Human Violence and the Divine Project

There are two very significant theme words in the book of Revelation. These are *martys* and *nikaō*, both with their cognates.[53] *Martys*, although providing the etymology for our English word *martyr*, is best translated "witness" or, in its verbal form, "to testify." From the very beginning of the book, this theme is foregrounded, both in John's declaration that he bears witness, and by applying the title to Jesus himself just a few verses later.

> The revelation from Jesus Christ, which God gave him to show his servants what must soon take place. He made it known by sending his angel to his servant John, who testifies [*martyreō*] to everything he saw—that is, the word of God and the testimony [*martyria*] of Jesus Christ. . . .
>
> Grace and peace to you from him who is, and who was, and who is to come, and from the seven spirits before his throne, and from Jesus Christ, who is the faithful witness [*martys*], the firstborn from the dead, and the ruler of the kings of the earth. (Rev 1:1–5)

Martys and its cognates are repeated on multiple occasions throughout the book and are frequently linked with death.[54]

Throughout Revelation the language of conquering (*nikaō*) is closely tied up with that of witness. The seven churches of Revelation 2–3 are called to conquer by their faithfulness, which is a key element of *martys*. We see the association most explicitly in the proclamation of 12:11, where the saints conquer the accuser.

> They triumphed [*nikaō*] over him
>   by the blood of the Lamb
>   and by the word of their testimony [*martyria*];
> they did not love their lives so much
>   as to shrink from death.

---

53. See the discussion in Stephen Finamore, *God, Order and Chaos: René Girard and the Apocalypse* (Bletchley: Paternoster, 2009), 135–46.

54. E.g., Rev 1:5; 2:13; 6:9; 11:3–13; 12:11, 17; 20:4. See Finamore, *God, Order and Chaos*, 136.

Thus witnesses, or martyrs, are not simply passive spectators or beneficiaries of the eschatological events portrayed in Revelation.[55] Rather, they are active participants in the eschatological process.[56] *But this is not through violence.* Like all true prophets, they speak truth that unmasks the lies of the devil and his consorts.[57] And just as Jesus's faithful witness even to death was followed by divine vindication, so their faithful witness even to death is followed by their vindication, which brings the victory of the Lamb to bear upon the earth.[58]

Likewise, the army arrayed behind the heavenly rider at the battle of Armageddon plays no part in the fight (Rev 19:11–15).[59] This is in striking contrast to the books of Enoch and the War Scroll (1QM), which, as we have seen, seek to stir up human violence for the eschatological project. Revelation contains plenty of exhortations, but none of these is to violent action.[60]

At this point we should note a caveat. It is true of all texts, but never more so than of Revelation, that one's starting point conditions one's interpretation. What I have set out above—and what will follow—is not uncontested. Even among Christians who hold this text as Scripture (and there are many readers who don't), some would claim that the book promises a nonviolent eschaton, some believe it contains extremes of violence, and there are many points in between. For example, Paul Middleton, who does not position himself as a Christian scholar, argues that those who find a nonviolent theme in Revelation detect it only because they are "driven by a prior theological commitment that non-violence is integrally related to the heart of God's purpose."[61] Of course, nobody reads the text without some sort of prior ideological commitment. With this caution in mind, we will now continue by thinking further about the divine violence we have identified.

Revelation and Violence
Some Violence Is Corrective

In some cases, the divine violence might be serving a corrective or warning function within the narrative of the text. For example, the locusts of Revelation 9 are permitted

55. The word *martus* gradually developed in its meaning from a legal witness to one who testifies to their faith at the threat of death, to one whose testimony leads to death, and finally to one who is killed for their faith. In the book of Revelation it carries a middle connotation, where witness and death are both implied. See Allison A. Trites, "Μάρτυς and Martyrdom in the Apocalypse: A Semantic Study," *NovT* 15.1 (1973): 72–80.

56. John P. M. Sweet, "Maintaining the Testimony of Jesus: The Suffering of Christians in the Revelation of John," in *Suffering and Martyrdom in the New Testament: Studies Presented to G. M. Styler by the Cambridge New Testament Seminar*, ed. William Horbury and Brian McNeill (Cambridge: Cambridge University Press, 1981), 116.

57. Bauckham, *The Climax of Prophecy: Studies on the Book of Revelation* (London: T&T Clark, 1993), 275.

58. Bauckham, *Climax of Prophecy*, 280–81.

59. Simon Woodman, *The Book of Revelation*, SCM Core Text (London: SCM, 2008), 78.

60. Helen Morris, "Lions in Lambs' Clothing? A Response to Middleton's *The Violence of the Lamb: Martyrs as Agents of Divine Judgement in the Book of Revelation*," in *Map or Compass? The Bible on Violence*, ed. M. Spalione and H. Paynter (Sheffield: Sheffield Phoenix, 2022), 139–56.

61. Paul Middleton, *The Violence of the Lamb: Martyrs as Agents of Divine Judgement in the Book of Revelation* (London: Bloomsbury T&T Clark, 2018), 7.

to afflict those who are not marked with the divine seal, but only for five months, and not fatally (v. 5). This appears to echo the locust plague of Exodus 10:4–15, which clearly functioned as a warning to the people of Egypt.[62]

Metaphors of Violence

It is important to be attentive to the complex and sometimes conflicting set of metaphors that the book offers. As discussed above, metaphor and imagery are an integral part of apocalyptic writing. Alongside its evidently symbolic images, Revelation's more prosaic language of fire, battles, and so on also needs to be understood as metaphorical. John is writing within a thought-world—which we share—that has the operational metaphor, "ARGUMENT IS WAR." Such images shape the imagination, both of the ancient writer and of his readers. As Susan Hylen writes:

> In John's vision we never escape these violent metaphors. John is as embedded in them as we are. Yet exploring the conventional nature of John's metaphors may serve as a reminder that modern interpreters do not have the moral high ground, looking down upon John, who witlessly reinscribes the violence of Rome. All of us speak from within the limits of human language and culture.[63]

Within this metaphorical domain, not all the violence we encounter maps to actual violence in an actual future world. Violence in the *literary* world can have a nonviolent rhetorical effect in the *actual* world of the seer's original readers—and his twenty-first century ones.[64]

The Nonviolent Turn

A good example of Revelation's unexpected nonviolent turn is offered by Richard Bauckham, who considers that the writer is deliberately deploying military imagery to challenge the militaristic language of other war scrolls.[65] Viewed in this way, much of the warlike imagery becomes a deliberate, pacific turn rather than something that Christian apologists need to explain away. Bauckham demonstrates this in several ways.

First, in 5:5–6, the seer *hears* a message to expect a conquering lion, using two key Old Testament titles for the Davidic Messiah. But what he *sees*—surprise!—is not a lion but a slain lamb. This is the first of several "this is heard but that is seen" turns in the book, whereby the seer subverts the expectation of the reader.[66] Further, the image of a slain lamb brings the slaughtered lamb of Isaiah 53 into the reader's mind.

---

62. Woodman, *Book of Revelation*, 135–36.
63. Susan E. Hylen, "Metaphor Matters: Violence and Ethics in Revelation," *CBQ* 73.4 (2011): 796.
64. This point is ably made in Morris, "Lions in Lambs' Clothing?," 149.

65. Bauckham, *Climax of Prophecy*, 232.
66. Bauckham, *Climax of Prophecy*, 214.

Second, in 7:2–14, the seer *hears* about 144,000 sealed, who are then enumerated as 12,000 from each tribe of Israel. There are clear points that relate this list to the census of Numbers 1, which is explicitly a count of fighting men.[67] There are resonances here with the War Scroll, too, which lists an army by division into twelve tribes. But what the seer *sees* is actually a great multitude from "every nation, tribe, people and language" (7:9)—in other words, this is far beyond Israel. This multitude is dressed in white, like the festal garments of those who celebrate victory, and waving palm branches, like the Maccabees did after recapturing Jerusalem.[68] But what is the victory they are celebrating? Verse 14 reveals it—slowly, like all good punch lines.[69]

- "These are they who have come out of the great tribulation." Like Daniel 12:1, this can be understood as a reference to victory in the eschatological war.
- "They have washed their robes and made them white. . . ." The washing of robes was part of the ritual postwar purification, described in Numbers 31:19–20.
- ". . . in the blood . . ." The War Scroll also has a victorious army washing its robes in blood. This was the blood "of the guilty cadavers."
- ". . . of the Lamb." Surprise!—it is by the self-sacrifice of the Lamb that the multitude are victorious.

Thus, the seer is deliberately subverting the militaristic expectations of his readers.

The third example Bauckham offers is in Revelation 14, where we learn a little more about the 144,000 of the eschatological army. According to verses 4–5,

These are those who did not defile themselves with women, for they remained virgins. They follow the Lamb wherever he goes. They were purchased from among mankind and offered as firstfruits to God and the Lamb. No lie was found in their mouths; they are blameless.

Once again, the seer is subverting expectations.[70] The sexual abstinence of the men reflects the ritual purity required of Israel's armies (Deut 23:9–14), a requirement also reflected in the War Scroll. And it leads the reader to assume that this 144,000 will wage war. But the assertion that "no lie was found in their mouths" once again recalls the slain lamb of Isaiah 53:9, in whose mouth there was no deceit. Further, the word translated above "blameless" (*amōmos*) could equally be rendered "without physical defect," just as were the slain lambs of the Passover. The 144,000 do not wage war.

Nor does the great host of Revelation 19, who stand behind the heavenly rider. This rider conquers by means of the sword of his mouth, a subversion of the militaristic metaphor that has previously been signaled (1:16; 2:12, 16):

67. Bauckham, *Climax of Prophecy*, 216.
68. Bauckham, *Climax of Prophecy*, 225.
69. Bauckham, *Climax of Prophecy*, 226–27.
70. Bauckham, *Climax of Prophecy*, 231–32.

> I saw heaven standing open and there before me was a white horse, whose rider is called Faithful and True. With justice he judges and wages war. . . . He is dressed in a robe dipped in blood,[71] and his name is the Word of God. The armies of heaven were following him, riding on white horses and dressed in fine linen, white and clean. Coming out of his mouth is a sharp sword with which to strike down the nations. (Rev 19:11–15)

This, of course, is the fuller expression of the *martys* theme we picked up earlier. The witnesses (and here the faithful witness, Jesus Christ, 1:5) conquer by their faithful testimony that exposes the lie of the evil one.

The Revelatory Function of Literary Violence

Related to this is the possibility that some of the violence we encounter in Revelation is in fact not descriptive of divine judgment but rather is *revelatory* of *human* violence. One particular place where this may be the case is with the four riders (the notorious four horsemen of the apocalypse) of Revelation 6.[72]

Elisabeth Schüssler Fiorenza argues that the bow carried by the first rider (6:2) would evoke recollections in the mind of the original audience of the Parthians and Babylonians; in other words, of imperial power. Thus, the first four seals (the four horsemen of the apocalypse) *reveal* imperial brutality rather than describing divine judgment:

> They describe: the defeat of the expansionist military rule of the Roman Empire; the inner strife and war undermining Rome's claim to worldwide peace wrought by Augustus (Pax Romana); the concomitant inflation that deprived especially the poor of their essential food sustenance; and last but not least, pestilence and death as bitter consequences of imperialistic war, civil strife, and epidemics of hunger. . . . Although the seven seal plagues are set in motion by the Lamb as the agent who opens the seals, John does not assert that these calamities are decreed by God. God authorizes the calamities but does not will them. Rather, Revelation's visionary rhetoric reveals the true nature of the reality and power of Babylon/Rome in its inevitable collapse.[73]

The seven seals, therefore, depict both "*things brought to light* and processes set in motion by the Christ event," inextricably linked with the enthronement of Christ.[74] The violence in John's literary world uncovers the violence of the real world.

---

71. Whose blood stains are on the rider's robe is debated. Some consider that it is the blood of his enemies (cf. Rev 14:20) and others that it is his own blood (cf. Rev 7:14). If it is his own blood, which is the interpretation I favor, then this is another subversion of the eschatological warrior motif. See, e.g., Isa 63:1–6, where the eschatological warrior has his enemies' blood on his robes.

72. Finamore, *God, Order and Chaos*, 179–85.

73. Elisabeth Schüssler Fiorenza, *Revelation: Vision of a Just World*, Proclamation Commentaries (Minneapolis: Fortress, 1991), 63.

74. Finamore, *God, Order and Chaos*, 215 (emphasis added).

Violence in Revelation: Some Conclusions

What conclusions should we therefore draw about the book of Revelation and its use of violence by God and his allies? First, and perhaps most importantly, there is little evidence that the martyrs and the saints are employed in this. Second, a good proportion of the militaristic language is employed in order to *subvert* militarism. There is a strong, if not overwhelming, strand of anti-violence within the book. Third, within the literary world at least, God exercises the violence of judgment in order to bring about the eschaton.

Should we be troubled by this? Perhaps we are reaching beyond the scope of the book, which after all is about *human* violence. But the question begs some comment, and as we shall see, it has implications for human conduct. The problem that many perceive is neatly posed by David Barr, who writes, "If God triumphs over evil only because God has more power than evil, then power—not love or goodness or truth—is the ultimate value of the universe."[75]

Miroslav Volf takes a different stance. Although he acknowledges the violence of the book (he describes Rev 19 as a "veritable orgy of hatred, wrath, and vindictiveness"[76]), he argues that the divine violence it graphically represents is a necessity, because "without such judgment there can be no world of peace, of truth, and of justice."[77] For this reason, he suggests, the vision of Christ as the white rider who conquers (Rev 19) should not be regarded as contradictory to the Christ of Golgotha:

> The violence of the Rider on the white horse, I suggest, is the symbolic portrayal of the final exclusion of everything that refuses to be redeemed by God's suffering love. For the sake of the peace of God's good creation, we can and must affirm this divine anger and this divine violence.[78]

However, for Volf such divine violence emphatically does not provide a template for human action: "Preserving the fundamental difference between God and nonGod, the biblical tradition insists that there are things which only God may do."[79] Helen Morris takes this a step further in a bold move: "The notion of a transcendent judge who will one day exercise perfect justice is the *only foundation* on which a call to non-violent resistance can solidly stand."[80]

Ultimately, it is only the confidence that God will one day right all wrongs that emboldens us to defer our claim upon justice and act in nonviolent self-sacrifice.

75. David L. Barr, "The Lamb Who Looks Like a Dragon?," in *The Reality of Apocalypse: Rhetoric and Politics in the Book of Revelation*, ed. David L. Barr (Atlanta: SBL, 2006), 211.

76. Miroslav Volf, *Exclusion and Embrace: A Theological Exploration of Identity, Otherness, and Reconciliation* (Nashville: Abingdon, 1996), 228.

77. Volf, *Exclusion and Embrace*, 229.

78. Volf, *Exclusion and Embrace*, 231.

79. Volf, *Exclusion and Embrace*, 232.

80. Morris, "Lions in Lambs' Clothing?," 156.

CONCLUSION

In this chapter we have asked whether God uses violence as he makes all things new, and whether he co-opts human violence to the divine project of re-creation. We considered several of the creation–de-creation–re-creation cycles: flood, exodus, conquest, and exile, and noted that each of these entails a certain degree of divine violence. The conquest and exile also use human violence, although this is always subsidiary to the divine role. However, the return from exile is viewed by the prophets as an act of God alone, and this is also reflected in the eschatological goal set out by the prophets and the New Testament. While divine violence at the eschaton is difficult—some would say undesirable—to deny, there is little to no evidence that God's people have any violent role in the eschatological project. Rather, the exhortations of Revelation are to bear faithful witness to the kingship of Jesus, if necessary to the point of death.

We have not examined the eschatological parables of Jesus, but these align with the conclusions we have reached. Unlike the teachings of Jesus in (for example) the Sermon on the Mount, the eschatological parables relate to the final judgment and the time when the opportunity for conversion has passed. Here, too, the violence is all God's, and there is no human involvement.[81]

The questions we have addressed in this chapter will prove to be highly relevant as we move toward the later part of the book, where we will attempt to draw come conclusions about ethical conduct in the present day. If the building of a new world is a project that permits, nay requires, human violent action, then every visionary leader with a utopian goal can legitimately mobilize an army to their project. But as we have seen, the saints are called rather to faithful tenacity until the Lord returns.

> Be faithful, even to the point of death, and I will give you life as your victor's crown. (Rev 2:10)

RELEVANT QUESTIONS

1. Can you think of contemporary examples that reflect an eschatological (or utopian) vision and employ human violence to achieve it?
2. Can a God who is sometimes violent call for nonviolence from his people?
3. Might a violent God be good news?

---

81. Barbara E. Reid, "Violent Endings in Matthew's Parables and Christian Nonviolence," *CBQ* 66.2 (2004): 237–55.

CHAPTER 11

LIVING THE NEW REALITY

The earliest church that we see in the New Testament did not forget or neglect Jesus's message of peace.
—Ronald J. Sider, *If Jesus Is Lord*

Readers who have been following the argument developed in the book so far might be wondering why we have skipped wholly over the book of Acts, and largely omitted the epistles from our consideration, moving rapidly from the cross to the eschaton. While the eschaton might be considered to close the theological trajectory in theoretical terms, we have of course not yet arrived there in reality. We, the author and readers of this book, live in the "time between the times"—the era between the Christ event and the final judgment—and we have this in common with the first Christians. Therefore, this final chapter in the "Arriving at Answers" section of the book will seek to learn from the early church as they, like us, seek to answer the question, "How then should we live?"

In this pursuit we have two forms of evidence, which we need to treat differently. First, we have the authoritative apostolic teaching, as recorded in Scripture. We should not forget, however, that the epistles are all *occasional* letters, that is, they were written for specific pastoral situations. They were not systematic theology lectures; arguably none of the epistles is seeking to set out a definitive theology of anything, but each reflects the apostle's practical application of relevant theological principles to the problems in hand.[1]

Second, we have the practice of the early church, both as recorded in the Acts of the Apostles (or inferred from the epistles), and as recorded in the writings of the early church. We need not view this as necessarily normative,[2] but we would be foolish if we wholly disregarded the opinion of those whose lives overlapped

---

1. The occasional nature of the epistles is well summarized in the editors' series introduction at the start of the NIV Application Commentary on Acts: "God's Word is *timely*. The authors of Scripture spoke to specific situations, problems, and questions. . . . [This] enables us to hear God's Word in situations that were *concrete* rather than abstract. . . . Yet the timely nature of Scripture also creates problems. Our situations, difficulties, and questions are not always directly related to those faced by the people in the Bible. . . . Fortunately, Scripture is not only timely but *timeless*. Just as God spoke to the original audience, so he still speaks to us through the pages of Scripture. Because we share a common humanity with the people of the Bible, we discover a *universal dimension* in the problems they faced and the solutions God gave them. The timeless nature of Scripture enables it to speak with power in every time and in every culture" (in Ajith Fernando, *Acts*, NIVAC [Grand Rapids: Zondervan, 1998], 10–11 [emphases original]).

2. For a discussion on this matter, see Gordon Fee and Douglas Stuart, *How to Read the Bible for All Its Worth*, 4th ed. (New York: Harper Collins, 2016), 123–28.

with Jesus and the apostles and who were the very first interpreters of the teaching of Jesus.

In this chapter, then, we will briefly survey elements of the teaching and practice of the early church, using as two test cases military service (physical violence), and slavery (structural violence). We will extend our consideration of historical practice somewhat beyond the New Testament period, engaging with the patristic writers, but our survey ends before the conversion of Constantine in 312 CE. The change in policy and power structures that followed this event ended the church's position as an outsider in society and began a period where—arguably—her greatest temptation was to collude with the state in all its bloody apparatus. Whether the church made the right decisions in those days has been the subject of much debate, but it is beyond the scope of our survey here.[3]

We will begin by surveying the theme of peace as the apostles explore it.

PEACE AS A THEME IN THE NEW TESTAMENT

New Testament scholar David Wenham has shown that the teaching of the apostle Paul is deeply indebted to the tradition begun by Jesus.[4] The dominical tradition is also clear in the Petrine and Jacobite letters. One of the themes that echoes most clearly is the need to return good for evil, and the refusal of vengeance. The Sermon on the Mount, for example, with Jesus's radical exhortation to enemy love, echoes in much of the New Testament (e.g., Rom 12:14–20; 1 Cor 4:12–13; 1 Thess 5:15; 1 Pet 3:9).[5]

The Greek word usually translated "peace" is *eirēnē*, and its frequency of use in the New Testament indicates the priority placed upon it by the apostles. It occurs almost a hundred times in the New Testament, and to this we should add related themes such as the injunctions to unity and against quarreling.

The gospel heralded by the angels with the promise of peace on earth (Luke 2:10–14) is later described by Paul as the "gospel of peace" (Eph 6:15). Disturbingly for some, this phrase is found within Paul's military image of the Christian being equipped in spiritual armor. The apostle is here adapting the metaphor of the divine

---

3. As a British Baptist I reflexively look askance at the Constantinian development, but I was interested to read this comment by Tom Wright, then Bishop of Durham: "If you want to see what it looks like for God's renewed people in Christ to be 'royal,' to be 'rulers' in the sense indicated by the vocation to be a 'royal priesthood,' don't look at the fourth and fifth centuries, when the Roman emperors first became Christian. . . . Look instead at what the church was doing in the first two or three centuries, while being persecuted and harried by the authorities" (Tom Wright, *Virtue Reborn* [London: SPCK, 2010], 194–95).

4. David Wenham, *Paul: Follower of Jesus or Founder of Christianity?* (Grand Rapids: Eerdmans, 1995). Along with the undisputed letters, Wenham considers 2 Thessalonians, Colossians, and Ephesians. He uses the Pastoral Epistles more slightly (24).

5. Sider, *If Jesus Is Lord*, 70–71.

warrior found in Isaiah 11:5, 52:7, and 59:17 and offers this peroration to motivate the Ephesian believers in their resistance against evil.[6] By instructing them to equip themselves in this way, he is telling them to clothe themselves in the characteristics of God himself.[7]

Lest there be any doubt that the battle Paul has in mind is not a physical one, he emphasizes its spiritual nature:

> Put on the full armor of God, so that you can take your stand against the devil's schemes. For our struggle is not against flesh and blood, but against the rulers, against the authorities, against the powers of this dark world and against the spiritual forces of evil in the heavenly realms. (Eph 6:11–12)

Elsewhere in the New Testament, *eirēnē* is coupled with *theos* ("God") five times[8] and with *kyrios* ("Lord") once (2 Thess 3:16), including one reference that emphasizes that the association of peace with *spiritual* conflict is unproblematic in Paul's mind: "the God of peace will soon crush Satan under your feet" (Rom 16:20).

Closely linked with peace, reconciliation (*katallagē* and its cognates) is, for Paul, a feature of the new order instituted by Christ, which is made visible in the present age by the church (e.g., 2 Cor 5:17–19).[9] Of course, this means reconciliation between humans and God through Christ (v. 18), but it is also fundamental to the existence of the church, which is God's new community where the age-old enmity between Jew and gentile is abolished.

> For [Christ] himself is our peace, who has made the two groups one and has destroyed the barrier, the dividing wall of hostility, by setting aside in his flesh the law with its commands and regulations. His purpose was to create in himself one new humanity out of the two. (Eph 2:14–15)

We see this reconciliation at work in a remarkable way in the book of Acts, when Peter is summoned to the house of Cornelius, who is a centurion and thus part of the oppressive, occupying army (Acts 10). Remarkably, notwithstanding his alarming circumstances, the message that Peter preaches highlights the very things that Paul would be writing about in years to come: God's impartial love and the gospel of peace.

---

6. Klyne Snodgrass, *Ephesians*, NIVAC (Grand Rapids: Zondervan, 1996), 334–36.

7. Snodgrass, *Ephesians*, 339.

8. Rom 15:33; 16:20; Phil 4:9; 1 Thess 5:23; Heb 13:20.

9. In Rom 8:6 and 14:17, Paul makes it clear that the very nature of this new Spirit-given life is peace.

> I have read the story of Peter and Cornelius many times, but it acquired a whole new depth of meaning for me in 2018 when I heard it preached (via translation) in a church in Lebanon. The speaker was a Syrian Christian, who described the terror of receiving a knock on the door in the middle of the night by Assad's police. He powerfully communicated the raw fear of being rudely awoken by those who hold power over you and have no goodwill toward you. This, we might imagine, would be how Peter and his friends would have experienced the visitation by the centurion's messengers. His natural reluctance would have been not simply a religious or ethical repulsion but also because the occupying Roman forces were, in very real terms, the enemy, who generally displayed no love for the Jewish people and who bore the power of arbitrary death and detention.

I now realize how true it is that God does not show favoritism but accepts from every nation the one who fears him and does what is right. You know the message God sent to the people of Israel, proclaiming peace through Jesus Christ, who is Lord of all. (Acts 10:34–36, adapted from the NIV)

Peter's words are no empty gesture; he has chosen the most pertinent and striking message to declare to this household. Proclaiming peace would have been understood by Jewish[10] and gentile listeners alike to refer to the cessation of hostilities.[11] To Peter's soldier host, the words would have been a deeply poignant expression of the unexpected hospitality of God, a hospitality that is shortly enacted as he is baptized into the name of the same Lord as his Jewish guest was. As Willie Jennings so beautifully puts it,

> The waters of baptism signify the joining of Jew and Gentile, not simply the acceptance of the gospel message. Yet both are miracle. Both are grace in the raw. . . . In a quiet corner of the Roman Empire, in the home of a centurion, a rip in the fabric of space and time has occurred. All those who would worship Jesus may enter a new vision of intimate space and a new time that will open up endless new possibilities of life with others.[12]

Romans 13

With this strong emphasis on peace and reconciliation in the apostolic literature in mind, Romans 13 may seem to strike a jarring note, with its emphasis on compliance with (by definition, corrupt) governments. It begins thus:

10. Deut 2:26; Judg 21:13.
11. Craig Keener, *Acts: An Exegetical Commentary: 3:1–14:28* (Grand Rapids: Baker Academic, 2013), 801.
12. Willie James Jennings, *Acts: A Theological Commentary on the Bible* (Louisville: Westminster John Knox, 2017), 93–94.

Let everyone be subject to the governing authorities, for there is no authority except that which God has established. The authorities that exist have been established by God. Consequently, whoever rebels against the authority is rebelling against what God has instituted, and those who do so will bring judgment on themselves. (Rom 13:1–2)

On the face of it, Paul seems to have taken a wrong turn here. Unlike Peter and John, who firmly tell the ruling officials that their duty is to obey God rather than human authorities (Acts 4:18–19), here Paul seems to be advocating compliance with the Roman Empire, in all its brutal strength. Accordingly, this passage has become well-loved by heavy-handed regimes seeking a biddable population. In the 1990s, it was even called "apartheid's last biblical refuge."[13]

Scholars have taken a number of different approaches to this conundrum. Walter Wink, whose exegesis of "turn the other cheek" we considered in chapter 9, considers that the verbs *antitassō* and *anthistēmi*, rendered "rebel" and "rebelling" in the NIV quotation above, refer to violent uprising rather than more peaceful forms of resistance. Accordingly, he translates verse 2 like this:

Therefore the person who engages in armed revolt against the political system commits insurrection against what God has ordained.[14]

Others, such as Douglas Moo, draw a distinction between specific *obedience* in all circumstances and *submission*, which is a more generalized posture.

Paul calls on believers to "submit" to governing authorities rather than to "obey" them; and Paul's choice of words may be important to our interpretation and application of Paul's exhortation. To submit is to recognize one's subordinate place in a hierarchy, to acknowledge as a general rule that certain people or institutions have "authority" over us.[15]

Moo, along with many scholars, points to the occasional nature of the letter. Paul is not (necessarily) making a declaration of a universal instruction but rather is responding to the particular circumstances in which the Roman church was operating. Laboring under the misapprehension that the return of the Lord Jesus was imminent, they were perhaps tempted to throw off all restraint and civic obedience.

13. Winsome Munro, "Romans 13:1–7: Apartheid's Last Biblical Refuge," *BTB* 20.4 (1990): 161–68. The text was also used by the German church during the rise of the Third Reich to justify collusion with Hitler (Richard N. Longenecker, *The Epistle to the Romans: A Commentary on the Greek Text* [Grand Rapids: Eerdmans, 2016], 962). More recently, it was quoted by the then US Attorney General Jeff Sessions to attempt to quell resistance to the Trump administration's bullish policy toward immigrants (Julie Zauzmer and Keith McMillan, "Sessions Cites Bible Passage Used to Defend Slavery in Defense of Separating Immigrant Families," *Washington Post*, June 15, 2018, www.washingtonpost.com/news/acts-of-faith/wp/2018/06/14/jeff-sessions-points-to-the-bible-in-defense-of-separating-immigrant-families/).

14. Walter Wink, *Violence and Non-Violence in South Africa: Jesus' Third Way* (Philadelphia: New Society, 1987), 58–61.

15. Douglas Moo, *The Epistle to the Romans*, NICNT (Grand Rapids: Eerdmans, 1996), 797.

They might, in fact, have been inclined to take Paul's instructions not to conform to the present age (Rom 12:1–2) rather too far.

> To the degree that this age is dominated by Satan and sin, Christians must resolutely refuse to adopt its values. But the world in which Christians continue to live out their bodily existence (see 12:1) has not been wholly abandoned by God. As a manifestation of his common grace, God has established in this world certain institutions, such as marriage and government, that have a positive role to play even after the inauguration of the new age.[16]

Further, it is likely that Paul was writing as early as 57–58 CE, well before the persecution under Nero, which began in 64 CE. In these circumstances it was reasonable to suggest that compliance with the state was not only theologically justifiable but also pragmatically wise.[17]

It is not possible to review here the full range of opinions on what Paul intends in this text, but some broader points can be made. First, the culmination of his argument here is in verse 7, which makes it clear that he is referring primarily to taxation.[18] Second, his exhortation in these verses needs to be read in conjunction with his broader theological argument: the Roman Christians should *not* conform to the pattern of this world but rather seek to obey God's "good, pleasing and perfect will" (12:2). Moreover, they are to operate with love, that is, in generosity, hospitality, peaceableness, and non-vengeance (vv. 9–21). Third, Paul's words here need to be read alongside the evidence that he later gets into serious trouble with the authorities. While he worked hard to bear witness to his innocence when he could, and operated within the parameters of law as best he was able,[19] his actions more than once resulted in imprisonment, and—by generally accepted tradition—martyrdom.

Tom Wright considers that Paul's words in Romans 13 reflect a desire to see the church in Rome engage its challenges with theological maturity.

> A robust monotheism knows that the Creator wants there to be [civic] authorities, and that they are themselves responsible, whether they know it or not, to God himself. The gospel does not sanction the apolitical spirituality of gnosis, nor does it sanction the one-dimensional revolution for which many of Paul's countrymen were even then preparing. [Paul] does not want the Jesus movement to be confused with the zealotry of Jerusalem.[20]

So, in the light of the turbulent times in which the early Christians lived, to what extent did their practice and teaching bear witness to the dominical and apostolic

16. Moo, *Epistle to the Romans*, 791.
17. For a fuller discussion, see Walter E. Pilgrim, *Uneasy Neighbors: Church and State in the New Testament* (Minneapolis: Fortress, 1999), 27–36.
18. Longenecker, *Romans*, 967.
19. See, e.g., Acts 22:22–23:11.
20. Tom Wright, *Paul: A Biography* (London: SPCK, 2018), 335.

emphasis upon peace and peacemaking? We now turn our attention to the next generation of Christians.

MILITARY SERVICE IN THE EARLY CHURCH[21]

Very shortly after the apostles came the next wave of Christian leaders. The perspectives and practices they offer need not necessarily be viewed as normative and certainly should not be received as canonical, but they deserve serious consideration because of their proximity to the time of Jesus and the apostolic age. The evidence we will consider can be grouped into two broad categories: evidence *about* the practice of the early church, and teaching that was written *for* the church.

Practice

From sources dated prior to around 172 CE, there is no evidence of Christians serving in the army. However, arguments from silence can be misleading and should be interpreted with caution. Part of the reason for the absence of Christians from the army may have been that the early church was largely comprised of slaves and freedmen, who were ineligible for military service.[22]

Probably the first clear indication of Christians serving in the army is found in the writings of Tertullian (ca. 155–220 CE) and Eusebius (ca. 260–339 CE). They both describe an incident that took place in 172 CE, where Marcus Aurelius's army was saved by a sudden rainstorm, and they ascribe this to the prayers offered by the Christians serving in his legion.[23] Written about twenty-five years after that incident, Tertullian's *Apology*, which attempts to defend Christians from the charges of atheism, treason, and other crimes, makes a passing reference to Christians serving in the army.

> We sojourn with you in the world, abjuring neither forum, nor shambles, nor bath, nor booth, nor workshop, nor inn, nor weekly market, nor any other places of commerce. We sail with you, *and fight with you*, and till the ground with you; and in like manner we unite with you in your traffickings.[24]

---

21. I am grateful to Brandon Hurlbert, whose excellent masters dissertation *Dulce et Decorum Est Pro Christo Mori: The Nonviolent Rule of Faith of the Ante-Nicene Fathers* (Durham University, 2018) helped inform my understanding of the patristic views on war. I was also guided by the unpublished essay by T. C. Moore titled "Christ, the Church, and the Sword: Evidence for a Consistent Nonviolent Kingdom Ethic in the New Testament and the Early Church," November 2007, which is available here: www.academia.edu/3343871/Christ_the_Church_and_the_Sword_Evidence_for _a_Consistent_Nonviolent_Kingdom_Ethic_in_the_New _Testament_and_the_Early_Church.

22. Roland H. Bainton, *Christian Attitudes toward War and Peace: A Historical Survey and Critical Reevaluation* (New York: Abingdon, 1960), 68.

23. F. Cross and E. Livingstone, eds., "Thundering Legion," in *The Oxford Dictionary of the Christian Church* (Oxford: Oxford University Press, 2005), 1631.

24. Tertullian, "The Apology," in *Latin Christianity: Its Founder, Tertullian*, ed. A. Roberts, J. Donaldson, and A. C. Coxe, trans. S. Thelwall (Buffalo: Christian Literature Company, 1885), 49 (emphasis added).

De Corona (or *The Crown*) written by Tertullian in 211, provides further evidence for Christian involvement in the military. Here, Tertullian refers to the case of a Christian soldier imprisoned and facing execution for refusing to carry the laurel crown. In 295 CE, a twenty-one-year-old recruit from North Africa, Maximilian, was brought to trial and executed for refusing to serve in the army on the grounds of his Christian faith. It is unclear whether his objections lay in his unwillingness to wear the imperial seal or to fight.[25] The proconsul who was trying him pointed out that Christians were known to be serving in the imperial guard. Whatever the young man's exact reasons, his calm and repeated refusal to do what he considered wrong, even to the point of martyrdom, later earned him canonization, and he is widely regarded today as the first known conscientious objector.

This brief survey would seem to indicate that early Christian *practice* was somewhat mixed. But what were the early church fathers actually *teaching*? (There is nothing new about church congregations acting in ways that are contrary to the preaching and teaching they receive!)

Teaching

It is a striking fact that prior to the time of Constantine, none of the patristic writers wrote in favor of military service.[26] The ante-Nicene church fathers appear to be of one mind in preaching nonresistance and nonviolence. Some spoke in terms of a new law of Christ, which prohibited violence and mandated enemy love.[27] Here are examples from the writings of Justin Martyr (ca. 100–165 CE) and Irenaeus (ca. 130–202 CE).

> We patiently endure all things contrived against us by wicked men and demons, so that even amid cruelties unutterable, death and torments, we pray for mercy to those who inflict such things upon us, and do not wish to give the least retort to any one, even as the new Lawgiver commanded us.[28]

> From the Lord's advent, the new covenant which brings back peace, and the law which gives life, has gone forth over the whole earth, as the prophets said: "For out of Zion shall go forth the law, and the word of the Lord from Jerusalem; and He shall rebuke many people; and they shall break down their

---

25. Peter Brock, "Why Did St Maximilian Refuse to Serve in the Roman Army?," *JEH* 45.2 (1994): 195–209.

26. Indeed, a Greek critic of Christianity, Celsus, appears to have argued that Christians were irresponsible in their refusal of military duty and that the empire would be left defenseless if it were entirely in their hands. Celsus's arguments have not survived and can only be reconstructed by reading his opponents' refutations, most notably those of Origen. See John Friesen, "War and Peace in the Patristic Age," in *Essays on War and Peace: Bible and Early Church*, ed. Willard M. Swartley (Elkhart: Institute of Mennonite Studies, 1986), 132–33.

27. William L. Elster, "The New Law of Christ and Early Christian Pacifism," in Swartley, *Essays on War and Peace*, 108–29.

28. Justin Martyr, "Dialogue of Justin with Trypho, a Jew," in *The Apostolic Fathers with Justin Martyr and Irenaeus*, ed. A. Roberts, J. Donaldson, and A. C. Coxe, vol. 1 (Buffalo: Christian Literature Company, 1885), 203.

swords into ploughshares, and their spears into pruning-hooks, and they shall no longer learn to fight."[29]

Of the extant writings from the early fathers, it was Tertullian who wrote most on the subject of nonviolence. He argued that, notwithstanding the evidence of Old Testament violence, Jesus had now forbidden it. Indeed, military service was antithetical to true Christian faith.

> There is no agreement between the divine and the human sacrament,[30] the standard of Christ and the standard of the devil, the camp of light and the camp of darkness. One soul cannot be due to two *masters*—God and Caesar. . . . The Lord, in disarming Peter, disarmed every soldier.[31]

In the matter mentioned above, where a soldier stood in jeopardy of his life for refusing to wear the laurel crown, Tertullian argued again that military service was incompatible with Christian faithfulness.

> I think we must first inquire whether warfare is proper at all for Christians. . . . Do we believe it lawful for a human oath to be superadded to one divine? . . . Shall it be held lawful to make an occupation of the sword, when the Lord proclaims that he who uses the sword shall perish by the sword? And shall the son of peace take part in the battle when it does not become him even to sue at law?[32]

Indeed, he states that a soldier who comes to faith must leave the army.

> When a man has become a believer, and faith has been sealed, there must be either an immediate abandonment of it, which has been the course with many; or all sorts of quibbling will have to be resorted to in order to avoid offending God.[33]

Tertullian's emphasis is that the Christian's rule of life leans toward martyrdom rather than violence. Christians had good reason to act in violent vengeance, but their rule of life forbade it.

> Banded together as we are, ever so ready to sacrifice our lives, what single case of revenge for injury are you able to point to, though, if it were held right among us to repay evil by evil, a single night with a torch or two could achieve

29. Irenaeus, "Irenæus against Heresies," in Roberts, Donaldson, and Coxe, *Apostolic Fathers with Justin Martyr and Irenaeus*, 512.

30. Here Tertullian is playing on words. *Sacramentum* in Latin can refer to a military oath.

31. Tertullian, "On Idolatry," in Roberts, Donaldson, and Coxe, *Latin Christianity*, 73.

32. Tertullian, "The Chaplet, or De Corona," in Roberts, Donaldson, and Coxe, *Latin Christianity*, 99.

33. Tertullian, "The Chaplet, or De Corona," 100.

an ample vengeance? . . . For what wars should we not be fit, not eager, even with unequal forces, we who so willingly yield ourselves to the sword, if in our religion[34] it were not counted better to be slain than to slay?[35]

It is clear from even this relatively small set of samples that the church fathers' reasons for forbidding military participation are diverse. This is further complicated by the fact that many of the writings we have were *apologias*, addressed to pagan authorities. Because of this intended audience, they tend to argue from natural law rather than Scripture.

For some of the church fathers, the sticking point appears to have been the incompatibility between allegiance to Christ and the unconditional loyalty that the army demands, expressed in the oath to Caesar. Similar to this is Maximilian's reluctance to bear the imperial seal. For many in the early church, such actions were considered idolatrous.

But for others, it was the mismatch between the bearing of fatal weapons and Jesus's commands and example that caused them to defy conscription, even to the point of death. Preeminently, the Sermon on the Mount and Jesus's instruction to Peter to put away his sword were the texts used and quoted. They also used the "spiritual armor" text from Ephesians 6, and in various ways reconfigured the Old Testament texts of violence. Origen is perhaps the clearest example of this; he at least partially dehistoricizes the wars of Joshua and uses them to make a point about spiritual warfare.

> Unless those physical wars bore the figure of spiritual wars, I do not think the books of Jewish history would ever have been handed down by the apostles to the disciples of Christ, who came to teach peace, so that they could be read in the churches. For what good was that description of wars to those to whom Jesus says, "My peace I give to you; My peace I leave to you," and to whom it is commended and said through the Apostle, "Not avenging your own selves," and, "Rather, you receive injury," and, "You suffer offence"? In short, knowing that now we do not have to wage physical wars, but that the struggles of the soul have to be exerted against spiritual adversaries, the Apostle, just as a military leader, gives an order to the soldiers of Christ, saying, "Put on the armor of God so that you may be able to stand firm against the cunning devices of the Devil."[36]

With the accession of Constantine and his reported dream where he saw a cross in the sky and was told "in this sign, conquer" came the end to this solid

34. The Latin underlying this is *disciplinam*. In the English translation I quote, it is translated "religion," but perhaps "rule of life" might be more appropriate.

35. Tertullian, "Apology," 45.

36. Origen, "Homily 15," in *Homilies on Joshua*, ed. Cynthia White and Barbara J. Bruce (Washington, DC: Catholic University of America Press, 2002), 138.

tradition of Christian pacifism.[37] From this point on, the Christian faith was first tolerated and then became the official religion, and so Christianity found itself aligned with the ruling body. It suddenly became in the state's interest to permit Christians to serve in the military. Depending on one's viewpoint, it might be considered that the church made a Faustian bargain at this point from which it has never recovered.

> When the power of the empire became joined to the ideology of the Church, the empire was immediately recast and re-energized, as the Church became an entity so different from what had preceded it as to be almost unrecognizable.[38]

In summary, the early church before Constantine appears to have taken very seriously Jesus's words about enemy love and surrendering the sword, and as a result was largely—at least at the leadership level—in opposition to Christian participation in the military. Consideration must be given as to whether the early church's practice should be viewed as normative or contextually determined. Are other practices permissible in different situations? We will be considering such questions further in future chapters.

Having examined the matter of bearing arms as a test case for the early church's stance on physical violence, we now turn to a consideration of one of the most egregious situations of structural violence extant in its day.

SLAVERY

The institution of slavery offers us a case study in structural violence. Readers are reminded of the discussion in chapter 6, however, where we discussed the evolving nature of human slavery and the differences between the experience of Roman slaves and the enslavement of Black people in the transatlantic slave trade. This should be borne in mind in the following discussion.

Slavery in the New Testament

Slavery as a metaphor is frequently employed by the writers of the New Testament epistles.[39] But the use of this imagery need not imply that the writers were indifferent to the suffering or condition of actual slaves. For example, on the basis that most slaves were only "freed" by death, Paul uses the slavery metaphor to indicate our utter entrapment by sin (Rom 6:6–7).

---

37. Bainton, *Christian Attitudes*, 85.

38. James Carroll, *Constantine's Sword* (Boston: Mariner, 2001), 171.

39. E.g., Paul employs the metaphor in Rom 6 to discuss the new ethical reality for the one who has "died with Christ" (vv. 1–18).

New Humanity

As we shall see, the Pauline letters appear to assume the ongoing existence of slavery within society and within the church. Paul's interest, in the main, is in the spiritual condition of slaves who were baptized into the church. He repeatedly insists that their status as slaves is irrelevant to their status in God's kingdom (1 Cor 12:13; Gal 3:28–29; Col 3:11).

In legal terms, a slave had no father and no children, whatever their actual biological relationships.[40] So it is remarkable that Paul tells (mainly gentile) slaves that they are "Abraham's seed"—full members of the family of God (Gal 3:29). Not only that, but they are *heirs* in the kingdom of God. Paul is employing the same logic that he uses in Ephesians, where he sets out the new humanity achieved by Christ, here expressed in terms of Jew and gentile (Eph 2:14–18).

Paul's emphasis on the equal status of slaves seems to correspond with what we know of the practice of the early church. The list of prominent Christians whom Paul greets at the end of his letter to Rome contains a large number of names typically given to slaves.[41] His instructions to wealthy Corinthian Christians that they should not start the Eucharist meal until the poorer people had arrived (1 Cor 11:17–22) might well have been intended to allow time for household slaves to make their way to the gathering—individuals who would not finish their work until the evening.[42]

Gain Your Freedom If You Can

However, Paul's failure to offer an explicit critique of slavery should not be inferred as indifference about the practice. He encourages slaves who are able to gain their freedom to do so (1 Cor 7:21–22). As ever, Paul is eager to offer reassurance that their slave status does not mean they are in any way "second class" Christians—a highly countercultural assertion to the status-conscious Corinthians. His emphasis in the wider passage (vv. 10–24) is that no one need seek to change their status—married to unmarried, uncircumcised to circumcised, or free to slave. As so often, his argument is angled toward gospel usefulness. To the Christian married to an unbeliever, he writes, "How do you know, wife, whether you will save your husband? Or, how do you know, husband, whether you will save your wife?" (v. 16).

Gospel usefulness is a huge priority for Paul, a principle he himself lived by. Using the slavery motif, Paul writes:

40. Jennifer Glancy, *Slavery in Early Christianity* (Oxford: Oxford University Press, 2002), 25.

41. Robert Jewett, *Romans: A Commentary on the Book of Romans* (Minneapolis: Fortress, 2007), 965.

42. There is little in the Pauline corpus that would seem to relate to slaves working in an agricultural context (Glancy, *Slavery in Early Christianity*, 40).

Though I am free and belong to no one, I have made myself a slave to everyone, to win as many as possible. . . . To the weak I became weak, to win the weak. I have become all things to all people so that by all possible means I might save some. I do all this for the sake of the gospel, that I may share in its blessings. (1 Cor 9:19–23)

For Paul, the call of Christ, with all its attendant suffering, trumps all other considerations.

Slaves, Obey

But what are we to make of the repeated apostolic exhortations to slaves to obey their masters? There are five places in the epistles where such instructions are given, and three different rationales are offered. Ephesians 6:5 and Colossians 3:22 are very similar texts, set within passages dealing with household codes. In both, Paul commends obedience because the slave is to understand that their work is ultimately directed to Christ, and it is God who will reward obedience. In both of these commands, masters are also addressed and reminded that God shows no partiality.

The Pastoral Epistles offer another reason for slaves to be obedient to their masters—so as not to bring the gospel into disrepute. Writing to Timothy, Paul[43] urges obedience by slaves in order that "God's name and our teaching may not be slandered" (1 Tim 6:1). Similarly, in his letter to Titus he instructs obedience so that "in every way they will make the teaching about God our Savior attractive" (Titus 2:9). Once again Paul demonstrates his concern that the gospel should not be hindered by anything.

Perhaps the hardest of these apostolic instructions is found in 1 Peter, although it is fully in line with the teaching of Jesus in the Sermon on the Mount. In Peter's letter, slaves are instructed to submit to their masters, even when those masters are harsh. Peter points to the pattern of Christ's submission to unjust suffering and shares Paul's belief that God will reward such obedience (1 Pet 2:18–21).

We discussed in chapter 9 that giving instructions such as these is perhaps the prerogative of those who suffer for the faith themselves. It is noteworthy that the Greek word *hypophero*, here in 1 Peter 2:19 translated "bear up under," was later used by Clement of Alexandria about Peter's own faithful suffering to death.[44] It should also be noted that Peter nowhere implies that the Christian should seek to suffer; he simply assumes that suffering is likely to attend the discipleship of the faithful Christian.

---

43. I am using the name "Paul" for the author of the letter here, without assuming the debate over the authorship of the Pastoral Epistles has been settled.

44. Dennis R. Edwards, *1 Peter*, SGBC (Grand Rapids: Zondervan, 2017), 117.

Onesimus

Paul's most direct and prolonged treatment of the slavery question is found in his epistle to the slaveowner Philemon, a letter which contains little overt exposition of theology but is richly informed by deep theological reflection.[45] Philemon, a Christian believer, had lost his slave Onesimus, who appears to have run away[46] and found his way to Paul, becoming a believer at some point in that process. In his letter to the wealthy slaveowner, Paul asks Philemon to welcome Onesimus back as he would welcome Paul himself (v. 17).

Is Paul asking Philemon to set Onesimus free on his return? Possibly, although manumission may not have been the unmitigated blessing that twenty-first century Westerners imagine. Once freed, an ex-slave was cast upon their own resources and often struggled to gain a toehold in the economy.[47] But Paul's priority seems to be the reconciliation of Christian brothers, offering an instruction that "chips away at the brick wall of slavery, even if it falls short of a full denunciation."[48]

> Perhaps the reason he was separated from you for a little while was that you might have him back for good—no longer as a slave, but better than a slave, as a dear brother" (vv. 15–16).

This is an expression of Paul's conviction that the church constitutes an eschatological foretaste of the new humanity wrought in Christ.[49] Any decision to manumit Onesimus would follow from his understanding of this. Keeping a brother Christian in slavery would hardly be compatible with this belief.[50]

Slavery in the Postapostolic Church

Turning our attention now to the postapostolic era, it cannot be denied that the church's record on slavery was rather poor. The Didache, a second-generation (probably late first century) Christian manual, said nothing about manumission but followed the apostles in urging slaves to obedience and masters to leniency.

> Thou shalt not lay commands in thy bitterness upon thy bondman or bondmaid, who hope in the same God, lest they perchance shall not fear the God who is over you both; for he cometh not to call men according to the appearance, but to those whom the Spirit hath made ready. And ye, bondmen, ye shall be subject to your lords, as to God's image, in modesty and fear.[51]

45. Marianne Meye Thompson, *Colossians and Philemon* (Grand Rapids: Eerdmans, 2005), 229.
46. For a discussion of alternative possibilities, see Douglas J. Moo, *The Letters to the Colossians and to Philemon*, Pillar New Testament Commentary (Grand Rapids: Eerdmans, 2008), 366–68.
47. Moo, *Letters to the Colossians and to Philemon*, 371.
48. Edwards, *1 Peter*, 122n22.
49. See Eph 2:14–18. This argument is made in Thompson, *Colossians and Philemon*, 230.
50. Moo, *Letters to the Colossians and to Philemon*, 373.
51. Didache 4.10–11, as found in H. D. M. Spence-Jones, *The Teaching of the Twelve Apostles: A Translation with Notes; and Excursus (I. to IX.) Illustrative of the "Teaching"; and the Greek Text* (London: James Nisbet, 1885), 11.

Writing at about the same time, Ignatius appears to forbid the use of church funds to purchase manumission for slaves.[52] His motivations for this edict are disputed. Some consider that he was attempting to protect slaves from the moral compromises that they might have to make in order to survive after obtaining their freedom. Others consider his intentions to be more sinister.[53]

More troubling still is the story recounted in the Acts of Andrew (late second or early third century), which tell of a Christian woman, Maximilla, who used her slave girl Euclia as a body double in her bed, in order to avoid becoming polluted by her vile and unbelieving husband Aegeates. The Acts of Andrew condemns Euclia for her attempt to blackmail her mistress but implicitly endorses the actions of Maximilla.[54] We should, of course, remember that most Christians had little opportunity to exercise political power or influence societal structures in those days. Nevertheless, within the constraints that were operative, the early church's record seems to be patchy, at best.

Slavery and the Early Church: Some Conclusions

It cannot be denied that many of us would be a lot more comfortable if the apostles had raged against slavery as a dehumanizing practice. It may be that they could not imagine a society where the institution did not exist.[55] There is evidence that even slaves themselves do not appear to have been able to imagine an end to slavery; even the slave revolts (e.g., the one led by Spartacus in 73–71 BCE) were about working conditions rather than aiming toward abolition.[56]

As we read about the early church's ineffectual response to slavery, it may not become us to throw the first stone, since the evils of our own day have often exercised us insufficiently. Consider, for instance, our failure to tackle climate change. N. T. (Tom) Wright draws the comparison:

> Slavery in the ancient world did, more or less, everything that is done in our world by oil, gas, or electricity, everything that we accomplished through our technology. Denouncing slavery would have been like denouncing electricity and the internal combustion engine.[57]

---

52. Ignatius of Antioch, "The Epistle of Ignatius to Polycarp," in Roberts, Donaldson, and Coxe, *Apostolic Fathers with Justin Martyr and Irenaeus*, 94–95.

53. For a helpful discussion, see John Francis Super, "Slavery and Manumission in the Pre-Constantine Church," *Eleutheria* 2.2 (2013): 3–17.

54. Glancy, *Slavery in Early Christianity*, 22.

55. Zvi Yavetz, *Slaves and Slavery in Ancient Rome* (New Brunswick: Transaction, 1991), 117.

56. Ben Witherington III, *Conflict and Community in Corinth: A Socio-Rhetorical Commentary on 1 and 2 Corinthians* (Grand Rapids: Eerdmans, 1995), 183.

57. Tom Wright, *Paul: A Biography* (London: SPCK, 2018), 281.

What the apostles did was address slaves as morally competent agents, affirm their equal status in the church, and call on masters to regard their believing slaves as brother Christians. These texts were remarkable in their time; William Webb describes them as "quietly suggestive" in that they opened up the possibility for future generations to take the ethic to a new level.[58]

They did this by laying theological foundations for the dismantling of slavery, not simply within the texts that explicitly speak on the matter but more broadly in the eschatological vision of the new humanity that they offer. Joel Green makes this point.

> When one considers the warrants for slavery in the Roman world (particularly the alleged distinction between slave and free with regard to inherent capacities and status), it is obvious that Peter's theological perspective . . . must trigger the unraveling of the institution of slavery.[59]

Green's comments are made about the first Petrine letter, but they would apply equally, perhaps even more intensely, to the Pauline corpus. In fact, there is perhaps an important principle to discover here. Paul's practical theology for the churches is *always* rooted in his understanding of the deep theology of the incarnation, death, and resurrection of Jesus Christ (which I will here term the Christ-event). It is as this event is worked out that the church will discover how to live.[60]

In his book, *Cruciformity: Paul's Narrative Spirituality of the Cross*, Michael Gorman shows how verses 6–8 of the christological hymn of Philippians 2 forms a sort of theological grammar for Paul. The structure of the hymn could be paraphrased:

> Although Jesus was God,
>   yet he did not take advantage of his entitlements,
>   but rather he took the journey to the cross.

These three elements, "although . . . yet not . . . but rather," form a paradigm for the way that Paul approaches many of the pastoral issues he addresses. See, for example, 1 Corinthians 8:4–13, where Paul applies this cruciform grammar to the question of the eating of idol meat. While idol meat may not be a pressing problem in our generation, how we should approach those who are weaker in one way or another is always relevant.[61]

---

58. William J. Webb, *Slaves, Women, Homosexuals: Exploring the Hermeneutics of Cultural Analysis* (Downers Grove, IL: InterVarsity Press, 2001), 85.

59. Joel B. Green, *1 Peter*, Two Horizons New Testament Commentary (Grand Rapids: Eerdmans, 2007), 78–79.

60. For an exploration of this theme, see Michael Gorman, *Cruciformity: Paul's Narrative Spirituality of the Cross* (Grand Rapids: Eerdmans, 2001).

61. Gorman, *Cruciformity*, 203–4.

| Theology of the Christ event | Practical theology for the church |

But Paul shows no interest in directly confronting the morality of wider society. As Ben Witherington writes, Paul is no revolutionary.

> Paul's approach is to put the leaven of the gospel into the structure of the Christian community, not into the larger society directly, and let it do its work over the course of time. As with the matter of women, Paul believes in living a true Christian life and letting the natural implications of that bring transformation to the patriarchal and slave society. He meant for the Christian community to live out its new freedom, thus bearing witness to the larger community about their values. Apparently, no early Christian, by litigation or by appeal to governing authorities or by revolt, ever tried to change the social fabric of ancient society. It was by means of witness and *change within the Christian community* that a new worldview was promulgated.[62]

This is in accordance with the teaching of Jesus, that the kingdom of God works like yeast within society (Matt 13:33). Good theology shapes the practice of the church (although we might wish it had shaped it more quickly), and the church functions as prophetic witness to the eschatological reality instituted in Christ. In other words, the order of effect is this:

| Theology of the Christ event | Practical theology for the church | Witness to wider society |

This approach, of course, emerged within an early church that existed at the margins of society and did not possess the social capital to make direct appeals to the center of power. Nonetheless, we might have wished that there were clearer evidence of the "yeast" working in the first centuries after Christ.

CONCLUSION

In regard to physical violence, there is good evidence that the teaching of the early church fathers was in line with the nonviolent ethic of Jesus that we considered in chapters 8 and 9. The actual practice of early Christians seems more mixed, however, probably reflecting the morally ambiguous world in which they were operating.

With regard to structural violence, the early church was slower to enact meaningful change, although the apostolic teaching directed the trajectory of the church

---

62. Witherington, *Conflict and Community in Corinth*, 185 (emphasis added).

toward justice. To switch metaphors, the New Testament church set rolling the first stones that were, over the centuries, to become an avalanche.[63] Lest we be critical of a perceived sluggishness by the early church on these matters, we should note that the circumstances in which they lived were very different from the world that most of the readers of this book inhabit. Most of them occupied places at the margins of society, often slaves themselves; and Christians of all classes endured the waves of brutal persecutions that crashed down upon them in the reigns of the emperors Nero, Marcus Aurelius, and some of their successors. As we saw in the previous chapter, for such people true discipleship looks like faithful witness even to the endurance of death.

We should not imagine, however, that the early church valorized suffering and martyrdom. Not every Christian who died violently at Roman hands was regarded as a martyr for the faith. Key to their understanding of martyrdom was that it was a death that could not (faithfully) be avoided *but was not sought out*.[64] This is consonant with the theology of innocent suffering we identified in chapters 8 and 9, and which does not valorize suffering for its own sake. The passion of Christ was redemptive; our human suffering is not.

Like us, the early Christians lived in the "time between the times," seeking to live in the reality of the kingdom of God that has been inaugurated by Jesus Christ and is yet to be fully consummated at the eschaton. Like us, they operated in a morally ambiguous world, with often limited power and agency, and yet with the commands of Jesus ringing in their ears:

> Blessed are the peacemakers,
>   for they will be called children of God. . . .

> You are the salt of the earth. But if the salt loses its saltiness, how can it be made salty again? (Matt 5:9, 13)

Like us, they came to a variety of conclusions on how to live faithfully in their time. How we navigate these questions is the subject of the final part of this book.

---

63. A number of scholars have in recent years made an argument for the centrality of the Christian gospel in the great social changes that have shaped the Western world through history to the present day. Three of them include the agnostic historian Tom Holland, *Dominion: How the Christian Revolution Remade the World* (New York: Basic Books, 2019); the Eastern orthodox philosopher and religious essayist David Bentley Hart, *Atheist Delusions: The Christian Revolution and Its Fashionable Enemies* (New Haven: Yale University Press, 2009); and the evangelical apologist Glen Scrivener, *The*

Air We Breathe: How We All Came to Believe in Freedom, Kindness, Progress and Equality (London: The Good Book Company, 2022).

64. Jason Brunner, *Imagining Persecution: Why American Christians Believe There Is a Global War against Their Faith* (New Brunswick: Rutgers University Press, 2021), 37. See, e.g., Clement of Alexandria, "The Stromata, or Miscellanies," in *Fathers of the Second Century: Hermas, Tatian, Athenagoras, Theophilus, and Clement of Alexandria*, ed. A. Roberts, J. Donaldson, and A. C. Coxe, vol. 2 (Buffalo: Christian Literature Company, 1885), 423 (iv.x).

RELEVANT QUESTIONS

1. If the waters of baptism join Jew and Greek, slave and free, male and female, whom do you encounter there that you would rather not—and how do you respond to that?

2. From a twenty-first century perspective, we might say that the early church was blind to the structural injustice of slavery. What structural injustices will future generations judge that we were blind to?

REFLECTING ON RELEVANCE

TOWARD A PRAXIS

As we move into the third section of this book, "Reflecting on Relevance," it seems important to stop and consider where we have got to so far. We have looked at the question of human violence in the Bible as addressed in myth, narrative, law, psalm, wisdom, prophecy, gospel, epistle, and apocalypse.

Our findings from these extensive studies cannot be boiled down into a simple answer. We have seen wars commanded and peacemaking exhorted. We have seen the violent punished and rewarded. Weapons have been celebrated and denigrated. How are we to move forward?

COHERENCE AND DISPARITY IN SCRIPTURE

Perhaps the canonical shape of Scripture can help us. In the course of our studies of the biblical testimony on violence, we have noted the strikingly generous, hospitable, and nonviolent creation shown in Genesis 1 and 2, and how these themes are recapitulated in the final two chapters of Revelation, where the new heavens and new earth manifest the eschatological climax of *shalom*. As I view Scripture, these four chapters form twin peaks, poking above the clouds, gloriously exemplifying God's original purpose and his ultimate intent for his creation (albeit expressed in finite human speech).

But between these chapters, we are always watching humanity living in a nonideal world, struggling with God and one another. At times we face the brutality of that world in all its darkness. At other times we see humans, under the guidance of God, rising above that violence and demonstrating greater qualities of love, peacemaking, and humility. Throughout God speaks, guides, leads, and rebukes. Humanity is never left to its own devices. Ultimately, having spoken through the prophets at various times and in various ways, God speaks by his Son. But always in these in-between times, humans fail to inhabit their calling. Even Jesus's disciples, three years into a close-quarters training program, pull a sword at the first sign of threat. And as we shall discuss shortly, always in these in-between times, ethical demands will strain away from one another. Justice seems only to be attainable by disturbing the peace; peacemaking often seems to necessitate the setting aside of justice claims.

So how are humans to navigate this in-between time, as we await the eschaton? How are we to resolve these tensions? In "Queuing the Questions," we considered three ways that we might interrogate Scripture where it does not seem to speak with a single voice. Should we seek coherence, at the risk of marginalizing deviant texts? Should we attend to polyphony within the text, trusting that truth will be discerned in the clash of voices? Should we look for the emerging theme, aiming to plot the developing trajectory and allowing later texts to trump earlier ones? At times, each of these approaches will be helpful, although as we have discussed each one carries inherent risk if it is allowed to eclipse the other approaches.

Therefore, as we begin to move from the study of the texts to a consideration of their application, I propose the following brief conclusions, framed using the three hermeneutical approaches above.

Coherence

The coherent testimony of Scripture is that violence is an inescapable part of life in the postlapsarian world. The Bible shows throughout, by example and instruction, that violence begets violence and that left to our own devices, humans spiral downward into a vortex of mutual destruction. However, the testimony is also coherent that the eschatological goal, spoken of by prophets, seers, and Jesus himself, is a nonviolent, just, and peaceful new heavens and earth. There is a theological development in the exploration of how that will ultimately be achieved, but Scripture seems coherent in its assertion that it will necessitate some *divine* violence.

Polyphony

There are a number of places where Scripture seems to be in dialogue with itself. For example, recall the disparate accounts of the conquest of Canaan in the books of Joshua and Judges concerning how complete the territory was taken and how total the extermination. The violence of the conquest appears to be—in part—deprecated by the text.

Development

The theme of warfare shows development within Scripture, with physical warfare being endorsed and commanded by God, then undergoing narrative subversion, and then being spiritualized into the believers' struggle with evil and the eschatological battle. Similarly, the theme of vengeance is developed; first by the limitation of personal vengeance by the law of talion and then by the extension of that limitation into an ethic of enemy love and forgiveness. Third, the theme of human involvement in the violence of the divine project appears to undergo considerable development until the book of Revelation, where humans are (arguably) not involved at all.

In chapter 2, we considered a particular canonical method: Richard Hays's approach to New Testament ethics. This begins with a detailed analysis of the theme within each biblical document on its own terms. This is similar to the approach that we took throughout the "Arriving at Answers" section. Hays's next step is to attempt a synthesis of the biblical witness. In this chapter we will attempt to do this by drawing out some eschatological themes from the sum of our study: justice, peace, and holiness.[1]

Like the biblical writers, we too live between the first and last times. It is therefore the proposal of this chapter that there is no single faithful way to live with regard to violence. Instead, we might approach the question using the metaphor of improvisation.

IMPROVISATION

With fear and trembling we must work out a life of faithfulness to God through responsive and creative reappropriation of the New Testament in a world far removed from the world of the original writers and readers.[2]

As we saw in chapter 2, we are not intended to live by a rule book (though rules can provide valuable guardrails), nor are we intended to determine the best possible outcome for the maximum number of people by the application of some incalculable equation. Rather, by the work of the Spirit who forms the character of Christ within us, we are to develop the virtues which will help us to make Christlike decisions in each moment.

N. T. Wright has famously offered the metaphor of the unfolding purposes of God being a drama in five acts, where the first four are the great scriptural moves of creation, fall, Israel, and Jesus. In Wright's scheme, the fifth act is an improvisation by the church.[3] The church of the New Testament provides the first scene in that final act, as God's people begin to tease out what it means to be faithful and Christ-shaped in their generation. But every subsequent generation of the church has its own scene to play. The faithful task is to improvise in a way which is consonant with the trajectory of the first four acts but does not rest in the first century. Rather, it continues to develop the great themes which were begun in the Old Testament, brought to a climax in Jesus Christ, and applied by the apostles, toward the eschaton.

Wright's metaphor is particularly helpful because it positions the task of improvisation within a *narrative* framework. The task "require[s] sensitivity of a high order to the whole nature of the story and to the ways in which it would be (of course) inappropriate simply to repeat verbatim passages from earlier sections."[4]

1. Richard Hays, *The Moral Vision of the New Testament: Community, Cross, New Creation: A Contemporary Introduction to New Testament Ethics* (San Francisco: HarperSanFrancisco, 1996), 3–7.

2. Hays, *Moral Vision of the New Testament*, 6.

3. N. T. Wright, "How Can the Bible Be Authoritative?," *Vox Evangelica* 21 (1991): 7–29.

4. Wright, "How Can the Bible Be Authoritative?," 11.

Wright's approach would be consistent with the work of William Webb and Gordon Oeste on the "redemptive trajectories" of Scripture. As they set out their scheme, in each new phase of the developing story God is tugging his people forward, moving their ethics and conduct a little closer to an as-yet-unrealized ultimate destination. In the final chapter of Webb and Oeste's book, they acknowledge the limited, incomplete journey of that trajectory so far. Their response is to point to the radical discontinuity of the eschaton and to the final judgment when God will right all wrongs.

> This is our final better answer: the justice story is not yet finished. . . . The biblical story line encourages us to believe in a God of complete and profoundly pristine justice who will someday right all wrongs.[5]

This is indeed the trajectory of Scripture and the destination toward which we are to orient ourselves. But we are not intended passively to wait for that time, whether in a posture of hopefulness or of dogged perseverance. Rather, we are invited to *participate* in the task of bringing the kingdom of God to bear upon the earth. And the eschatological vision is essential in orienting us. As Trevor Hart writes:

> The performance has a vital eschatological dimension and energy. In our Christian "will to meaning," we do not just look backward, but perform hopefully toward a promised and imagined end.[6]

Our task, then, is not to carve out from Scripture a "truth" about peace and violence and then stand still, holding it in our hands like a precious thing. Our task is to journey forward, battling through the jungle of confusion, pain, despair, and moral complexity that our world presents, setting off in the direction we have been pointed toward and moving onward toward the destination we have glimpsed. There is no single path, not because God's standards are flexible but because we are seeking to discern how to apply them in a broken world. But there are routes that will take us forward and others that will sidetrack us or lose us altogether. There is no map, because this way has not been trodden before—nobody has lived these years before us. Fortunately, though, there is a Guide, and we travel in community.

So here are some key principles for improvisation: it is to be conducted under the guidance of the Spirit, among the community of God's people, with attention to the scriptural trajectory, and straining toward the eschaton. With these in mind, I now venture to offer a framework for making decisions about violence.

5. William J. Webb and Gordon K. Oeste, *Bloody, Brutal and Barbaric? Wrestling with Troubling War Texts* (Downers Grove, IL: InterVarsity Press, 2019), 360.
6. Trevor A. Hart, "The Sense of an Ending: Finitude and the Authentic Performance of Life," in *Faithful Performances: Enacting Christian Tradition*, ed. Trevor A. Hart and Stephen R. Guthrie (London: Routledge, 2007), 185. See also Samuel Wells, *Improvisation: The Drama of Christian Ethics* (London: SPCK, 2004).

A PROPOSED FRAMEWORK

Three Eschatological Goals

I propose that our studies of Scripture have revealed three eschatological goals which, in the new heavens and the new earth, will be perfectly fulfilled.[7] They are: holiness, justice, and peace. In the end, God's now perfectly holy people will live in God's perfect new world, in perfect justice and perfect peace. These goals can only be understood in their biblical-theological setting; in other words, the narrative of the whole of Scripture exercises a control over our understanding of what they mean. Here we will briefly revisit a few key texts that we have already considered.

Consider Isaiah 11:1–9,[8] which speaks of the eschatological reign of the Messiah.[9] This reign will be characterized by perfect justice, through the wisdom of the Spirit.

> With righteousness he will judge the needy,
> > with justice he will give decisions for the poor of the earth.
> > > (Isa 11:4)

Yet at the same time, this reign will be characterized by peace, with divine shalom envisaged in what we today might characterize as cosmic-ecological terms.

> The infant will play near the cobra's den,
> > the young child will put its hand into the viper's nest.
> They will neither harm nor destroy
> > on all my holy mountain. (Isa 11:8–9)

In this final phrase, the goal of holiness is also indicated. God's king will be reigning from, and God's people will be inhabiting, God's "holy mountain." This term is commonly used in the prophets to refer to mount Zion and the temple. The use of the term here points toward the holiness that must characterize the eschaton because God's holy reign will be accomplished.

Not all of the eschatological texts in Scripture have all three goals clearly in view; some focus on just one. But overall, the testimony of Scripture appears to be that these three things will be perfectly coterminous in the world established by the eschaton. John the seer's vision of the new heavens and earth clearly show all three goals fully attained. There will be righteous judgment (Rev 20:11–12). The new Jerusalem is

---

7. I would not wish to claim that these are the *only* eschatological goals, but with regard to our investigation into human violence they seem to be the significant ones.

8. Cf. also Isa 2:2–4.

9. Although the Hebrew word *mashiakh* is not used in this passage, its messianic focus is clear: the anticipated one is a "root from the stump of Jesse" (i.e., a Davidic king), and he is endued with the Spirit (i.e., anointed).

represented as a bride in perfect purity, representing holiness (21:9–11, 27). And there is also perfect shalom. The city is unthreatened, her gates never needing to close (21:25), because those who commit violence are excluded (22:15). This peace is also emphasized in the comforting and unthreatening presence of God, where no grief is necessary (21:3–4; see also vv. 6–7, 22–23).

We will shortly move from this discussion of the eschatological goals to the virtues we need to practice now in order to move toward them. But while I shall argue that nobody is able to hold these together perfectly and that they always pull apart in our hands, we should of course note that there is One who did indeed manage to embody all of these at once.

When Jesus began his ministry by saying "the kingdom of God is at hand," he was in a very real sense not announcing its approach but declaring its arrival. This is borne out in a number of places, particularly where Jesus exhibits the signs of the eschaton, such as the raising of the dead, as well as on occasions when he explicitly states the presence of the kingdom (e.g., Luke 11:20; 17:21). And so, in the person of Jesus, all the marks of the eschaton are present, perfect in quality though still limited in scope (i.e., not yet cosmic).

Thus, Jesus demonstrates perfect justice. Consider his responses on occasions when he is asked to act in that capacity (e.g., John 8:16). He also demonstrates complete holiness. This is both the testimony in the epistles (e.g., 2 Cor 5:21; Heb 4:15; 1 Pet 2:22) and the narrative conclusion to which the Gospels direct us (e.g., Matt 8:3; Luke 23:13–15). And he exemplifies perfect peace. Not only does he speak peace into troubled situations (e.g., Mark 4:39; Luke 24:36), but he also lives the peaceable, nonviolent way that he teaches (e.g., Luke 22:47–53; 23:34).

In Jesus, then, all the eschatological goals coalesce. But we are not Jesus. So how then shall we live?

Three Present Virtues

While in eschatological terms justice, peace, and holiness are *goals*, in the here and now we are called to exercise related *virtues* to shape our praxis as we strain eschatologically. And as we have seen, Scripture speaks a great deal about the application of these virtues.

Justice-Making

Justice-making is a key value that underlies the Torah and is perhaps best exemplified in the law of talion (Exod 21:22–25; Lev 24:17–22; Deut 19:16–21)—a value that shapes the prayers of the psalmists and the prophets. The king of Israel was to exemplify justice in his righteous judgments, especially protecting those who were marginalized in various ways (e.g., Ps 72). In addition, the prophets (e.g., Amos) raged against injustice in the nation. Jesus commends those who "hunger and thirst for righteousness,"[10] and the concern for justice toward the weak and vulnerable was a mark of the early church (e.g., Acts 6:1–4) and the epistles (e.g., Jas 5:1–6).

Peaceableness

We have extensively studied the ways in which the arc of Scripture bends toward peace, including the gradual devalorization of warfare and subversion of vengeance. The society that the Old Testament law is attempting to build and the sages are promoting is one of neighborly cooperation and coexistence, where everyone sits under *their own* vine and fig tree (1 Kgs 4:25, cf. Mic 4:4). We have seen the way in which Jesus takes this trajectory to a whole new level, calling peacemakers "children of God" (Matt 5:9) and both commanding and enacting enemy love (e.g., Matt 5:38–48; Luke 23:34). This is explicated in Paul's theology of the church, which unexpectedly contains Jew and gentile as equal coinhabitants (e.g., Eph 3:1–6).

Purity

Finally, purity[11] as a step toward holiness is a key theme that runs through the whole of Scripture. Many of the cultic laws operated to enable the people to maneuver in the world where both sinful actions and normal bodily functions rendered one impure before a holy God. The covenant people of God, called into relationship with him (which is the very heart of covenant), were to be holy as he is holy (e.g., Lev 11:44, 45; 19:2; 20:26). This injunction is reflected in Jesus's words, "Be perfect as your heavenly Father is perfect" (Matt 5:48; cf. 5:20), as well as in the epistles (e.g., 1 Pet 1:15–16). Similar themes are found in the Pauline writings (e.g., Rom 12:1–2; 1 Thess 4:3–7) and in the other epistles (e.g., 1 John 1:5–7; Jude 23).

The Limitations of the Virtues

But there are two important differences between the eschatological goals we have been discussing and the virtues that lead toward them. First, in this "time between the times," the virtues "pull apart" from one another. The demands of justice may—and often do—compete with the demands of peace and purity. The pursuit of holiness may strain the virtues of justice and peace. And so on. Sometimes two of the virtues can be satisfied, and yet it is rare for all three to be in cohesion.

But none of these virtues is dispensable in the walk of faithful discipleship; no one of them may be prioritized at the expense of the other two. This is the nature of the complex and morally ambiguous world in which we operate. We could represent the tension in this way:

10. "Righteousness" here carries connotations of a just social order, possibly eschatological (John Nolland, *The Gospel of Matthew: A Commentary on the Greek Text*, NIGTC [Grand Rapids: Eerdmans, 2005], 203).

11. I trust that it is obvious that I am using this term broadly, and not in the narrow sense that is exclusively concerned with sexual conduct.

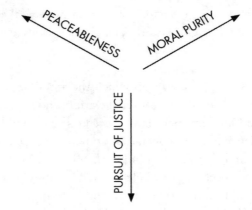

The second difference between the virtue and its matching goal is that each of the virtues carries an inherent danger when it is exercised by fallible people on this side of the eschaton. This is particularly true when it is exercised in isolation from the other virtues. Let us consider them one at a time.

Justice-Making

When equality and appropriate punishment become a goal above all other goals, the human tendency is to enforce this with coercion, causing harm in the process. We might recall the brutal pogroms of Stalin, ostensibly in the pursuit of a communist ideal of equality for all. But we do not need to look to such extreme examples. Many of us have experienced—or colluded with—the harsh rule of mini-tyrants in the form of a boss, teacher, or parent. Until it is perfected by the eschaton, justice will always carry the inherent threat of becoming utilitarian brute force. Scripture is full of examples of powerful men executing more or less dubious claims to justice with little mercy. We might consider David laying the defeated Moabites on the ground to measure two thirds of them for slaughter (2 Sam 8:2), or the brutal use of the "shibboleth"/"sibboleth" dialect difference to mark out the Ephraimites for killing at the fords of the Jordan (Judg 12:1–6). Justice, then, must be tempered with mercy.

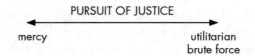

Peaceableness

If peace is equated with the absence of (overt) conflict, peaceableness can become a convenient pretext for inaction and collusion with evil. We might recall how David said and did nothing when his daughter Tamar was raped by his son, the crown prince Amnon. He is said to have been "furious" (2 Sam 13:21), but he did not set in motion the judicial procedures that would have vindicated Tamar and punished Amnon.[12] Here was the triumph of "peace" (or, rather, a quiet life) over the claims of justice.

As we will discuss in chapter 14, there is a huge difference between true pacifism and passivism. Peacemaking is an active, energetic, and often dangerous calling. Ignorance or indifference are inadmissible excuses.

> Rescue those being led away to death;
>> hold back those staggering toward slaughter.
> If you say, "But we knew nothing about this,"
>> does not he who weighs the heart perceive it? (Prov 24:11–12)

Peace, then, must be pursued with boldness, lest peaceableness become a euphemism for pusillanimity.

PEACEABLENESS

boldness   pusillanimity

Purity

Moral or ethical purity is grown through obedience to the teaching of Christ and cooperation with the Spirit who forms us in the likeness of Christ. But this is not an individualistic pursuit. Purity must be lived out incarnationally—it must have dirty hands—lest it become privatized piety and lead to social indifference. We might consider Pontius Pilate's very public washing of his hands as he sent Jesus to his crucifixion (Matt 27:24). In so doing, he attempted to signal his own innocence while simultaneously failing to take the very actions which could render him truly innocent of Jesus's blood. Or in the familiar parable of Jesus, we see the priest and the Levite who both walk past the (potentially dead) man on the road, prioritizing their lawful and appropriate concern for corpse impurity over their (also lawful) responsibility to love their neighbor (Luke 10:25–37).[13] Purity, then, is not something that can be cultivated in the cloister or the ivory tower. It must always have dirty hands; it must always be embedded in the messy reality of life.

MORAL PURITY

dirty hands   privatized piety

---

12. It is just such favoritism that the law of talion, often regarded as harsh, was framed to eliminate. It states, "Your eye shall not pity. It shall be life for life, eye for eye, tooth for tooth, hand for hand, foot for foot" (Deut 19:21 ESV).

13. Matthew Thiessen helpfully points out that this parable does not invite the reader (or Jesus's listeners) to pit love over law as if they were somehow opposed. See *Jesus and the Forces of Death: The Gospels Portrayal of Ritual Purity within First-Century Judaism* (Grand Rapids: Baker, 2020), 95–99.

Toward a Proposal

We can now put these three virtues back into the matrix we are building, showing how they continually operate in tension with one another. The diagram attempts to show that the three virtues pull apart less when they are tempered in the ways I have indicated. When justice is merciful, when peaceableness is bold, and when purity is willing to have dirty hands, they are more able to work together.

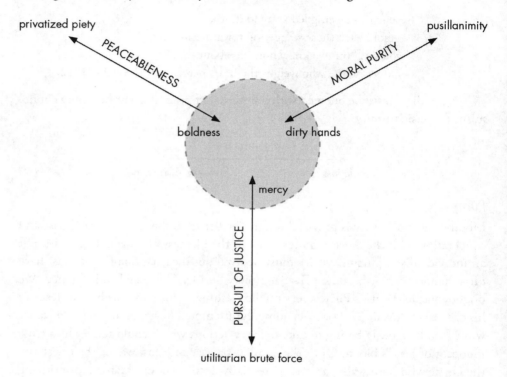

At the center of the matrix, I have added a shaded circle, which overlaps the ends of the three arrows. I suggest that this area represents the space for legitimate, faithful Christian action, the place where improvisation may take place. It will be readily observed that the shaded area has a finite size. There are positions that lie beyond it; there are actions which lie outside faithful Christian discipleship. But conversely there is no single point on the matrix that marks the ethical sweet spot. This reflects what I think is the biblical testimony that the priorities of justice, holiness, and peaceableness will need to be balanced differently in different situations. Equally faithful believers might come to different answers to the same set of questions. Within a limited range, these can be equally valid.

How is the decision to be made on any given occasion? Once again, we return to the principles outlined above. Improvisation is conducted along the trajectory indicated by Scripture, oriented toward the eschaton, is guided by the Spirit, and worked out within the community of God's people. This allows us to add the final pieces to the framework.

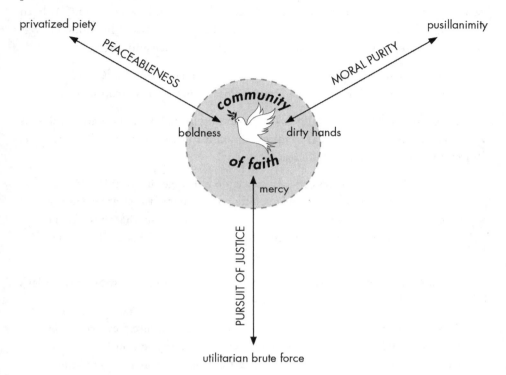

Some readers will wonder why the word *love* does not appear in the scheme above. This is because there is no single place to situate it. Love does not belong more clearly to the domain of peace than it does to that of justice. And, with the double love command in mind, the domain of purity also entails love. As Jesus said, "If you love me, you will keep my commandments" (John 14:15 ESV). Perhaps it would be better to say that the task of love is to discern the operational position within the framework above, in every given set of circumstances.

Considering the Tensions

The oppositional pull of justice and peace probably requires little explanation. To a large extent it is this tension that charges the just war-pacifism debate, which we will consider in chapter 14. The role of purity, however, might require more comment. The question is, to what extent should one prioritize one's own pristine conscience when compromise might alleviate injustice or effect peace? A tension might arise here too. Perhaps a good biblical parallel is when David and his men ate the forbidden Bread of the Presence (1 Sam 21:1–6), an action which Jesus endorsed (Matt 12:3–8).

In July and August 1932, the German pastor Dietrich Bonhoeffer addressed two international youth conferences, in Czechoslovakia and Switzerland.[14] At both events he reflected on the church's response to the global crisis of his time. He was evidently aware of the tension that can exist between peace and justice.

> A peace that violates justice and truth is no peace, and the church of Christ must protest against such peace. There can be a peace that is worse than struggle.[15]

But he was also aware of the dangers of responding to such unfathomable problems with passive withdrawal for fear of taking an ethical misstep. Rather, he urged, the church must be prepared to take risks.

> The church thus dares to say, for instance: do not wage this war; be socialists today, this commandment as God's commandment out of the clear recognition that it is possible therewith to take the name of God in vain, that the church is in error and is sinful, but it may speak it in faith in the word of the forgiveness of sins that holds true for the church as well.[16]

This was an early prefiguration of Bonhoeffer's decision to conspire against Hitler's life, a decision he made after much soul-searching:

> Because Jesus took the guilt of all human beings upon himself, everyone who acts responsibly becomes guilty. Those who, in acting responsibly, seek to avoid becoming guilty divorce themselves from the ultimate reality of human existence. . . . They place their personal innocence above their responsibility for other human beings and are blind to the fact that precisely in so doing they become even more egregiously guilty.[17]

Bonhoeffer's theology of sin and guilt is too complex for us to address in detail here,[18] but this relatively modern example is offered in order to demonstrate the interaction of the three poles I have outlined above.

14. I am indebted to Christopher Wilson, whose paper on Bonhoeffer's Christology in relation to Northern Ireland nationalism, presented at the Trinity College/Bristol Baptist College postgraduate research conference of 2021, drew my attention to this work of Bonhoeffer's.

15. Dietrich Bonhoeffer, *Ecumenical, Academic, and Pastoral Work Book: 1931–1932*, ed. E. Amelung, C. Strohm, V. Barnett, M. Brocker, and M. Lukens, Dietrich Bonhoeffer Works 11 (Minneapolis: Fortress, 2012), 380.

16. Bonhoeffer, *Ecumenical, Academic, and Pastoral Work Book*, 361.

17. Dietrich Bonhoeffer, *Ethics*, ed. C. Green, Dietrich Bonhoeffer Works 6 (Minneapolis: Fortress, 2005), 275–76.

18. The interested reader is directed to Christine Schliesser, *Everyone Who Acts Responsibly Becomes Guilty: Bonhoeffer's Concept of Accepting Guilt* (Louisville: Westminster John Knox, 2008).

CONCLUSION

Our detailed survey of Scripture over the previous chapters has shown that there is no simple answer to the question of human violence. Perhaps this should reassure rather than perplex us, however. Instead of a rigid set of rules that we might attempt to circumvent, or a utopian model that we might struggle to apply to modern realities, we have a rich, layered narrative that both reflects ultimate reality and offers staging posts to help to direct us there. Above all, this is an invitation to faithful improvisation, to participate with God in the task of peacemaking in the world.

A determined commitment to the three eschatological goals we have identified should help us to avoid the danger of fixation on proxy goals, which can become idolatrous. Centuries ago Augustine wrote of the ultimate good (*summum bonum*), which was found in God alone and to which all other lesser goods point.[19] But in day-to-day life, we substitute proxy goals for ultimate ones all the time. In pragmatic terms we need to do this in order to function. For example, I have to complete my academic marking by a particular deadline. At certain times of the year, this goal becomes almost all-consuming. But it is a proxy goal, not an ultimate one. It is, I hope, in pursuit of a greater goal—the training of men and women for ministry and hence for the building up of the church and evangelism in the world. The marking is not, itself, the ultimate goal. (Even the building up of the church and its task of evangelism, if we think about them, are not eschatological goals, but they are a lot closer to being ultimate than my marking is!) But danger emerges when those proxy goals become all-consuming. If my determination to complete my marking to a deadline means that I fail to attend to a family member who is in crisis, I have probably overemphasized the proxy at the expense of the ultimate.

What proxy goals do we employ in our day-to-day lives? Here are some suggestions (the reader will be able to add others): freedom, democracy, and human rights. These are all good things; I doubt that many readers of this book would disagree with that. But none of them is an eschatological reality. None of them should become an all-consuming pursuit for its own sake. Many of our culture wars, I would suggest, arise from a determined pursuit of a proxy goal at the expense of an ultimate one.

But there is a converse danger. Undue focus on ultimate goals could lead to a sort of consequentialism, a willingness to tread any path in pursuit of what is seen as ultimately good. Such a thing is seen in movements that are oriented toward utopianism, from the far left ("Why wail over broken eggs when we are trying to make an omelette?")[20] to the far right (the Third Reich was built upon a vision of

---

19. Augustine of Hippo, "The City of God," in *St. Augustin's City of God and Christian Doctrine*, ed. P. Schaff, trans. M. Dods (Buffalo: Christian Literature Company, 1887), 397 (19.1.1).

20. These words were reportedly spoken by Stalin's right-hand man Lazar Kaganovitch. See "Russia: Stalin's Omelette," *Time*, October 24, 1932.

a glorious future of peace and prosperity, for which great sacrifices were demanded in the short term).[21]

There are several things that will mitigate this danger. First, it is important to keep under review the question of whether proxy goals have slipped into the status of ultimate goals in our minds. Personal interest and hidden agendas are far more likely to be manifest in pursuit of proxy goals (such as the passing of a law or the removal of a regime) rather than true eschatological goods (such as peace). Second, the eschatological goals identified above (which are not the only ones that the Bible teaches but are the ones that seem most relevant to violence studies) must act in concert with one another. As we have already seen, the prioritizing of one at the expense of others leads to a dangerous imbalance. And third, it is worth restating that the model outlined above indicates that the praxis is to be worked out *in the community of the church* and *under the guidance of the Spirit.*

This relates to the church's role as prophetic community, and it is this that we will next consider.

RELEVANT QUESTIONS

1. Why are the Spirit and the community of the saints so important for working out our praxis?
2. Can you identify examples from your own experience where justice has failed to be tempered with mercy, peaceableness with boldness, or holiness with dirty hands?
3. Above I suggested that three of the proxy goals that can become all-consuming are freedom, democracy, and human rights. Can you identify others? Can you see this tendency in other people? Can you see it in yourself?
4. What are some issues involving violence in contemporary society that cry out for the thoughtful application of the matrix outlined in this chapter?

---

21. David Redles, "National Socialist Millennialism," in *The Oxford Handbook of Millennialism,* ed. Catherine Wessinger (Oxford: Oxford University Press, 2011), 529–48.

CHAPTER 13

THE CHURCH AS PROPHETIC ACTOR

> *The church, as the body of Christ, acts by the power of the Holy Spirit to continue its life-giving mission in prophetic and compassionate ministry and so participates in God's work of healing a broken world. Communion, whose source is the very life of the Holy Trinity, is both the gift by which the church lives and, at the same time, the gift that God calls the church to offer a wounded and divided humanity, in hope of reconciliation and healing.*
>
> —World Council of Churches, *The Church Toward a Common Vision*

It may be that readers of this book picked it up with the hope of finding out "what the Bible says" about just war, capital punishment, and so on. If so, and you are still reading, thank you for your patience, and please continue to exercise it a little longer. Before we can attend to the great conundrums of violence in our time, before we may presume to address issues of national and international import, we should turn our focus to the heart of our calling as the church: to glorify God by being a living sign of the eschaton.

As we began to discuss in chapter 11, this is a prophetic task. The church is called into being by God to be a prophetic community that both points to and incompletely manifests the life of the world to come. The church's role is not identical to that of the prophets, but our calling is in continuity with theirs—to represent the truth of God by word and deed.

While the mission of Jesus was unique in its redemptive action, the church is also called to continue his work in the world. It is the Christ event that shapes the praxis of the church, which in turn serves as a witness to the world.

Theology of the Christ event	Practical theology for the church	Witness to wider society

This is the import of Jesus's words to his disciples in John 14:

> Whoever believes in me will do the works I have been doing, and they will do even greater things than these, because I am going to the Father. (John 14:12)

One example of the church's continuation of the mission of Jesus is found in the call to be the light of the world. Isaiah's promised servant of the Lord was to be a light to the nations (Isa 49:6), a promise that is fulfilled in Jesus (John 8:12), and the commission is then passed on to his disciples (Matt 5:14).

A common New Testament metaphor describes the church as the firstfruits of the new creation;[1] that is, the church is called to *anticipate* the eschaton. Thus, we are to witness by word and action to the peaceful, just, and holy world that God is inaugurating. And what this means is that things that we do behind the closed doors of our church buildings—our practices and rituals that we might imagine are relevant only to ourselves—are in fact a powerful participation in the reign of the Prince of Peace, and, crucially, *a gift to the world*.

THREE PROPHETIC PRACTICES OF THE CHURCH

In consideration of the issues of violence and peace, the church has three great prophetic practices to offer the world. These are existing, hospitality, and reconciliation.

Existing

Perhaps calling "existing" a "practice" of the church seems oxymoronic, but the word was chosen to attempt to express the biblical idea that the church *by her very existence* is a sign and statement to "the powers of this dark world and . . . the spiritual forces of evil in the heavenly realms" (Eph 6:12).

We frequently encounter calls for Christian unity, and rightly so, as we will discuss shortly. But these should all be framed within the understanding that the church, ontologically, is united. To say otherwise is like calling water "dry." This is a subject that preoccupies Paul in his letter to the Ephesians. As is characteristic of Paul, he heaps metaphors upon one another as he warms to his theme. Fundamentally, what has been achieved at the cross is a new humanity, which encompasses both Jew and gentile (Eph 2:15); it is a whole building made up of God's diverse people (vv. 20–22); a family where all the children are coheirs (3:6); a single body where every part is equally valued (2:16). This, Paul says, is a mystery that has been concealed for generations (1:9; 3:1–6).

---

1. E.g., 2 Thess 2:13; Jas 1:18; cf. Rev 14:4.

Having served as minister in two churches, I have always found this truth of the ontological unity of the church to be encouraging. As Paul makes very clear, God has accomplished unity, not imposed uniformity; and that unity is seen most clearly when we are diverse. So when tensions arose because people brought different cultural assumptions or had different theological emphases, as difficult as those might be to navigate I was perversely cheered. This is because these tensions were themselves a demonstration of the diversity of people whom God had brought together into the new humanity in Christ.

Working from Paul's typical indicative-imperative logic, we are therefore called to live in the reality of that unity-in-diversity.

The Peacemaking Possibilities of Ephesians 2

Werner Mischke and Kristin Caynor lead the Ephesians 2 Gospel Project for Mission One.[2] The project works to help bring the gospel values of reconciliation to bear in situations of community identity conflict. Core to their work is the understanding that Ephesians 2 shows the gospel to have horizontal as well as vertical dimensions. Often, Christ's work on the cross is viewed as reconciling humans with God (vertical), with horizontal (human-human) reconciliation considered to be an ethical outworking of that. Mischke and Caynor argue that Ephesians 2 shows the two elements of reconciliation are indivisible and that reconciliation of all things is a core gospel reality.[3]

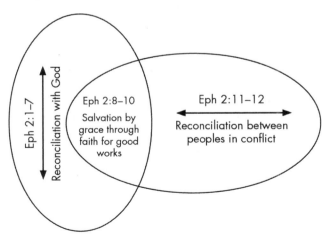

2. "Ephesians 2 Gospel Project," MissionOne, https://mission1 .org/ephesians-2-gospel-project/.

3. Diagram adapted from fig. 2.37 in Werner Mischke, "Two Dimensions of Honor-Status Reversal for Believers in Eph 2," in *The Global Gospel: Achieving Missional Impact in Our Multicultural World* (Scottsdale, AZ: Mission ONE, 2015), 198. Used by permission.

In Mischke and Caynor's work, this becomes a practical tool for the healing of ethnic identity conflicts. They partner with and seek to learn from people in a variety of global contexts where this truth is being applied in transformative ways.

> Werner Mischke describes a discussion he had with Ugandan Christian leader Calvin Echodu. During their conversation, Mischke commented that he did not recall ever hearing a sermon preached on Ephesians 2:13–17. "I do," said Echodu. "I grew up where that text was preached. And this is why there is tribal reconciliation in the church in Uganda. The hatred was so bad. The racial and tribal divisions in Uganda were so bad. But in the last 25 years, the church has taught this text and it has brought healing. The tribal distinctions and differences are still there, but the hostility is gone."[4]

Multiculturality: From Ontology to Praxis

How do we live out the reality of our ontological unity in meaningful ways in the local church? One of the most important steps we can take is to try to make our churches more multicultural.

The word *multicultural* is a broad term. There are many lines of difference in society and church, and it is hard but important to be attentive to them all. While the term is not generally used to include generational differences, these are important too. True diversity will attend to the wisdom and the particular needs of the elderly as well as to the wisdom and particular needs of the young.

Important also is class diversity. I have observed a tendency in the UK for churches in deprived areas to draw onto their leadership teams those who are most educated and business-savvy. This is generally the middle-class people who are not representative of the majority of the congregation. Such people shouldn't be *excluded*, of course, but it is key to being a truly multicultural church that the more articulate voices are not privileged.

Primarily, a multicultural church will include and celebrate racial diversity. But this, too, is difficult to do well, because of the sorts of power dynamics that are at play.[5] It is, I think, particularly hard for a majority-White church to learn to become racially diverse. It might be easy for them to *seem* to be inclusive of other ethnicities, but in practice that welcome often stops at the friendly handshake at the

---

4. Werner Mischke tells this story in a webinar presented to the Hindustan Bible Institute in October 2021. The video can be found here https://mission1.org/ephesians-2-gospel-project/.

5. For a sensitive discussion of the power dynamics at work in multiethnic churches, see Korie L. Edwards, *The Elusive Dream: The Power of Race in Interracial Churches* (Oxford: Oxford University Press, 2008).

door. As Laurene Bowers describes, this is, in effect, a sort of unexamined cultural imperialism.

> The dominant group in a church, which seemingly represents the interests of the entire congregation, perceives that everyone benefits because they run the church.[6]

A different but coexistent danger is that of fetishizing the ethnic other. Sometimes, in an effort to be ultra-inclusive, people in ethnic minorities are stereotyped for their perceived dress, music, or food preferences, and attention is continually called to these things.[7] This is reflected in the first two of Laurene Bowers's "Ten Commandments for a Multicultural Church":

> Thou Shall Not Deny Difference
>   Thou Shall Not Categorize by Cultural Grouping[8]

It is hard to navigate between these and other pitfalls. But one of the surest ways of avoiding them is to listen genuinely to a diversity of perspectives. We should not be doing things *to* people but *with* them.[9]

Three Black American Christians, Christina Edmondson, Ekemini Uwan, and Michelle Higgins, run a helpful podcast series called *Truth's Table*. In a conversation recorded in 2018, they discuss their experiences of being part of multiethnic churches.[10] They speak with great affection for their churches, but they make no attempt to conceal the difficulties that they have experienced there or their strong sense of being called by God to a challenging context. Even though two of them are pastors' wives, they still describe the feeling that their presence at the front of the church is performative for the church to demonstrate its inclusiveness. They sense an expectation upon them to "affirm the politeness of white folks who don't want to be challenged, they want a photo op." Their conversation provides both challenge and encouragement, and I recommend listening to the podcast.

---

6. Laurene Beth Bowers, *Becoming a Multicultural Church* (Cleveland: Pilgrim, 2006), 25.

7. This sort of romanticized stereotyping of the ethnic other is known as *Orientalism*, in terms paradigmatically set out by Edward Said in his *Orientalism* (New York: Vintage Books, 1978).

8. Laurene Beth Bowers, *Becoming a Multicultural Church* (Cleveland: Pilgrim, 2006), 83–85.

9. These power imbalances are very similar to those in the model of European mission that has been dominant until recent years and still persists in certain places. See Analzira Nascimento, *Evangelization or Colonization?*, trans. John Clark, David Grainger, and Elídia Grainger (Oxford: Regnum, 2021).

10. "Multiethnic Churches: A Foretaste of Heaven or Bulwarks of White Supremacy Part 1," *Truth's Table*, September 16, 2017, https://soundcloud.com/truthstable/multiethnic-churches-a-foretaste-of-heaven-or-bulwarks-of-white-supremacy-part-1.

Hospitality

As the church seeks to inhabit its God-given identity of diversity in unity, this brings us to a discussion of what we might term *hospitality*. By this term I mean the welcoming of the "other" from a place of relative power. It is a concept far more extensive than having friends around for dinner! It encompasses some of the dynamics of multicultural church, relates to contexts of migration, and even overlaps with questions around ecumenical relations and interfaith dialogue.

Hospitality appears to have been important to the early church. Paul commends it to the church in Rome alongside peaceable living (Rom 12:9–21). Peter similarly urges his readers to practice the same (1 Pet 4:9). Hospitality is one of the core virtues listed as a prerequisite to the office of overseer (1 Tim 3:2; Titus 1:8) and is expected to be demonstrated by widows hoping to be supported by the church (1 Tim 5:10). But the decision to offer hospitality was not always straightforward. Compare these two passages from the Johannine literature.

> Dear friend, you are faithful in what you are doing for the brothers and sisters, even though they are strangers to you. They have told the church about your love. Please send them on their way in a manner that honors God. It was for the sake of the Name that they went out, receiving no help from the pagans. We ought therefore to show hospitality to such people so that we may work together for the truth. (3 John 5–8).

> Many deceivers, who do not acknowledge Jesus Christ as coming in the flesh, have gone out into the world. . . . If anyone comes to you and does not bring this [sound] teaching, do not take them into your house or welcome them. Anyone who welcomes them shares in their wicked work. (2 John 7, 10–11)

Hospitality in the early church is seen as facilitating the ministry of the guest (cf. Rom 15:24). For this reason, the priorities of hospitality and godly truth might sometimes be in tension. The guest may present a threat to the church, particularly to those younger or weaker in faith. But this warning appears to be limited to the prevention of dangerous heretical teaching. Certainly, Paul appears to envision hospitality being offered to "enemies," presumably who are outside the believing community. He quotes Proverbs:

> If your enemy is hungry, feed him; if he is thirsty, give him something to drink. (Rom 12:20)

Hospitality is complex in more ways than this. It is never—and never can be—offered without explicit or implicit conditions. If I welcome someone into my home, I am simultaneously asserting my ownership of the house and my prerogative to determine who may and may not enter. There are always power dynamics at work when hospitality is being offered and received.[11] But it is not optional, and Scripture provides compelling evidence that we must take it seriously.

Why Hospitality?

The first reason why we should exercise hospitality is because we are recipients of divine hospitality. By the same logic as the parable of the ungrateful servant (Matt 18:21–35), our generosity of spirit toward others should reflect the generosity with which we have been treated.

We are recipients of divine hospitality first at creation. Paul Fiddes points out that in creation God chooses to limit himself to make room for the created world;[12] or as Reinhard Hütter beautifully puts it, creation is "the sharing of the divine life with those who are dust."[13] This divine hospitality is then offered to Israel, who is given "a good and spacious land, a land flowing with milk and honey" (Exod 3:8). The land is indeed bountiful, bearing bunches of grapes so large that it takes two men to bear them (Num 13:23–24). Further, the land contains "large, flourishing cities you did not build, houses filled with all kinds of good things you did not provide, wells you did not dig, and vineyards and olive groves you did not plant" (Deut 6:10–11).

Leviticus 25 places the generous act of Jubilee in three important contexts. In practical terms, it would only be possible to celebrate it because in every Sabbath year God promised to bless the people abundantly in advance:

> You may ask, "What will we eat in the seventh year if we do not plant or harvest our crops?" I will send you such a blessing in the sixth year that the land will yield enough for three years. (Lev 25:20–21)

In narrative terms, the Jubilee was to emerge out of gratitude for their own redemption from slavery (Lev 25:1–2, 38, 55). This story was ethically formative for them. (And, as a result, they were to be hospitable even to the Egyptians themselves! See Deut 23:7–8.) And in liturgical terms, the Jubilee was proclaimed on the Day of Atonement (Lev 25:8–12), the day in all the year when the people were most aware of their own indebtedness to God.

As the story continues to the New Testament, all who are included in the new covenant are recipients of divine hospitality, ultimately destined for the most perfect

---

11. This is explored in more detail in Helen Paynter, "'Make Yourself at Home': The Tensions and Paradoxes of Hospitality in Dialogue with the Bible," *The Bible and Critical Theory* 14.1 (2018): 42–61.

12. Paul Fiddes, "Creation out of Love," in *The Work of Love: Creation as Kenosis*, ed. J. Polkinghorne (Grand Rapids: Eerdmans, 2001), 176–91.

13. Reinhard Hütter, "Hospitality and Truth: The Disclosure of Practices in Worship and Doctrine," in *Practicing Theology: Beliefs and Practices in Christian Life*, ed. M. Volf and D. Bass (Grand Rapids: Eerdmans, 2002), 219.

hospitality of all (Rev 21:4; 22:1–5). As Paul reminded the Corinthians, "What do you have that you did not receive?" (1 Cor 4:7). And we who are gentile Christians have been admitted to a covenant that was not ours originally; we have been grafted into the olive tree (Rom 11:11–24).

A second compelling reason to exercise hospitality toward the stranger is that we thereby find ourselves hosting the Lord himself, in what might be considered a glorious, divine bait and switch. The writer of Hebrews probably has this instance in mind when they write, "Do not forget to show hospitality to strangers, for by so doing some people have shown hospitality to angels without knowing it" (Heb 13:2). Yet perhaps the fullest exposition of the principle is in these words of Jesus, in the parable of the sheep and the goats, where the king concludes by saying, "Whatever you did for one of the least of these brothers and sisters of mine, you did for me." (Matt 25:40).[14] Probably the most wonderful application was when two dejected travelers invited a stranger into their home in Emmaus one Sunday just after Passover (Luke 24:13–35).

Good-News Hospitality

This brings us to a discussion of Jesus's hospitality. We will discover the centrality of generous hospitality to his ministry and that the practical and tangible reality of that hospitality cannot be separated from his gospel proclamation; the gospel is embodied in hospitality. As usual with Jesus, again and again he surprises our expectations.

The first thing to notice is that every time someone hosts Jesus, the binary roles of guest and host become blurred or even inverted. Having Jesus to dinner is always good news (which, of course, is the meaning of the word *gospel*) for the host. Consider the meal with Zacchaeus, which culminates in Jesus's words, "Today salvation has come to this house" (Luke 19:9). Or note the wedding at Cana in Galilee, where wine was poured in vast abundance (John 2:1–11). Again, perhaps the supreme example takes place at that house in Emmaus on Resurrection Sunday, when the friends' hearts burned within them as the Lord taught them and then became known to them as he broke the bread (Luke 24:13–35).

This relates to a second unexpected feature of Jesus's hospitality, which is that it is journeying, not static. It does not wait passively for the guests to arrive but goes out after them, "to the roads and country lanes" (Luke 14:23), "to seek and to save the lost" (Luke 19:10). The shepherd seeks out the lost sheep to bring it to safety (Luke 15:1–7), and the forgiving father hitches up his robes to run and welcome his son

---

14. Jesus is probably here referring to hospitality offered toward his disciples (cf. Matt 10:40–42).

home (15:11–32). This gospel pattern of hospitality takes place on a grand scale, too, in Jesus's downward journey from equality with God to the status of a servant, and then to "death, even death on a cross" (Phil 2:6–8)—a journey undertaken "while we were still sinners" (Rom 5:8).

This brings us to the third feature: the unexpected guests whom Jesus gathers around him. Levitical law prohibited the physically blemished from serving in the tabernacle.

> No man who has any defect may come near: no man who is blind or lame, disfigured or deformed; no man with a crippled foot or hand, or who is a hunchback or a dwarf, or who has any eye defect, or who has festering or running sores or damaged testicles. (Lev 21:18–20)

The War Scroll found at Qumran has a similar list of those excluded from participating in the eschatological battle:

> No man who is lame, or blind, or crippled, or afflicted with a lasting bodily blemish, or smitten with a bodily impurity, none of these shall march out to war with them.[15]

By contrast, it is just such people that Jesus gathers around him, as always, for good news.

> The blind receive sight, the lame walk, those who have leprosy are cleansed, the deaf hear, the dead are raised, and the good news is proclaimed to the poor. (Luke 7:22)

It is almost exactly the same list of people whom Jesus commends as dinner guests, going on to list them as the participants at the eschatological banquet (Luke 14:12–14, 21).

When Jesus received these unexpected guests, a sort of reverse contagion took place. Uncleanness in the Old Testament law was transmissible. In Leviticus 15:19–30, for example, we read that contact with a menstruating woman made people, bedding, and seating unclean. By contrast, when the woman with the issue of blood touched Jesus, it was holiness that was transmitted, not uncleanness (Mark 5:24–34).

Finally, the gospel hospitality that Jesus offered was often in a context of his own physical need. He is humble enough to rely upon the generosity of others (Mark 11:11; Luke 8:2–3; cf. Luke 7:36–50; John 12:1–2) and often had nowhere to lay his head (Luke 9:58). He fed five thousand people when he did not even have his

---

15. 1QM 7.4–5, cited in Geza Vermes, *The Dead Sea Scrolls in English*, 4th ed. (Sheffield: Sheffield Academic Press, 1995), 132.

own packed lunch (Mark 8:5), and he ministered to the Samaritan woman when he was tired and thirsty (John 4:6–7). Even on the cross, at his weakest moment, he performed one of his most profound acts of hospitality: "Truly I tell you, today you will be with me in paradise" (Luke 23:43). And this pattern of receiving hospitality on the basis of need but then becoming the bringer of good news (gospel) is one that he commands his disciples to follow.

> Do not take a purse or bag or sandals; and do not greet anyone on the road.
>
> When you enter a house, first say, "Peace to this house." If someone who promotes peace is there, your peace will rest on them; if not, it will return to you. Stay there, eating and drinking whatever they give you, for the worker deserves his wages. Do not move around from house to house.
>
> When you enter a town and are welcomed, eat what is offered to you. Heal the sick who are there and tell them, "The kingdom of God has come near to you." (Luke 10:4–9)

Gospel proclamation is inseparable from the act of generous, embodied hospitality.

Reconciliation

Closely linked with the generous, good-news practice of hospitality is a third prophetic practice of the church: reconciliation. In this section we will focus on some actions and habits that should be central to the practice of every church.

While he had much to say about the significance of his death, Jesus did not focus on that alone at his last meal with his friends. The gospel accounts of the supper, with their diverse emphases, reveal some fundamentals of the nature of the community he would be leaving behind to continue his work after his ascension. They are summarized in a command, a practice, and an ordinance.

A Command

> A new command I give you: Love one another. As I have loved you, so you must love one another. By this everyone will know that you are my disciples, if you love one another. (John 13:34–35)

In his book *Fight Like Jesus*, Jason Porterfield considers the final week of Jesus's life through a peacemaking lens. He reflects on the community that Jesus was establishing, which would one day become the church. Given that the command to love is by no means novel, what makes this command "new"? It is the establishment of a community explicitly founded upon love like Jesus's, Porterfield argues. The strength of this pattern of modeling peace to the world lies in the exponential multiplicity of loving relationships, which form a structure within which Christ's love can be encountered by others.

On your own, all you can do is talk about peace and demand justice. But in community you can actually embody peace and do justice. Your personal attempts to contend for peace will forever be stunted unless done as part of a community that endeavors to serve in this world as a living expression of that peace.[16]

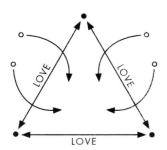

From *Fight Like Jesus: How Jesus Waged Peace Throughout Holy Week* by Jason Porterfield. Used by permission of Herald Press.

This model helps to make sense of Jesus's logic: "By this everyone will know that you are my disciples." As we saw above, the church embodies the mystery of unity-in-diversity. It is by her obedient participation in that reality that the gospel is revealed to the watching world.

This is true not simply at the level of the local church, of course. Baptist ecumenist Steven Harmon argues that our baptisms involve a paradox. As we are baptized into the one holy catholic and apostolic church of the Prince of Peace, we are simultaneously baptized into all the bloody divisions that have plagued it over the years. Viewed in this way, the task of ecumenical peacemaking becomes core to the church's mission—and one which is costly.

Seeking the unity of the church at a time when the divisions of the church seem inconsequential to many . . . is often a cruciform practice. It requires entering into the suffering inflicted by division, and even taking these divisions upon ourselves that we might participate in Christ's work of making us into one body through the cross.[17]

It is unsurprising that this should be costly, of course. If we are to love one another as Christ loves us, this love must necessarily be cross-shaped.

When we think of reconciliation, it is important not to be too backward-looking. Sometimes there is no idyllic past to summon contending people back to. David Tombs explains:

Etymologically reconciliation is rooted in the Latin for "Calling together again" or "Calling back together." Some would criticise this as suggesting that reconciliation is backward-looking not forward-looking. Too much emphasis on the "re" of reconciliation can make it open to the criticism that it suggests a simple return to the past is a sufficient response to the problems of the present. This criticism recognises a real danger. What is

16. Jason Porterfield, *Fight Like Jesus: How Jesus Waged Peace Throughout Holy Week* (Harrisonburg, VA: Herald Press, 2022), 130.

17. Steven Harmon, "Ecclesial Peacemaking: A Cross-Bearing Practice for Lent and Beyond," Centre for the Study of Bible and Violence, Lent Lectures 2022, fourth lecture, delivered March, 24 2022. Available here https://youtu.be/JdT1emwt574.

the purpose of a return to past relationships and structures when these were part of the underlying problem?

Restoring these relationships and structures does not address the issue. Thus "restoring" needs to be balanced with "transforming," because transformation points forward and highlights a sense of positive change. To speak of transformation is to suggest that a return to the past is not enough; it is something new and better that is required.[18]

A Practice

When [Jesus] had finished washing their feet, he put on his clothes and returned to his place. "Do you understand what I have done for you?" he asked them. "You call me 'Teacher' and 'Lord,' and rightly so, for that is what I am. Now that I, your Lord and Teacher, have washed your feet, you also should wash one another's feet. I have set you an example that you should do as I have done for you." (John 13:12–15)

Throughout John's Gospel, Jesus shapes his disciples' ethics not simply by teaching right actions but by forming their worldview.[19] To follow Jesus is to be transformed from the inside out and all the way through. Through washing his disciples' feet and his accompanying teaching, Jesus is shaping their understanding of what it means to live humbly with one another.

The literal practice of footwashing has been considered valuable in many church contexts, since the very early days of the church. First Timothy 5:10, which lists the activities undertaken by worthy widows, speaks of footwashing as one of them. Augustine commended it as a practice to be emulated:

We have learned, brethren, humility from the Highest; let us, as humble, do to one another what He, the Highest, did in His humility. . . . For when the body is bent at a brother's feet, the feeling of such humility is either awakened in the heart itself, or is strengthened if already present.[20]

18. David Tombs, "Toward a Public Theology of Reconciliation in Northern Ireland," in *Mining Truths: Festschrift in Honour of Geraldine Smyth OP—Ecumenical Theologian and Peacebuilder*, ed. John O'Grady, Cathy Higgins, and Jude Lal Fernando (Reichenbach: EOS, 2015), 126.

19. Jan van der Watt, "'Thou Shalt . . . Do the Will of God': Do New Testament Ethics Have Anything to Say Today?," Radboud University Nijmegan, lecture delivered on September 16, 2010, available here as a PDF at https://repository.ubn.ru.nl/bitstream/handle/2066/84460/84460.pdf (see p. 34 for source of the statement above).

20. Augustine of Hippo, "Lectures or Tractates on the Gospel according to St. John," in *St. Augustin: Homilies on the Gospel of John, Homilies on the First Epistle of John, Soliloquies*, ed. P. Schaff, trans. J. Gibb and J. Innes (New York: Christian Literature Company, 1888), 306.

The theological significance of this moment at the Last Supper is manifold. For instance, it has been said to speak of postbaptismal cleansing, of forgiveness, and of humility. But it has also been used as a peacemaking practice. Christopher Landau considers this practice to be essential to the life of the church, which inevitably has disagreements.

> In the context of human communities that unavoidably become places of tension and disagreement, Jesus offers a sacramental ritual that overturns convention and emphasises mutuality and solidarity.[21]

Both as paradigm for humble service and as liturgical practice, footwashing is a gift to a church that is seeking to embody unity and reconciliation.

The primates' meeting of the Anglican communion, held in early 2016, was a difficult and divided affair, with feelings (and theological convictions) running very high about the question of same-sex marriage. In his address to the general synod of the Church of England in February 2016, Archbishop of Canterbury Justin Welby spoke of a moment which took place during the final Eucharist.

> We washed each other's feet, and each prayed a blessing on the one who had washed our feet, before washing the feet of other Primates; a great contrast to what is often portrayed as the conflicts within the [Anglican] Communion. Many of us were moved to tears.

Following this moment, although deep divisions remained, there was a renewed sense of shared love and purpose, which Welby went on to describe.

> For me, apart from the final Eucharist, the most remarkable aspect of the Primates' Meeting was the energy that was released when we acted together. For the first time, I experienced the beauty of the Communion when, on issues affecting us very widely—often issues of life and death—there was a sharing and an outpouring of mutual support.[22]

---

21. Christopher Landau, *A Theology of Disagreement: New Testament Ethics for Ecclesial Conflicts* (London: SCM, 2021), 40–41.

22. "Archbishop Reflects on Primates' Meeting in Synod Address," The Archbishop of Canterbury, February 15, 2016, www.archbishopofcanterbury.org/speaking-and-writing/speeches/archbishop-reflects-primates-meeting-synod-address-video. Both the full text as well as a video presentation of the address is available.

An Ordinance

> Because there is one loaf, we, who are many, are one body, for we all share the
> one loaf. (1 Cor 10:17)

And finally, we turn to Jesus's institution of one of the two great practices or sacraments of the Christian church; variously called the Lord's Supper, Communion, Mass, or the Eucharist.

As the gospel accounts relate this moment, it is explicitly loaded with covenant imagery. Just as Moses sprinkled the people with blood at Sinai, saying, "This is the blood of the covenant" (Exod 24:8), so Jesus offers the cup, telling his disciples, "This cup is the new covenant in my blood" (Luke 22:20; cf. Matt 26:28). Our celebration of Communion is a liturgical restatement or renewing of that new covenant, which encompasses all who follow Christ.

All participate in this covenant renewal on equal terms, just as all entered it on equal terms. All who partake must—literally or figuratively—kneel. We must acknowledge our own unworthiness and position ourselves as people under judgment and in need of mercy. We all eat and drink the same bread and wine; there is no budget version of the bread for some or luxury label of the wine for others. In eating of the one bread, we assert our essential unity (1 Cor 10:17). We line up side by side at the altar rail or sit cheek by jowl with people who irritate us, patronize us, let us down, and whom we have irritated, patronized, or failed in our turn. We all suffer with the same affliction and must partake of the same cure. As we hold out our hands to be supplied with spiritual food, we acknowledge our dependence on our brothers and sisters, and that we are a means of grace to one another.

But we do not simply share the meal with our brothers and sisters in the same congregation. The bread we eat, we share with the whole church—those who eat wafers and those who eat matzah; those who break bread in prisons and hospitals; those who eat in the tropics and in the antipodes; and with those who have gone before us. We share it with those whose doctrines we disagree with and those whose worship styles bemuse us. Our participation in this meal re-situates us in the one holy catholic and apostolic church and reminds us we are all one.

Elsewhere in the Gospels, Jesus commands that anyone who is going to offer worship to God, and recalls that they have a relationship that requires amendment, must go and attend to that before they can continue with their worship (Matt 5:23). Likewise, Paul instructs that all who approach the Lord's table must examine themselves before they may eat or drink.

> Everyone ought to examine themselves before they eat of the bread and drink
> from the cup. For those who eat and drink without discerning the body of
> Christ eat and drink judgment on themselves. (1 Cor 11:28–29)

It is impossible to eat and drink authentically without recognizing the body of Christ, which is not simply that which is symbolically or literally contained in the bread or the wafer but is also the body of Christ on earth.[23] This is why Paul takes the Corinthian church to task in this chapter. By participating in communion in socially stratified ways, they are denying the unity to which the Lord's Supper testifies and which it makes real.[24]

Just as sin, when it entered the world, ruptured all relationships, so its cure, remembered, celebrated, and reenacted at this meal is the cure for all ruptured relationships. In our regular participation in this meal, we become enculturated in the narrative of our faith, our identities are re-formed in Christ, and we are reoriented to the life of the peaceable kingdom. To partake of the Lord's Supper is a public, political, and eschatological act.

Writing in the context of Chilean suffering under Pinochet, William Cavanaugh offers a rich theological exploration of the way the Eucharist's counter-practice presents a challenge to the script offered by the state, one which stands prophetically against the fragmentation of personhood that torture inscribes upon its victims. His exploration of the *reality* of Christ in the Eucharist is not dependent upon a particularly Catholic theology of the mass but points rather to the eschatological reality which it draws into the present.

In the Eucharist one is fellow citizen not of other present "Chileans" but of other members of the body of Christ, past, present, and future. The Christian wanders among the earthly nations on the way to her eternal *patria*, the Kingdom of God. The Eucharist makes clear, however, that this Kingdom does not simply stand outside of history, nor is heaven simply a goal for the individual to achieve at death. Under the sign of the Eucharist the kingdom becomes present in history through the action of Christ, the heavenly high Priest. In the Eucharist the heavens are opened, and the church of all times and places is gathered around the altar.[25]

23. Roy E. Ciampa and Brian S. Rosner, *The First Letter to the Corinthians*, Pillar New Testament Commentary (Grand Rapids: Eerdmans, 2010), 555.

24. Ben Witherington III, *Conflict and Community in Corinth: A Socio-Rhetorical Commentary on 1 and 2 Corinthians* (Grand Rapids: Eerdmans, 1995), 244.

25. William T. Cavanaugh, *Torture and Eucharist: Theology, Politics, and the Body of Christ* (Oxford: Blackwell, 1998), 16–17.

CONCLUSION

Steeped though he was in the Jewish worldview, learned though he was in the law, and trained though he was in the Greek rhetorical tradition, the apostle Paul sounds endearingly flabbergasted in the book of Ephesians. His opening doxology floods out like water from a ruptured dam; his superlatives heap up—you have to pity his poor amanuensis who was trying to take his dictation.

At the heart of Paul's wonderment in Ephesians is what he heralds in 1:9 as a "mystery," something planned from of old but only now brought into fulfillment. He hints at its meaning: "to bring unity to all things in heaven and on earth under Christ" (1:10), but it is not yet clear from his letter what this really means. His golden prose rolls on: "the riches of his glorious inheritance . . . the church, which is his body, the fullness of him who fills everything in every way . . . the incomparable riches of his grace" (1:18–23; 2:7). And then come these words, at once glorious and inspiring, and yet sobering in their weight for us.

> We are God's handiwork, created in Christ Jesus to do good works, which God prepared in advance for us to do. (Eph 2:10)

No pressure there, then!

Paul continues to develop this theme in Ephesians 3, and in doing this he returns to the motif of mystery:

> This mystery is that through the gospel the Gentiles are heirs together with Israel, members together of one body, and sharers together in the promise in Christ Jesus. . . .
>
> [God's] intent was that now, through the church, the manifold wisdom of God should be made known to the rulers and authorities in the heavenly realms, according to his eternal purpose that he accomplished in Christ Jesus our Lord. (Eph 3:6, 10–11)

We cannot get around this. The ontological unity of the church is God's revelation to the world, a foretaste of that eschatological unity that will be when God places all things under Christ's feet. By her existence, and in her practices, the church testifies to that.

In the chapters which follow, we will explore the ways that we should view and respond to the many forms of violence in the world around (and within) us. But first, we must attend to the church, because we are called not just to speak but to *be*, namely, God's good news to a violent world.

> In Christ there is no east or west,
> in him no south or north,

but one great fellowship of love
throughout the whole wide earth.

In Christ shall true hearts ev'rywhere
their high communion find.
His service is the golden cord
close binding humankind.

Join hands, then, people of the faith,
whate'er your race may be.
All children of the living God
are surely kin to me.

In Christ now meet both east and west,
in him meet south and north.
All Christly souls are joined as one
throughout the whole wide earth.[26]

RELEVANT QUESTIONS

1. Reflecting on your own church, to what extent is your self-understanding shaped by Paul's vision of the reason God called it into being?
2. To what extent do you see yourself as part of the universal church? What boundaries do you place around that?
3. How well does your church reflect the multiculturality of the church?
4. What would be true of your local church if its members celebrated Communion in all of its theological and ethical richness?

---

26. "In Christ There Is No East or West," by John Oxenham, 1908. Public domain. There are plenty of tunes to this traditional hymn, but my particular favorite is the swing version (Andrew Remillard, "In Christ There Is No East or West [McKee]," YouTube, www.youtube.com/watch?v=RsEJOHXE8kg).

CHAPTER 14

HOW TO RESIST EVIL

Pressing the battle in Jesus' name,
A victory to win
Raising our banner of Truth and Love
O'er fields of vice and sin;
Onward our soldiers in bright array,
Marching, yes, marching from day to day,
Tramp, tramp, tramp, tramp,
The victory to win.
Tramp, tramp, tramp, tramp,
The victory to win!
—Mark D. Ussery, "The Victory to Win"

Would you go back in time to shoot Hitler if you had the chance? This familiar thought experiment epitomizes the conundrum that we will grapple with in this chapter. How should we respond to evil that can only be stopped by violence? Even in the absence of a time machine, the question is nontheoretical, for the individual and for the nation-state. Is it ever justified to go to war? Should a criminal justice system use capital punishment? We might phrase the question like this: What should we do when the cheek that is slapped is not our own? In this chapter and the one that follows we will attempt to tease out some of the issues raised by this question, applying what we have learned from Scripture and the various types of resistance that we discovered in chapter 7.[1]

First, we will consider the question of what our stance should be when allegations of harm are made close to home.

ON MILLSTONES AND HOLY RAGE

In recent years, many denominations of the church have been rocked by abuse scandals. These include, but are by no means confined to, the unmarked mass graves discovered in the grounds of Canadian schools for indigenous children;[2] widespread

---

1. Lament, protest, memory, satire, civil disobedience, and physical violence.
2. Ian Austen, "'Horrible History': Mass Grave of Indigenous Children Reported in Canada," *New York Times*, May 28, 2021, www.nytimes.com/2021/05/28/world/canada/kamloops-mass-grave-residential-schools.html.

sexual abuse perpetrated by clergy against particularly young boys in the Catholic church;[3] and sexual abuse principally against seven hundred teenage girls and women in the Southern Baptist Convention.[4]

One of the common features of almost any of these scandals is the church's attempted concealment of the issue or its scramble to defend itself when it comes to light. Sometimes this is institutional: clergy discovered to be committing abuse have often been quietly moved on to another position. Sometimes it takes place on the local or individual level. Many women who have made accusations of abuse against a pastor or church leader discover the church rallying to their abuser's support and themselves ostracized.[5] It is not uncommon for the victim-offender role to be switched in such circumstances.

After his death, the famous evangelist Ravi Zacharias was discovered to have abused many women with sexual coercion. Allegations made during his lifetime to his organization, RZIM, had been hushed up and closed down. RZIM was "stubbornly incurious" about these allegations, to the extent that they redirected nearly one million dollars donated for the ministry to mount an expensive legal defense against one particular complainant, Lori Anne Thompson.[6] With RZIM's blessing, this legal team mounted a countersuit against Thompson, suing her for defamation and attempted blackmail. Even after Thompson's complaint was settled out of court with Zacharias paying her significant damages in exchange for a nondisclosure agreement, RZIM ministries failed to investigate what was not being disclosed, and Zacharias was free to continue his abuse.[7]

We have seen much in our survey of Scripture to persuade us of the inappropriate nature of such responses. We have discussed the rage of the prophets, and of Jesus himself, when the innocent are abused: "If anyone causes one of these little ones—those who believe in me—to stumble, it would be better for them to have a large millstone hung around their neck and to be drowned in the depths of the sea" (Matt 18:6). God's concern for the weak and defenseless is reflected in the high

3. "The Roman Catholic Church Investigation Report: Executive Summary," Independent Inquiry Child Sexual Abuse, January 2023, www.iicsa.org.uk/reports-recommendations/publications/investigation/roman-catholic-church/executive-summary.

4. Robert Downen, Lise Olsen, and John Tedesco, "Abuse of Faith," *Houston Chronicle*, February 10, 2019, www.houstonchronicle.com/news/investigations/article/Southern-Baptist-sexual-abuse-spreads-as-leaders-13588038.php.

5. I document and discuss examples of this in Helen Paynter, *The Bible Doesn't Tell Me So: Why You Don't Have to Submit to Domestic Abuse and Coercive Control* (Abingdon: Bible Reading Fellowship, 2020).

6. Daniel Silliman, "RZIM Spent Nearly $1M Suing Ravi Zacharias Abuse Victim," *Christianity Today*, February 23, 2022, www.christianitytoday.com/news/2022/february/rzim-board-donor-money-guidepost-report-ravi.html.

7. The report by Guidepost Solutions was published on the RZIM website, along with an apology from RZIM. However, at the time of going to press, the RZIM website appears to be defunct.

standard to which he calls those who lead in his name.[8] The abuse of others should disturb and enrage us; when this happens within institutions for which we have some responsibility, it should stir us to action in their defense.

> "The multitude of your sacrifices—
>   what are they to me?" says the LORD. . . .
> "When you spread out your hands in prayer,
>   I hide my eyes from you;
> even when you offer many prayers,
>   I am not listening.
> Your hands are full of blood!" (Isa 1:11, 15)

Failure to be proactive on behalf of those who are being harmed within our spheres of influence will render our prayers invalid. This is grave indeed.

CAN VIOLENCE SOLVE VIOLENCE?

In the examples discussed above, the appropriate response, in broad terms, should be fairly clear. There are robust processes for dealing with such matters, including preeminently the civil criminal justice system. The key thing is that the church must respond with compassion and humility and cooperate fully with any criminal investigation. But what of cases where an abuse or an injustice cannot be addressed in such ways, such as the example of Hitler that we opened the chapter with? Is it ever appropriate to use violence in such circumstances?

In chapter 3 we looked at some of the *Chaoskämpfe* of the ancient Near Eastern cultures such as the *Enuma Elish*. It will be recalled that in this Babylonian myth, the creation of the world takes place through the slaughter of a primordial monster. Violence is the means by which good is achieved. The *Enuma Elish* is just one of many such myths from the ancient world.

As we have discussed, some scholars, led by Walter Wink, have termed this idea that violence can be legitimately employed to achieve good the "myth of redemptive violence," and have sought to reject all violence on this basis. However, Scripture is not straightforward on the matter; the idea that human violence can solve violence can neither be wholly rejected nor uncritically endorsed from the pages of the Bible.

Certainly, as we saw in chapter 10, the *Chaoskampf* is continually subverted in Scripture. Unlike its pagan equivalents, the Genesis creation account does not view evil as ontological, nor violence primal. The trajectory of Scripture is from the ontological peace of creation to the ontological peace of new creation. And although

---

8. See, e.g., God's denunciation of Hophni and Phinehas for their abuse of the women who came to serve in the sanctuary (1 Sam 2:22–34; cf. Ezek 34; Luke 12:42–48).

humans are drawn into participation in the divine project of re-creation in its early iterations, the conquest of evil is gradually evacuated of human participation as the canonical story unfolds until the eschatological battle, which is entirely divine. And as we have seen throughout, Scripture testifies to the way that violence tends to be multiplicative and that we should be very wary of employing it.

This tension between the eschaton and the present is relevant to our consideration of the way we respond to evil that is threatening others. In the framework set out in chapter 12, I suggested that between the three eschatological goals of justice, holiness, and peace there is a bounded area within which faithful action might be situated, and that this does not collapse into a single point but is subject to the prayerful discernment of the church in its own context, under the guidance of the Spirit.

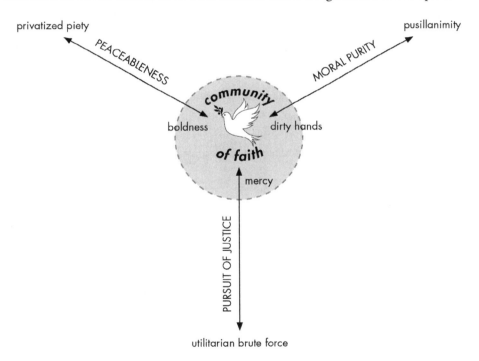

We will now consider some of the approaches taken by Christians to an evil that they feel some responsibility toward, and which lies beyond the reach of the criminal justice system. Principally this is a question of Christian attitudes to state-sponsored military action.

A TAXONOMY OF CHRISTIAN ATTITUDES TO WAR

Traditionally, Christian approaches to the question of war have fallen into three main camps: *crusade* (which is a category far broader than the medieval campaigns by that name), *just war*, and *pacifism*.[9] Each of these headline terms embraces a range of stances, and the issue is made more complex by the different ways that writers use the same terms. We will consider each of these in turn, before considering some case studies in the following chapter.

Crusade

Roland Bainton defines *crusade* as an intensely religious type of war, which emerges from the biblical holy-war tradition. However, it differs from the biblical holy war in that the crusade is conducted *on God's behalf*, for a divine rather than a human goal, whereas the holy war is divinely instigated and can only be won *with God's assistance*. Harold O. J. Brown offers several definitions, but he suggests that crusades tend to be waged to correct a historic wrong; it is "a war fought to undo something that no one had the right to do in the first place."[10]

Daniel Heimbach offers twelve characteristic features of crusade, which I have summarized below.[11]

1. Crusade is viewed as an ultimate means of defeating evil.
2. It takes place by divine command ("divine" here is a broad term that can include a human authority, if considered ultimate).
3. Therefore, it does not need to observe human conventions of warfare, such as the declaration of war.
4. Crusade is conceived in universal, not local, terms; this war is part of the great cosmic battle.
5. It accepts no restraint in pursuit of this ultimate goal, . . .
6. . . . therefore, it takes no prisoners, . . .
7. . . . and is not interested in compromise with the enemy . . .
8. . . . because its goals are conquest, punishment, conversion, or destruction.
9. Crusade opposes the entire social order of the enemy and therefore does not distinguish between combatants and noncombatants.
10. It is fought by zealous volunteers, not by conscripts.
11. The war is simultaneously material and spiritual or ideological, . . .
12. . . . and therefore it never really ends, because the cosmic goal is never attained.

9. See, e.g., Roland H. Bainton, *Christian Attitudes toward War and Peace: A Historical Survey and Critical Re-evaluation* (New York: Abingdon, 1960). This tripartite distinction is also broadly observed in Robert G. Clouse, ed., *War: Four Christian Views* (Downers Grove, IL: InterVarsity Press, 1981), although the "pacifist" position here is separated into two strands. The more recent version of the "Four Views" volume identifies Christian Realism as a separate strand from just war, but the distinctions are relatively minor. This will be discussed further below. See A. J. Nolte, "A Christian Realism View: Just War and 'Dirty Hands,'" in *War and Peace: Four Christian Views*, ed. Paul Copan (Downers Grove, IL: InterVarsity Press, 2022), 116–45.

10. Harold O. J. Brown, "The Crusade or Preventive War," in Clouse, *War: Four Christian Views*, 158.

11. Daniel Heimbach, "Crusade in the Old Testament and Today," in *Holy War in the Bible: Christian Morality and an Old Testament Problem*, ed. Heath A. Thomas, Jeremy Evans, and Paul Copan (Downers Grove, IL: InterVarsity Press, 2013), 184–85.

As may already be apparent, the category we are considering is somewhat imprecise, and the terms are used by scholars in slightly different ways. Yet we are now in a position to make a number of broad points.

Objections to Crusade

First, and most significantly, the Bible offers no support for crusade war in our time. There are two principal places in Scripture where proponents might appeal. One is Israel's divinely mandated conquest of Canaan. As we saw in chapter 1, these texts have indeed been used historically for just such a purpose, but we have also seen that they are part of a developing trajectory through the two testaments that gradually subverts human violence. Further, God's mandate for Joshua's military action was publicly verifiable in ways that have never been reproduced in modern times.[12] War conceived in these terms bears no connection to widely conceived definitions of justice.

A second possible justification for crusade is the biblical idea of cosmic war, which we have discussed in chapters 3 and 10. One example of its use is by the Norwegian mass-murderer Anders Behring Breivik. Of his "manifesto," Hannah Strømmen writes,

> Breivik's Bible emerges with a clear message: God is not a pacifist, the Bible encourages violence as self-defence of the Christian God and his seemingly exclusively European people; additionally, proponents of an anti-multiculturalist and anti-Muslim position are effectively soldiers of Christ, following a biblical tradition of righteous warfare.[13]

It will be remembered that in contrast to many of the apocalypses of the time, the book of Revelation excludes humans from participation in the divine war. And as we saw in chapter 3, the creation account in Genesis is deliberately and polemically set in opposition to the myth of creation by combat.

Dividing people into binary categories of "good" and "evil" fails to do justice to what Scripture teaches about the human condition. It leads us into the dangerous trap of casting our enemies as ontologically evil, and the equally toxic lie that we are wholly aligned with God and his purposes. This is very dangerous to our own fallible psyches. As Walter Wink puts it, "Resistance to evil . . . combines in our own depths with whatever is similar to the outer evil we oppose. Our very resistance *feeds* the inner shadow."[14] In short, if we believe that we are agents in a cosmic battle for good and evil, we will quickly become the enemy that we deprecate. We will turn into the dragon.[15]

12. Matthew Rowley, "On the Impossibility of Imitating Biblical Violence," in *The Bible on Violence: A Thick Description*, ed. Helen Paynter and Michael Spalione (Sheffield: Sheffield Phoenix Press, 2020), 42–61.

13. Hannah Strømmen, "Christian Terror in Europe? The Bible in Anders Behring Breivik's Manifesto," *The Journal of the Bible and Its Reception* 4.1 (2017): 155.

14. Walter Wink, *The Powers That Be: Theology for a New Millennium* (New York: Doubleday, 1998), 125–26.

15. This is exactly the mistake made by Moses in Exod 2:11–12. He had not yet learned the lesson of the Red Sea: "Stand firm and you will see the deliverance the LORD will bring you today" (Exod 14:13).

> Military language is common in the worship songs of the church in most Protestant denominations. Of course, there is good biblical precedence for this in the book of Psalms. Nonetheless, responsible church leaders and worship leaders should exercise caution. Which battles does the writer have in mind? What is the congregation imagining?
>
> As Carolyn Whitnall has written,
>
> No text exists in a vacuum, but especially not one purposed for use in multiple communal contexts—even less so when that text, aided by modern technology and social media, has achieved global, cross-denominational popularity. Whatever the "intended" meaning of the words, their signification to worshippers and onlookers will be influenced by the immediate context in which the song is played, as well as by the broader and/or intersecting social contexts that the individuals experience.[16]

As Heimbach suggested in his twelve features of crusade war, the narrative of cosmic conflict permits the laying aside of all restraint, as we have become part of a totalizing war where any means are justified. This is an ultimately utilitarian ethic, which we rejected in chapter one as sub-Christian.

A further problem is that crusade ideology relies upon an illegitimate model of the nature and calling of the church. It emerges from a confusion between the church and the kingdom of God, with the attendant secular authority that God's kingdom commands.[17]

> A crusade assumes either that private parties or agencies adopt force or else that government adopts religious causes. The first is illegal and (by just war principles) immoral, and it would tend to proliferate violence. The second is something neither a pluralistic society nor [the USA's] constitutional separation of church and state could allow.[18]

Most Christians will reject the crusade approach to war. The next model we will consider, however, enjoys a lot more favor within Christian circles: just war.

---

16. Carolyn Whitnall, "In the Presence of Whose Enemies? A Discourse Analysis of a Popular Christian Song in the Context of a 'Worship Protest,'" *Journal for the Study of Bible and Violence* 1.1 (2022): 6–42.

17. Herman Hoyt, "'A Non-Resistant Response' to Harold O. J. Brown, 'The Crusade or Preventive War,'" in Clouse, *War: Four Christian Views*, 171.

18. Arthur F. Holmes, "'A Just-War Response' to Harold O. J. Brown, 'The Crusade or Preventive War,'" in Clouse, *War: Four Christian Views*, 183.

Just War

War is evil. Its causes are evil. . . . Its consequences are evil. . . . The issue that tears the Christian conscience is not whether war is good, but whether it is in all cases entirely avoidable.[19]

Not all evil can be avoided in this world. Just-war theory is borne out of this realism. In this it differs from both crusade and pacifism, which are each primarily ideological in nature. Just-war theorists shape their philosophy in response to the world as it is, rather than attempting by force to shape the world into what it should be, or living as if that utopia has arrived.

In the face of this real-life problem, just-war proponents take it as read that violence may be necessary to prevent greater harm. But such a consequentialist position cannot be sufficient; rules for the conduct of this unwelcome war are also necessary. Importantly, just-war theory is not attempting to justify war but to bring it under regulation.[20] From classical times (Plato, Aristotle, and Cicero), attempts have been made to put limits around the causes and conduct of war. Early Christian writers such as Ambrose and Augustine developed this, and Christian just-war theory first found full expression with Thomas Aquinas, although it has been restated and developed by many Catholic and Protestant theologians since.

A just war must be a war fought reluctantly, and in the spirit of love.[21] It is conducted not because it is morally permissible but because it is morally *necessary*. These principles can be set out more formally with the following criteria:

Jus ad bellum (a just cause for war)
> A just cause: only defensive
> Just intention: for a just peace for all involved
> Probability of success: there must be a reasonable expectation that the just peace is attainable
> Last resort: only when all other avenues have been attempted

Jus in bello (just conduct of war)
> Formal declaration of war by legitimate authority
> Limited objectives: prevents "mission creep" toward total destruction of the enemy's society
> Proportionate means: excludes total war
> Noncombatant immunity: individuals not contributing to the conflict are immune from attack[22]

---

19. Arthur F. Holmes, "The Just War," in Clouse, *War: Four Christian Views*, 117.

20. Holmes, "Just War," 119.

21. Bainton, *Christian Attitudes*, 246.

22. See, e.g., Thomas Aquinas, *Summa Theologica*, trans. Fathers of the English Dominican Province (London: Burns Oates & Washbourne, 1912), 40.1; Holmes, "Just War," 120–21.

Arthur Holmes offers a scriptural basis for just war.[23] He notes that both testaments deprecate violence as an evil, but argues that the Old Testament provision for capital punishment in certain circumstances proves that the sixth commandment ("you shall not kill") cannot be an absolute prohibition on taking a human life. The New Testament, particularly the Gospels, teaches that *individuals* may not use violence, but does permit its use by the proper authority. Romans 13:1–7 and 1 Peter 2:13–14 show that the civil authorities are divinely commissioned to restrain evil. Holmes concludes that just-war theory takes proper account of both testaments, whereas the pacifist position tends to prioritize the New Testament.

Just-war theory offers a protocol for *state* violence; it explicitly prohibits private enterprise in these matters. However, although war is waged by states, it is conducted by individual actors, whose two extreme options of complete pacifism and blind obedience both involve the abrogation of personal moral responsibility.[24] At least in theory, each actor has to decide on their own level of complicity. But it is commonly difficult from this on-the-ground and in-the-moment perspective to evaluate whether the *jus ad bellum* is truly just or not. A good modern example would be the Russian invasion of Ukraine in early 2022, where many Russian soldiers apparently genuinely believed that they were responding to an act of aggression by Ukraine. The state that seeks to wage war bears great responsibility for ensuring that it is indeed just.

Objections to Just War

Because of its classical origins, just-war theory is constructed with a significant dependence on natural law.[25] This is both a strength and a weakness. Its value is that the theory can make meaningful contact with the ethical systems of those who do not operate within a Christian theological framework. The problem, however, is that it takes a broadly positive view of humanity's ability to discern and willingness to do the right thing. The optimism of early modern scholars such as John Locke has not been borne out by the events of the twentieth and twenty-first centuries.

This leads us to a second problem with just-war theory, which is the simple and pragmatic observation that no truly just war has ever been waged. Wars which might, arguably, have had a *jus ad bellum* rapidly lose any claim to the moral high ground as they universally abandon the *jus in bello*. Indeed, many would say that the ideal of love in war is laughable. Roland Bainton quotes Lord John Fisher, first sea lord of the royal navy in the lead-up to World War I:

> The humanizing of War! You might as well talk of the humanizing of Hell! When a silly ass at the Hague got up and talked about the amenities of civilized warfare . . . my reply, I regret to say, was considered totally unfit for publication.

23. Holmes, "Just War," 122–24.
24. Brown, "Crusade or Preventive War," 165.

25. Holmes, "Just War," 125.

As if war could be civilized! If I'm in command when war breaks out I shall issue my order:

"The essence of war is violence.

Moderation in war is imbecility.

Hit first, hit hard, and hit everywhere."[26]

Does history's failure to enact just war invalidate the model? Some say no; the Ten Commandments are imperfectly observed, but this does not lessen their intrinsic value.[27] However, if just war is realistically unattainable, this might lessen its practical usefulness. This is particularly relevant, given that just-war theory is essentially a pragmatic or realistic response set between the ideological poles represented by crusade and pacifism.

The necessary "dirtiness" of war underlies a stance known as Christian realism. While it has similarities to just war in its acknowledgement that war may be necessary, Christian realism places a greater emphasis on the dirty means that may be necessary. It is more consequentialist than just war.[28] This might be problematic, as it "could lead to a diminished concern over morality of the means this actor uses to win, so long as victory is swift, decisive, and ultimately leads to peace."[29]

A related objection to just war focuses on its effect upon the combatants. In recent decades therapists have become more aware of the extreme psychological effects that often follow combat. These may drive former combatants toward addiction, lifelong guilt and shame, or suicide. The effects fall into two related conditions: post-traumatic stress disorder (PTSD) and moral injury, which have been characterized respectively as "terror of one's own vulnerability" and "horror of one's own immorality."[30] PTSD is relatively well understood in the popular imagination, so we will here make a few remarks about moral injury.

Moral injury results from a breach of one's internal moral code by oneself or someone in authority in a high-stakes situation.[31] Combatants who have witnessed or perpetrated atrocities are likely to demonstrate moral injury, but it is by no means confined to those who have been involved in such illegitimate actions. Moral injury is also experienced in what the combatants believe to be a just war. This reflects the very tension that we have been grappling with in this section: doing something reprehensible in the pursuit of a "good" goal.

War is the realm of the paradoxical: the morally repugnant is the morally permissible, and even the morally necessary. . . . War justifies—more importantly, demands—what, in peacetime, would be unjustifiable: the destruction of the

26. Bainton, *Christian Attitudes*, 247.
27. Holmes, "Just War," 119.
28. Nolte, "Christian Realism View," 143.
29. Nolte, "Christian Realism View," 144.

30. Duane Larson and Jeff Zust, *Care for the Sorrowing Soul: Healing Moral Injuries from Military Service and Implications for the Rest of Us* (Eugene, OR: Cascade, 2017), 3.
31. Jonathan Shay, "Moral Injury," *Intertexts* 16.1 (2012): 57.

lives and happiness of others. Those who fight live this paradox day in and day out. In a very real way, war is the abnormal ruled normal.[32]

When the cost of war is waged, its psychological effects on the men and women who bear the brunt of the task must not be underestimated.[33]

Perhaps it is evidence of the human tendency to push at boundaries that a number of amendments to the just-war criteria have been proposed. We will consider two of them.

Amendments to Just War

One variation of just-war theory is preemptive or "preventive" war in the face of a threatened evil. We saw above that one of the *jus ad bellum* criteria was that the war must only ever be defensive in nature. A number of voices have proposed setting this aside under certain circumstances. One is Harold O. J. Brown's, who considers that an appropriate aggressive war is a logical and theoretically valid extension of just-war theory.

> If war is ever justified to prevent a greater evil, then we can conceive of situations in which a crusade not provoked by any direct act of international aggression, might also be justified.[34]

However, what might sound nobly dispassionate here is somewhat undermined by Brown's ready application of the principle to *Christian* self-determination and self-defense:

> If we accept the idea that there are some conditions that are so terrible that those who suffer from them are justified in beginning a violent rebellion, and their friends in other countries are justified in bringing force to aid them, then we are not pacifists. In that case, it is unwise to deny ourselves as Christians the same recourse to force to secure justice that we allow to others.[35]

Brown is by no means alone in offering such an argument. For instance, Charles Wendell (Chuck) Colson, previously special counsel to Richard Nixon, wrote these words in the lead-up to the Iraq war: "Out of love of neighbor . . . Christians can and should support a preemptive strike, if ordered by the appropriate magistrate to prevent an imminent attack."[36] Ironically, his argument was based upon the intelligence that Saddam had acquired an arsenal of weapons of mass destruction, a claim that was subsequently proved invalid. Perhaps this demonstrates the frailty of such an approach.

There is arguably something oxymoronic about the concept of "preventive war."

---

32. Lieutenant James M. Dubik (retired), quoted in Larson and Zust, *Care for the Sorrowing Soul*, 16.

33. For a helpful review of moral injury from a biblical perspective, see Brad E. Kelle, *The Bible and Moral Injury: Reading Scripture alongside War's Unseen Wounds* (Nashville: Abingdon, 2020).

34. Brown, "Crusade or Preventive War," 161.

35. Brown, "Crusade or Preventive War," 159.

36. Charles Colson, "Just War in Iraq: Sometimes Going to War Is the Charitable Thing to Do (The Back Page)," *Christianity Today*, December 9, 2002, 72.

The optimism that took the Allies to war in 1914, that this would be "a war to end all war," soon dissipated into pessimism as it proved not only to be the bloodiest war in history but also to be the war that triggered another world war. In pragmatic terms, history shows us that conflicts commonly escalate in the absence of dogged peacemaking, just as entropy tends to increase unless there is an injection of energy into the system.[37] A better preventive strategy might be heavy investment in, say, healthcare in the relevant region.[38] We will consider such ideas later, in our discussion of just peacemaking.

A second adaptation of the just-war principles was offered by Michael Walzer in his book *Just and Unjust Wars*. Walzer proposed that in a "supreme emergency," when the *jus ad bellum* principles were satisfied, the *jus in bello* criteria could be set aside. In other words, in these extreme instances, war could be waged without restraint: "when conventional means of resistance are hopeless or worn out, anything goes."[39] Walzer's use of the term "supreme emergency" follows Winston Churchill's use of the same phrase in 1939, and he concurs with the British prime minister that the Nazi threat did indeed constitute just such an exceptional exigency. Having coined the term, Churchill later used it to justify the area bombing of German cities; Walzer created a theoretical framework for this action.

The idea of setting aside the *jus in bello* criteria might—rightly, I think—be morally distasteful to us. But this is just one example among many that Walzer provides. The honest reader will find it hard to choose the "correct" response to many of the cases. This ably demonstrates the extreme moral complexity of war and the impossibility of conducting it in a pristine manner.

Nuclear Weapons and Just War

All of the houses were demolished. The crumbled walls and heaps of tiles stretched for many miles. Many people rushed from the centre. Their bodies were burnt. Their skin was hanging down like rags. Their faces were swollen to twice normal size. They were holding their hands to their breasts. They were walking, embracing one another and crying out with pain.

—testimony of Mrs. Hizume of Hiroshima[40]

The development of nuclear weapons in the second half of the twentieth century brought a whole new set of questions to the just-war proposal. The key historical developments are summarized in the table below.[41]

---

37. The second law of thermodynamics states that systems become more disorganized over time (entropy increases), and it takes an input of energy to increase structure (enthalpy).

38. Myron S. Augsburger, "'A Christian Pacifist Response' to Harold O. J. Brown, 'The Crusade or Preventive War,'" in Clouse, *War: Four Christian Views*, 178.

39. Michael Walzer, *Just and Unjust Wars: A Moral Argument with Historical Illustrations*, 4th ed. (New York: Basic Books, 1977), 252.

40. Quoted in Roland H. Bainton, *Christian Attitudes toward War and Peace: A Historical Survey and Critical Re-evaluation* (New York: Abingdon, 1960), 228–29.

41. Most of the elements in this table were drawn from the

1942	Manhattan Project established in USA to develop the world's first nuclear weapon
1945	Atomic bombs deployed over Hiroshima and Nagasaki, with immediate deaths (within the year) an estimated 225,000
1946	UN General Assembly calls for a ban on nuclear weapons
1949	USSR conducts first nuclear weapon test in Kazakhstan
1952	UK conducts first nuclear weapon test in Australia USA tests world's first hydrogen bomb in Marshall Islands
1955	Bertrand Russell, Albert Einstein, and other nuclear scientists issue a manifesto warning of the dangers of nuclear war
1958	Campaign for Nuclear Disarmament established
1959	**Antarctic Treaty** opens for signature, banning nuclear tests in Antarctica
1962	Cuban Missile Crisis
1963	**Partial Test Ban Treaty** opens for signature
1967	Latin America becomes nuclear free
1968	**Non-Proliferation Treaty** opens for signature
1982	A million people gather in New York to support the nuclear freeze movement
1985	South Pacific becomes nuclear free
1987	USSR and USA sign the **Intermediate-Range Nuclear Forces Treaty**
1995	Southeast Asia becomes nuclear free
1996	Africa becomes nuclear free The **Comprehensive Test Ban Treaty** opens for signature
2017	The **Treaty on the Prohibition of Nuclear Weapons** opens for signature

In bold are marked the main international treaties that have limited the acquisition and testing of nuclear weapons. The first major step forward came in 1968, when the Nuclear Non-Proliferation Treaty opened for signature. The treaty entered into force in 1970 and was extended indefinitely in 1995. A total of 191 states have now signed, including the five nuclear-weapon states. Signatory states that do not currently possess nuclear weapons undertake never to acquire them, and signatory states with nuclear weapons agree to share the benefits of peaceful nuclear technology and to pursue disarmament.

The Treaty on the Prohibition of Nuclear Weapons, also known as the Nuclear

historical timeline provided by the International Campaign to Abolish Nuclear Weapons ("The Road to a World Free of Nuclear Weapons," ICAN, www.icanw.org/nuclear_weapons_history). The table is simplified; the acquisition of nuclear weapons by the other nuclear powers are omitted for the sake of brevity.

Ban Treaty, entered into force in 2021, having been ratified by fifty states. As a result of this treaty coming into effect, nuclear weapons are now banned by international law. Neither the USA nor the UK is yet a signatory. These treaties, and the enormous international efforts which they represent, have resulted in a decrease in the number of nuclear weapons over recent decades by over 75 percent. Today there are approximately fifteen thousand nuclear weapons in the world.

The use of nuclear weapons breaches at least two of the just-war criteria. From the *jus in bello*, the use of a nuclear weapon against civilians would always fail the proportionality test. Likewise, the *jus ad bellum* cannot all be satisfied, because nuclear war cannot offer a reasonable hope of attaining just peace.[42]

By those who possess it, the nuclear deterrent has generally been justified as essential for national defense, much as Denethor described his ill-fated plans for the ring of power in this quotation from the *Lord of the Rings* trilogy:

> It should have been kept, hidden, hidden dark and deep. Not used, I say, unless at the uttermost end of need. . . . If I had this thing now in the deep vaults of this citadel, we should not then shake with dread under this gloom, fearing the worst, and our counsels would be undisturbed.[43]

However, other factors such as national ambition are also clearly in play. For instance, in a 2006 op-ed in the *Sunday Times* (of London), the prospect of abandoning the UK's nuclear weapons was criticized for forfeiting Britain's place "at the top table."[44]

The Nuclear Ban Treaty has reversed the general narrative that the USA and UK are moral leaders in the world. Along with the other nations that have refused to sign the treaty, we are now in breach of international law, which since January 2021 has prohibited the possession, development, or threat of using nuclear weapons.

Church groups have generally been wan at most in their support of the nuclear deterrent. The pastoral letter published by the Catholic bishops suggests that it might be a step toward disarmament but is emphatically not an end in itself: "[Nuclear deterrence] is a transitional strategy justifiable only in conjunction with resolute determination to pursue arms control and disarmament."[45] The British free church interdenominational campaign group, JPIT, puts it even more strongly: "A threat of violence is not a non-violent act."[46]

These are examples of many of the ways that the church is speaking and campaigning about the international arms race. In many places the church has been

---

42. National Conference of Catholic Bishops, "The Challenge of Peace: God's Promise and Our Response: A Pastoral Letter on War and Peace by the National Conference of Catholic Bishops, May 3, 1983," United States Catholic Conference, 1983, https://pdf4pro.com/amp/view/the-challenge-of-peace-usccb-org-155fff.html.

43. John Ronald Reuel Tolkien, *Return of the King* (London: Allen & Unwin, 1966), 87.

44. "The Case for Trident," *Sunday Times*, March 12, 2006.

45. National Conference of Catholic Bishops, "Challenge of Peace."

46. Joint Public Issues Team, "Better Off without Trident," 2018, www.jointpublicissues.org.uk/wp-content/uploads/2018/01/Better-off-without-Trident.pdf.

instrumental in the movements for disarmament and international bans. Particularly when its activities transcend national borders and traditional hostilities, these are exemplary instances of the church occupying its prophetic calling. This is not universally the case, of course. As Walter Wink writes, "The sorry record reveals that Christian churches have usually simply endorsed the side on which they happened to find themselves."[47] In such circumstances, the church may lend theological weight to the war and even to the nuclear armament. For instance, Patriarch Kirill of the Russian Orthodox Church is notorious for blessing his country's nuclear warheads with holy water.

An opportunity that perhaps has not yet been fully explored is the possibility of developing *and sharing* defensive technology. If a greater proportion of nations' military development budgets could be spent on developing defensive rather than aggressive weapons, this might be a small step forward. Something like this was attempted in 1983, in the failed Strategic Defense Initiative, which was promoted by Ronald Reagan with great fanfare. The SDI ("Star Wars") program failed partly for technical reasons, but also because thousands of scientists boycotted the program, claiming that America's unilateral possession of defensive technology would drive the accelerated development of weapons by the USSR in response.[48] A significant factor in this aggravation of the arms race, however, was the projected *unilateral* possession of the defensive technology. I offer these comments as a theologian, not as a defense strategist, but it seems to me that the scope for the shared development of such technology has not yet been fully explored, particularly in this new world with fewer weapons and shifted geopolitical realities.

Pacifisms

A true war story is never moral. It does not instruct, nor encourage virtue, nor suggest models of proper human behavior. . . . If a story seems moral, do not believe it. If at the end of a war story you feel uplifted, or if you feel that some small bit of rectitude has been salvaged from the larger waste, then you have been made the victim of a very old and terrible lie.[49]

The third broad position that some Christians have taken is to choose not to meet violence with violence, by adopting one of the various forms of principled

47. Walter Wink, *The Powers That Be: Theology for a New Millennium* (New York: Doubleday, 1998), 131.
48. John B. Kogut, "The Scientists' Campaign against the Strategic Defense Initiative," *Journal of the American Medical Association* 258.5 (1987): 658–60.
49. Tim O'Brien, *How to Tell a True War Story*, quoted in David C. Cramer and Myles Werntz, *A Field Guide to Christian Nonviolence: Key Thinkers, Activists and Movements for the Gospel of Peace* (Grand Rapids: Baker, 2022), 31.

nonviolence. This has a long and honorable history within the church, but Christians arrive at this stance by a number of different routes. David Cramer and Myles Werntz have recently offered a very helpful taxonomy of the types of nonviolence that have been proposed, and the interested reader is directed to their work.[50] We will briefly outline several different approaches before focusing more closely on the one offered by Glen Stassen.

The Mennonite J. Denny Weaver is one of several writers who share the conviction that Jesus did not simply set an example of nonviolence but that his nature and mission was fundamentally predicated upon it. This means that the church is essentially constructed upon nonviolence.

> Since rejection of violence is intrinsic to the story and work of Jesus, I do not separate it from the confession of Jesus as Lord and norm.[51]

This perspective on the church has much in common with its prophetic role that we discussed in chapter 13. However, it can verge toward marginalizing the Old Testament's witness; indeed, it sometimes drives a wedge within the Gospels between the "violent messianism of Mary and Elizabeth" and the nonviolence of Jesus.[52]

André Trocmé was pastor of the French Reformed Church at Le Chambon-sur-Lignon during the Second World War and a convinced pacifist. Trocmé mobilized not simply his church members but several entire villages to defy the Nazi-controlled Vichy regime. More than five thousand Jews and other hunted persons were saved from deportation to the death camps through this action.[53]

A somewhat different perspective is offered by the Methodist theologian and ethicist Stanley Hauerwas, who focuses upon the cultivation of virtue and the way it forms character. Christian virtues are fundamentally nonviolent, because there is a deep logic of nonviolence at the heart of God.

> Christians are called to nonviolence not because we think nonviolence is a strategy to rid the world of war; but rather in a world of war, as faithful followers of Christ, we cannot imagine being anything other than nonviolent.[54]

---

50. Cramer and Werntz, *Field Guide to Christian Nonviolence*.
51. J. Denny Weaver, *The Nonviolent God* (Grand Rapids: Eerdmans, 2013), 155.
52. Cramer and Werntz, *Field Guide to Christian Nonviolence*, 13. The quoted phrase belongs to the Catholic New Testament scholar, J. Massyngbaerde Ford.
53. The story is told in Caroline Moorehead, *Village of Secrets: Defying the Nazis in Vichy France* (New York: Random House, 2014).
54. Stanley Hauerwas, *Performing the Faith: Bonhoeffer and the Practice of Nonviolence* (Eugene, OR: Wipf & Stock, 2004), 236.

Such virtue is not acquired in isolation but cultivated and embodied within the confessional community.[55] It becomes a habit which shapes the character in times of peace, to be drawn upon in times of conflict. This emphasis is particularly helpful. The model of training the heart and mind after the ways of Christ is deeply written into the New Testament, particularly the Pauline writings.

A third approach to nonviolence was proposed by the Baptist civil-rights activist Howard Thurman. Perhaps surprisingly, Thurman was a mystic. He believed that it is out of deep communion with God that the violence within our own hearts can be transformed, and guidance received. "The wise man [*sic*] acts in the light of his best judgment illumined by the integrity of his profoundest spiritual insights."[56] It is impossible to criticize any movement that promotes deep prayer and worship. But whether such contemplation must inevitably lead to a wholly nonviolent position is unclear.

A different approach to nonviolence is what Cramer and Werntz term "apocalyptic non-violence."[57] This is the performative practice of nonviolence for the sake of its revelatory function, in that it uncovers the reality of God's nonviolent kingdom. Nonviolence that is embraced because of its likelihood to have persuasive power depends upon the acquiescence of amenable political bodies. By contrast the apocalyptic approach is more concerned with "exposing the rot" within political systems that depend on violence. This is the approach offered by the Catholic anthropologist René Girard, whose thought we have engaged with in some detail, and by activists such as the Plowshares movement.[58]

> "The Plowshares members utilized tactics such as burglarizing an FBI office, hammering on warplanes and nuclear warheads, burning draft cards, and refusing to pay taxes in support of the Vietnam War. But none of these actions were designed first and foremost to influence lawmakers, though opposing unjust laws drew attention to their injustice. . . . Rather, the dramatic actions were meant to enact the ways of God over against Death by quite literally beating a weapon into some other instrument."[59]

There is something attractive in the bold defiance of such activism, which echoes many of the dramatic actions of the Old Testament prophets. However, one

55. Stanley Hauerwas, *The Peaceable Kingdom: A Primer in Christian Ethics* (Notre Dame: University of Notre Dame Press, 1983), 97.

56. Howard Thurman, *Meditations of the Heart* (Boston: Beacon Press, 1953), 80.

57. David C. Cramer and Myles Werntz, *A Field Guide to Christian Nonviolence: Key Thinkers, Activists and Movements for the Gospel of Peace* (Grand Rapids: Baker, 2022), 59–74.

58. Trident Ploughshares, https://tridentploughshares.org/.

59. Cramer and Werntz, *Field Guide to Christian Nonviolence*, 66.

consideration to bear in mind is the extent to which truth-telling is valuable for its own sake, as opposed to any further tangible benefits that it might achieve.

Other nonviolent activists work with a more pragmatic goal in mind. A good example is the political nonviolence practiced *par excellence* by Martin Luther King Jr., the Baptist minister and Nobel Prize-winning, civil-rights campaigner who was murdered at the age of thirty-nine. King's convictions arose from a deep engagement with Scripture, but he combined this with a pragmatic, natural-law approach to nonviolence, informed in particular by the practice of Mohandas Gandhi.[60] King viewed violence as not simply morally wrong, but also inherently self-defeating. By this logic, nonviolent practice is not simply virtuous but also useful, particularly because it enables the nonviolent protagonist to occupy the moral high ground.

> King bemoaned the church's failure to accept this responsibility and prophetically speak for peace.
>
> > When the man in the parable knocked on his friend's door and asked for the three loaves of bread, he received the impatient retort, "Do not bother me; the door is now shut, and my children are with me in bed; I cannot get up and give you anything." How often have men experienced a similar disappointment when at midnight they knock on the door of the church. . . . In the terrible midnight of war, men have knocked on the door of the church to ask for the bread of peace, but the church has often disappointed them.[61]

King's legacy extends well beyond the original cause for which he campaigned. Inspired by his teaching and example, nonviolent resistance has spread around the world, influencing campaigners as diverse as Nelson Mandela and Desmond Tutu in South Africa and Srdja Popovic in Serbia.

Cramer and Werntz's taxonomy helpfully demonstrates the ideological and practical diversity of Christian approaches to nonviolence. They should not be homogenized. Some of the approaches are clearly "utopian,"[62] in that they are reaching toward an unachievable ideal. This need not inherently be a criticism, but it is certainly a relevant consideration. To what extent does the pristine conscience trump practical benefit? We are back to our framework of balancing the virtues of justice, peacemaking, and moral purity. Some, but not all, of these approaches can tend

60. Martin Luther King Jr., *Stride toward Freedom: The Montgomery Story* (Boston: Beacon, 1958), 84.

61. Martin Luther King Jr., "A Knock at Midnight," in *Strength to Love* (Boston: Beacon, 1981), 58.

62. D. Heimbach and K. Keithley, "Daniel R. Heimbach: The Ethics of War and Peace," *Christ and Culture Podcast*, May 7, 2021, https://cfc.sebts.edu/faith-and-politics/daniel-heimbach-ethics-war-peace/.

toward passivism, that is, the temptation to remain aloof from the woes of the world. Therein lies the danger of pursuing "peace" at the expense of justice, and perhaps straying beyond the circle of faithful Christian response that our framework models.

With this in mind, we now turn to consider a very proactive response proposed by the Baptist theologian Glen Stassen.

Just Peacemaking

Stassen's just peacemaking is a creative way for Christian engagement. He considered just-war argumentation to be a capitulation to "the game set by the principalities and powers," while traditional pacifist approaches depend upon "an ethics of 'if only.'"[63]

In Stassen's view, Scripture is fundamentally pro-life.[64] Jesus's healing miracles and blessing on peacemakers are evidence of this, as are his instructions to be proactive in making peace with an adversary (Matt 5:21–26). Stassen sees these as *transforming initiatives*; not simply illustrations of the broader theme of enemy love but concrete steps toward peacemaking.[65] His challenge to be specific and active rather than speak in vague generalizations is hard-hitting:

> Watching Christians rationalize their vagueness in the face of Adolf Hitler and the Nazis, Dietrich Bonhoeffer said Jesus was incarnate not vaguely but concretely: If the church is not speaking concretely, it is not speaking the word of the living Jesus Christ; it should admit that it has no business speaking some other word, and shut up.[66]

Stassen makes an ingenious if somewhat reductive argument from the letter to the Romans, viewing the vices identified by Paul in the early chapters—malice, murder, envy, and so on—as *idolatries* (cf. Rom 1:23, 25) that lead to war. In his own late twentieth-century context, Stassen considered them to be manifest in three particular ways: the idolatry of secularism (a pseudo-Christian perspective that places trust in weaponry rather than God); the idolatry of abstractionism (where the statement "Jesus is Lord" has no ethical or moral content); and the idolatry of silversmithing (with reference to the silversmith of Acts 19, the groups and individuals who profit directly from the arms trade).[67]

The apostle Paul, steeped as always in the dominical tradition, echoes Jesus's words of nonviolence and non-vengeance. Stassen identifies eight such "transforming initiatives" in Romans 12. I have summarized these, with a single example of each (Stassen provides many), in the table below.[68]

---

63. Glen Stassen, "A Theological Rationale for Peacemaking," *Review & Expositor* 79.4 (1982): 623.

64. Stassen uses the term in the general, rather than pregnancy-related, sense.

65. Glen Stassen, *Just Peacemaking: Transforming Initiatives for Justice and Peace* (Louisville: Westminster John Knox, 1992), 53.

66. Stassen, *Just Peacemaking*, 54.

67. Stassen, "Theological Rationale for Peacemaking," 627–28.

68. Stassen, *Just Peacemaking*, 56–57.

Offer your bodies as a living sacrifice, holy and pleasing to God. (Rom 12:1; cf. Luke 6:25)	→ Acknowledge your alienation and God's grace
As far as it depends on you, live at peace with everyone. (Rom 12:18; cf. Matt 5:24)	→ Go, talk, welcome, and seek reconciliation
If your enemy is hungry, feed him. (Rom 12:20; cf. Matt 5:40)	→ Don't resist vengefully but take transforming initiatives
Live in harmony with one another. Do not be proud, but be willing to associate with people of low position. (Rom 12:16; cf. Matt 5:42)	→ Invest in delivering justice
Rejoice with those who rejoice; mourn with those who mourn. (Rom 12:15; Matt 5:44a)	→ Love your enemies with actions; affirm their valid interests
Bless those who persecute you; bless and do not curse. (Rom 12:14; cf. Matt 5:44b)	→ Pray for your enemies
Do not repay anyone evil for evil. (Rom 12:17; cf. Matt 6:14)	→ Don't judge but repent and forgive
In Christ we, though many, form one body, and each member belongs to all the others. (Rom 12:5; cf. Matt 5:1)	→ Do peacemaking in a church or group of disciples

The pattern appears a little strained at times, but the overall point is well made. Developing these principles, Stassen identifies ten initiatives for our own day, which together constitute the practice of just peacemaking.[69] These are:

- Support nonviolent direct action.
- Take independent initiatives to reduce threat.
- Use cooperative conflict resolution.
- Acknowledge responsibility for conflict and injustice; seek repentance and forgiveness.
- Promote democracy, human rights, and religious liberty.
- Foster just and sustainable economic development.
- Work with emerging cooperative forces in the international system.
- Strengthen the United Nations and international efforts for cooperation and human rights.
- Reduce offensive weapons and the weapons trade.
- Encourage grassroots peacemaking groups and voluntary associations.

---

69. See, e.g., Glen Stassen, ed., *Just Peacemaking: Ten Practices for Abolishing War* (Cleveland: Pilgrim, 1998).

This approach to violence and peace is a welcome positive movement. It is not primarily a reaction against the evil that needs to be confronted nor a protest against the urge to violent intervention. Rather it is a move *for* proactive, positive measures to increase the shalom of the community and the world. Even if it proves ultimately insufficient in a particular instance, it provides a very good starting place for the church or individual who is seeking to live faithfully.

Stassen demonstrated his own commitment to such action in his engagement with the international disarmament movement. The high point of the US arm of that movement was a protest in Central Park, New York in 1982, which drew over a million protestors. Stassen believed this demonstration to have been a key factor in driving the Reagan government toward the Intermediate-Range Nuclear Forces Treaty that he signed with Mikhail Gorbachev in 1987.[70]

CONCLUSION

In this chapter we have surveyed some of the principal Christian approaches to the question, *What do we do when the cheek that is slapped is not our own?*

The tensions we have previously identified between the pursuit of justice, moral purity, and peaceableness have been evident throughout this chapter. We began by considering the tendency of some churches and other institutions to be slow to respond to abuse allegations. In such circumstances the value of "peaceableness" (or a simulacrum of it) has been promoted with insufficient attention to the imperatives of justice and moral integrity.

We then considered crusade war, where—arguably—none of the three virtues is genuinely in evidence; and just war, where there is (or may be) a genuine concern for justice, and perhaps peace.

The religious historian Matthew Rowley encourages us to distinguish between a war that is considered just because it is holy (by appeal to some transcendent revelation), and a war which is, in a sense "holy" because it is driven by a just cause.[71] In both of these patterns, war may be justified in sacred terms. But whereas in the first category it is the transcendent call to war that constructs a sufficient cause for war; in the second, the divine revelation (in Scripture and so on) provides a framework for justice that might render war necessary. Such a framework is compatible with a public understanding of what constitutes justice. So, a crusader who believed that

---

70. Paul Vitello, "Glen Stassen, Theologian, Dies at 78; Champ_pioned Nuclear Disarmament," *New York Times*, May 7, 2014.

71. Matthew Rowley, *God, Religious Extremism and Violence* (Cambridge: Cambridge University Press, forthcoming).

taking Jerusalem for the pope was a holy act would consider his war just for that reason. By contrast, a soldier who signs up to try to stop a genocide considers the war just and (if he thinks in such terms) therefore a holy endeavor.

As we consider the relative merits of these approaches to war, Rowley's model serves as a potent warning. Our survey of the scriptural narrative on war and peace has identified no holy cause in Scripture that serves to justify war. If war is ever to be permissible, it must be reluctantly pursued in the cause of justice.

We concluded by considering a range of Christian nonviolence philosophies and movements. These vary in their underlying theology and purpose. Some are vigorously proactive, and others lean toward passivity.

It will have become apparent that while some approaches may be better than others, none of them is ideal. Some will work well under certain circumstances but not in other situations. Always there is the need to balance principle with pragmatism, or—to put it another way—to improvise faithfully in the "time between the times," in the tension between the eschatological goal and the real, messy world that we live in and to whose messiness we contribute.

Whether the world is becoming less violent or not, as we discussed in chapter 1, will probably remain a moot point. What is clear is that in our generation there has never been a greater need for a prophetic people who will seek to enact justice with mercy, to work for peace with boldness, and to strive toward holiness with dirty hands.

> In a world of pain and sorrow
> Where power conquers right
> We receive the fresh commission
> To fight the cause of Light—
> With the weapons you permit us:
> Patient love, self-sacrifice;
> By the stirring of the Spirit
> Our fortitude will rise.
> As by love and grace and mercy,
> The captives we release
> Most of all, our Master, teach us
> The things that make for peace.
>
> May we live the deep reality,
> The realm we cannot see;
> Your peaceful reign of freedom
> And hospitality.
> Where the government is Justice
> With a bias to the poor,
> Where we celebrate our difference

And hasten not to war;
Where suspicion, fear and prejudice,
The seeds of hatred, cease;
So above all, Master, teach us
The things that make for peace.

To the foes of God and humankind,
Pride and hostility
We will raise the cross of Jesus Christ:
Weakness, humility;
All the broken and fragmented
Find their purpose in that place;
Lost are found, sick find healing,
And prodigals find grace.
Here is reconciliation
Of former enemies;
Here we find our Master's remedy—
The cross that makes for peace.[72]

RELEVANT QUESTIONS

1. How effectively and compassionately would/does your church respond if someone made an allegation of abuse? Do you have robust systems already in place?
2. Where have you seen crusade war in recent years?
3. We highlighted above the enormous responsibility that rests upon state actors in evaluating the possible causes for military engagement. In what ways can you support your government and hold it to account as it operates on the international stage?
4. What value (if any) do you see in nonviolent actions that are performative rather than designed to effect direct change?
5. What experience do you have of the just peacemaking initiatives that Glen Stassen outlines? Can you see areas where you could lean into these?

---

72. Lyrics © Helen Paynter 2013. Tune: Thaxted (Gustav Holst, 1926; public domain). Reproduction of the song for congregational use is welcome provided the author is attributed.

CHAPTER 15

RESISTING EVIL: TWO CASE STUDIES

We have considered three broad approaches to the question of how to resist evil, how to respond when violence is being enacted against others. These discussions were far from theoretical, and history is full of people who have aligned themselves with one or the other of the approaches. However, in this chapter we will consider two particular case studies: the question of gun ownership in the US, and the issue of capital punishment.

These are issues over which Christians are divided. The question I will attempt to address in each case is what stances are contained within the central circle of faithful action, and what lie beyond it. For each case, I will set out the theological case made by proponents of the more violent stance (gun ownership and capital punishment) before attempting to evaluate that argument using the principles we have been developing. I will finish by offering my own conclusions and inviting you, the reader, to develop your own opinion.

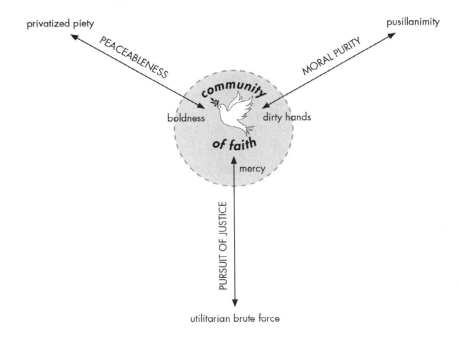

Worked Example: Gun Control

I live and work in the United Kingdom, where gun ownership is very tightly restricted. Following a school shooting in Dunblane in 1996 that killed sixteen pupils and one teacher, handgun ownership was banned. Our police are not routinely armed. This is the context with which I am most familiar, and like most people in the UK I find myself bewildered at the US's resistance to enact gun control. However, I aim here to be completely fair and examine the Christian gun lobby's debate at its strongest point.

In May 2022, the Gospel Coalition hosted a debate between Rev. Bob Thune and Rev. Dr. Andrew Wilson on the question of gun control. Both participants made their case strongly, clearly, and irenically, and the debate, which can be viewed on YouTube,[1] offers a microcosm of the diverse perspectives held by Christians as the debate relates to the US today.

The Case for the Right to Bear Arms

Bob Thune, speaking for the right to bear arms, made three main points to support his overall thesis that love of neighbor ***necessitates*** the bearing of arms.

1. All beings have the *right* "by creation" to preserve their existence, and therefore there is a fundamental right to self-defense. Thune quoted Exodus 22:2 in favor of this argument: "If a thief is caught breaking in at night and is struck a fatal blow, the defender is not guilty of bloodshed; but if it happens after sunrise, the defender is guilty of bloodshed." He also cited arguments from Thomas Aquinas and Francis Turretin in favor of the right to self-defense.
2. Christians have a moral *duty* to protect their neighbors against unjust violence, citing Calvin in support of this argument. (Thune described this as a duty "by redemption," which leaves open in my mind the possibility that he considers Christians to have a particular privilege in terms of gun-bearing rights.)
3. Because of the presence of guns in high numbers in the US, fulfillment of the duty (point 2) and exercise of the right (point 1) necessitate a weapon proportional to the threat, that is, a gun. Thune augmented this point by speaking of the purpose of gun ownership to prevent governmental overreach.

The Case for Gun Control

Andrew Wilson, speaking for gun control, made four points; the first three by natural law and the final one a theological point.

---

1. The Gospel Coalition, "Gun Control and the Right to Bear Arms—Good Faith Debates," YouTube, May 4, 2022, www.youtube .com/watch?v=xOMePdBBLnI.

1. The ready availability of guns in the US means that it has a disproportionately large death toll compared to other developed countries. Much of the brunt of this is borne by the already disadvantaged: the poor, African Americans, women, and children.[2]

2. In 1996, Australia, which shares many cultural similarities with the US, responded to a mass shooting by banning the ownership of automatic and semiautomatic weapons and tightening the rules around ownership of other guns. The overall homicide rate has halved.

3. Wilson's third point was around the balancing of rights and responsibilities. He argued that the bearing of arms was not considered an absolute right by anybody. Arm-bearing ranges from the ownership of a baseball bat, to which nobody objects, to the private ownership of a nuclear weapon, which nobody proposes. The sliding scale of "rights," then, needs to be balanced by the needs and rights of others.

4. Finally, Wilson turned to Scripture to demonstrate the call and example of Jesus to nonviolence, seeking to call into question Thune's assumption of the right to self-defense. Wilson quoted a large number of texts (to balance Thune's use of Exodus 22), including Hebrews 10:34, where the Christians are commended for "joyfully accepting the confiscation of your property." The sum of Wilson's argument, then, was that *Christian discipleship requires the laying down of arms.*

Thune's case is partly based on principle and partly on pragmatism. His argument for rights and duties are principles, but his third point is a pragmatic one. In fact, there are striking resemblances between the just-war argument and the third point that Thune makes. By his argument, gun ownership is necessary to defend the neighbor from the gun violence that already exists.

In response to this, there are perhaps five points in addition to Wilson's which I would make.

1. It will be recalled that one of the *jus in bello* conditions is that war is conducted by a legitimate authority. As we have discussed, the just-war argument does not provide a legitimation for vigilante justice. By contrast, the argument made by Thune was highly individualistic: an *individual* has both the right and the duty to bear arms. Society appears to be irrelevant to his argument, and government is viewed as a threat rather than both being seen as a cooperative means of limiting the threat of violence. (While I understand the good historical reasons that underlie this position, many of those historic conditions

2. Jason E. Goldstick, Rebecca M. Cunningham, and Patrick M. Carter, "Current Causes of Death in Children and Adolescents in the United States," *New England Journal of Medicine* 386 (2022): 1955–56.

are no longer relevant. America is no longer a frontier society, and the guns that the founding fathers had in mind had a very different killing capacity from the ones now widely available for purchase.) Thune's stance appears to me to take insufficient account of both the common good that a democratic society offers, and of the priority of community over individualism that the New Testament assumes.

2. Building on this, the use of the language of "rights" should give us pause for thought. The New Testament would urge that while rights are things we might defend for others, they are things that we are frequently called to lay down ourselves. In chapter 11 we considered the cruciform logic of Philippians 2 (although I have this entitlement . . . yet I will not exercise it . . . but rather I will lay it down) with which the apostle Paul shapes just about all of his pastoral theology. The prioritization of "my rights" over "their harm" is sub-Christian.

3. If gun ownership is a *pragmatic* response to a nonideal situation, it can only be sustained if there is evidence that it is actually working. To the contrary, there is ample evidence that it is not overall effectively protecting the weak and the vulnerable, but rather is having the opposite effect. This bears similarity to just war's *jus ad bellum* of "probability of success," which is clearly not met.

4. We have seen again and again that violence tends to spiral, or as Girard would put it, we come to imitate one another in our violence. This is certainly a pattern that is observable in the US, and indeed in Thune's argument. Even if we do not reject the use of violence to restrain violence in the most desperate of situations, there must be a very high threshold indeed for doing so. This relates to just war's *jus ad bellum* of "last resort." The balance of evidence from the US would suggest that this condition has not been met. The gun-control lobby offers plenty of options (including the Australian model), which have not yet been attempted.

5. The rhetoric of the gun lobby in the US bears substantial similarity to the language of the arms race, and there may be something we can learn from this. Just as there has been some success in gradually de-escalating the nuclear threat, the very least that a responsible gun-owner should be doing is proactively working to de-escalate the gun situation nationally. This, of course, may already be taking place quietly at the grassroots level, but it is very evident that significant voices from the evangelical church are vocally promoting guns rather than deprecating their putative necessity.

In conclusion, I believe the argument is overwhelming that the current availability and use of guns in the US is, to use Andrew Wilson's term, a "grievous injustice."

Worked Example: Capital Punishment

Juan Roberto Melendez spent almost 18 years on Florida's death row for a crime he didn't commit. A Puerto Rican migrant farmer raised in New York City, Melendez struggled to participate in his defense because he spoke no English and was never offered an interpreter. There was no physical evidence in his case. He was finally released after it was revealed that the prosecutor withheld evidence of his innocence, including a confession by the person who committed the crime.[3]

The Case for Capital Punishment

The case for capital punishment, when made theologically, largely rests upon three parts of Scripture.[4]

1. First, it invokes Genesis 9:6:

   > Whoever sheds human blood,
   >> by humans shall their blood be shed;
   > for in the image of God
   >> has God made mankind.

   However, this verse is, no pun intended, a double-edged sword for the death penalty argument, in its vigorous assertion of the supreme value of human life.

2. The second place where death-penalty proponents will tend to look in Scripture is the Mosaic law and its prescription of the death penalty for a number of offenses.[5] We have considered at some length the role that the Old Testament law plays for the Christian individual today and should be wary of simplistically applying it in legal situations. On what basis might the death penalty be justified for homicide (Num 35:16–28), if not also for incorrigible delinquency (Deut 21:18–21)? Further, the context in which these laws were handed down is extremely different from our own. The Sinai law was given to a nomadic people, who would have no opportunity to set up a system for incarceration for many years.[6] As we have seen, the Old Testament law provides a valuable guide for Christian discipleship, but its selective application to twenty-first century contexts is deeply flawed.

---

3. Case history provided by Equal Justice USA, EJUSA, https://ejusa.org/resource/latinos-and-the-death-penalty/.

4. The case is set out in the briefing paper, Dan Van Ness, "A Call to Dialogue on Capital Punishment," Dallas Baptist University, Sociology professor Jean Humphrey's online course materials, www3.dbu.edu/jeanhumphreys/juvenile/captialpunishment.htm#back3.

5. Van Ness lists sixteen offenses for which the Torah prescribes the death penalty.

6. There is one example of legal detention during those desert years (Num 15:34), and it appears to have been both exceptional and ad hoc.

3. Finally, in Romans 13 Paul speaks of the state's responsibility under God to exercise justice.

> If you do wrong, be afraid, for rulers do not bear the sword for no reason. They are God's servants, agents of wrath to bring punishment on the wrongdoer. (Rom 13:4)

> One of the weaknesses of this argument is the lack of clarity around what Paul means by "bearing the sword." It seems doubtful that he is expressly referring to the death penalty.[7] In any case, Paul is making an argument about how Christians should conduct themselves under legitimate government. Any reference he is making to the death penalty is somewhat tangential to his broader point. What is clear is that Paul is far from universally approving of the state's actions in oppressing Christians.

The pro-death penalty argument relies on a presumption about what constitutes "justice." Charles Colson, for example, argues for the death penalty much as I have outlined above, but then describes how his encounter with an unrepentant death-row inmate clinched the argument for him.

> The testimony in the trial, of course, was overwhelming. I don't think anyone could possibly believe he didn't commit those unspeakably barbaric crimes. What I realized in the days prior to Gacy's execution was that there was simply no other appropriate response than execution if justice was to be served.[8]

Justice, for Colson, is talionic. The man in question would not receive justice if he was locked up for his crimes, even if that detention lasted for his entire life. His crimes must be paid for with his death, otherwise justice had not been served.

Beyond the theological argument, the case for the death penalty rests on the consequential arguments that it serves as a deterrent and prevents reoffending, and that it provides closure for the families of the victims.

The Case against Capital Punishment

Many arguments have been made against the death penalty, and I will briefly set out the key ones here. In theological terms, as we have seen, the trajectory of Scripture is toward peace. Even from the very first murder, there is a tendency of mercy toward the offender (Gen 4:13–16). Jesus explicitly refuses the death penalty for the woman taken in adultery by setting an unattainable bar to those who would exercise it.

---

7. Leon Morris, *The Epistle to the Romans*, The Pillar New Testament Commentary (Grand Rapids: Eerdmans, 1988), 464.

8. Charles Colson, "Why I Support Capital Punishment," The Gospel Coalition, February 21, 2017, www.thegospelcoalition.org /article/why-i-support-capital-punishment/.

Let any one of you who is without sin be the first to throw a stone at her. (John 8:7)

Interestingly, Jesus's approach here is similar to that of some of the later rabbis, who added layers of preconditions that had to be satisfied before a capital sentence could be passed. For instance, of the man collecting sticks on the Sabbath (Num 15:32–36), Alan Mittleman writes:

In the hands of the rabbis, layers of legal procedure are added to the spare narrative. The overall thrust of rabbinic law is to diminish, to the vanishing point, the possibility of imposing a death sentence.[9]

Moving on toward more practical considerations, we will locate our discussion in the criminal justice system of the US. The violent death that the death penalty necessarily entails evidences a striking lack of mercy—to be blunt, it is cruel. But the executions are often far more traumatic than they need be.[10] We should also consider the extended confinement on death row (usually well over a decade). By the time most prisoners are executed in the US, they would have been eligible for a parole hearing in the UK.

Nor should we overlook the effect of the execution on those who are responsible for administering it and witnessing it—jurors, prison officer, chaplains, medics, the families of the prisoner, and independent witnesses. There is clear evidence that it can cause PTSD.[11] Two wrongs don't make a right; they just double the number of victims and the amount of secondary trauma.[12]

Some of these practical problems might be written off as an unfortunate by-product of a worthy process if there was evidence that the death penalty did more than provide an outlet for the vengeful rage of society. But on every measure, the death penalty fails to deliver.

It is monumentally expensive. A 2008 study of capital-eligible cases in Maryland showed that a case resulting in a death sentence cost approximately $1.9 million *more* than a case where the death penalty was not sought.[13] This diverts resources that could be used, for example, to fund investigation of cold cases or victim support.

9. Alan Mittleman, "Jewish Interpretations of Biblical Violence," in *Violence and Peace in Sacred Texts: Interreligious Perspectives*, ed. Maria Power and Helen Paynter (London: Palgrave, 2023), 53–72.

10. "Examples of such problems include, among other things, inmates catching fire while being electrocuted, being strangled during hangings (instead of having their necks broken), and being administered the wrong dosages of specific drugs for lethal injections" (Death Penalty Information Centre, "Botched Executions," https://deathpenaltyinfo.org/executions/botched-executions).

11. A. Freinkel, C. Koopman, and D. Spiegel, "Dissociative Symptoms in Media Eyewitnesses of an Execution," *The American Journal of Psychiatry* 151.9 (1994): 1335–339.

12. For stories of those involved in executions, see Kim Bellware, "This Is What It Feels Like to Spend Your Life Working on Death Row," Huffington Post, December 7, 2017, www.huffingtonpost.co.uk/entry/death-row-stories_n_7043620.

13. John Roman, Aaron Chalfin, Aaron Sundquist, Carly Knight, and Askar Darmenov, "The Cost of the Death Penalty in Maryland," Urban Institute, Justice Policy Center, March 2008. https://files.deathpenaltyinfo.org/legacy/files/pdf/CostsDPMaryland.pdf.

It does not provide closure for families. For families of victims, the long-delayed process of execution actually tends to prolong the healing process. Multiple post-conviction hearings continually dredge up the crime for the family, and the public focus is on the murderer rather than their victim.[14] These are the words of Celeste Dixon, whose mother, Marguerite Dixon, was murdered.

> Before my mother's murder, I hadn't thought much about capital punishment. But starting with the trial, doubts crept in that an execution ever would bring me any comfort. Enduring over two decades of appeals and waiting cemented my belief that pursuing the death penalty did me no good.[15]

It is not fair. The death penalty is applied arbitrarily.

> The system is little better than a lottery: an accomplice gets death while the person who actually pulled the trigger is sent to prison; a convenience store robbery gone awry results in execution, while a methodical serial killer gets a life sentence; two equivalent crimes occur on different sides of the county line—one sentenced to die, the other to prison. Such disparities are the norm, not the exception.[16]

In fact, it is even worse than arbitrary. There is consistent evidence that there is a strong racial bias built in to the process. In 1983 the now-famous Baldus study, an extremely cautious and thorough statistical analysis of more than two thousand murder cases, demonstrated a striking inequality of death-penalty decisions according to the race of the victim: "Our data strongly suggests that Georgia is operating a dual system, based upon the race of the victim, for processing homicide cases."[17] Another analysis, which examined every execution for homicide in the US between 1976 and 2013, reported similar findings.[18] Other groups disproportionately represented on death row include those with mental disabilities and those unable to afford good-quality legal representation.

Worst of all is the undeniable fact that innocent people are sometimes executed. Since 1975, the US has seen at least thirty-one innocent people convicted in capital cases; some of them have been executed.[19]

Nor does the death penalty act as an effective deterrent. States that use the death penalty do not have a lower offending rate. States that abolish the death penalty do not see a spike in crime afterward. It is widely agreed among criminologists that the

14. Gardner C. Hanks, *Against the Death Penalty: Christian and Secular Arguments against Capital Punishment* (Scottdale, PA: Herald Press, 1997), 91.

15. "The Closure Myth: How the Death Penalty Fails Victims' Families," EJUSA, https://ejusa.org/resource/the-closure-myth/.

16. "People Are Asking Tough Questions about the Death Penalty," EJUSA, https://ejusa.org/resource/people-are-asking/.

17. David C. Baldus, Charles Pulaski, and George Woodworth, "Comparative Review of Death Sentences: An Empirical Study of the Georgia Experience," *Journal of Criminal Law and Criminology* 74.3 (1983): 709–10.

18. Frank R. Baumgartner, Amanda J. Grigg, and Alisa Mastro, "#BlackLivesDon'tMatter: Race-of-Victim Effects in US Executions, 1976–2013," *Politics, Groups, and Identities* 3.2 (2015): 209–21.

19. Hanks, *Against the Death Penalty*, 120.

death penalty has no deterrent effect.[20] In chapter 1 we surveyed the work of James Gilligan in his psychological evaluation of violent offenders. He described them as the "living dead," for whom physical death can offer no new terrors.[21] Even in some of the most egregious instances—cases of terrorism—execution seems to be counterproductive. Here Audrey Cronin evaluates the relative merits of capturing or assassinating a terrorist leader.

> From a counter-terrorism perspective, rather than leading to a group's demise, the killing of a leader can backfire, resulting in increased publicity for the group's cause and the creation of a martyr.[22]

These arguments that the death penalty does not achieve what it sets out to do would matter a lot less if there were a clear theological justification or biblical mandate for it. But as we have seen, it rests on a weak biblical argument. This was understood by many theologians of the early church, including Tertullian.[23]

> Shall it be held lawful to make an occupation of the sword, when the Lord proclaims that he who uses the sword shall perish by the sword? And shall the son of peace take part in the battle when it does not become him even to sue at law? And shall he apply the chain, and the prison, and the torture, and the punishment, who is not the avenger even of his own wrongs?[24]

Even if verdicts were absolutely reliable, sentencing was irreproachably impartial, and executions were conducted with expediency and no unnecessary cruelty, the taking of a human life would be a grave, grave matter and has very dubious theological justification or practical benefit. But since none of those conditions is consistently satisfied, the death penalty has no place in a civilized society, especially one that claims to be built on Christian principles.

RELEVANT QUESTIONS

1. In each of the two case studies above, where do you see the application of the eschatological goals of justice, peace, and holiness? What possibilities lie within the central circle of faithful action?
2. Have your convictions about these issues been affected in some ways by the discussion of this whole book and this chapter in particular?

---

20. Michael L. Radelet and Traci L. Lacock, "Do Executions Lower Homicide Rates: The Views of Leading Criminologists," *Journal of Criminal Law and Criminology* 99.2 (2008): 489–508.

21. James Gilligan, *Violence: Reflections on a National Epidemic* (New York: Random House, 1996), 42.

22. Audrey Kurth Cronin, *How Terrorism Ends: Understanding the Decline and Demise of Terrorist Campaigns* (Princeton: Princeton University Press, 2009), 32.

23. Roland H. Bainton, *Christian Attitudes toward War and Peace: A Historical Survey and Critical Re-evaluation* (New York: Abingdon, 1960), 78.

24. Tertullian, "The Chaplet, or De Corona," in *Latin Christianity: Its Founder, Tertullian*, ed. A. Roberts, J. Donaldson, and A. C. Coxe (Buffalo: Christian Literature Company, 1885), 99.

CHAPTER 16

"PEACE PEACE," BUT THERE IS NO PEACE

If anyone, then, knows the good they ought to do and doesn't do it, it is sin for them.
James 4:17

Throughout this book we have been noting the universality of human violence. It is sometimes mighty and world-changing, but it is often petty and seemingly trivial. But as we have seen, often it is the petty and seemingly trivial actions or inactions that enable the mighty and world-changing acts and structures of violence. And some violence is baked into our communities and our cultures. We call this structural violence.

In this chapter, we consider this structural violence that is sometimes so pervasive that we don't notice it any more than the air we breathe. How do we learn to identify it, and how do we respond to it? What responses represent faithful improvisation between the pulls of justice, peace, and holiness?

THE ENTANGLEMENTS OF VIOLENCE

In chapter 1 we discussed Hannah Arendt's description of Adolf Eichmann and her use of the term "banality of evil." This is not, of course, because his diabolical work didn't matter, but because it was bureaucratic and pen pushing. Eichmann "just" made sure the (Jewish deportation) trains ran on time. The Eichmann incident is an example of a far more universal phenomenon. Violent systems co-opt others to make them complicit and thus to shore up their own power.

They may do this by use of threat. Violent regimes around the world have found the threat of arrest, confiscation of goods, or other loss of entitlement to be an effective deterrent against those who might speak out against atrocities. The right to scrutinize government policy and peacefully protest against it are important elements of democracy that we should not take for granted.

They may do it by offering enticements. Much of the opposition to the abolition movement was offered by those whose wealth was generated through plantation slavery. Governments will often attempt to leverage our own self-interest to mute any dissent.

And they do it by propagating the lie that there is no alternative. As we saw in our discussion of Roman slavery, violence can shape whole societies and become so integral to their survival that any alternative is unthinkable. It becomes the water in which we swim. Comparing the abusive reign of Solomon to the court of the Pharoah who enslaved the Hebrews, Walter Brueggemann argues that such hegemonic ideologies propagate a "royal consciousness." It totalizes, numbs, and seeks to shut down all alternative imaginations.[1]

Violence grows, expands, co-opts, and forms systems in which we are entangled. But we are not simply flies caught in a web that we can't escape. When we allow violent systems to flourish without our protest, we become predators. This is the dangerous power of silence.

Silence

The German pastor Martin Niemöller, who was imprisoned in Sachsenhausen and Dachau concentration camps under the Nazis, famously wrote these words:

> First they came for the socialists, and I did not speak out—
> Because I was not a socialist.
> Then they came for the trade unionists, and I did not speak out—
> Because I was not a trade unionist.
> Then they came for the Jews, and I did not speak out—
> Because I was not a Jew.
> Then they came for me—and there was no one left to speak
> for me.[2]

In this quotation, Niemöller at once critiques and employs self-interest. The notional speaker (who may have been Niemöller himself, since he initially supported national socialism) did not speak out initially, because the matter did not touch him personally. But at the same time, the denouement is an appeal to self-interest: "and then they came for me." Yet long before the final line, the *moral* disaster has happened. The willingness to speak out should not be contingent on having "skin in the game." We should refuse to keep silent because it is the right thing to do.

The witness of both testaments stands against those who are hard-hearted toward those who are less privileged, who are represented in the following quotations about poverty and imprisonment:

> Whoever shuts their ears to the cry of the poor
> will also cry out and not be answered. (Prov 21:13)

---

1. See, e.g., Walter Brueggemann, *The Prophetic Imagination*, 40th anniversary ed. (Minneapolis: Fortress, 2018).

2. There are several versions of Niemöller's quotation. This one is from the United States Holocaust Memorial Museum and can be found here: https://encyclopedia.ushmm.org/content/en/article/martin-niemoeller-first-they-came-for-the-socialists.

Depart from me, you cursed, into the eternal fire prepared for the devil and his angels. For I was hungry and you gave me no food, I was thirsty and you gave me no drink, I was a stranger and you did not welcome me, naked and you did not clothe me, sick and in prison and you did not visit me. (Matt 25:41–43)

Indeed, through the prophet Isaiah God warns his people that if they fail to release the chains of oppression, he will not heed their religious practices.

> You cannot fast as you do today
>   and expect your voice to be heard on high. . . .
> Is not this the kind of fasting I have chosen:
> to loose the chains of injustice
>   and untie the cords of the yoke,
> to set the oppressed free
>   and break every yoke? (Isa 58:4, 6)

Overlooking the structurally baked-in suffering of people in our own societies is incompatible with offering authentic worship.

With the judgment of God in the form of the Babylonian army looming large over the people of Judah, the false prophets in Jerusalem sought to deny that there was anything wrong. Jeremiah expressed God's fury and indignation about the violence in the city and those who denied that there was anything to worry about:

> Violence and destruction resound in her;
>   her sickness and wounds are ever before me. . . .
> Prophets and priests alike,
>   all practice deceit.
> They dress the wound of my people
>   as though it were not serious.
> "Peace, peace," they say,
>   when there is no peace. (Jer 6:7, 13–14)

This is a sobering warning to any of us who would seek to deny the reality of violence and God's consequent judgment in our own society.

Silence in the face of injustice is one form of sinning by omission, but it is not the only one. In Deuteronomy there is an odd little law that sounds like ancient health and safety:

> When you build a new house, make a parapet around your roof so that you may not bring the guilt of bloodshed on your house if someone falls from the roof. (Deut 22:8)

Health and safety it may be, but the underlying and rather radical idea is that individual Israelite householders are responsible for the well-being of unknown others, who might simply be passing by. The relevance to structural violence should be apparent: we carry a responsibility to people we have never met. It is all the more important to bear this in mind when urban design or class boundaries function to keep us apart from the people who are most vulnerable in our cities and nations.

So, with these warnings ringing in our ears, we now turn to take a deeper look at one representative form of structural violence.

WORKED EXAMPLE: RACISM

On the principle of not criticizing others before facing our own culpability, I will begin with a story from the United Kingdom, where I live. On the evening of April 22, 1993, a young Black teenager stood at a bus stop in London, waiting to catch a bus home from his uncle's house, where he had spent the evening with a friend. As he stood quietly waiting, a group of about five young White men attacked him in a vicious, unprovoked assault, during which he was stabbed four times. He bled to death within a few minutes. The young man's name was Stephen Lawrence, and he was studying for his final school exams with the hope of becoming an architect.

Prime suspects were identified within a few days of the incident, but it was to take nineteen years before two—and to this day only two—of his murderers were convicted of the crime. The police handling of the case was riddled with corruption, delays, and ineffectiveness. The police did not give Stephen first aid when they arrived, but they did place an undercover officer to monitor the activity of the bereaved Lawrence family. An independent inquiry ordered by the home secretary, which received over a hundred thousand pages of evidence, concluded that the investigation had been incompetent and that the reason for this was that the Metropolitan Police was institutionally racist. The report also accused the British civil service, local governments, the National Health Service, schools, and the judicial system of institutional racism and called for reform in each of them.[3]

I select the Stephen Lawrence story as one of many that I could have chosen. More recently, what has been dubbed the "Windrush scandal" has seen many British subjects from the Caribbean, who were invited to make their home in the United Kingdom in the 1950s and 60s, unceremoniously returned to their countries of origin, due to the deliberate policy of creating a "hostile environment" against immigrants.[4]

---

3. For some of the story, see "Stephen Lawrence Murder: A Timeline of How the Story Unfolded," BBC, April 13, 2018, www.bbc.co.uk/news/uk-26465916.

4. "Windrush Scandal Explained," Joint Council for the Welfare of Immigrants, www.jcwi.org.uk/windrush-scandal-explained.

In some cases they were unable to prove their entitlement to stay in the UK because the Home Office had "lost" their documentation.[5]

We turn now to the United States, and as a case study we will consider the issue of racism in the criminal justice system. Here I summarize the argument made by American civil-rights lawyer Michelle Alexander that the Jim Crow laws effectively perpetuated the structural abuse of slavery.[6] She then goes on to show that these abuses were reinvented once again in Reagan's "war on drugs," which instituted a racially prejudiced criminal justice system that is present to this day.

The war on drugs caused a massive uptick in prosecutions and criminalization, but most were for minor possession offenses of the least harmful drugs.[7] Hefty financial incentives for drug arrests resulted in enormous sweeps to catch minor offenders and the use of SWAT teams for even trivial offenses. Large incentives were offered to those who provided information leading to an arrest. Despite crack cocaine use being eight times higher among White college students than Black students,[8] the police—permitted an enormous amount of discretion—conducted their searches in a racially targeted manner, principally focused on the ghettoes.

> From the outset, the drug war could have been waged primarily in overwhelmingly white suburbs or on college campuses. SWAT teams could have rappelled from helicopters in gated suburban communities and raided the homes of high school lacrosse players known for hosting coke and ecstasy parties after their games. The police could have seized televisions, furniture, and cash from fraternity houses based on an anonymous tip that a few joints or a stash of cocaine could be found hidden in someone's dresser drawer. Suburban homemakers could have been placed under surveillance and subjected to undercover operations designed to catch them violating laws regulating the use and sale of prescription "uppers." All of this could have happened as a matter of routine in white communities, but it did not. Instead, when police go looking for drugs, they look in the 'hood.[9]

After arrest, a large proportion of suspects are unable to access legal assistance. Alexander cites the example of Ohio where 90 percent of juveniles are unrepresented in court. Innocent suspects often plea-bargain rather than risk the consequences of an unfavorable trial, where sentencing even for first-time minor drugs offenses often exceeds other countries' sentences for a far more serious crime.

5. Amelia Gentleman, "Home Office Destroyed Windrush Landing Cards, Says Ex-Staffer," *Guardian*, April 17, 2018, www.theguardian.com/uk-news/2018/apr/17/home-office-destroyed-windrush-landing-cards-says-ex-staffer.

6. Michelle Alexander, *The New Jim Crow: Mass Incarceration in the Age of Colorblindness* (New York: New Press, 2012).

7. Alexander, *New Jim Crow*, 60.
8. Alexander, *New Jim Crow*, 99.
9. Alexander, *New Jim Crow*, 124.

Once an individual has a criminal record, they are ineligible for food stamps, they may be evicted from their housing, and they are unable to vote. Then there is the "three strikes and you're out" policy. A drug addict who has accepted a plea-bargain for a crime of which she's innocent (strike one) in order to get back out of prison to see her children, and is then found with a single tablet of two different drugs in her pocket (strikes two and three), will stay in prison until she dies. And, to belabor the point, Black people are targeted far more than Whites. Here is a single piece of evidence out of many, relating to the use of minor traffic violations as a pretext for random drug searches.

> In Volusia County, Florida, a reporter obtained 148 hours of video footage documenting more than 1,000 highway stops conducted by state troopers. Only 5 percent of the drivers on the road were African American or Latino, but more than 80 percent of the people stopped and searched were minorities.[10]

In short, the American criminal justice system is stacked against African Americans in every stage of the process.

Just as I could have given many more instances from the UK, so this single example from the US is just the tip of the iceberg. What have we learned from our survey of Scripture that will help us to understand the issue and how to respond to it?

The Bible and Racism

In the beginning, humans were made in the image of God, and there was no hierarchy between them. But the very first visible consequence of humanity's disobedience was the murder of one man by his brother, which the narrative quickly goes on to denounce as a crime against God's image.

> Whoever sheds human blood,
> > by humans shall their blood be shed;
> for in the image of God
> > has God made mankind. (Gen 9:6)

Perhaps one of the greatest and most effective lies that the enemy tells us is that some people (those who own something that we desire, those who have wronged us, those who do not look like us) bear the image of God in a lesser way; they are disposable or exploitable.

In our study of the Old Testament, we have noticed that God's people are commanded to be loving toward not only their Hebrew neighbors but also those who live among them who are not Israelites. We noted the mixed multitude who came out of Egypt (Exod 12:38) and the provision for aliens in the poor laws (Lev 25:35). We noted

---

10. Alexander, *New Jim Crow*, 134.

the unexpected moments when those who were not God's people became part of God's people (Exod 12:49; Josh 6:22–25; see Josh 9). This trajectory continues into the New Testament, where Peter is rebuked that God makes no distinction between people on the basis of their ethnic origin (Acts 10:13–15, 34–35). Similarly, Paul reminds the gentile Christians that they are the unexpected (but very welcome) guests at the table:

> Formerly you who are Gentiles by birth and called "uncircumcised" by those who call themselves "the circumcision" (which is done in the body by human hands)—remember that at that time you were separate from Christ, excluded from citizenship in Israel and foreigners to the covenants of the promise, without hope and without God in the world. But now in Christ Jesus you who once were far away have been brought near by the blood of Christ. (Eph 2:11–13)

God's move is always toward tearing down walls of separation.

Willie Jennings uses this repeated "outsiders brought inside" move of Scripture to challenge White Christians, as we can tend to position ourselves at the center of the church, and regard non-White others as peripheral. Speaking of Jesus's conversation with the Canaanite woman (Matt 15:21–28), Jennings writes:

> The story of the Canaanite woman is especially provocative as it carries with it the clear sense not only of Israel's election, but also of the undomesticated God of Israel, one who cannot be approached except on the terms established by the divine word. . . . The colonialist moment helped to solidify a form of Christian existence that read this text as though we were standing with Jesus looking down on the woman in her desperation, when in fact we, the Gentiles, are the woman.[11]

Positioning ourselves where we actually are, as outsiders who have been brought in, should engender a humility within us that makes us less amenable to narratives of racial (or other forms of) superiority.

In chapter 6 we considered various forms of structural violence that existed in ancient Israel and how the Bible both describes and condemns these injustices. The very existence of structural violence is disputed by some Christians, who prefer to speak of there being a "problem of sin" rather than a "problem of race." This is a false dichotomy, of course. As we saw in chapter 4, the consequence of the fall was that violence entered every part of society, and this was quickly manifested not simply in individual violence but in structures of violence, such as polygamy and hegemonic oppression.

It is important to understand that individual ideologies and actions influence the actions and structures of organizations, and that conversely the ideological ethos

---

11. Willie Jennings, *The Christian Imagination: Theology and the Origins of Race* (New Haven: Yale University Press, 2010), 267.

of those institutions act on the individuals whom they encompass. In other words, human sin and structural violence are intimately connected. This is the very crude outline of an idea from complexity theory. Using these arguments with reference to racism, Matthew Croasmun writes:

> The consequences of racism . . . propagate in all directions: "upward" from racist individuals to social institutions; "downward" from those institutions to racialized actors; and even to the unconscious neurological activity within their brains.[12]

So "solving" a structural injustice such as racism can never have simple answers. It is, in fact, a task too great for us. As Paul says of his own heart of sin, "who will rescue me from this body of death?" (Rom 7:24 NRSV). For this, as for every other evil in our societies and our hearts, there is one ultimate solution, and that is the hope offered by the present gospel and future coming of our Lord Jesus Christ. But what does this mean for those of us who have pledged our allegiance to this kingdom above all others and who seek to live obediently and prophetically in the time between the times?

The Church's Response to Racism

How are we to respond to systematic racism in our societies? A first step is to acknowledge that we need to look inward as well as outward. Martin Luther King Jr. famously described eleven o'clock on a Sunday morning as the most segregated hour of the week in America.[13] Much has changed in the sixty years since he said that, but racism still exists within the church on both sides of the Atlantic (and beyond). In his book *Ghost Ship: Institutional Racism and the Church of England*, the British Anglican priest Azariah France-Williams describes many instances of racism from his own experience and others. Here are two examples:

> At BAP [the three-day residential assessment for prospective clergy], I was asked why I didn't consider working in software or tech as "your sort are good at it." Talking about a vacancy: "They had issues about an African priest but you're okay, no one would think you were an ethnic minority."[14]

Writing in the US context, Jemar Tisby gives a historic survey of Christian complicity with racism through the centuries, concluding thus:

> Racism never goes away; it just adapts. [From the mid-twentieth century] many politically and theologically conservative Christians strayed away from

---

12. Matthew Croasmun, *The Emergence of Sin: The Cosmic Tyrant in Romans* (Oxford: Oxford University Press, 2017), 51.

13. Martin Luther King Jr, "11 AM Sunday Is Our Most Segregated Hour," *New York Times*, August 2, 1964.

14. A. D. A. France-Williams, *Ghost Ship: Institutional Racism and the Church of England* (London: SCM, 2020), 7.

the use of explicitly race-based language and appeals. Yet those appeals did not disappear. Instead they mobilized around the issue of taxation of private Christian schools, many of which remained racially segregated or made only token efforts at integration. They supported presidents and legal policies that disproportionately and negatively impacted black people. They accepted a color-blind rhetoric that still utilized racially coded messages. . . . Simply by allowing the political system to work as it was designed—to grant advantages to white people and to put people of color at various disadvantages—many well-meaning Christians were complicit in racism.[15]

Tisby closes his book by offering some very practical steps that Christians might take to combat racism in their own contexts. Some are very specific to the US context, but the broadly applicable headlines are: awareness, relationships, and commitment.[16]

Awareness involves an active willingness to listen and learn. In particular, in a context where many evangelicals neglect the possibility of structural evil because of their focus on individual sin, awareness involves a willingness to learn from those who have studied the ways that organizations and whole societies can have racism (or other injustice) built into them, from their roots to their operational practice.[17]

Building relationships requires a willingness to move beyond one's normal circles of work and social interactions, to lay aside one's natural preferences, and to be willing to spend time with, making friends with, and listening to the "other." But friendship must be genuine. It is not acceptable to treat relationships as opportunities to mine other people for information.

Start with the people you know. Most of us know someone of a different race or ethnicity. Have you talked with them specifically about their experiences and perspectives of race and justice? These individuals cannot merely be projects or sources of information. They are real people with whom to pursue a meaningful friendship. Still, it takes intentionality to diversify our social networks, and we should start with those nearest us.[18]

Third, we need to commit to act. "If anyone, then, knows the good they ought to do and doesn't do it, it is sin for them" (Jas 4:17). Committing to act isn't necessarily comfortable. This might involve changing our own practice and habits, speaking out in formal and informal settings, and working actively to make sure that our churches are as multicultural as possible, in ways that we discussed in chapter 13. It might involve political engagement in one form or another.

---

15. Jemar Tisby, *The Color of Compromise: The Truth about the American Church's Complicity in Racism* (Grand Rapids: Zondervan, 2019), 171.

16. Tisby, *Color of Compromise*, 194.

17. Michael O. Emerson and J. Russel Hawkins, "Viewed in Black and White: Conservative Protestantism, Racial Issues, and Oppositional Politics," in *Religion and American Politics: From the Colonial Period to the Present*, ed. Mark A. Knoll and Luke E. Harlow, 2nd ed. (Oxford: Oxford University Press, 2007), 327–43.

18. Tisby, *Color of Compromise*, 195–96.

The examples here offered are from the US and UK contexts. But racism is an egregious, structural sin that is present far beyond these two nations. We must have the courage to confront it within the church before we can be an authentic prophetic presence in society more widely.

CONCLUSION

We are not called to combat structural injustice simply as individuals. As we have discussed, in all societies, at all times, the church is called to be a prophetic presence in society. This is never more true than at times when there is deep structural violence in that culture.

But, as we have seen, there is a long tradition of false prophets who claim to speak in God's name but actually ape the systems of injustice and untruth around them. To Jeremiah's indictment of those who cry "Peace, peace," when there is no peace, we might add these sobering words from the poet who lamented over broken Jerusalem.

> Your prophets have seen for you
> > false and deceptive visions;
> they have not exposed your iniquity
> > to restore your fortunes,
> but have seen for you oracles
> > that are false and misleading. (Lam 2:14 ESV)

Racism is just one of many forms of structural violence that we could have considered. The call to become more aware is just as applicable to other forms. How many of us can be confident that we are not complicit in egregious violence of one form or another? Do you know where your savings are invested? Are they in the pornography industry?[19] In the arms industry? In fossil-fuel companies?

As one more example, consider the issue of modern-day slavery. Are we sure that our clothes have not been made in a sweatshop? In the UK where I live, many of the high street labels use factories in the Indian subcontinent that employ children for long hours and in abusive conditions.[20] In the US, some clothing companies' pursuit of cheap labor in the Caribbean basin has been described as "not merely opportunistic . . . also sometimes actively parasitic."[21] Much of the candy we buy or the cobalt in the batteries of our electronic devices were made using child slave

---

19. For a searing indictment of the abuses within the pornography industry, see Sheila Jeffreys, *The Industrial Vagina: The Political Economy of the Global Sex Trade* (Abingdon: Routledge, 2008).

20. For stories about slavery and poor working conditions in the fashion industry, see Safia Minney, *Slave to Fashion* (Oxford: New Internationalist, 2017) and the resources at https://safia-minney.com/slave-to-fashion/.

21. Sofi Thanhauser, "Behind the Label: How the US Stitched Up the Honduras Garment Industry," *Guardian*, January 25, 2022, www.theguardian.com/news/2022/jan/25/behind-the-label-how-the-us-stitched-up-the-honduras-garment-industry.

labor. To become better informed or find ways of helping, you might like to visit one or more of these websites.

- www.endslaverynow.org
- www.fairtradefederation.org
- www.fairtrade.org.uk/

A prophetic church will be prepared to weep over the sins of society and over her own complicity in them, and to refuse to be complicit with the forces that would urge us to keep silent. To that end, I close with these powerful words of confession from the Book of Common Worship of the Presbyterian Church in Canada.

> Merciful God,
> in your gracious presence
> we confess our sin and the sins of this world.
> Although Christ is among us as our peace,
> we are a people divided against ourselves
> as we cling to the values of a broken world.
> The profits and pleasures we pursue
> lay waste the lands and pollute the seas.
> The fears and jealousies that we harbor
> set neighbour against neighbour
> and nation against nation.
> We abuse your good gifts of imagination and freedom,
> of intellect and reason.
> We turn them into bonds of oppression.
> Lord, have mercy upon us;
> heal and forgive us. Set us free to serve you in the world
> as agents of your reconciling love in Jesus Christ. Amen.[22]

RELEVANT QUESTIONS

1. What structural violence are you aware of in your own culture and society? What steps can you take to speak and act prophetically into these circumstances?
2. This is a hard one! How might you discover forms of structural violence around you that you have not yet noticed? Whose voices might you need to listen to, in order to do this?

---

22. Book of Common Worship (Presbyterian Church in Canada, 1991), 28. Used with kind permission.

CHAPTER 17

LOVING OUR NEIGHBORS

When a foreigner resides among you in your land, do not mistreat them. The foreigner residing among you must be treated as your native-born. Love them as yourself, for you were foreigners in Egypt. I am the LORD your God.
Leviticus 19:33–34

The second [great commandment] is this: "Love your neighbor as yourself." There is no commandment greater than these.
Mark 12:31

You have heard that it was said, "Love your neighbor and hate your enemy." But I tell you, love your enemies and pray for those who persecute you, that you may be children of your Father in heaven.
Matthew 5:43–45

Love your neighbor. This is the great commandment, second only to the call to love God with the whole of our being. This is clear.

But as these three great passages show us, who our neighbor actually *is* might surprise us. And when we discover the answer, it may strain our neighborliness. In Leviticus, the instruction to neighbor love is expanded to include non-Hebrews living within the confines of Israel. In Jesus's conversation with the lawyer, quoted above from Mark 12 but also found in Matthew 22:34–40, Jesus expands the category to include those with whom there is traditional hostility (such as the Samaritan in the parable). In the Sermon on the Mount, Jesus pushes this to another dimension: your enemy is also your neighbor.

What does this look like in practice for us? In this chapter we will investigate some of the complexity of these questions. We will do this by using the case study of global migration, offering some positive practices and some negative parameters that the church might consider in its attempts to offer a faithful response to the challenging questions this poses.

WORKED EXAMPLE: MIGRATION

I live in Bristol, England in a short cul-de-sac (dead-end street), which has just ten houses. Number one is owned by the council and is currently rented to a family who came as refugees from an African country. A family of Pakistani origin own and live in number five. Number six has an elderly German woman who fled the Second World War as a baby. Number ten has a Dutch woman and her British husband. This is the reality of Britain today, and a similar story is reflected in many countries across the world.

In 2020, 3.6 percent of the world's population, approximately 281 million people, were migrants. This figure has been rising steadily over the last thirty years. Approximately 48 percent of international migrants are female, and 14.6 percent are children.[1] Beneath these statistics lie millions of human stories of despair and hope.

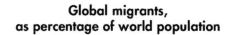

**Global migrants,
as percentage of world population**

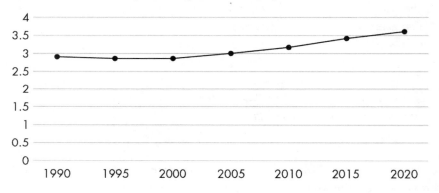

In order for us to make sense of all of this, some definitions might be helpful.

The International Organization for Migration (IOM) considers *migrancy* to be an umbrella term:

> A person who moves away from his or her place of usual residence, whether within a country or across an international border, temporarily or permanently, and for a variety of reasons. The term includes a number of well-defined legal categories of people, such as migrant workers; persons whose particular types of movements are legally-defined, such as smuggled migrants; as well as those whose status or means of movement are not specifically defined under international law, such as international students.[2]

---

1. All of these statistics, and the data for the graph, are taken from the 2022 World Migration Report of the International Organization for Migration (https://worldmigrationreport.iom.int/).

2. "Key Migration Terms," International Organization for Migration, www.iom.int/key-migration-terms.

Not everyone who leaves their home to live in another place has the same story. Well over five million students are studying abroad worldwide.[3] The headline figures for 2020 include 169 million migrant workers, 26.4 million refugees, and 55 million internally displaced peoples. A subset of *migrant* is *refugee*:

> A person who, owing to a well-founded fear of persecution for reasons of race, religion, nationality, membership of a particular social group or political opinion, is outside the country of his nationality and is unable or, owing to such fear, is unwilling to avail himself of the protection of that country; or who, not having a nationality and being outside the country of his former habitual residence as a result of such events, is unable or, owing to such fear, is unwilling to return to it.[4]

It is important to note that different organizations categorize migrancy and refugees differently. The UNHCR, for example, uses the term *migrant* to refer to those who choose to move not because of a direct threat of persecution or death but mainly to improve their lives by finding work, or in some cases for education, family reunion, or other reasons. This term therefore excludes refugees.[5] In this chapter I will use the term *migrants* in the broad meaning defined by the International Organization for Migration.

Two other definitions would also be useful. *Internally displaced persons* (IDPs) are:

> Persons or groups of persons who have been forced or obliged to flee or to leave their homes or places of habitual residence, in particular as a result of or in order to avoid the effects of armed conflict, situations of generalized violence, violations of human rights or natural or human-made disasters, and who have not crossed an internationally recognized State border.[6]

Finally, *asylum seekers* are those seeking refugee status:

> An individual who is seeking international protection. In countries with individualized procedures, an asylum seeker is someone whose claim has not yet been finally decided on by the country in which he or she has submitted it. Not every asylum seeker will ultimately be recognized as a refugee, but every recognized refugee is initially an asylum seeker.[7]

These definitions are summarized in the following table.

---

3. "International Students," Migration Data Portal, June 9, 2020, www.migrationdataportal.org/themes/international-students.

4. "Key Migration Terms," www.iom.int/key-migration-terms.

5. See "Asylum and Migration," UNHCR, www.unhcr.org/uk/asylum-and-migration.html.

6. "IDP Definition," UNHCR Emergency Handbook, https://emergency.unhcr.org/entry/250553/idp-definition.

7. "Asylum-seeker," UNHCR Glossary, www.unhcr.org/51b1d62c13.pdf.

Migrant	Someone who moves away from their home for any reason.
Refugee	Someone forced to flee to another country because of a well-founded fear of danger.
Internally displaced person (IDP)	Someone forced to flee their home who remains within their home country.
Asylum seeker	An individual seeking international protection whose claim has not been decided.

Sadly, the experience of arriving in a foreign country has not always been positive for people. Sometimes they are viewed with suspicion, and sometimes even with hostility. And tragically, sometimes a theological justification is given for these responses.

Theological Entanglements of the Far-Right

In their book *The Claim to Christianity*, Hannah Strømmen and Ulrich Schmiedel examine the theological claims made by a sample of the far-right groups in Europe. These groups are by no means homogenous; they range from the mainstream UK Independence Party to the terrorist Anders Behring Breivik, who murdered sixty-nine people—most of them under the age of twenty—in Oslo and Utøya on July 22, 2011. Nonetheless, they share some common features in their arguments and rationales. Disturbingly, some of these are expressed in terms of Christian theology. It should be noted, as relevant background to what follows, that a large proportion of refugees, asylum seekers, and economic migrants coming to Europe at present are from Muslim-majority countries.

In 1982 the right-wing German politician Alfred Dregger gave a speech in the Bundestag. Here, for perhaps the first time in European political discourse, the previously *racial* issue of immigration began to be reexpressed in *religious* terms.[8] With many immigrants to Germany at the time coming from Turkey, Dregger argued that there was an incompatibility between German culture and Turkish culture:

> The Turks were not shaped by Christianity, rather by Islam—another high culture, and I stress, high culture. . . . Even in its more secular form, the cultural impulses of Christian and Islamic high culture have a lasting effect on our peoples. This contributes, in addition to a pronounced national pride of the Turks, to the fact that they are not assimilable. They want to remain what they are, namely Turks. And we should respect this.[9]

On the surface, this may seem like a respectful articulation of difference. But, as Strømmen and Schmiedel argue, Dregger's claim essentializes the Turk. It reduces him or her to a simple irreducible "other"-ness, which cannot assimilate into German

---

8. Rita Chin, *The Crisis of Multiculturalism in Europe: A History* (Princeton: Princeton University Press, 2017), 160.

9. Quoted in Rita Chin, *Crisis of Multiculturalism in Europe*, 159.

society *because of their* "*Muslimness.*" Whether they are in fact Muslim, secular, or Christian makes no difference. In this worldview, "religion—just like race—is something that is *not* chosen. Our religions choose us."[10] This has been termed the "new racism," which uses "culture-coded" language rather than color-coded language to essentialize "the Muslim." It is used to justify unequal treatment.

> If "the Turks" . . . cannot be assimilated into our culture, then we don't have to offer them opportunities for integration. Here, the far right's racist essentialization of who we are and of who we aren't pays off. While one can continue to assume that all persons should be treated equally in the abstract . . . one actually treats "the other" differently. This treatment is legitimized with reference to her otherness.[11]

Far-right movements build on this by framing Islam as a threat to Christianity. They speak and act on the assumption that both religions are "strong, stable, and static," displaying no regional or chronological variations in their presentation.[12] They imply that two cultures represented by the two faiths are locked in a perpetual battle, and that Muslims are secretly (or not so secretly) working to undermine stability and the liberal project. They promote the narrative of a "global war on Christianity" being waged, particularly in Islamic countries, but also threatening Christians in countries where they have been hitherto free to practice their faith.[13]

Broadly speaking, far-right theological claims fall into two types, which Strømmen and Schmiedel term "Culture Christianity" and "Crusader Christianity." Culture Christianity identifies the British nation (for example) as essentially Christian in its cultural manifestations and looks back to an idyllic golden age of "Christian values," now under threat. This then becomes a marker of identity that marks "us" out from "them." For example, in the 2015 UK elections, the UK Independence Party[14] published a so-called "Christian Manifesto" entitled "Valuing our Christian Heritage." Similar ideology is being found elsewhere in Europe. Here are representative excerpts from the speeches of two highly prominent European political leaders.[15]

> The masses arriving from other civilizations endanger our way of life, our culture, our customs and our Christian traditions. (Viktor Orbán, prime minister of Hungary, 2016)

---

10. Hannah Strømmen and Ulrich Schmiedel, *The Claim to Christianity: Responding to the Far Right* (London: SCM, 2020), 21.

11. Strømmen and Schmiedel, *Claim to Christianity*, 21.

12. Strømmen and Schmiedel, *Claim to Christianity*, 25.

13. Jason Brunner, *Imagining Persecution: Why American Christians Believe There Is a Global War against Their Faith* (New Brunswick: Rutgers University Press, 2021).

14. For context, UK Independence Party obtained 12.6 percent of the vote and won one parliamentary seat in the UK's "first past the post" system.

15. Both quotations are taken from Christel Lamère Ngnambi, "Populists, Christians and Christianity—A Bird's Eye View," in *Is God a Populist? Christianity, Populism and the Future of Europe*, ed. Susan Kerr (Oslo: Frekk Forlag Skaperkraft, 2019), 86–87.

Our identity and that of the whole of Europe is Christian and that must be preserved because our values are superior and dignify man. I do not want the Islamisation of Europe because it goes against who we are, against the best of us. The separation between Church and state is clearly a Christian principle. Islam is a political ideology that seeks the conquest of the state. (Santiago Abascal, leader of the Spanish right-wing populist party Vox, 2019)

It may be seen that although Abascal names Islam, Orbán does not. Here, the Christian-culture language is operating as a proxy for racist sentiment, which Strømmen and Schmiedel identify as a common trope:

If Christianity or Judaeo-Christianity is central to the Constitution, the culture and the character of the country, what is it that's unconstitutional, uncultured and uncharacteristic? The answer is, of course, the Muslim migrant. There's no need for the manifesto to name Islam. The claim to Christianity as Judaeo-Christianity does the trick.[16]

The second ideology, more obviously dangerous, Strømmen and Schmiedel term "Crusader Christianity." As we might expect from our discussion of crusade in chapter 14, this employs biblical language and imagery to cast the "Muslim threat" in existential terms. There is a struggle against the evil other, in which the faithful must enlist. God trains our hands for battle (e.g., Ps 18:34); an apocalyptic showdown is coming. This ideology was explicitly employed by Anders Behring Breivik in his Christian manifesto.[17]

Although the examples above have all been drawn from the European context, many parallels can be found in the US—both in relation to Islam and with regard to other outsider groups. The attack upon the Twin Towers in 2001 prompted a sharp turn in popular opinion against Muslims, one that has been particularly spearheaded by evangelical Christians, who often characterize Islam as violent, regressive, and anti-American.[18] Of course, the characterization of the Qur'an as a violent text, in contrast to a peaceful Bible, is entirely unfair. As we have seen, there is plenty of violence in both testaments, and all sacred texts require interpretation with hermeneutical wisdom. It is important to understand that believers of all faiths struggle to interpret their texts in ways that are both faithful and peaceful.[19]

---

16. Strømmen and Schmiedel, *Claim to Christianity*, 101.

17. The Breivik manifesto is widely available, but I decline to provide a link to hate literature.

18. E.g., see this newspaper report from two years after the Twin Towers attack: Laurie Goodstein, "Seeing Islam as 'Evil' Faith, Evangelicals Seek Converts," *New York Times*, May 27, 2003, www.nytimes.com/2003/05/27/us/seeing-islam-as-evil-faith-evangelicals-seek-converts.html.

19. See, e.g., Maria Power and Helen Paynter, eds., *Violence and Peace in Sacred Texts* (London: Palgrave McMillan, 2023).

The Church's Response to Immigration

This raises two questions, which are deeply intertwined. How should the church respond to the far right? And how should the church relate to its Muslim neighbors? What might faithful improvisation look like in this context?

In response to the rise of far-right rhetoric, churches in Europe have adopted a range of strategies, which Strømmen and Schmiedel group into two main categories that they term "consolidating" and "challenging."[20]

Consolidating churches seek to strengthen democracy by bringing diverse people together for conversation. They welcome contestation, on the basis that the moral and logical flaws in far-right rhetoric will be exposed when democratic processes work well. In this model, churches seek to provide neutral spaces and occupy neutral positions to facilitate these conversations and must also therefore avoid alignment with either side in the dispute.

However, there are some weaknesses in this model. First, it is easy to overlook the power that needs to be wielded in order to bring about such apparently democratic conversations. Who is excluded and who is included—and who gets to decide? Second, and related to this, is another, more insidious, danger:

> The commendation of Christianity as a faith that consolidates democracy—a commendation that we would expect from churches—runs the risk of complacency or complicity with the theology of the far right. From the mainstream to the margins, the far right insists that Christianity is the one and only religion that produces democratic culture. . . . Where Christianity is characterized as a consolidation of democracy, however, Muslims are easily evaluated as anti-democratic aliens.[21]

An alternative to this potentially demonizing approach could be termed the "Challenging Church" model—challenging in that it seeks to confront the rhetoric of the far right head-on. It begins from a position of acknowledging Christianity's historic complicity in Islamophobia, and also its latent, residual power in (British or European) society. Therefore, it chooses to stand with the marginalized, while taking a sophisticated and nuanced approach to identifying who actually is marginalized. (The loudest voices, for instance, may not always be those who are most disadvantaged. On the other hand, it is important to recognize that marginalization is not the "prerogative" of any one group in society.) This approach chooses, then, to take what the liberation theologians have termed "the preferential option for the poor,"[22] necessitating the decision to trust that "the gospel is strong enough to stand on its

---

20. Strømmen and Schmiedel, *Claim to Christianity*, 121–27.
21. Strømmen and Schmiedel, *Claim to Christianity*, 124.
22. This phrase relates to the active decision to attend to the voices of the poor and to read Scripture from the perspective of the weak, not the strong. "Poor," then, might connote more than just economic deprivation.

own legs."[23] Therefore, it refuses to pit itself against Islam or to view it as something that needs to be overcome in any way.

This approach is also open to criticism and particularly needs to reckon with the question of what it means to *bring*—as well as *be*—"good news" to our Muslim neighbors. So, does the belief that the gospel is strong enough to stand on its own legs nullify the need to express that gospel lovingly? Has the task of gospel proclamation had its day? If not, how is that to be combined with the "challenging" approach? Or are these separate tasks that should be separated from one another, employing the diversity of gift and calling within the body of Christ?

Martin Accad, a Christian theologian who lives and works in the Muslim-majority part of Beirut, has a great deal of experience in operating in cross-faith contexts. He has developed what he terms a "kerygmatic" approach to interfaith dialogue, taking a view on Islam that refuses both demonization and idolization. Key to this kerygmatic stance is the boldness to be Christ-centered (which he distinguishes from necessarily being church-centered), while being humble, honest, respectful, and loving.[24] So it is possible—by the logic of the gospel it *must be* possible!—to act humbly, lovingly, and hospitably toward our Muslim neighbor without denying the call to allegiance to Jesus Christ, which is at the heart of all evangelism.

There is no simple recipe for how we love neighbors who are not like us. Nor does the Bible give us a prescription for the optimally loving immigration policy. In what follows, I will attempt to sketch out some parameters that might be relevant as we seek the faithful way.

Truth

The issue of global migration has become the focus of a good deal of misinformation, fed by knowledge gaps, definitional ambiguities like the ones mentioned above, and "bad actors" (people who intentionally create and propagate disinformation), particularly those from the far right.[25] Perhaps the first thing that loving our neighbor means, in this context, is being sure that we are well-informed about the truth of any narratives we propagate, particularly on social media.

This might relate in particular to misperceptions about the numbers of people traveling. About 20 percent of all migrants today are IDPs, so they have not crossed an international border. Many more remain in neighboring countries or in the same continent.[26] And our perception of our own nation's intake of refugees is often

23. This phrase is used by the Church of Norway in its material published to help its members respond to the far right. Quoted in Strømmen and Schmiedel, *Claim to Christianity*, 125.

24. Martin Accad and Jonathan Andrews, eds., *The Religious Other: A Biblical Understanding of Islam, the Qur'an and Muhammad* (Carlisle: Langham Global Library, 2020), 2–6.

25. International Organization for Migration, "World Migration Report 2022," 217–32 (https://worldmigrationreport.iom.int/).

26. The Za'atari refugee camp in Jordan, for example, hosts around eighty thousand people, mainly from Syria ("Refugee Camps," UNHCR Jordan, www.unhcr.org/jo/refugee-camps). The Dadaab camp in Kenya has hosted generations of people, mainly displaced from Somalia. At its peak it had well over two hundred thousand inhabitants ("Dadaab Refugee Camp," UNHCR Kenya, www.unhcr.org/ke/dadaab-refugee-complex).

distorted. Consider this graph, which charts Turkey and the UK's gross domestic product in proportion to one another, and alongside this, the two nations' relative intake of Syrian refugees, as of 2020.

By 2020, the UK (GDP USD 2.7 trillion) had taken 11,412 Syrian refugees, while Turkey (GDP USD 720 billion) had a massive 369,500.[27] Yet the narrative in certain parts of the population here was that we in the UK were being "inundated" and overwhelmed by people seeking asylum. The UK population's far more enthusiastic embrace of Ukrainians displaced by the 2022 invasion by Russia lends credibility to the accusation that racial motivation lies behind much of our resistance to immigration.[28]

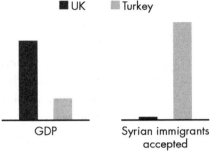

Proportional Comparison of GDP and Immigrant Hospitality: UK And Turkey

■ UK   ■ Turkey

GDP   Syrian immigrants accepted

Humanization

One of the tools of the misinformation propagated by bad actors is the use of dehumanizing language:

> Make no mistake, these migrants are like cockroaches. (Popular commentator Katie Hopkins in *The Sun* newspaper, April 17, 2015)

> . . . a swarm of people coming across the Mediterranean, seeking a better life. . . (prime minister David Cameron on the BBC news on July 30, 2015)

> . . . large numbers of pretty desperate migrants marauding around the area. . . (foreign secretary Philip Hammond on the BBC news on August 9, 2015)[29]

Often the language is of water: migrants are a "flood," a "tide," a "wave." Or, notoriously, they are "rapists" from "shit-hole countries."[30] Use of language like this makes it easier for societies to view migrants as less than human. I offer two other brief examples of such dehumanization; as before, one is from UK/Europe and one is from the US.

One of the chief travel routes for migrants seeking to enter the UK is the English Channel. This is the world's busiest shipping lane and an extremely dangerous place to try to cross in an inflatable dinghy or by swimming. (It is twenty-one miles across at its narrowest point.) Another major route for people trying to enter Europe is across the Mediterranean from Turkey or north Africa, usually to the Greek islands. One in

27. "Ranking of the Largest Syrian Refugee-Hosting Countries in 2022," Statista, June 2022, www.statista.com/statistics/740233/major-syrian-refugee-hosting-countries-worldwide/.

28. See, e.g., Eva Połońska-Kimunguyi, "War, Resistance and Refuge: Racism and Double Standards in Western Media Coverage of Ukraine," Media@LSE, May 10, 2022, https://blogs.lse.ac.uk/medialse/2022/05/10/war-resistance-and-refuge-racism-and-double-standards-in-western-media-coverage-of-ukraine/.

29. These quotations were assembled and quoted in Vesna Lazović, "Refugee Crisis in Terms of Language: From Empathy to Intolerance," *British and American Studies* 23 (2017): 284.

30. Michael Finnegan and Mark Z. Barabak, "'Shithole' and

twenty-three people who begin that crossing dies in the attempt. And people die in other ways trying to cross borders too. Some fall from the undersides of lorries. Some die in scuffles with lorry drivers or sailors. Some die at the hands of people smugglers or even coastguards. Undoubtedly some are murdered. Many countries fail to publish statistics on migrant fatalities; some do not collect the data, and—most disturbingly—some do not investigate violent deaths. If a person dies unexpectedly on British or French soil, their death is likely to be the subject of a police investigation and/or inquest. But if they die at sea or on the coastline between the two countries, it is quite possible that nobody will bother.[31] It has been suggested that such policies are aimed to provide nation-states with a moral alibi for migrant deaths.[32] Similarly it has been argued that the conditions endured within many of the refugee camps are due to a violence of inaction by the authorities.[33]

Turning to the United States, in July 2019 Clara Long gave testimony to the US House Committee on Oversight and Reform, Subcommittee on Civil Rights and Civil Liberties. With over a decade of experience monitoring and reporting on prison and detention conditions both globally and in the US, Long was then serving as acting deputy Washington director and senior researcher on immigration in the US program at Human Rights Watch. Her eyewitness account of the conditions endured by children being detained at the US-Mexican border is harrowing. Here is a brief excerpt, but the whole article is worth reading if you can stomach it.

> The US Border Patrol is holding many children, including some who are much too young to take care of themselves, in jail-like border facilities for weeks at a time without contact with family members, or regular access to showers, clean clothes, toothbrushes, or proper beds. Many were sick. Many, including children as young as 2 or 3, were separated from adult caretakers without any provisions for their care besides that provided by unrelated older children also being held in detention.[34]

Both of these cases are examples of what can happen when people are dehumanized in public discourse.[35] Loving our neighbor means that we will speak truthfully and kindly about them, because the consequences if we do not are truly terrifying.

Other Racist Things Trump Has Said—So Far," *Los Angeles Times*, January 11, 2018, www.latimes.com/politics/la-na-trump-racism -remarks-20180111-htmlstory.html.

31. Many of the ideas in this section are expanded more substantially in Helen Paynter, *Immigration and the Church: Reflecting Faithfully in Our Generation*, Grove Pastoral 149 (Cambridge: Grove, 2017).

32. R. L. Doty, "Bare Life: Border-Crossing Deaths and Spaces of Moral Alibi," *Environment and Planning D: Society and Space* 29 (2011): 599–612.

33. Thom Davies, Arshad Isakjee, and Surindar Dhesi, "Violent Inaction: The Necropolitical Experience of Refugees in Europe," *Antipode: A Radical Journal of Geography* 49.5 (2017): 1263–284.

34. Clara Long, "Written Testimony: 'Kids in Cages: Inhumane Treatment at the Border,'" Human Rights Watch, July 11, 2019, www.hrw.org/news/2019/07/11/written-testimony-kids-cages -inhumane-treatment-border. It should be stated that the Biden administration has at least partially reversed some of the policies of his predecessor.

35. The link between dehumanizing language and dehumanizing treatment has been clearly described. See, e.g., Beverly Crawford Ames, "The Dehumanization of Immigrants and the Rise of the

Compassion and Humility

A second step in loving our neighbor is to try to understand them. What has caused them to travel so far from home? Climate change and conflict have been two of the principal factors in driving worldwide people movements. But the causes are often multiple, layered, and mixed.[36]

Major environmental events and processes	Mobility Drivers	Conflict and Violence
Floods	Food insecurity	Direct displacement
Landslides	Water insecurity	Fear
Earthquakes	Economic insecurity	Environmental damage
Storms	Personal/Political insecurity	Political oppression
Droughts	Global environmental insecurity	Societal breakdown
Forest fires	Energy insecurity	Infrastructure failure
Industrial accidents		Income loss
Pollution		Family disruption
Sea-level rise		
Change in temperature		
Coastal erosion		

Sometimes I reflect on small things that I have done to protect my family, particularly my daughters as they were growing up. I went into school to talk to staff when my daughter was being bullied. My husband or I drove or walked with our daughters if they went out after dark. When a noisy drunk got into the London Underground carriage we were sitting in, I drew them close. These are normal things that most of us would do to protect the people we love most. But the threats we're talking about here are small ones: playground bullying, the remote chance of a stranger attack, the possibility of someone acting unpredictably in a public space when the British Transport Police are within easy call. What would I have done for my children if something terrible threatened them? If ISIS were approaching our village? If there were no food for days on end? If they could not attend school because of their gender? What would it take to make me pack up and move them somewhere safer?

Extreme Right," American Institute for Contemporary German Studies: John Hopkins University, September 11, 2019, www.aicgs .org/publication/the-dehumanization-of-immigrants-and-the-rise -of-the-extreme-right/.

36. Part of this diagram is simplified from the International Organization for Migration, "World Migration Report 2022," 235.

In 1943 Abraham Maslow published a paper entitled, "A Theory of Human Motivation," where he described how human motivation is based upon the fulfillment of an ordered set of needs:

1. Physiological needs (e.g., hunger, thirst)
2. Safety needs
3. Love needs (including societal relationships)
4. Esteem needs (self-respect and the esteem of others)
5. Self-actualization needs (doing what one is fitted for)[37]

Natálie Reichlová has used this theory to model human migration, which enables us to take account of the complexity of factors that contribute to the decision to move.[38] A potential migrant will carefully weigh the perhaps oppositional priorities before deciding whether to travel. These decisions are not taken lightly. Asylum seekers and refugees are people who have been driven by the most basic of human needs: physiological and safety. People traveling for family reunification are following the third of Maslow's list. Which of us could say that we would make different choices?

So-called "economic migrants" are particularly subject to vilification in the media and popular discourse. (They are "coming over here, taking our jobs," "driven by greed.") But isn't it greed that drives the capitalist project?[39] Isn't it greed, or at least aspiration, that propels the "American Dream"? It is our disordered desires in the West that are the root of many of the evils in the world, including many of those that are causing people to leave their homelands. Such anti-migrant rhetoric frequently exposes the speaker's own moral failure. Loving our neighbors means viewing them with compassion and with humility about our own failings.

Refusing Abjection

Such violent rhetoric is an example of something known as *abjection*, a term first used by Julia Kristeva, building upon the work of Sigmund Freud.[40] Kristeva's work relates to the individual psyche in the first instance, but it is also instructive for the observation of societies in general.

Kristeva argues that the proximity of strangers provokes anxiety because we are unable to categorize them; we struggle to place their behavior, dress, customs, and worldview within our own frames of reference. As a result, the world feels unpredictable. Our response to this anxiety is *abjection*.

In abjection, we separate out from our society those people who make us feel

37. Abraham Maslow, "A Theory of Human Motivation," *Psychology Review* 50.4 (1943): 370–96.

38. Natálie Reichlová, "Can the Theory of Motivation Explain Migration Decisions?," *IES Working Papers* 27 (2005): 1–24.

39. This is also true of Marxism, of course, but that political ideology is not the one under discussion here.

40. Julia Kristeva, *Powers of Horror: An Essay on Abjection*, trans. L. Roudiez (New York: Columbia University Press, 1982). Kristeva's observations have such explanatory power that I suggest they should be taken seriously, even by those who have methodological or ideological reservations about Freud's work.

uncomfortable, those who threaten our preferred self-image. We establish boundaries between us and them, and across those boundaries we project negative aspects of ourselves. In this way we create our own ideal identity, affirming ourselves based on our rejection of what is undesirable. The boundaries we establish may be real or representational: walls, the fences of detention facilities, ghettoes, or simply psychological barriers. We tend to seek out and gather with those who are like us, and we ascribe to those who are not like us negative motives, habits, or other characteristics. We define ourselves by what (whom) we are not. This is the process of *othering*.

As we have seen, in its worst manifestations othering will cause us to dehumanize people. It predisposes us to act toward them with violence—and vice versa. Indeed, these processes are important elements in the journey of radicalization. Andrew Silke has shown how marginalization and enclave formation, coupled with a sense of grievance, are key factors in the development of a potential terrorist.[41] By means of abjection, the group-self is formed and bonded.

This process is typically at work in more than one place in society at the same time. Take, for instance, the abjection with which far-right groups view Muslims in UK society (and beyond). This extreme form of othering results in some within those far-right groups being radicalized to commit acts of violence against Muslims. Conversely, the experience of abjection and othering contributes to the radicalization of a minority of Muslims. And so, the cycle continues. To illustrate this, here is a timeline of six significant terrorist incidents on British soil.[42] Note the pattern of Islamist attack and far-right response.

It is ironic that abjection and othering conducted by the in-group against the out-group nourishes othering and objection in the marginalized out-group. Or it is utterly predictable, as Girard

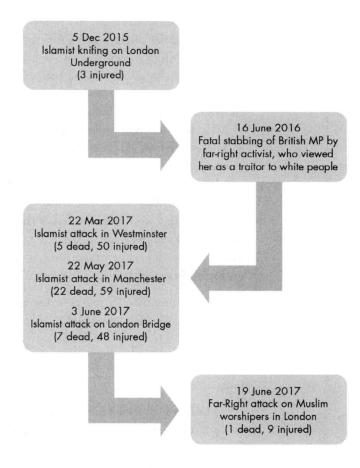

5 Dec 2015
Islamist knifing on London Underground
(3 injured)

16 June 2016
Fatal stabbing of British MP by far-right activist, who viewed her as a traitor to white people

22 Mar 2017
Islamist attack in Westminster
(5 dead, 50 injured)

22 May 2017
Islamist attack in Manchester
(22 dead, 59 injured)

3 June 2017
Islamist attack on London Bridge
(7 dead, 48 injured)

19 June 2017
Far-Right attack on Muslim worshipers in London
(1 dead, 9 injured)

41. Andrew Silke, *All That Matters: Terrorism* (London: Hodder & Stoughton, 2014).

42. "London Bridge Attack: Timeline of British Terror Attacks," BBC, June 19, 2017, www.bbc.co.uk/news/uk-40013040.

would say. Loving our neighbor means refusing to be drawn into that deadly cycle and learning to honor the image of God in people who differ from us in religion, culture, and ethnic background.

In chapter 13 we discussed the biblical call to hospitality. The complexities we have been discussing here should make us thoughtful around how we do that, but they do not get us off the hook. However, there are narratives in public discourse that seek to do just that. In our own time there are some important myths in society and the church that the scriptural testimony firmly contests.

Rejecting Dangerous Myths

The first myth is that of *blood purity*. This ideology has benighted many societies at different points in history, and—tragically—the church has been drawn into this at certain times. In chapter 8 we saw how porous the ethnic boundaries of Israel were, with the inclusion of many peoples. It is remarkable that even the relatively tight boundaries of the covenant people of God in the Old Testament were never determined on race grounds. And once the new covenant is instituted, the prophets' visions of the kingdom of God being for people of all tribes and tongues (e.g., Isa 2:1–5; 19:19–25; Joel 2:28–32) are realized. There is nothing in Scripture that can support an ideology of blood purity.[43]

The second myth, less egregious but perhaps more pervasive, is what I term the *myth of entitlement*. This centers our imagination on our own ownership of our land, our homes, our wealth and marginalizes the need of others into something that we can (or perhaps should) choose to care about. Ownership is a "given" and generosity is an "option." But thoughtful reading of Scripture cannot sustain such a narrative. Consider Israel, to whose forefather the land of Canaan had been promised (e.g., Gen 12:7). Even in this very particular case, God continued to assert his sovereignty over the land. It was never irrevocably given to them to use as they saw fit. See, for example, these words from Leviticus 25:23:

> The land must not be sold permanently, because the land is mine and you reside in my land as foreigners and strangers.

If even Israel could not regard herself as having entitlement to the land and its resources, how much less may we, to whom no such promise has been made? Indeed, God's covenant people themselves belonged to God as his bondservants.

> The Israelites belong to me as servants. They are my servants, whom I brought out of Egypt. I am the LORD your God. (Lev 25:55)

---

43. Israelite prohibitions on intermarriage, which might seem to contradict this statement, need to be understood as primarily intended to prevent religious syncretism. As we have seen, there are plenty of counterexamples that fly in the face of the prohibition and are celebrated, not condemned. The example of the sending away of the foreign wives by Ezra (chs. 9–10) is a distressing text of othering, but it should be noted that the voice of God is not heard to endorse this action in the text.

Likewise, at our baptism, we give over to God everything that we thought we owned. There is no space for an ideology of entitlement here.

> The dangerous narrative of entitlement is particularly prevalent in countries that have a popular myth of exceptionalism or "manifest destiny." In the time of the Pilgrim Fathers, God's election of biblical Israel became mapped onto the New World through the language of "New Israel."[44] In his lecture of March 21, 1630, delivered in Southampton to a group of travelers bound for Boston, the Puritan John Winthrop referred to these New World colonists as "a city on a hill." Based upon this belief that America had a peculiar role in God's purposes, the language of "manifest destiny" became prevalent in the nineteenth century.[45] The phrase "city on a hill" has since been used of the USA by many presidents, including John F. Kennedy, Ronald Reagan, Barack Obama, and others. Countless commentators have linked this ideology with what they describe as America's aggressive foreign policy, particularly its use of force in an attempt to democratize the world.

A third myth that is in common currency in discussions about immigration is about the *ordering of our priorities*. "Our own poor are our first priority." Such a statement arises from a zero-sum gain perspective, where giving is a one-way act that rapidly depletes the giver's resources. If we "give" to refugees, then we cannot "give" to our own homeless, goes the logic. And this is not without truth, of course. The public purse does indeed have limitations, and prudence is a fiscal virtue, although there are also many ways that immigrants enrich their host societies (in the broadest sense of the term).[46]

But this narrow focus on "our own" is challenged, too, by the perspective of Scripture, which—as so often—inverts our expectations. We have already read several parts of Leviticus 25. Here is another verse from this extraordinary chapter in an unfairly overlooked book of the Bible.

> If any of your fellow Israelites become poor and are unable to support themselves among you, help them as you would a foreigner and stranger, so they can continue to live among you. Do not take interest or any profit from them, but

44. Roger Chapman, "American Exceptionalism," in *Culture Wars in America: An Encyclopedia of Issues, Viewpoints, and Voices*, ed. Roger Chapman and James Ciment, 2nd ed. (Abingdon: Routledge, 2013), 25.
45. Glenn Hastedt, "Manifest Destiny," in *Encyclopedia of American Foreign Policy*, ed. Glenn Hastedt, 2nd ed. (New York: Facts on File, 2004), 302–3.

46. In purely financial terms, a number of countries recently have come to realize that immigration can help to solve their pension crisis, where there are currently insufficient working people to pay for the support of an aging population. It should also be noted that the people who emigrate for work prospects are often the most motivated and entrepreneurial of individuals, who bring great benefit to their new countries of residence.

fear your God, so that they may continue to live among you. You must not lend them money at interest or sell them food at a profit. I am the LORD your God, who brought you out of Egypt to give you the land of Canaan and to be your God. (Lev 25:35–38)

It would be striking if the text were to state that resident aliens should be cared for as well as native-born people. But this text says something even more radical. The benchmark for Israel for how their own were to be treated was the treatment of the aliens among them.

CONCLUSION

Those who migrate from their place of birth often do so out of one degree or another of compulsion. They are frequently traumatized, bereaved, scared, and disoriented. Their journeys are likely to increase those feelings. They are susceptible to predation from human traffickers. Particularly for women migrants, sexual assault and rape are common, almost routine, at every stage in their journey. When they cross borders they may risk their lives, and if they do die their families may never find out the truth about what happened to them. And when they arrive in their destination country, they may then be separated from their families, even from their children. They may be subject to detention and further abuse in that setting. They are likely to have prolonged, often fruitless, engagement with legal immigration processes. And they may encounter a lack of welcome in the communities where they settle.

Situations like these are taking place all over the world, and in each place the church needs to grapple for itself with the question: What does it mean to love my immigrant neighbor? In this chapter, we have attempted to sketch out some theological and practical parameters by way of a worked example. In the following chapter, we will turn the spotlight back on ourselves, as we consider our own complicity in violence.

> It came upon the midnight clear,
> that glorious song of old,
> from angels bending near the earth
> to touch their harps of gold:
> "Peace on the earth, good will to men
> from heaven's all-gracious King."
> The world in solemn stillness lay,
> to hear the angels sing.
>
> Still through the cloven skies they come
> with peaceful wings unfurled,
> and still their heavenly music floats

o'er all the weary world;
above its sad and lowly plains,
they bend on hovering wing,
and ever o'er its Babel sounds
the blessed angels sing.

Yet with the woes of sin and strife,
the world has suffered long;
beneath the angel strain have rolled
two thousand years of wrong,
and man, at war with man, hears not
the love song which they bring.
O hush the noise, ye men of strife,
and hear the angels sing!

—Edmund Hamilton Sears, "It Came upon the
Midnight Clear" (1849, public domain)

RELEVANT QUESTIONS

1. What are the narratives around immigration that you have heard recently? Whose voices are you hearing? Are they truthful? Are they loving? Do you need to research some statistics to do some fact-checking?

2. Who, for you, are the "others" that you struggle to love? How can you take some positive steps in this direction?

CHAPTER 18

REORDERING OUR DESIRES

I am for peace;
but when I speak, they are for war.
Psalm 120:7

The psalmist may well have been evaluating his own heart truthfully when he wrote this, but if we are honest, the tendency to view violence as "other people's problem" lies within us all. *The argument wasn't of our making. . . . We would never respond with our fists like they did. . . . They fired the first shot. . . . We are only acting in self-defense.*

Our capacity for self-delusion is expressed in deep, internal, psychological ways and in the play of nation-states. It is such self-delusion that enables a dictator to take his country into an aggressive war while claiming it as "self-defense."[1]

REMOVING THE PLANK FROM OUR OWN EYE

Our studies in Scripture and our engagement with some of the work of violence theorists should have taught us to see through such claims. They should also have taught us that before we can hope to offer any value to the more generalized debate on violence, war, and peace, we need to acknowledge and begin to address the violence in our own hearts—to take the plank out of our own eyes first. In this chapter, I will pull together some of the threads from our studies and invite us all to consider how that might challenge our own life and practice.

Violence Stems from Desire

Recall the words of James:

> What causes fights and quarrels among you? Don't they come from your desires that battle within you? You desire but do not have, so you kill. You covet but you cannot get what you want, so you quarrel and fight. (Jas 4:1–2)

---

1. At the time of writing this chapter (summer of 2022), the example that I have in mind is the Russian war of aggression against Ukraine, framed as a defensive action by Russia's leader, Vladimir Putin. But history can offer many similar examples, and no doubt future readers of this book will be able to add new ones.

The root of much of the violence in our world lies in the problem of disordered desire. This is first seen in Genesis 3, when the woman and the man desire the fruit and all that it offers, rather than fixing their desire upon God himself. We see it played out again and again through Scripture. David saw and desired Bathsheba, raped her, and murdered her husband. Ahab saw and desired Naboth's vineyard and colluded in his murder. And disordered desire leads to rivalry and enmity. This brings us to the insightful work of the anthropologist René Girard, discussed in chapter 1, who identifies the ways that rivalries start: first we imitate one another in our desires before then becoming like one another in our violence.

Violence Is Mimetic

As we have seen repeatedly, violence begets violence. From Lamech's song of revenge in Genesis 4 onward, the Bible reveals the human tendency to respond to a perceived wrong with vengeance. In our biblical survey, we noted many of the ways in which the Bible acts progressively to restrict the impulse of vengeance. But the first thing the Bible does is diagnose the problem, and we need to receive that diagnosis for ourselves.

There is a Billy Joel song titled, "We Didn't Start the Fire."[2] This reflects the universal tendency of humanity to consider our own actions to be simply a response to those of others. And, in a sense, this is true. Whatever our upbringing, our violence has been learned from the cradle and arises in response to violence that came before us. But our violence will teach the next generations. We may not have started the fire, but each of us helps it spread a little further.

Taking these insights together, then, leads us to the first remediating step which we might take as we seek to be people of peace, justice, and holiness in this time between the times: we need to learn to reorder our desires.

REORDERING OUR DESIRES
From Covetousness to Contentment

For many people, the tenth commandment, "you shall not covet," comes as a bit of an anticlimax. Why does this deserve a mention alongside the towering crimes of murder, adultery, and blasphemy? The Decalogue reveals a deep understanding of the ways that humans operate. Learning not to covet what belongs to our neighbor is a very good way of curbing our own violent instincts. How can we learn not to covet? Perhaps the first step is to become more aware of the ways in which desire is instrumentalized in our societies.

---

2. "We Didn't Start the Fire" was released by Billy Joel as a single in 1989, and later the same year it was contained in his album *Storm Front*.

Stephen Finamore has written on the theology of advertising, drawing in some of the thought of Girard. Finamore argues that modern advertising employs and perpetuates a disordered anthropology. This is the lie that replaces the biblical anthropology of finding human purpose and meaning through relationship with our Creator and one another (creatureliness and relatedness) with an anthropology that defines human purpose and meaning—"being"—through acquisition.

> The advertisement functions by telling the audience that they should be dissatisfied; they lack *being* and this lack can be remedied through the acquisition of a commodity or the purchase of an experience. This is a strategy that encourages people to be discontent with their own lives, their own bodies, their own possessions, and the long-term consequences of a culture's exposure to such a practice needs to be carefully considered.[3]

Our own desires, harmful as they might be in their individual ways, coalesce to cause great harm and global instability. Consider the financial crisis of 2008. Mark Slatter argues that the collapse of Lehman Brothers and other great financial institutions was driven by "a culture wholly fetishized by greed," which was "socialized into an anthropology of deficiency."[4] That crisis played an important role in triggering many of the global populist movements that continue to cause international instability to this day.[5]

Nor can we ignore the role of our desires in driving climate change, and the role of climate change in contributing to global instability. We are already experiencing some of the greatest people movements ever seen, and there is intense international competition for a number of basic human necessities, particularly water. In his exploration of the links between Girardian mimesis and climate change, Michael Northcott writes an excoriating indictment of Western consumerism:

> It is the very success of the consumer society in generating an abundance of available objects that necessitates the constant creation of new objects. . . . As everyone becomes the possessor of a fridge or a television, the capacity of consumer objects to diffuse rivalry is devalued, and people lose interest in the "universally available" objects. This process of devaluing requires that new objects—designer fridges, smart phones, luxury cars—are created. This constant need for reinvention, also undergirded by designed obsolescence, is the motive power that drives the market society into devouring the earth's

3. Stephen Finamore, "Hope: Prophetic Vision and the Lie of the Land," in *Mission in Marginal Places: The Theory*, ed. Paul Cloke and Mike Pears (Milton Keynes: Paternoster, 2016), 225.

4. Mark Slatter, "The Secret Life of Greed," *Anglican Theological Review* 96.3 (2014): 483, 490.

5. See John Cassidy, "The Real Cost of the 2008 Financial Crisis," *The New Yorker*, September 10, 2018, www.newyorker.com /magazine/2018/09/17/the-real-cost-of-the-2008-financial-crisis.

resources. . . . One buys objects with one hand, and throws them away with the other—in a world where half of the human population goes hungry.[6]

This unending cycle of mimetic greed is proving catastrophically harmful not just in our own generation but for generations to come.

The antidote to covetousness is the cultivation of contentment and generosity. We have previously mentioned Micah 4:4, which refers to everyone sitting under their own vine and fig tree. This is an image of rest, calm, and contentment.

Contentment is a virtue promoted by the apostles and the sages (1 Tim 6:6–10; Prov 30:8–9). But it is not simply about financial means. Equally dangerous for the soul, and equally likely to provoke violence, is covetousness of status or position, and with it, the vice of ambition. The Old Testament warns us of this by negative example; we might think of Absalom or Ziba,[7] for instance. And the New Testament writers urge us by word and example to contentment in difficult circumstances and indeed to be willing to seek the lower path. Note two examples from the letter to the Philippians (Phil 2:3–8; 4:11–12).

This is about cultivating the virtue of generosity, too—generosity with our means and also generosity of spirit. To live with contentment is to be unambitious (for personal status and wealth, at least). It means living noncompetitively. "There is no limit to what a person can achieve if they don't mind who gets the credit." I spent some time on Google trying to work out who said that, and it is unclear. How fitting!

The Gift of Sabbath

Scripture gives us some practices to help us cultivate the virtues of contentment and generosity. They are Sabbath and Jubilee.

In chapter 6 we explored the significance of Sabbath for slaves and for a people who used to be slaves. Far from being the sort of burden that Christians have made the practice from time to time, for the Israelites the Sabbath was a gift that asserted the freedom that God had achieved for them. But it was also a discipline. For a subsistence farmer whose crop is ready for harvest, it must have been an enormous challenge to put down their tools on Friday before sunset and not take them up again until Sunday morning. Sabbath, then, was an act of faith and reorientation. It was a weekly reminder that:

> In vain you rise early
> and stay up late,

---

6. Michael Northcott, "Girard, Climate Change, and Apocalypse," in *Can we Survive our Origins?: Readings in René Girard's Theory of Violence and the Sacred*, ed. Pierpaolo Antonello and Paul Gifford (East Lansing: Michigan State University Press, 2015), 300.

7. The story of Absalom's coup against his father David is found in 2 Sam 15–18. The story of Ziba and Mephibosheth his master, whom he betrays through ambition, begins in 2 Sam 16:1–4 and concludes in ch. 19.

>   toiling for food to eat—
>   for he grants sleep to those he loves. (Ps 127:2)

It was a weekly opportunity to reorient oneself before God as the beneficiary of his love and goodness. Such a reorientation helps to protect us from the pride and arrogance of the servant who chased down his friend for a small debt when he had been forgiven an enormous one (Matt 18:21–35). Sabbath, then, promotes a God-oriented anthropology. It centers us on our creatureliness and provides opportunity to renew our relatedness.

The Gift of Jubilee

The second practice that the Old Testament provides to help reorder our desires is that of the Jubilee. This intermittent act of freeing bonded laborers and restoring land pressed a sort of reboot button on society. It prevented families from growing richer and richer over multiple generations. It freed the poor from the burden of their poverty and the rich from the burden of their wealth.

The author and the majority of the readers of this book will fall within the top 15 percent of global household incomes. We are probably familiar with the idea that the poor might need "saving" from their poverty. But how might we be freed from the burden of our wealth and from the potency of our desires? And lest we bristle at the notion that we might need saving from our acquisitiveness, let us remember the warning of Jesus: "How hard it is for the rich to enter the kingdom of God!" (Mark 10:23).

CONCLUSION

I was in two minds about whether to begin the "Reflecting on Relevance" section with this chapter, or to end here. Perhaps we need both. Before we should consider the violence of the world around us we need to face the violence in our own hearts. But this is a good place to end too. We will never move on from needing to confront our own sinful desires—the way that we "curve in upon ourselves," as several of the great theologians have written.

But we might very well ask the question: How can my actions, so small on a global scale, really make any difference? What is the point? There are at least three answers to that question. The first is that we are individuals in a world made up of individuals. The global effect is the sum of the total, and while the role of global corporations should not be overlooked, they are frequently responding to market forces driven by individuals. It is for each individual to play his or her part.

The second response is that the actions of individuals or churches can be prophetic. In chapter 14 we looked at so-called apocalyptic nonviolence—actions chosen for their revelatory effect rather than their utility. Our choices—to not retaliate, to live generously, to not covet—can be quietly influential on others. Virtue can be mimetic too!

But third, and most importantly, we act in certain ways because they are the right things to do. This is the point of virtue ethics, which we discussed in chapter 2. When undertaken as community, this is the action of the prophetic church as we saw in chapter 13. We act in virtuous ways because it is by the regular, faithful practice of these virtues that we are formed into the likeness of Christ.

May our reflections lead us to humility. If we have never committed any great act of violence, it is not principally because we lack the tendency. Far more likely it is because we have been blessed with a stable upbringing, with money to buy the things we need, with a life that is not threatened, with a home in a country at peace. Not, of course, that all people who lack these things are violent, but if we have not been tested in these ways and found peaceful, the moral high ground does not belong to us.

> Who will deliver me from this body of death? Thanks be to God through Jesus
> Christ our Lord! (Rom 7:24–25 ESV)

May God have mercy upon us.

> Dear Lord and Father of mankind,
> forgive our foolish ways;
> reclothe us in our rightful mind,
> in purer lives thy service find,
> in deeper reverence, praise.
>
> In simple trust like theirs who heard
> beside the Syrian sea
> the gracious calling of the Lord,
> let us, like them, without a word
> rise up and follow thee.
>
> O Sabbath rest by Galilee,
> O calm of hills above,
> where Jesus knelt to share with thee
> the silence of eternity,
> interpreted by love!
>
> Drop thy still dews of quietness,
> till all our strivings cease;
> take from our souls the strain and stress,
> and let our ordered lives confess
> the beauty of thy peace.

Breathe through the heats of our desire
thy coolness and thy balm;
let sense be dumb, let flesh retire;
speak through the earthquake, wind, and fire,
O still, small voice of calm![8]

RELEVANT QUESTIONS

1. Can you identify spirals of ambition or aggression in your own life that need to be addressed?
2. How can you cultivate contentment in your life?
3. How might you receive the gift of Sabbath more meaningfully?
4. Reflecting on the immense grace toward you in Christ, how might he be summoning you to respond to the message of this book?

---

8. "Dear Lord and Father of Mankind," by John Greenleaf Whittier, 1872 (public domain).

CHAPTER 19

THIS IS TRUE

We also glory in our sufferings, because we know that suffering produces perseverance; perseverance, character; and character, hope. And hope does not put us to shame, because God's love has been poured out into our hearts through the Holy Spirit, who has been given to us.

Romans 5:3–5

In J. R. R. Tolkien's majestic *Lord of the Rings* trilogy, he describes a battle (the battle of Helm's Deep) where the enemy's attack is relentless, coming in wave after wave, seemingly inexhaustible and unstoppable.

> The enemy before them seemed to have grown rather than diminished, and still more were pressing up from the valley through the breach. . . . The assault on the gates was redoubled. Against the Deeping Wall the hosts of Isengard roared like a sea. Orcs and hillmen swarmed about its feet from end to end. Ropes with grappling hooks were hauled over the parapet faster than men could cut them or fling them back. Hundreds of long ladders were lifted up. Many were cast down in ruin but many more replaced them. . . . Before the wall's foot the dead and broken were piled like shingle in a storm; ever higher rose the hideous mounds, and still the enemy came on.[1]

Maybe this is how we feel about violence in the world today. No sooner have we recovered from the shock of one atrocity than another fills our newsfeeds. A terrorist attack here; a bruised and battered wife there; a war in this place; a racist murder in that place; child labor and sex trafficking; genocide and coups. Wave upon wave throughout history; the dead piling up like shingle in a storm.

It is all too easy to despair in the teeth of such an onslaught, to doubt that anything can ever change, to live in fear or rage, and to submit to the violence by becoming part of it, even if in opposition to it. Or alternatively, it is tempting to allow our despair to shut us down, to refuse to listen to the news or engage with the realities of the world, to resist the clamor and harden our hearts against pain that we cannot ease, to submit to the violence by choosing to ignore it.

---

1. J. R. R. Tolkien, *The Two Towers: Being the Second Part of the Lord of the Rings* (New York: HarperCollins, 1997), 523.

Perhaps such hopelessness was experienced by the seer in Revelation, who saw the scroll of God's good purposes but knew that there was nobody to open and enact it.

> Then I saw in the right hand of him who sat on the throne a scroll with writing on both sides and sealed with seven seals. And I saw a mighty angel proclaiming in a loud voice, "Who is worthy to break the seals and open the scroll?" But no one in heaven or on earth or under the earth could open the scroll or even look inside it. I wept and wept because no one was found who was worthy to open the scroll or look inside. (Rev 5:1–4)

This would be our predicament if God had not sent a Savior. There would be nobody to enact God's good will, nobody to stand in the breach against the forces of death. And wave upon wave of evil and violence would crash down upon us, again and again, until the descending darkness would be met by the rising darkness in our own souls, and all would be night.

But thanks be to God, he did not leave us in such a predicament.

> Then one of the elders said to me, "Do not weep! See, the Lion of the tribe of Judah, the Root of David, has triumphed. He is able to open the scroll and its seven seals."
>
> Then I saw a Lamb, looking as if it had been slain. (Rev 5:5–6)

History is not cyclical; it is headed toward a destination. We have been given a glimpse of that destination, and the forces of death are nowhere in the picture. This is because the will of God has been enacted by the only true human there has ever been—by the Lion of Judah who commands all dominion, but who is also—marvelously—the Lamb who has been slain. He is not one who is aloof from the violence of the world but is one who has drunk the bitter cup to its dregs.

We have spent a long while in the last few chapters reflecting on how we as the church and as individuals should respond to human violence. And it is, indeed, our privilege and responsibility to labor together for the cause of peace and to follow the Spirit where he leads us in that difficult, creative endeavor. But we must never imagine that ultimately it all relies on us.

Violence entered the world hard on the heels of the first lie. But our hope is in the one who is truth.

> He who was seated on the throne said, "I am making everything new!" Then he said, "Write this down, for these words are trustworthy and true." (Rev 21:5)

The promises of God are true. He is making all things new. And to this we cling. Come, Lord Jesus.

ADVENT CREDO

It is not true that creation and the human family are doomed to destruction and loss—

This is true: For God so loved the world that He gave his only begotten Son, that whoever believes in Him shall not perish but have everlasting life;

It is not true that we must accept inhumanity and discrimination, hunger and poverty, death and destruction—

This is true: I have come that they may have life, and that abundantly.

It is not true that violence and hatred should have the last word, and that war and destruction rule forever—

This is true: Unto us a child is born, unto us a Son is given, and the government shall be upon his shoulder, his name shall be called wonderful councilor, mighty God, the Everlasting, the Prince of peace.

It is not true that we are simply victims of the powers of evil who seek to rule the world—

This is true: To me is given authority in heaven and on earth, and lo I am with you, even until the end of the world.

It is not true that we have to wait for those who are specially gifted, who are the prophets of the Church before we can be peacemakers—

This is true: I will pour out my spirit on all flesh and your sons and daughters shall prophesy, your young men shall see visions and your old men shall have dreams.

It is not true that our hopes for liberation of humankind, of justice, of human dignity of peace are not meant for this earth and for this history—

This is true: The hour comes, and it is now, that the true worshipers shall worship God in spirit and in truth.

So let us enter Advent in hope, even hope against hope. Let us see visions of love and peace and justice. Let us affirm with humility, with joy, with faith, with courage: Jesus Christ—the life of the world.[2]

---

2. From Allan Boesak, "Advent Credo," from *Walking on Thorns*, ed. Allan Boesak (Grand Rapids: Eerdmans; Geneva: World Council of Churches, 1984). Used here with the kind permission of the World Council of Churches.

SCRIPTURE INDEX

SUBJECT INDEX

AUTHOR INDEX